ALL · IN · ONE

CCFP^{SM} Certified Cyber Forensics Professional Certification

Exam Guide

Chuck Easttom

New York   Chicago   San Francisco
Athens   London   Madrid   Mexico City
Milan   New Delhi   Singapore   Sydney   Toronto

Cataloging-in-Publication Data is on file with the Library of Congress

McGraw-Hill Education books are available at special quantity discounts to use as premiums and sales promotions, or for use in corporate training programs. To contact a representative, please visit the Contact Us pages at www.mhprofessional.com.

CCFP^{SM} Certified Cyber Forensics Professional Certification All-in-One Exam Guide

1234567890 DOC DOC 10987654

ISBN: Book p/n 978-0-07-183611-1 and CD p/n 978-0-07-183974-7
of set 978-0-07-183976-1

MHID: Book p/n 0-07-183611-X and CD p/n 0-07-183974-7
of set 0-07-183976-3

Sponsoring Editor Meghan Riley Manfre	**Technical Editor** George (Buzz) Murphy	**Production Supervisor** Jean Bodeaux
Editorial Supervisor Patty Mon	**Copy Editor** Lisa McCoy	**Composition** Cenveo Publisher Services
Project Manager Harleen Chopra, Cenveo® Publisher Services	**Proofreader** Paul Tyler	**Illustration** Cenveo Publisher Services
Acquisitions Coordinator Mary Demery	**Indexer** Karin Arrigoni	**Art Director, Cover** Jeff Weeks

CONTENTS

Acknowledgments   xi
Introduction   xiii

Part 1 Legal and Ethical Principles   1

Chapter 1 Introduction to Forensics   3
What Is Cyber Forensics?   3
Understanding the Science of Forensics   4
Elements of the Crime   5
    Law   5
    Intent   5
    Burden of Proof   5
    Exculpatory Evidence   6
Knowledge Base Needed for Cyber Forensics   6
    Hardware   6
    Operating Systems   9
    Networks   13
The Fundamental Principles of Cyber Forensics   21
    Maintaining Chain of Custody   23
The Law and Cyber Forensics   23
    General Legal Issues   24
    Discovery   24
    Warrants   25
Federal Guidelines Forensics Investigators Need to Know   26
    FBI   26
    Secret Service   27
The Need for Cyber Forensics Certification   27
Chapter Review   29
Questions   29
Answers   30
References   30

Chapter 2 The Investigative Process   31
Chain of Custody   31
Securing the Scene   33
Documentation   33
Authority and Objectives   35
Examination   36

Code of Ethics 36
   (ISC)² Ethics 37
   American Academy of Forensic Science Ethics 37
   ISO Code of Ethics 38
Ethical Conduct Outside the Investigation 40
   Civil Matters 40
   Criminal Matters 40
   Other Issues 41
Ethical Investigations 41
   The Chinese Wall 41
   Relevant Regulations for Ethical Investigations 42
The Evidence 43
   Criminal Investigations 43
   Civil Investigations 44
   Administrative Investigations 44
   Intellectual Property Investigations 45
   The Daubert Standard 46
The Forensic Investigator as an Expert 46
   Qualities of an Expert 47
Chapter Review 51
Questions 51
Answers 53
References 53

Chapter 3   **Evidence Management** **55**
Evidence Collection 55
   Evidence Documentation 55
   Evidence Preservation 57
Evidence Transport 64
   Evidence Tracking 65
Evidence Storage 67
   Environmental Hazards 67
   Unauthorized Access 69
   Electromagnetic Interference 69
   U.S. Army Digital Evidence Storage 70
Evidence Access Control 71
Evidence Disposition 71
Chapter Review 71
Questions 72
Answers 73
References 73

Part II   Forensic Science   75

Chapter 4   Principles and Methods   77
   Scientific Approach to Forensics   77
      The Scientific Method   77
      The Philosophy of Science   78
      Peer Review.. 78
      Locard's Principle of Transference   79
      Inman-Rudin Paradigm   81
   Identify and Classify Evidence   82
   Locations Where Evidence May Reside   82
      Storage Media   83
      Hardware Interfaces   87
      File Systems   89
      File Format   90
      File Types   91
      Header Analysis   92
   Recovering Data   95
      Physical Damage   95
      Logical Damage   95
      File and Metadata Carving   96
      Known File Filtering   99
   Media File Forensic Steps   99
      Running Processes   100
      Netstat   101
   Chapter Review   102
   Questions   102
   Answers   103
   References   103

Chapter 5   Forensic Analysis   105
   Planning   105
      Collecting the Evidence   105
      Analyze the Evidence   106
   Case Notes and Reports   108
      Case Notes   108
      Reports   109
   Quality Control   114
      Lab Quality   114
      Investigator Quality Control   116
      Examination Quality Control   120
   Chapter Review   121
   Questions   121
   Answers   122
   References   123

Part III Digital Forensics 125

Chapter 6 Hardware Forensics 127

Hard Drive Specifications 127
General Hard Drive Facts.......................... 127
RAID 130
Recovering from Damaged Media 132
CMOS/BIOS 133
The Swap File 134
Operating System Specifics 135
Operating System Essentials 135
The Kernel 136
The GUI 137
Interrupts 137
API 138
Extracting Deleted Files 138
Windows 138
Windows Tools 140
Scrubbing Files 144
Linux 145
Macintosh 147
MacKeeper 147
Encrypted Files 148
EFS 148
TrueCrypt 149
How to Deal with Encrypted Drives and Files 150
Chapter Review 151
Questions 151
Answers 152
References 152

Chapter 7 Hidden Files and Antiforensics 153

Cryptography 153
The History of Encryption 154
Modern Cryptography 157
Symmetric Encryption 159
Asymmetric Cryptography 163
Cryptographic Hash 167
Windows Passwords 169
Steganography 170
Historical Steganography 170
Methods and Tools 171
Steganalysis 175
Cryptanalysis 176
Frequency Analysis 177
Kasiski 177
Modern Methods 177

Log Tampering 179
   Log Deletion 179
   Auditpol 179
   Winzapper 179
Other Techniques 179
   Onion Routing 179
   Spoofing 180
   Wiping 181
   Tunneling 181
Chapter Review 181
Questions 181
Answers 182
References 182

Chapter 8 Network Forensics 183
Network Packet Analysis 183
   What Is a Packet? 183
   Ports 186
   Network Traffic Analysis 188
   Log Files 190
   Web Traffic 191
   HTTP Sniffer 194
   Web Traffic 194
   Nmap 196
   Snort 197
Wireless 198
   Network-Related Cybercrimes 199
Router Forensics 200
   Router Basics 200
   Types of Router Attacks 202
   Getting Evidence from the Router 202
Firewall Forensics 204
   Firewall Basics 204
Logs to Examine 205
   Windows Logs 205
   Linux Logs 207
Operating System Utilities 207
   Netstat 208
   Net sessions 208
   Openfiles 209
Network Structure 210
   Types of Networks 210
   Network Topology 210
   Shares 213
   Services 214
   P2P Networks and Proxies 214
   SANS 214

	Social Networks	214
	Chapter Review	215
	Questions	215
	Answers	216
	References	216
Chapter 9	Virtual Systems	**217**
	Types of Virtual Systems	217
	Virtual Machines	217
	Service-Based Systems	220
	The Cloud	222
	Forensic Issues	225
	Technical Issues	225
	VMware	226
	VirtualBox	226
	Virtual PC	227
	Legal/Procedural Issues	227
	Chapter Review	229
	Questions	230
	Answers	230
	References	231
Chapter 10	Mobile Forensics	**233**
	Cellular Device Concepts	233
	The Basics	234
	Networks	236
	Operating Systems	237
	Apps	243
	What Evidence Can You Get from a Mobile Device?	243
	Cell Phone Records	243
	Photos and Videos	243
	GPS Records	244
	Evidence from Apps	244
	What You Should Look For	245
	Device Status	246
	Seizing Evidence from a Phone	246
	Imaging a Phone	247
	Windows 8 Phone	257
	The iPhone	257
	Android Forensics	259
	Embedded Devices	260
	Summary	260
	Questions	261
	Answers	261
	References	262

Part IV Application Forensics and Emerging Technologies 263

Chapter 11 Application Forensics 265

File Formats 265
The Registry 265
Windows Swap File 272
Index.dat 272
Other Files That Provide Evidence 273
Memory Analysis 274
Windows File Copying 276
Web Forensics 277
Basics of Web Applications 277
SQL Injection 277
Cross-Site Scripting 279
Cookie Manipulation 280
Forceful Browsing 281
XML Injection 281
E-mail Forensics 281
How E-mail Works 282
E-mail headers 283
E-mail Files 289
Tracing E-mail 290
E-mail Server Forensics 290
Database Forensics 291
Database Types 291
What to Look For 292
Record Carving and Database Reconstruction 293
Chapter Review 293
Questions 294
Answers 295
References 295

Chapter 12 Malware Forensics 297

Viruses 297
How a Virus Spreads 297
Real-World Cases 298
Types of Viruses 301
History of Viruses 302
Modern Virus Creation 304
Trojan Horses 305
Spyware 306
The Buffer Overflow 307
Rootkit 307
Logic Bombs 308
Ransomware 308

Advanced Persistent Threats 309
Malware Analysis 310
    Static Analysis 310
    Dynamic Analysis 310
Chapter Review 312
Questions 313
Answers 313
References 314

Chapter 13 New and Emerging Forensics Technology 315
Social Networks 315
    Types and Applications of Social Networks 315
    Direct Evidence of Crimes 317
    Commission of Crimes 318
New Devices 320
    Google Glass 320
    Cars 320
    Medical Devices 321
Control Systems and Infrastructure 321
Online Gaming 321
Electronic Discovery 322
    Types of Investigation 323
    Liability and Proof 325
    Relevant Laws 325
    Big Data 327
    Steps in Electronic Data Discover 328
    Disaster Recovery 328
Chapter Review 328
Questions 329
Answers 330
References 330

Appendix About the CD-ROM 331
System Requirements 331
Total Tester Premium Practice Exam Software 331
Installing and Running Total Tester
   Premium Practice Exam Software 331
PDF Copy of the Book 332
Technical Support 332
    Total Seminars Technical Support 332
    McGraw-Hill Education Content Support 332

Glossary 333

Index 337

ABOUT THE AUTHOR

Chuck Easttom has over 20 years of practical experience in all aspects of the IT industry. That experience includes teaching and practicing all aspects of computer security, including forensics. In addition to the practical experience, he has been teaching IT topics for over 14 years. Most notably, he has taught forensics to the U.S. Secret Service and to the Internal Revenue Service, as well as private companies. This is his eighteenth book and his second forensics book. He also has 29 different IT certifications, including CISSP, CISSP- ISSAP, CHFI, and CEH, and three computer-related patents. Mr. Easttom also frequently serves as an expert witness in computer-related cases. You can find out more about him at www.ChuckEasttom.com.

About the Technical Editor

George (Buzz) Murphy, CISSP, CASP, is a sought-after public speaker, corporate trainer, author, and cybersecurity evangelist who has touched the lives of thousands of adult learners across the country over the past 20 years with courses, seminars, and consulting presentations on a variety of technology topics. A former Dell technology training executive, he has addressed audiences at Comdex, NetWorld, and the National Computer Conference. Buzz has earned more than 19 IT and cybersecurity certifications from (ISC)², CompTIA, and many other industry organizations. Having held a top-secret security clearance in both U.S. and NATO intelligence, he has trained network cybersecurity ops for the U.S. Army, various government security agencies, and foreign military personnel across Conus and EMEA, and has been involved with facilitating such subjects as site EMP hardening, cryptographic methodology, and computer forensic sciences as well as cyber-warfare training.

ACKNOWLEDGMENTS

Writing a book is an arduous task. It is always my goal to make each book better than the last. While a single author's name may go on the cover, many people helped make this book a success. I have to thank several people for aiding me in this endeavor. First, the very helpful editorial staff at McGraw-Hill Education. They were simply wonderful to work with! And their commitment to quality is unsurpassed in the publishing world. The team included copy editors, layout editors, graphics design people, etc., all working to make sure no mistakes crept into the book. Also, thanks to Buzz Murphy for doing a tech edit of the chapters. Finally, I must thank my wife Teresa, who was so patient when I spent long hours working on this book.

INTRODUCTION

Cyber forensics is a growing field. Reaffirming this, (ISC)², creators of the CISSP credential, have created a comprehensive cyber forensics certification, the Certified Cyber Forensics Professional (CCFP). This certification is not a vendor tool certification, but rather a broad-based general cyber forensics certification. The certification requires a four-year degree with three years of experience in cyber forensics or IT security in at least three out of the six (ISC)² CCFP domains. If you don't have a degree, then six years of experience are required. If you have no experience, you can take the test and become an Associate of (ISC)². The test consists of 125 multiple-choice questions. You have four hours and must pass with a 70 percent (700 points) or greater. After you've passed the exam successfully, you must also agree to adhere to the (ISC)² Code of Ethics (discussed in Chapter 2 of this book). Your application must then be endorsed by a current (ISC)² member (someone with the CCFP, CISSP, or similar certification) in order to achieve the credential.

This book is intended to thoroughly prepare you to take the CCFP exam. In this book, you will learn about forensics concepts, how to create forensics reports, various forensics techniques, computer forensics, mobile device forensics, and emerging trends. While we assume general IT security knowledge, we don't assume prior cyber forensics knowledge, although the CCFP exam assumes three years' experience. We will teach you everything you need to know to function effectively as a cyber forensics professional.

This book starts with general concepts in Chapter 1. Chapter 2 makes certain you have the appropriate technical background for cyber forensics. For most readers, Chapter 2 should be a review. As you progress through the chapters, you will see a mixture of theory along with practical techniques and advice. Look for extra test tips and notes in the chapters—these are meant to provide some extra information for you.

 EXAM TIP Chapter 10 gives you a good introduction to mobile forensics. This is an increasingly important topic in forensics, and for the CCFP exam. You should pay particular attention to this chapter, and I recommend memorizing all the various terms found therein.

In addition to the book, I have created a website designed to be an aid to readers and forensics practitioners: www.digitalforensicscert.com/. This website will be updated from time to time and expanded as needed. You can also visit my personal website: www.ChuckEasttom.com.

How to Use This Book

As you read the book, you will encounter all the material you need to know to successfully take and pass the CCFP exam. I recommend you give each chapter a casual read and then return and spend time studying topics that were new to you or were difficult. If there are hands-on exercises or labs in a chapter (and there are several), whenever possible actually execute the exercise or the lab. Anytime you encounter a new term or acronym, it is important that you memorize it. Don't just read it—make sure you commit it to memory.

Each chapter ends with review questions, and there are additional questions that accompany the book in electronic format. These questions will test your knowledge related to the CCFP domains, but these are not actual questions from the CCFP exam. The point is not to memorize the questions and answers, but use them to probe your knowledge and see how much has been retained. While the test assumes you have experience in cyber forensics, this book does not. My experience has been that a lot of working professionals, in any field, have very deep knowledge of some areas, and gaps in others. This book should review what you already know and fill in gaps in other areas.

As I mentioned, pay special attention to the Exam Tips in the chapters. These are specific guidelines discussing what you will need to know for the test, and in some cases, things you don't need to know for the test. When you finish a chapter, take a moment to reflect on it. Make sure you fully understood the chapter and memorized any new terms or acronyms before you move on to the next chapter.

The Examination

I have taken many certification tests (29 as of this writing) and successfully taught many certification courses. Let me give you a few exam tips. First and foremost, make sure you are relaxed. Don't schedule the exam until you are really ready. And then schedule it at the best time for you. If you are a morning person, schedule it as early as you can. If you are not a morning person, then under no circumstances should you take a difficult test in the morning!

The day of the test, try to relax. On your way to the test, listen to your favorite music and relax. You will notice a few things when the test starts. The first is that occasionally you will see a question essentially repeated but worded a different way. That's okay and actually helps you. One way the question is worded might not be clear to you, but the other way is. This gives you a second chance to see what the question is asking and to answer it appropriately. Make sure you fully read each question. Four hours is plenty of time—don't rush.

You may have heard the old adage, never change your answer. That is only partially true. If a subsequent question is clearer to you and you know, absolutely know, that you need to change an answer, then do it. However, if your second answer is just a guess, stick with your first guess. Also, keep in mind that no matter how hard you study, you will probably encounter a question or two that you just don't know. Don't panic. You have a one in four chance of guessing right. Can you see at least one answer that you are certain is *not* correct? Well, you just raised your odds to one in three!

If you've read this book, you should feel confident that you've prepared, and prepared well. Last but not least, good luck!

CCFP Exam Objective Map

Official Exam Objective	All-in-One Coverage	Chapter Numbers	Page Numbers
1.0 Legal and Ethical Principles			
1.1 Analyze the Nature of Evidence and Its Characteristics	1. What Is Computer Forensics? 1. Understanding the Field of Forensics 4. Identify and Classify Evidence	1, 4	3-5, 82
1.2 Analyze the Chain of Custody	1. Maintaining Chain of Custody 2. Chain of Custody	1, 2	23, 31-33
1.3 Analyze the Significance of Rules of Procedure	1. The Law and Cyber Forensics 1. General Legal Issues	1	23-26
1.4 Analyze the Role of Expert Witness	2. The Forensic Investigator as an Expert 13. Administrative Investigations	2, 13	46-51, 324
1.5 Apply Codes of Ethics	2. Code of Ethics 2. Ethical Conduct Outside the Investigation 2. Ethical Investigations	2	36-43
2.0 Investigations			
2.1 Analyze the Investigative Process	2. Examination	2	36
2.2 Analyze Evidence Management	2. The Evidence 3. Evidence Collection 3. Evidence Preservation 3. Evidence Transport 3. Evidence Tracking 3. Evidence Storage 5. Collecting the Evidence 5. Analyze the Evidence	2, 3, 5	43-46, 55-70, 105-106
2.3 Analyze Criminal Investigations	1. Elements of the Crime	1	5-6
2.4 Analyze Civil Investigations	2. Civil Investigations 13. Types of Investigations	2, 13	44, 323-325
2.5 Analyze Administrative Investigations	2. Administrative Investigations 13. Administrative Investigations	2, 13	
2.6 Analyze Forensic Response to Security Incidents	13. Disaster Recovery	13	328
2.7 Analyze Electronic Discovery	13. Electronic Discovery	13	322-325
2.8 Analyze Intellectual Property (IP) Investigation	2. Intellectual Property Investigations 13. Types of Investigations	2, 13	45-46, 323-325

Official Exam Objective	All-in-One Coverage	Chapter Numbers	Page Numbers
3.0 Forensic Science			
3.1 Analyze Fundamental Principles	2. Scientific Approach to Forensics 4. Scientific Approach to Forensics	2, 4	46-51, 77-81
3.2 Analyze Forensic Methods	4. Media File Forensic Steps 5. Planning	4, 5	99-102, 105-108
3.3 Evaluate Report Writing and Presentation	2. Documentation 5. Case Notes and Reports	2, 5	33-35, 108-114
3.4 Analyze Quality Assurance Control Management and Accreditation Procedures	5. Quality Control 5. Validation of Findings	5	106-107, 114-121
4.0 Digital Forensics			
4.1 Analyze Media and File System Forensics	1. Files and File Systems 6. Extracting Deleted Files	1, 6	11, 138-147
4.2 Analyze Computer and Operating System Forensics	6. Operating System Specifics	6	135-138
4.3 Analyze Network Forensics	8. Network Packet Analysis 8. Wireless 8. Router Forensics 8. Network Structure	8	183-204, 210-214
4.4 Apply Mobile Device Forensics	10. Cellular Device Concepts 10. What Evidence Can You Get From a Mobile Device? 10. Seizing Evidence From a Phone	10	233-260
4.5 Understand Embedded Device Forensics	10. Embedded Devices	10	260
4.6 Apply Virtual System Forensics	9. Types of Virtual Systems 9. The Cloud 9. Forensic Issues	9	217-229
4.7 Analyze Forensic Techniques and Tools	6. Windows Tools 9. Forensic Issues 10. Types of Acquisition	6, 9, 10	140-142, 225-229, 247-248
4.8 Understand Antiforensic Techniques and Tools	6. Encrypted Files 7. Cryptography 7. Steganography 7. Log Tampering 7. Other Methods	6, 7	148-150, 153-176, 179-181

Official Exam Objective	All-in-One Coverage	Chapter Numbers	Page Numbers
5.0 Application Forensics			
5.1 Apply Software Forensics	11. File Formats 11. Windows File Copying	11	265-277
5.2 Analyze Web, E-mail and Message Forensics	11. Web Forensics	11	277-281
5.3 Understand Database Forensics	11. Database Forensics	11	291-293
5.4 Understand Malware Forensics	12. Viruses 12. Trojan Horses 12. Spyware 12. Buffer Overflow 12. Rootkit 12. Logic Bomb 12. Ransomware 12. Advanced Persistent Threats 12. Malware Analysis	12	297-312
6.0 Hybrid and Emerging Technologies			
6.1 Understand Cloud Forensics	9. The Cloud	9	227
6.2 Understand Social Networks	8. Social Networks 13. Social Networks	8, 13	214-215, 315-321
6.3 Understand the Big Data Paradigm	13. Online Gaming	13	
6.4 Understand Control Systems	13. Control Systems and Infrastructure	13	321-322
6.5 Understand Critical Infrastructure	13. Control Systems and Infrastructure	13	321-322
6.6 Understand Online Gaming and Virtual/ Augmented Reality	13. Online Gaming	13	312-322

PART I

Legal and Ethical Principles

■ **Chapter 1**   Introduction to Forensics
■ **Chapter 2**   The Investigative Process
■ **Chapter 3**   Evidence Management

Introduction to Forensics

In this chapter you will learn:

- The definition of cyber forensics
- The science of forensics
- The knowledge base needed for cyber forensics
- Two fundamental principles of cyber forensics
- The relationship between the law and cyber forensics
- Federal guidelines forensic investigators need to know
- The need for certification

Cyber forensics is a comparatively new field. Widespread use of computers dates back to the 1970s, and widespread computer crime to the 1990s. The field of cyber forensics has evolved only in the past 25 years. However, it is a branch of the science of forensics. As such, it takes forensics principles and applies them to cybercrimes. This brings up the question of what forensics is. The American Heritage Dictionary defines forensics as "the use of science and technology to investigate and establish facts in criminal or civil courts of law."[1]

That still might not be a satisfying definition. So let's put it another way. Essentially, forensics is the process whereby scientific principles are applied to the task of gathering and processing evidence. Whether the evidence is DNA, matching bullets to guns, or fingerprint analysis, the concept is the same. The investigator applies well-tested scientific principles to analyze the data and formulate conclusions.

What Is Cyber Forensics?

CERT (Computer Emergency Response Team) defines cyber forensics in this manner: "If you manage or administer information systems and networks, you should understand cyber forensics. Forensics is the process of using scientific knowledge for collecting, analyzing, and presenting evidence to the courts. (The word *forensics* means "to bring to the court.") Forensics deals primarily with the recovery and analysis of latent evidence. Latent evidence can take many forms, from fingerprints left on a window to DNA evidence recovered from blood stains to the files on a hard drive."[2]

There are really two primary objectives in cyber forensics. The first is to find out what happened. What data was affected, what files, what was done? Was there a denial-of-service attack, a virus, or perhaps sensitive files stolen? The first goal is to gather facts, to know what occurred and, if possible, to know how and when it occurred. The second objective is to collect data in a manner that is acceptable to a court. As you continue in this book, we will discuss how to ensure that the data is collected in the appropriate manner.

 EXAM TIP Various organizations have established their own guidelines for digital forensics. The Certified Cyber Forensics Professional test focuses heavily on the standards published by the Scientific Working Group on Digital Evidence (www.swgde.org), and you will see their standards referenced frequently within this book.

Cyber forensics is a more appropriate term than computer forensics. Computers are not the only objects of forensic investigations. Any device that can store data is potentially the object of cyber forensics. That includes computers, but also includes smart phones, routers, tablets, printers, tablets, and GPS devices, even vehicle GPSs.

While the subject of cyber forensics, as well as the tools and techniques used, is significantly different from traditional forensics (like DNA analysis and bullet examination), the goal is the same: to obtain evidence that can be used in some legal proceeding. However, a few principles will be introduced now and dealt with in more detail later.

The first is securing the scene. You have to ensure that the crime scene is secure before proceeding to collect evidence. In the case of cybercrime, the "crime scene" could be a PC, cell phone, or server. It is imperative to make sure the device is not being monitored, and most importantly, that evidence is not being destroyed.

The other concept that is critical to forensics investigations is the chain of custody. Chain of custody is a documentation trail from the time that you secure the crime scene to the time the evidence is presented at court. You must be able to show clear documentation of every place the evidence was at, how it was stored, how it was secured, who accessed the evidence, and how they accessed it. Any break in the chain of custody is likely to render the evidence inadmissible in court.

Understanding the Science of Forensics

Forensics, of any type, is first and foremost a science. This means there are well-established scientific principles one must adhere to when conducting a forensic investigation. This is not an art, and there is no place for "gut feelings." Chapters 2 and 3 will delve more deeply into these topics.

What do we mean when we say "well-established scientific principles"? First, scientific investigation is a very special way of thinking. In a scientific investigation, one forms a hypothesis, tests that hypothesis, and then records the results. A hypothesis must be a testable question. Questions that cannot be subjected to testing have no place in science. For example, in a cyber forensic investigation, you may hypothesize that there are deleted files on a suspect PC that can be recovered. You test that hypothesis by using an undelete tool to recover those files. If you find there are no files to recover, then you must reject your hypothesis. The nature of any scientific inquiry is to follow the evidence, even if it leads to conclusions we did not expect, or did not even want.

This brings us to the topic of "testing the hypothesis." How do you test it? In any forensic investigation, you can only use well-established scientific tests. This means tools and techniques that have been widely accepted in the relevant scientific discipline—in this case, in the fields of computer science and engineering.

Elements of the Crime

What are the essential elements of the crime? This may seem a bit removed from forensic analysis. And it is true that not all forensics involves criminal cases. However, if a criminal case is involved, you should at least be aware of the elements of a crime. There are two main factors needed for a crime to be committed, which the following sections discuss.

Law

There must be some law that was broken. That may sound obvious, but you might find some conduct objectionable but not criminal. For example, it is legal for someone to provide biased stock advice on the Internet, as long as somewhere on their website they disclose the nature of the bias. That might be unethical, but it is not criminal.

Intent

Someone cannot accidentally commit a crime. They can accidentally commit a civil tort and be sued, but criminal law requires intent. For example, in a case of alleged child pornography, it may not be enough that a single image exists on the suspect's computer. Forensics can help establish intent by showing when the suspect last accessed the image, if the suspect deliberately downloaded it, etc.

Burden of Proof

Depending on the case, the burden of proof might be a bit different. For example, in criminal cases, the burden of proof is "beyond a reasonable doubt." It is not enough to show that the accused could have committed the crime, and might have committed the crime; you have to show "beyond a reasonable doubt" that they did commit the crime. Usually, defense attorneys attempt to introduce alternative theories of the crime in order to introduce reasonable doubt.

With civil cases, the standard is "by a preponderance of the evidence." This is less than the "beyond a reasonable doubt" standard. Essentially, in a civil case, you just have to show that it is highly likely that the accused committed the offense in question.

Exculpatory Evidence

This is a rather simple concept, but an important one. Exculpatory evidence is evidence that proves the accused innocent. Let us assume you are investigating a computer wherein the suspect is accused of creating a virus and releasing it. Yet in your investigation, you find evidence that the suspect may have actually been a victim of the virus himself and accidentally downloaded it. That would constitute exculpatory evidence. In criminal cases, prosecutors have a legal duty to turn over exculpatory evidence to the defense.

Knowledge Base Needed for Cyber Forensics

Cyber forensics is not an area for novices. If you are new to computer science in general, you should get a solid background in hardware, basic networking, and operating systems before pursuing forensics. In this book (and on the CCFP exam), it is assumed that you have that background. If you don't, the following section gives a brief overview of the bare minimum knowledge you should have. This is also useful if it has been a while since you studied one or more of these topics and need a refresher.

Hardware

It should be obvious that it is impossible to perform forensic analysis of computers without some knowledge of computers. In general, this means a working knowledge of motherboards, hard drives, RAM, expansion slots, etc. This would be equivalent to the knowledge gained from a basic PC course at a university or the level of knowledge tested on the CompTIA A+ certification. This merely covers computers, however. If you intend to perform forensic analysis of cell phones, vehicle GPS devices, routers, tablets, or other devices, you will need to be familiar with the hardware in those devices. For routers, a basic Cisco course and certification, like the CCNA, is a good place to start. At a minimum, you should familiarize yourself with the hardware in any device you intend to examine.

In this section, we will give you a general overview of hardware for PCs, servers, and laptops. The information presented herein should be considered the absolute minimum level of knowledge for a forensic investigator, and you are strongly advised to gain as deep an understanding of computer hardware as you can.

Hard Drives

Since evidence is often found on hard drives, let's begin by looking at hard drives. The first step is simply to categorize the various types of hard drives you are likely to find.

- **SCSI**   Small Computer System Interface. It is pronounced "scuzzy." This has been around for many years, and is particularly popular in high-end servers. This standard is actually pretty old—it was established in 1986. SCSI devices must have a terminator at the end of the chain of devices to work and are limited to 16 chained devices. There is also an enhancement to the SCSI standard called Serial SCSI.

- **IDE**   Integrated Drive Electronics. This is an older standard but one that was commonly used on PCs for many years. It is obvious you are dealing with an

IDE or EIDE drive if you see a 40-pin drive connector. This was supplanted years ago by Extended IDE (EIDE). Chances are if you find any IDE drives, they will be EIDE. However, neither standard has been used in a long time.

- **SATA** Serial Advanced Technology Attachment. SATA and solid state are the two most common drives in use today. These devices are commonly found in workstations and many servers. The internals of the hard drive are very similar to IDE and EIDE—it is the connectivity to the computer's motherboard that is different. Also, unlike IDE or EIDE drives, this type of drive has no jumpers to set the drive.

- **Solid State** These are becoming more common—in fact, many tablets use solid-state drives (SSDs) because they have a longer battery lifespan (they use less electricity). Unlike the other drive types discussed, SSDs don't have moving parts like platters, spindles, etc. Since 2010, most SSDs use NAND (Negated AND gate)–based flash memory, which retains memory even without power. Unfortunately, this type of memory has a shorter lifespan than traditional hard drives.

Hard drives record data by magnetizing ferromagnetic material directionally to represent either a 0 or a 1 binary digit. The magnetic data is stored on platters; the platters are organized on a spindle with a read/write head that reads and writes data to and from the platters. The data is organized as follows:

- A *sector* is the basic unit of data storage on a hard disk, usually 512 bytes.
- A *cluster* is a logical grouping of sectors. Clusters can be one sector in size to 128 sectors. That means 512 bytes up to 64KB. The minimum size a file can use is one cluster. If the file is less than the size of a cluster, the remaining space is simply unused.
- Sectors are in turn organized by *tracks*.

The first practical thing you can use from this information is the issue of the cluster. For any computer operating system, files are stored in clusters. And once a cluster is allocated for a given file, the entire cluster is considered "used" even if it is not being used by that file. For example, assume you have 64KB clusters, and you save a file that is 70KB in size. Two clusters totaling 128KB will be allocated for that file. However, 58KB is not being used. As far as the file system is concerned, that space is allocated for the file. We call this "slack space," and there are techniques for hiding data in slack space, which we will examine later.

A few other terms you should be familiar with include the following:

- **Drive Geometry** This term refers to the functional dimensions of a drive in terms of the number of heads, cylinders, and sectors per track.
- **Low-Level Format** This creates a structure of sectors, tracks, and clusters.
- **High-Level Format** This is the process of setting up an empty file system on the disk and installing a boot sector. This alone takes little time, and is sometimes referred to as a "quick format."

EXAM TIP Asking about drive geometry is actually common to not just the CCFP exam, but other forensics tests as well.

The real issue with forensic examination of hard drives is preventing damage to evidence. Knowing that the data is stored magnetically explains why you must keep hard drives away from magnetic sources that could destroy evidence.

It is also important to understand the relationship when there are multiple hard drives. When you have more than one drive, the primary drive (the one that the system boots from) is called the master and the other drive(s) are slaves.

TIP If you have a drive that can no longer boot for whatever reason, take it out and plug it into one of your forensic lab machines as a slave. Then you can boot your lab machine and try to access that drive's data as a slave.

RAM

RAM, or random access memory, is actually quite important in forensic investigations. It is frequently necessary to do a live memory capture. That means to take what is currently in memory, with the computer still running, and create an image of this. In the early days of cyber forensics, some guidelines suggested you should always shut down a running computer immediately. Eventually, it was realized that there might be things happening in memory that are very important to the investigation and are lost upon shutdown. So live memory captures have become quite important. Therefore, it is important that you have a good understanding of RAM.

There are a variety of ways to categorize RAM. One way is to look at the method whereby data is written to and read from the RAM (these are presented in sequential order from older to newer technologies):

- **Extended Data Out (EDO) DRAM** Single-cycle EDO has the ability to carry out a complete memory transaction in one clock cycle. Otherwise, each sequential RAM access within the same page takes two clock cycles instead of three once the page has been selected.

- **Burst EDO (BEDO)** An evolution of EDO, burst EDO DRAM, could process four memory addresses in one burst.

- **DRAM (Dynamic Random Access Memory)** This is the most common type of memory today, and it has been around for many years, with various improvements, some of which are described here.

  - **ADRAM** Asynchronous DRAM is not synchronized to the CPU clock. This memory is no longer found, and is mentioned only for historical purposes.

  - **SDRAM** Synchronous dynamic random access memory was a replacement for EDO.

  - **Double Data Rate (DDR)** DDR was a later development of SDRAM. We now have DDR2 and DDR3

- **Synchronous Graphics RAM (SGRAM)** This type of memory is used primarily in certain graphics cards.
- **Pseudo-static RAM (PSRAM)** This is dynamic RAM with built-in refresh and address-control circuitry to make it behave similarly to static RAM. It is used in various devices, including the iPhone.
- **Reduced Latency DRAM (RLDRAM)** This type of memory has a high-performance double data rate.

These are the major types of RAM. All of these are volatile memory, and you must keep that in mind when working with live memory capture. We will discuss live memory capture in later chapters in great detail.

Operating Systems

Operating systems are a critical factor in forensics. In this section, we will discuss a basic overview of the major operating systems available today. However, you should absolutely not attempt to perform forensics on a system if you don't truly understand the operating system. And, as you will see in later chapters, there is no such thing as learning "too much." Every detail about an operating system might enhance your forensic investigation.

Windows

The Windows operating system has gone through many changes over the years. The first version of Windows that many people are familiar with is Windows 3.1. This was not really an operating system, but more of a graphical user interface that rested on the DOS operating system. With Windows 95 and beyond, there is no separation between operating system and graphical user interface. Rather, the operating system and the graphical user interface are intertwined. However, one can still open up a command prompt and utilize DOS commands. As we explore forensic methods, you will be introduced to specific DOS commands that can be quite useful.

We will get into more details on Windows in later chapters, where we discuss extracting information from Windows, but we can cover a few essentials now. The most critical part of Windows from a forensics perspective is the Windows registry. From this registry, you can get all kinds of information, including the password for wireless networks and the serial numbers for all USB devices that have been connected to that computer.

 TIP Most forensics examiners have some knowledge of Windows. However, often their knowledge is not deep enough. The Windows registry is a treasure trove of information. You should delve into it as deeply as you possibly can.

In addition to the registry, Windows has a number of places you should look for evidence. There are certain folders and files (like the index.dat file that we will investigate later in this book) that are great places to find evidence. Even browser cookies and history can be useful. Given that Windows is such a common operating system, it is advisable to be very familiar with it.

Linux

While Linux may not be as common an operating system as Windows, it is very important forensically. There are open-source forensic tools that run on Linux, and even Linux commands that can be used for forensic purposes. You will find a lot of free forensics tools come on Linux, and we will be examining several in this book. In fact, there is a Linux distribution called BackTrack that has an extensive collection of forensics, security, and hacking tools.

Linux is a Unix clone developed originally by Linus Torvalds. There are now well over 100 different distributions (variations) of Linux. However, all have some commonalities. In the Linux world, command-line (called shell in Linux) work is far more important than it is in Windows.

Macintosh

For many years, Apple Macintosh was a complete operating system. However, beginning with OS X, the Macintosh system is based on Free BSD (a Unix clone very similar to Linux). The graphical user interface you interact with is just that, an interface. The underlying operating system is a Unix-like system.

This means that many forensics techniques you can use on Linux can also be used on Macintosh from the shell prompt. There are many such commands and techniques, which we will discuss later in this book.

A Very Brief History of Linux

Linux is a clone of Unix. Specifically, it is an open-source clone of Unix. In 1985, Richard Stallman published his famous "GNU Manifesto," a document outlining the parameters for open-source licensing. Stallman had begun working on his own operating system in 1983. He called this system GNU (GNU is Not Unix). His goal was to create an open-source version of Unix. His version had issues that later open-source Unix clones attempted to correct.

In 1987, a man named Andrew S. Tanenbaum created Minix, an operating system quite similar to Unix. Minix was a fairly stable, functional, and reasonably good Unix clone. Though Minix failed to gain the popularity of some other Unix variants, it was an inspiration for the creator of Linux, Linus Torvalds. Linus was introduced to Minix and, while still in graduate school, decided to create his own open-source Unix clone. Linus found many things he liked about the Minix operating system, but he believed that he could make a better Unix variant. He chose the name Linux as a combination of his first name, Linus, and the end of Unix, nix. He began by posting the operating system code on an Internet discussion board, allowing anyone to use it, play with it, or modify it. Finally, Linus Torvalds released Linux 0.01 on the Internet under a GNU public license.

iOS

iOS was developed by Apple and was released in 2007. It is the operating system used on iPhones, iPads, and the iPod Touch. The interface focuses on direct interaction, such as touching, swiping, tapping, pinching, etc., to make the operating system respond. It is derived from OS X but is significantly different. We will discuss iOS in more detail later in this book when we explore mobile forensics.

Android

Android is a mobile operating system based on the Linux kernel. It was developed by Android, Inc., but is now owned by Google. It is open source, so one can actually download the Android code from the Web; however, many vendors make their own proprietary alterations to it. We will explore Android in more depth later in this book when we discuss mobile forensics.

Files and File Systems

Files and file systems are just as critical as the operating system. It is important to realize that the computer organizes data on a disk according to the file system. The operating system must interact with that file system to interact with files. A few basic facts about files:

- File headers start at the first byte of a file. This is important in forensics, as a suspect may rename a file extension, but examining the first byte will still show what type of file it is.

- The Executable and Linkable Format (ELF, formerly called Extensible Linking Format) is a common standard file format for executables (i.e., programs, applications, etc.), object code, and shared libraries for Unix-based systems.

- Portable Executable (PE) is used in Windows for executables and DLLs (Dynamic Linked Libraries).

- The term area density refers to the data per area of disk.

- Windows Office files have a GUID (Globally Unique Identifier) to identify them.

There are actually quite a few different file systems, but they can be divided into two categories: journaling and nonjournaling. Journaling is basically the process whereby the file system keeps a record of what file transactions take place so that in the event of a hard drive crash the files can be recovered. Journaling file systems are fault tolerant because the file system will log all changes to files, directories, or file structures. The log in which changes are recorded is referred to as the file system's journal. Thus, the term journaling file systems.

There are two types of journaling: physical and logical. With physical journaling, the system logs a copy of every block that is about to be written to the storage device before it is written. The log also includes a checksum of those blocks to make sure there is no error in writing the block. With logical journaling, only changes to file metadata are stored in the journal.

Specific File Systems   This section will give you a brief look at some specific file systems:

- FAT (File Allocation Table) is an older system that was popular with Microsoft operating systems for many years. It was first implemented in Microsoft Stand-alone Disk BASIC.FAT stores file locations by sector in a file called, eponymously, the File Allocation Table. This table contains information about which clusters are being used by what particular files and which clusters are free to be used. The various extensions of FAT (FAT16, FAT32) differ in the number of bits available for filenames. For example, FAT16 only supports 16-bit filenames, whereas FAT32 supports 32-bit filenames. Note that floppy disks use FAT12.

 EXAM TIP   Floppy disks use FAT12. This is an important forensics fact, and you are likely to be tested on it.

- Microsoft eventually introduced a new file system to replace FAT. This file system is called New Technology File System (NTFS). This is the file system used by Windows NT 4, 2000, XP, Vista, 7, Server 2003, and Server 2008. One major improvement of NTFS over FAT was the increased volume sizes NTFS could support. The maximum NTFS volume size is $2^{64}-1$ clusters. As of this writing, no version of Windows currently supports volumes that large.

- Extended File System (EXT) was the first file system created specifically for Linux. There have been many versions of EXT—the current version is 4. The EXT 4 file system can support volumes with sizes up to 1 exabyte (10^{18} bytes, or 1 billion gigabytes) and files with sizes up to 16 terabytes. This is frankly a huge file and volume size, and no current hard drives come even close to that. For an administrator, one of the most exciting features of EXT 4 is that it is backward compatible with EXT 2 and EXT 3, making it possible to mount drives that use those earlier versions of EXT.

- The Reiser File System is a popular journaling file system, used primarily with Linux. Reiser was the first file system to be included with the standard Linux kernel and first appeared in kernel version 2.4.1. Unlike some file systems, Reiser supported journaling from its inception, whereas EXT did not support journaling until version 3. Reiser File System is open source and was invented by Hans Reiser.

- The Berkeley Fast File System is also known as the Unix File System. As its names suggest, it was developed at Berkeley specifically for Unix. Like many file systems, Berkeley uses a bitmap to track free clusters, indicating which clusters are available and which are not. Like EXT, Berkeley includes the File System Check (FSCK) utility. This is only one of many similarities between Berkeley and EXT. In fact, some sources consider EXT to just be a variant of the Berkeley Fast File System.

Networks

Modern cyber forensics is very much intertwined with network operations. Many computer crimes take place across the network. Thus, it is imperative that any forensic examiner have a strong understanding of basic networking—something equivalent to the depth and breadth of knowledge to be gained from a good general networking course at a university, or perhaps the level of knowledge tested on the CompTIA Network+ certification. In this section, we will cover the absolute bare minimums of networking knowledge you must have to function as a forensic analyst. It is strongly recommended that you continue your study of networking beyond what is given in this section.

The Physical Connection

One of the first things to understand is the actual physical connection. Of course, many networks are now wireless, but physical connections are still important. The first thing to examine is your network interface card, commonly called a NIC. This is the card on your computer that you plug a cable into.

The cable connection used with traditional NICs (meaning not wireless) is an RJ 45 connection. (RJ is short for "registered jack.") In contrast to the computer's RJ 45 jacks, standard telephone lines use RJ 11 jacks. The biggest difference between jacks involves the number of wires in the terminator. Phone lines have four wires or in some cases six, whereas RJ 45 connectors have eight.

This type of cable is also often referred to as unshielded twisted-pair (UTP) cable. In UTP, the wires in the cable are in pairs, twisted together without any additional shielding. Each subsequent category of cable is somewhat faster and more robust than the last. It should be noted that although Cat-4 can be used for networks, it almost never is used for that purpose. You will usually see Cat-5 cable, and increasingly Cat-6; however, Cat-7 is also available.

Cat-5 cable works at speeds of up to 100 megabits per second (mbps), whereas Cat-6 works at 1000 mbps. It is widely available now, and has been for several years. However, for it to truly function properly, you need hubs/switches and NICs that also transmit at gigabit speeds. Category 7 is the latest advance in twisted-pair cabling, with frequencies up to 1000 MHz and speeds of up to 40 Gigabit Ethernet at 50 meters (164 ft) and 100 Gigabit Ethernet at 15 meters. Cat-5 is still found in many networks, with Cat-6 also being very common.

Coax cable has also been used for networking. It looks much like the coax cable used for your television. Two primary types are used for networking. The first is RG (an abbreviation for Radio Guide) 58 for Thinnet and RG 8 for Thicknet. Both are very resistant to crosstalk and interference.

Fiber-optic cable is becoming more common. There are two primary modes for fiber optic: The single-mode fiber optic is more expensive than the multimode fiber-optic cables and requires a light source with a narrow spectral width for propagation. The single-mode fiber (SMF) is a single strand of glass fiber with a core diameter less than 10 microns and has one mode of transmission.

TIP Fiber-optic cables are also called optic cables (OC), and their bandwidth is denoted by an OC number such as OC 3. A few common OCs are
OC3 155 megabits per second.
OC12 622 megabits per second. The equivalent of 336 T1 lines or 8,064 phone lines.
OC48 2.5 gigabits per second. The equivalent of four OC12 lines.

WiFi

Wireless is obviously becoming more widespread. There are various types of WiFi connections, all of which are based on the 802.11 standard. A brief summary of the variations is as follows:

- **802.11a** WiFi 5 GHz wireless. This was the first 802.11 WiFi standard and is no longer used.

- **802.11b** WiFi 2.4 GHz wireless. This is the networking commonly used in homes and SOHO (small office/home office) environments. It is being replaced by the faster 802.11g standard. It uses a wireless access point (WAP) to connect to other wireless computers. It has an indoor range of 125 ft and a bandwidth of 11 mbps.

- **802.11g** WiFi 2.4 GHz wireless. This networking is also commonly used in homes and SOHO environments. It uses a WAP to connect to other wireless computers. It is backward compatible with 802.11b. It has an indoor range of 125 ft and a bandwidth of 54 mbps.

- **802.11n** WiFi 2.4 or 5.0 GHz wireless. This standard has a bandwidth of 100 to 140 mbps and an indoor range of 230 ft.

- **IEEE 802.11n-2009** This standard has a bandwidth of up to 600 Mbit/s with the use of four spatial streams at a channel width of 40 MHz. It uses multiple-input multiple-output (MIMO), which uses multiple antennas to coherently resolve more information than is possible using a single antenna.

Today, you are most likely to find 802.11n, usually just called "n" WiFi. There are three different WiFi security modes: WEP, WPA, and WPA2.

Wired Equivalent Privacy (WEP) uses the stream cipher RC4 to secure the data and a CRC-32 checksum for error checking. Standard WEP uses a 40-bit key (known as WEP-40) with a 24-bit initialization vector to effectively form 64-bit encryption. 128-bit WEP uses a 104-bit key with a 24-bit initialization vector. RC4 is a very good algorithm; however, it was implemented poorly in WEP. The initialization vector should be used once, but that is not the case with WEP. Therefore, WEP is relatively easy to crack.

WiFi Protected Access (WPA) uses the Temporal Key Integrity Protocol (TKIP). TKIP is a 128-bit-per-packet key, meaning that it dynamically generates a new key for each packet.

WPA2 is the only one of the three that fully implements the security features of the 802.11i standard. WPA2 uses the Advanced Encryption Standard (AES) with the Counter

Mode-Cipher Block Chaining (CBC)-Message Authentication Code (MAC) Protocol (CCMP) that provides data confidentiality, data origin authentication, and data integrity for wireless frames.

Connection Devices

There are three connection devices that should also be discussed: the hub, the switch, and the router.

The Hub   The simplest connection device is the *hub*. A hub is a device into which you can plug in network cables. It will have four or more ports, most likely RJ 45 jacks. You can also connect one hub to another; this strategy is referred to as "stacking" hubs. If you send a packet (we'll discuss packets in a following section) from one computer to another, a copy of that packet is actually sent out from every port on the hub. There is no routing of any type. This was an old network traffic method that is no longer used today.

 NOTE   If you go to an electronics store and request a hub, they will give you a switch.

The Switch   A *switch* is basically an intelligent hub. A switch works and looks exactly like a hub, but with one significant difference. When it receives a packet, it will send that packet out only on the port it needs to go out on. A switch accomplishes this routing by using the MAC address (described a little later in this chapter) to determine where the packet should be routed to.

The Router   Finally, if you wish to connect two or more networks together, you use a *router*. A router is much like a switch, except that it routes traffic based on the IP address. Routers can also incorporate all types of network functionality such as a firewall.

What Is a Packet?

Packets are used to transmit data. The basic purpose of cable is to transmit packets from one machine to another. It does not matter whether that packet is part of a document, a video, an image, or just some internal signal from one computer to another. A packet is a certain number of bytes divided into a header and a body. The header tells you where the packet is coming from, where it is going, what type of packet it is, and more. Modern packets often have multiple headers. For example, standard network traffic will have an Ethernet header, TCP header, and IP header. The body contains the actual data, in binary format, that you wish to send. The aforementioned routers and switches work by reading the header portion of any packets that come to them. Packets usually have a footer that does some sort of error checking.

Protocols

There are different types of communications for different purposes. The different types of network communications are called *protocols*. A protocol is, essentially, an agreed-upon method of communication. Each protocol has a specific purpose and normally operates on a specific networking port. There are a total of 65,535 possible ports— 1,024 are called "well-known ports." Some of the most important protocols are listed in Table 1-1.

As was already mentioned, there are 1,024 "well-known ports," so the list in Table 1-1 is not comprehensive. All of these protocols are part of a suite of protocols referred to as TCP/IP (Transmission Control Protocol/Internet Protocol). A port is, essentially, a channel through which communication can occur. The communication is still occurring via the NIC over either cable or wireless. As we will see in later chapters, the knowledge of ports can be very important in forensic investigation of network attacks.

IP Addresses

An IP (Internet Protocol) address is an address assigned to a machine (PC, laptop, server, tablet, smart phone, router, etc.). There are currently two types of IP addresses: IP v4, which is widely used, and IP v6, which is a new standard gaining wide acceptance.

Protocol	Purpose	Port(s)
FTP (File Transfer Protocol)	For transferring files between computers.	20, 21
SSH (Secure Shell)	A secure/encrypted way to transfer files.	22
Telnet	Used to remotely logon to a system. You can then use a command prompt or shell to execute commands on that system. Popular with network administrators.	23
SMTP (Simple Mail Transfer Protocol)	Sends e-mail.	25
DNS (Domain Name Service)	Translates URLs into web addresses.	53
HTTP (Hypertext Transfer Protocol)	Displays web pages.	80
POP3 (Post Office Protocol Version 3)	Retrieves e-mail.	110
NetBIOS	An older Microsoft protocol that is used for naming systems on a local network.	137, 138, 139
SNMP (Simple Network Management Protocol)	A protocol for gathering information about various nodes on the network.	160, 161
BGP (Border Gateway Protocol)	This is how gateway routers exchange routing information.	179
HTTPS (Hypertext Transfer Protocol Secure)	HTTP encrypted with SSL or TLS.	443
Secure SMTP	Encrypted SMTP using SSL or TLS.	465

Table 1-1 Protocols and Ports

An IP v4 address is a series of four 3-digit numbers, separated by periods. (An example would be 107.22.98.198.) Each of the three-digit numbers must be between 0 and 255. The reason for this number range is that the IP address is actually four binary numbers; you just see them in decimal format. Recall that a byte is 8 bits (1's and 0's), and an eight-bit binary number converted to decimal format will be between 0 and 255.

IP v4 The IP v4 addresses come in two groups: public and private. The public IP addresses are for computers connected to the Internet. No two public IP addresses can be the same. However, a private IP address, such as one on a private company network, only has to be unique in that network. It does not matter if other computers in the world have the same IP address because this computer is never connected to those other worldwide computers. Often, network administrators use private IP addresses that begin with a 10, such as 10.102.230.17. The other private IP addresses are 172.16.0.0–172.31.255.255 and 192.168.0.0–192.168.255.255.

When you, as a forensic investigator, are tracing an IP address, be aware of a few facts. The first is that ISPs (Internet Service Providers) buy pools of IP addresses and assign them as needed. So if you trace suspect communication back to an IP address belonging to some ISP, you will then need to obtain more information from that ISP, often through a subpoena. The second issue is that IP addresses are easy to spoof. Someone can fake an IP address so that their traffic appears to be coming from somewhere else. This is commonly done in denial-of-service attacks.

IP v6 IP v6 utilizes a 128-bit address instead of a 32-bit one and utilizes a hex numbering method in order to avoid long addresses such as 132.64.34.26.64.156.143.57.1.3.7 .44.122.111.201.5. The hex address format will appear in the form of 3FFE:B00:800:2::C, for example. This gives you 2^{128} possible address (many trillions of addresses), so there is no chance of running out of IP addresses in the foreseeable future.

MAC Addresses

A Media Access Control (MAC) address is a unique address for a NIC. Every NIC in the world has a unique address that is represented by a six-byte hexadecimal number. The Address Resolution Protocol (ARP) is used to convert IP addresses to MAC addresses. So when you type in a web address, the DNS protocol translates that into an IP address. Then, the ARP protocol will translate that IP address into a specific MAC address of an individual NIC.

TIP It is also possible for someone to spoof a MAC address, but this takes a bit more skill and is less common than spoofing an IP address. So when tracing down criminal activity, gathering MAC addresses is very important.

Basic Network Utilities

As already mentioned, there are network utilities that you can execute from a command prompt (Windows) or from a shell (Unix/Linux). Many readers are already familiar with Windows, so this discussion will execute the commands and discuss them from the Windows command-prompt perspective. However, it must be stressed that these utilities are available in all operating systems. In this section, you will learn about IPConfig, ping, and tracert utilities.

IPConfig   The first thing you will want to do when determining the network status of the system you are examining is to get some information about that system's network connection. This may include the MAC address, IP address, etc. To accomplish this fact-finding mission, you will need to get a command prompt. In Windows 7, you do this by going to the Start menu, selecting All Programs, and then choosing Accessories. You will then see an option called Command Prompt. For Windows 8 users, accessing the program requires clicking the Start menu on the bottom-left side and scrolling right until you see the program you are looking for. You may then need to right-click and select All Apps to find the command prompt.

However you find the command prompt, now you can type **ipconfig**. (You could input the same command in Unix or Linux by typing **ifconfig** from the shell.) After typing **ipconfig** (**ifconfig** in Linux), you should see something much like what is shown in Figure 1-1.

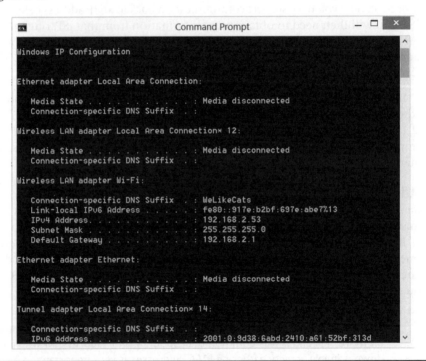

Figure 1-1   ipconfig

This command gives you some information about your connection to a network (or to the Internet). Most importantly, you find out your own IP address. The command also has the IP address for your default gateway, which is your connection to the outside world. Running the IPConfig command is a first step in determining your system's network configuration.

TIP There are also variations or command flags you can add. For example, ipconfig /all will give you more details. Ipconfig/release releases a dynamically assigned IP address.

Ping   Another commonly used command is ping. Ping is used to send an echo packet to a machine to find out if the machine is reachable and how long the packet takes to reach the machine. The command is shown in Figure 1-2.

```
                       Command Prompt              —  ☐  ✕

C:\Users\chuckeasttom>ping www.yahoo.com

Pinging ds-any-fp3-real.wa1.b.yahoo.com [206.190.36.45] with 32 bytes of data:
Reply from 206.190.36.45: bytes=32 time=68ms TTL=49
Reply from 206.190.36.45: bytes=32 time=67ms TTL=49
Reply from 206.190.36.45: bytes=32 time=67ms TTL=49
Reply from 206.190.36.45: bytes=32 time=70ms TTL=49

Ping statistics for 206.190.36.45:
    Packets: Sent = 4, Received = 4, Lost = 0 (0% loss),
Approximate round trip times in milli-seconds:
    Minimum = 67ms, Maximum = 70ms, Average = 68ms

C:\Users\chuckeasttom>
```

Figure 1-2   ping

This figure demonstrates that a 32-byte echo packet was sent to the destination and returned. The ttl item means "time to live." That time unit is how many intermediary steps, or hops, the packet should take to the destination before giving up. Remember that the Internet is a vast conglomerate of interconnected networks. Your packet probably won't go straight to its destination. It will have to take several hops to get there. As with all command-line utilities, you can type **ping -?** to find out various ways you can refine your ping.

Tracert   The final command we will examine is tracert. This command is sort of a ping "deluxe." Tracert not only tells you if the packet got there and how long it took, but also tells you all the intermediate hops it took to get there. (This same command can be executed in Linux or Unix, but there it is called "traceroute" rather than "tracert.") You can see this utility in Figure 1-3.

```
Command Prompt - tracert www.yahoo.com                    –  □  ×

C:\Users\chuckeasttom>tracert www.yahoo.com

Tracing route to ds-any-fp3-real.wa1.b.yahoo.com [98.138.253.109]
over a maximum of 30 hops:

  1     4 ms     6 ms     3 ms  router.WeLikeCats [192.168.2.1]
  2     7 ms     3 ms     7 ms  Wireless_Broadband_Router.home [192.168.1.1]
  3    12 ms    10 ms    10 ms  L100.DLLSTX-VFTTP-62.verizon-gni.net [96.226.241
.1]
  4    16 ms    18 ms    12 ms  G0-3-1-7.DLLSTX-LCR-21.verizon-gni.net [130.81.1
88.52]
  5    17 ms    14 ms    20 ms  ae3-0.DFW9-BB-RTR1.verizon-gni.net [130.81.199.5
8]
  6    15 ms    14 ms    15 ms  0.xe-3-3-0.BR2.DFW13.ALTER.NET [152.63.100.5]
  7   123 ms    18 ms    18 ms  ae8.edge10.dallas3.level3.com [4.68.62.33]
  8    37 ms    36 ms    56 ms  vlan60.csw1.Dallas1.Level3.net [4.69.145.62]
  9    37 ms    38 ms    36 ms  ae-61-61.ebr1.Dallas1.Level3.net [4.69.151.126]

 10    75 ms    35 ms    34 ms  ae-14-14.ebr2.Chicago2.Level3.net [4.69.151.117]

 11   141 ms    35 ms    34 ms  ae-2-52.edge3.Chicago3.Level3.net [4.69.138.168]

 12    43 ms    94 ms    36 ms  YAHOO-INC.edge3.Chicago3.Level3.net [4.53.96.158
]
 13   312 ms   201 ms   313 ms  ae-7.pat1.nez.yahoo.com [216.115.104.124]
 14   242 ms   207 ms   215 ms  xe-5-0-0.msr1.ne1.yahoo.com [216.115.100.1]
 15   186 ms   367 ms    52 ms  UNKNOWN-98-138-97-X.yahoo.com [98.138.97.3]
```

Figure 1-3   tracert

Netstat   Netstat is short for network status. It shows the current connections that machine is engaged in. This is very important from a forensic perspective. If you come upon a suspect machine that is running, before shutting that machine down, you should run netstat to determine connections. You can see netstat in Figure 1-4.

 TIP   All of these commands have flags that you can learn about by typing the command name followed by a question mark—for example, ipconfig -?. These commands are all useful in forensics, and you should become very familiar with them.

This section is just a brief overview of the hardware, software, and networking knowledge you should have in order to study forensics. If you find you are lacking in one or more areas, it is probably a good idea to review that material before proceeding beyond this chapter.

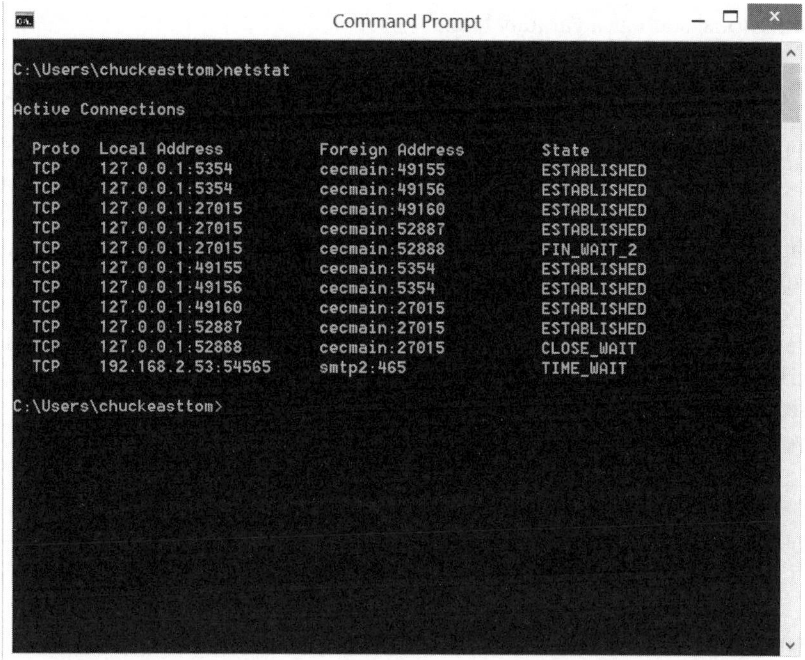

```
Command Prompt                                    _ □  x

C:\Users\chuckeasttom>netstat

Active Connections

  Proto  Local Address          Foreign Address        State
  TCP    127.0.0.1:5354         cecmain:49155          ESTABLISHED
  TCP    127.0.0.1:5354         cecmain:49156          ESTABLISHED
  TCP    127.0.0.1:27015        cecmain:49160          ESTABLISHED
  TCP    127.0.0.1:27015        cecmain:52887          ESTABLISHED
  TCP    127.0.0.1:27015        cecmain:52888          FIN_WAIT_2
  TCP    127.0.0.1:49155        cecmain:5354           ESTABLISHED
  TCP    127.0.0.1:49156        cecmain:5354           ESTABLISHED
  TCP    127.0.0.1:49160        cecmain:27015          ESTABLISHED
  TCP    127.0.0.1:52887        cecmain:27015          ESTABLISHED
  TCP    127.0.0.1:52888        cecmain:27015          CLOSE_WAIT
  TCP    192.168.2.53:54565     smtp2:465              TIME_WAIT

C:\Users\chuckeasttom>
```

Figure 1-4   Netstat

The Fundamental Principles of Cyber Forensics

We briefly mentioned earlier in this chapter the need to secure the crime scene and to maintain chain of custody. These are two fundamental principles of forensics. We will be examining various such principles in detail throughout this book. However, let's examine the two fundamental principles right now.

Securing the Crime Scene

The first, and perhaps most critical, step once you begin to actually analyze the evidence is to secure the crime scene. That usually means stopping access to the suspect system. In the past, various organizations have recommended immediately powering down the computer; however, it was discovered that this often led to a loss of evidence. So the recommendation now is to note all current connections, running software, processes, etc., and then shut down the system.

It is also important to then make sure the system is not accessible to any outside party. For laptops, this can mean turning off the wireless network card. For cell phones and other devices, it might mean transporting the device in some container that inhibits transmissions, such as a Faraday bag.

Limiting Interaction with the Evidence

Once the crime scene is secured, the next step is to make certain that you touch the actual evidence as little as possible. It is important that the investigator avoid any possibility of contaminating the evidence. For that reason, one of the first steps in a forensic investigation of a computer is to create a bit stream image of the hard drive; then the investigator investigates that image, not the original drive. This prevents any accidental tampering with the evidence. It is also important to use a write blocker. This is a device that prevents accidental writing of data to a storage device.

You can make a forensic copy with most major forensics tools, such as AccessData's Forensic Toolkit, or Guidance Software's EnCase. However, it can also be done with free tools using Linux. It is probably a good idea to understand how to do this manually even if you plan to use an automated forensic tool.

 TIP   One issue to keep in mind is testifying at deposition or trial. The opposing counsel might have a forensic expert advising them, and one common tactic is to ask you technical questions about your process. If you used an automated process, that is fine, as long as you can explain how it works. If not, you may find your testimony and your results excluded.

To make an image of a drive using Linux, you will need a bootable copy of Linux. Almost any Linux distribution will work. I personally use BackTrack. You will actually need two copies of a bootable Linux CD—one on the suspect machine and one on the target machine. Whichever version of Linux you use, the steps will be the same.

First, we have to completely wipe the target drive. This is done with the following command executed on the target drive:

```
dd if=/dev/zero of=/dev/hdb1 bs=2048
```

Now we need to set up that target drive to receive the copy of the suspected drive we wish to examine. The Netcat command helps with that. The specific syntax is as follows:

```
nc -l -p 8888 > evidence.dd
```

We are telling the machine to listen on port 8888 and put whatever it receives into the file evidence.dd.

Now on the suspect machine we have to start sending the drive's information to the forensics server:

```
dd if=/dev/hda1 | nc 192.168.0.2 8888 -w 3
```

Of course, this example assumes that the suspect drive is hda1. If this were not the case, then you would replace that part of the command with the partition you are using.

This example also assumes the server has an IP address of 192.168.0.2. If this were not the case, you would replace it with whatever your forensics server IP address is.

Now that we have made a copy, we need to ensure it was done properly. The method for this is to create a cryptographic hash of the original drive and the copy we just made. Most forensics toolkits will do this, but we can also do it from the Linux command line:

```
md5sum /dev/hda1 | nc 192.168.0.2 8888 -w
```

Maintaining Chain of Custody

We have already mentioned the need to maintain the chain of custody—this is done via a thorough document trail. A forensic investigator must document everything. The more documentation, the better. Document the scene where evidence is seized, the condition of equipment, and photograph as much as is practical. Then document how the evidence is seized and transported. Document the specifics of how the evidence is stored. And, of course, document the details of all tests performed on the suspect machine, beginning with the imaging of the machine.

The Law and Cyber Forensics

While state laws may vary, U.S. federal laws are not only consistent throughout the United States, but often supersede state laws in matters of computer crime. Computer crimes often involve interstate commerce, financial institutions, or other factors that render them federal crimes.

Many laws affect forensic investigation. For example, some jurisdictions have passed laws requiring that in order to extract the evidence, the investigator must be either a law enforcement officer or a licensed private investigator. Of course, that does not prevent a forensic investigator from either working with data someone else extracted or extracting evidence if the data owner gave their permission. It is important to be aware of the legal requirements in the jurisdiction you work in.

That is just one of many laws that will be important to you as a forensic investigator. It is impossible for any book to cover all the laws you should know. However, there is one principle that is key to forensics and is all too often overlooked in forensics books. That is the Daubert standard. The Cornell University Law School describes the Daubert standard in the following manner:[3]

> Standard used by a trial judge to make a preliminary assessment of whether an expert's scientific testimony is based on reasoning or methodology that is scientifically valid and can properly be applied to the facts at issue. Under this standard, the factors that may be considered in determining whether the methodology is valid are: (1) whether the theory or technique in question can be and has been tested; (2) whether it has been subjected to peer review and publication; (3) its known or potential error rate; (4) the existence and maintenance of standards controlling its operation; and (5) whether it has attracted widespread acceptance within a relevant scientific community.

What this means, in laymen's terms, is that you should only use tests, software, and equipment that has gained wide acceptance in the industry. If you conduct any part of your investigation with tools or techniques that have not been properly vetted by the scientific community, opposing counsel may issue a "Daubert challenge" claiming your evidence should be excluded. If they are successful, then any evidence you have collected will be excluded from the trial. Throughout this book, we will only use widely accepted tools and techniques.

General Legal Issues

There are two main branches of law: civil and criminal. Criminal law deals with intentional violations of law. Civil law deals with acts that may or may not be intentional, but the penalties don't involve incarceration. A civil wrong is called a tort.

"Torts are civil wrongs recognized by law as grounds for a lawsuit. These wrongs result in an injury or harm constituting the basis for a claim by the injured party."[4] Essentially, a tort results in a lawsuit where monetary damages may be awarded. In a civil case, the primary objective is to assess liability. Liability simply means who is responsible for the tort (if anyone) and then to assess the proper monetary value for that liability.

In any legal proceeding, the two parties are referred to as litigants. In a civil case, they are the plaintiff (the party that filed the lawsuit) and the defendant (the party being sued). It is not uncommon for there to be a countersuit where the defendant is also suing the plaintiff. It is also possible in civil law for one of the parties to be an organization or corporation rather than an individual.

In criminal law, the litigants are the prosecutor and the defendant. The prosecutor works for a government agency. When dealing with local crimes, that agency will be the district attorney's office. In federal crimes, it will be the U.S. Attorney's office. The defendant is represented by an attorney who is an advocate for their client. As a forensic analyst, you may work for either litigant. Keep in mind that, regardless of the attorney's role, you are not an advocate for either party. Your job is to dispassionately find the truth.

Discovery

In either a civil or criminal case, discovery is the process of each litigant finding out what evidence the other party has. In a criminal case, the prosecutor has a legal obligation to turn over all evidence to the defense attorney. The defense attorney does not have a reciprocal obligation. It is legal for the defense to hold on to exculpatory evidence until trial. Now there are some caveats to this, and they will vary from one jurisdiction to the next.

In a civil case, both parties are required to provide evidence if the opposing party asks for it. The first step in that is a simple request for documents. The next step includes what are called interrogatories. These are essentially a list of questions the opposing side is required to answer under oath. Finally, there are depositions. This is a chance for each side to question the opposing side under oath before trial.

NOTE The concept of "under oath" is very important. Lying under oath is a crime, and one that judges take very seriously.

The scope of discovery is not unlimited. A common objection attorneys make to an interrogatory or a request for documents is that it is beyond the scope of the case. Litigants are only entitled to relevant discovery, not an unfettered fishing expedition.

A related, and popular, trend is e-discovery. This is merely the electronic version of discovery. The litigants exchange documents in electronic format. This is becoming increasingly common as more and more law firms rely on computer technology.

Warrants

When seizing any property, including computers, cell phones, or other electronic devices, it is important to be sure you have the legal authority to do so. If you illegally seize evidence, then that evidence will most likely be excluded from any legal proceedings. The most common way to legally seize evidence is with a warrant issued by a court.

According to the Supreme Court, a "'seizure' of property occurs when there is some meaningful interference with an individual's possessory interests in that property" *United States v. Jacobsen*, 466 U.S. 109, 113 (1984), and the Court has also characterized the interception of intangible communications as a seizure in the case of *Berger v. New York*, 388 U.S. 41, 59–60 (1967). Now that means that law enforcement need not take property in order for it to be considered seizure. Merely interfering with an individual's access to his or her own property constitutes seizure. And *Berger v. New York* extends that to communications. Now if law enforcement's conduct does not violate a person's "reasonable expectation of privacy," then formally it does not constitute a Fourth Amendment "search" and no warrant is required.

There have been many cases where the issue of reasonable expectation of privacy has been argued. But to use an example that is quite clear, if I save a message in an electronic diary, I clearly have a reasonable expectation of privacy. However, if I post such a message on a public bulletin board, I can have no expectation of privacy. In less clear cases, a general rule is that courts have held that law enforcement officers are prohibited from accessing and viewing information stored in a computer if they would be prohibited from opening a closed container and examining its contents in the same situation.

In computer crime cases, two consent issues arise particularly often. First, when does a search exceed the scope of consent? For example, when a person agrees to the search of a location—for example, their apartment—does that consent authorize the retrieval of information stored in computers at the location? Second, who is the proper party to consent to a search? Can roommates, friends, and parents legally grant consent to a search of another person's computer files? These are all very critical questions that must be considered when searching a computer. In general, courts have held that the actual owner of a property can grant consent. For example, a parent of a minor child can grant consent to search the living quarters and computers. However, a roommate who shares rent can only grant consent to search living quarters and computers that are co-owned by both parties. A roommate cannot grant consent to search the private property of the other person.

Federal Guidelines Forensics Investigators Need to Know

If you are setting up a forensics lab, or if you are new to forensics, a good place to start would be the federal guidelines. Two agencies in particular—the FBI and the Secret Service—are important sources of guidelines.

FBI

While the Secret Service is now the premier federal agency responsible for cybercrime, the FBI is also involved in many computer crime cases. Prior to the Patriot Act, the FBI took the lead role in computer crime investigations. The FBI lists its own guidelines, though they are largely consistent with those of the Secret Service. Those guidelines are explained in this section.

If an incident occurs, the FBI recommends that the first responder preserve the state of the computer at the time of the incident by making a backup copy of any logs, damaged or altered files, and, of course, any files left by the intruder. This last part is critical. Hackers frequently use various tools and may leave traces of their presence. Furthermore, the FBI warns that if the incident is in progress, activate any auditing or recording software you might have available. Collect as much data about the incident as you can. In other words, this might be a case where you do not take the machine offline, but rather analyze the attack in progress.

The FBI computer forensic guidelines stress the importance of securing any evidence. They further stress that computer evidence can come in many forms. A few common forms are

- Hard drives
- System logs
- Portable storage (USB drives, external drives, etc.)
- Router logs
- E-mails
- Chat room logs
- Cell phones
- SIM cards for cell phones
- Logs from security devices such as firewalls and intrusion detection systems
- Databases and database logs

Obviously, what you secure will depend upon the nature of the cybercrime. For example, in the case of child predators, online stalkers, or online fraud, e-mail may be very important but router logs may be irrelevant. The FBI also stresses that you work with a copy of the hard drive, not the original.

 TIP The FBI has a cybercrimes5 web page, which is a very useful resource for learning more about trends in cybercrime and in cyber forensics.

Secret Service

The U.S. Secret Service is the premier federal agency tasked with combating cybercrime and with cyber forensics. They have a website devoted to cyber forensics[6] that includes forensics courses. These courses are usually for law enforcement personnel.

The Secret Service also has released a guide for first responders to computer crime.[7] They have listed their "golden rules" to begin the investigation. Those are

- Officer safety. Secure the scene and make it safe.
- If you reasonably believe that the computer is involved in the crime you are investigating, take immediate steps to preserve the evidence.
- Do you have a legal basis to seize this computer (plain view, search warrant, consent, etc.)?
- Do not access any computer files. If the computer is off, leave it off.
- If it is on, do not start searching through the computer. If the computer is on, go to the appropriate sections in this guide on how to properly shut down the computer and prepare it for transportation as evidence.
- If you reasonably believe that the computer is destroying evidence, immediately shut down the computer by pulling the power cord from the back of the computer.
- If a camera is available and the computer is on, take pictures of the computer screen. If the computer is off, take pictures of the computer, the location of the computer, and any electronic media attached.
- Do special legal considerations apply (doctor, attorney, clergy, psychiatrist, newspapers, publishers, etc.)?

These are all important first steps to both preserving the chain of custody and ensuring the integrity of the investigation from the outset.

The Need for Cyber Forensics Certification

Why certifications? This question has been bandied about the information technology field for years. Various pundits come down upon one extreme or the other, with some claiming certifications are invaluable and others claiming they are worthless. Also, some subindustries within IT have different attitudes about certifications. In the Cisco world, certifications are kingpin, while in the Linux community, certifications have negligible value. So what is the worth of certifications in forensics?

First, one must examine the purpose of certifications—what does it mean to be "certified"? Frequently, people who have a dim view of certifications have that view because they have encountered someone with some certification who was not very competent. This denotes a misunderstanding of what any certification is. Certification is supposed to indicate that the holder of that certification has met a minimum standard. It does not mean that the person in question is the master of that topic, but rather, that they are competent. A good analogy would be a medical degree. That does not guarantee the person is a great doctor, merely that they have obtained a minimum competency in medicine.

However, it is possible to pass a certification test and not be very good at the topic. But the same is true of any field and any educational endeavor. There are certainly some medical doctors (thankfully few) who are incompetent. But if you suddenly have chest pains, I bet you would prefer someone call you a medical doctor rather than a plumber. Why? Because the odds of a medical doctor having the requisite skill is much higher than that of a plumber. The same is true for IT certifications. While it is certainly possible that someone could be certified and not be competent, the odds that a certified person is competent are much higher. That is why employers frequently require or prefer certifications. It makes the job of filtering through applicants much easier.

So any IT certification can be one valuable indicator of a job applicant's skill. It is not the only indicator, and certainly should not be the only thing considered, but it is one factor. This brings us to forensic certifications. Is there a need for another one? First look at what cyber forensics certifications are currently available.

AccessData, the creators of the Forensic Toolkit, have multiple certifications for their product, as does Guidance Software, the creators of EnCase. Both of those vendor certifications are quite good. However, they are also both vendor certifications. The emphasis is on the particular proprietary suite of tools rather than on a general coverage of cyber forensics. If you are going to work with either tool, it is a very good idea to get the appropriate vendor certification, but that is not the same thing as a broad-based cyber forensics course/test.

The EC-Council has their Computer Hacking Forensic Investigator test, and it has been somewhat popular. However, as the name suggests, it has an emphasis on hacking and counter-hacking. The EC-Council's primary focus has always been hacking.

This brings us to the topic of (ISC)^2's Certified Cyber Forensics Professional. Is this certification test worth taking? The first thing to realize is that (ISC)^2 has a long history of well-respected certification courses/tests, starting with the CISSP, which is the oldest and most well-known computer security certification. This means the CCFP is backed by a strong support organization. The content of the course/test is also very good. The domains covered include forensic science, application forensics, investigatory procedures, law, and ethics. It is just the sort of broad coverage of cyber forensics that is needed.

Chapter Review

Forensics of any type is a science, and that is absolutely true with cyber forensics. Any sort of digital media can be the object of a cyber forensic investigation. This includes cell phones, routers, computers, tablets, even the new Google Glass. If an item can digitally store data, then it can be forensically examined by a cyber forensics investigator.

Cyber forensics requires a strong working knowledge of PCs, operating systems, and networking. That knowledge is the foundation of cyber forensics. The equivalent of a CompTIA A+ and Network+ certifications should be considered the base level of knowledge.

A variety of laws and principles are critical to cyber forensics, principles such as touch the evidence as little as possible; always work with an image of the drive, not the original; and document everything. There are also legal standards such as the Daubert standard that are critical to cyber forensic investigations.

Questions

1. What term describes the route that evidence takes from the time you find it until the case is closed or goes to court?

    A. Chain of custody

    B. Law of probability

    C. Daubert path

    D. Separation of duties

2. If a police officer without a warrant locks a door so that a suspect cannot access his (the suspect's) own computer, what would be the most likely outcome?

    A. The evidence will be excluded because the officer seized it without a warrant.

    B. The evidence will be excluded because it does not meet the Daubert standard.

    C. The evidence will be admitted; this is not a warrantless seizure.

    D. The evidence will be admitted; the officer acted in good faith.

3. What U.S. federal agency is most responsible for cybercrime investigation?

    A. The FBI

    B. Homeland Security

    C. NSA

    D. Secret Service

4. Which of the following refers to functional dimensions of a drive in terms of the number of heads, cylinders, and sectors per track?

   A. Drive layout

   B. Hard drive geometry

   C. Drive geometry

   D. Hard drive layout

5. Space in a cluster not used by a file is called _____.

   A. Slack space

   B. Unused space

   C. Ghost space

   D. Empty space

Answers

1. **A.** Chain of custody, which is a critical concept you must understand for the CCFP exam.

2. **A.** Yes, any interference with a person's property is a seizure

3. **D.** The U.S. Secret Service is the lead organization for cybercrime. This was implemented as part of the Patriot Act.

4. **C.** Drive geometry is the appropriate term.

5. **A.** Slack space is the term for unused space at the end of a cluster.

References

1. American Heritage Dictionary. http://education.yahoo.com/reference/dictionary/entry/forensics.

2. CERT Forensics Definition. http://www.us-cert.gov/reading_room/forensics.pdf.

3. Cornell Law School Daubert Standard. http://www.law.cornell.edu/wex/daubert_standard

4. http://www.law.cornell.edu/wex/tort.

5. FBI Cybercrime website. http://www.fbi.gov/about-us/investigate/cyber/cyber.

6. Secret Service, Cyber forensics. http://www.ncfi.usss.gov/.

7. First Responders Guide. http://www.forwardedge2.com/pdf/bestPractices.pdf.

The Investigative Process

In this chapter, you will learn:

- How to manage the chain of custody
- Proper investigative ethics
- How to manage criminal investigations
- The issues of civil investigations
- How to manage administrative investigations
- The essentials of intellectual property investigations

While cyber forensics is clearly a very technical process, technical prowess alone is not enough. Throughout this book, we will spend a great deal of time on specific technical processes, procedures, and techniques. However, the ethics of forensics is just as important as the technical process. In fact, one can do everything technically correct, but an ethical issue can render evidence inadmissible in court. And in some cases, a breach of ethics could, in fact, end a cyber forensics analyst's career. So the material in this chapter is quite critical, both for the Certified Cyber Forensics Professional certification test and for your career itself.

Chain of Custody

The concept of chain of custody is one of the cornerstones of forensic science, whether that is cyber forensics or some other forensic discipline. Chain of custody refers to detailed documentation showing the status of evidence at every point in time from the moment of seizure to the moment the evidence is presented in court. Any break in that chain of custody will likely render that evidence inadmissible at trial.

 TIP   Failure to maintain the chain of custody is an egregious error. I am certain you have seen police dramas on television wherein some key evidence was excluded due to some gap in the chain of custody. This part of crime dramas is accurate. You must be able to completely document the chain of custody from the point of seizure to the point of trial.

According to the Scientific Working Group on Digital Evidence Model Standard Operation Procedures for Computer Forensics:

> The chain of custody must include a description of the evidence and a documented history of each evidence transfer.[1]

This definition is worth further examination. Notice it states "history of each evidence transfer." Any time that evidence is transferred from one location to another, or from one person to another, that transfer must be documented. The first transfer is the seizure of evidence when the evidence is transferred to the investigator. Between that point in time and any trial, there may be any number of transfers.

The first transfer occurs when the evidence is initially seized. At that point, a complete documentation of the scene, the personnel involved, date, and time should be performed. Then, each time the evidence is moved to any new location, examined, or a different person accesses it, this all should be documented. In law enforcement, this is accomplished with an evidence tag. An example of an evidence tag is shown in Figure 2-1. Obviously, specific law enforcement agencies will have some slight differences in how they format their evidence tag (note this tag has the police department name redacted).

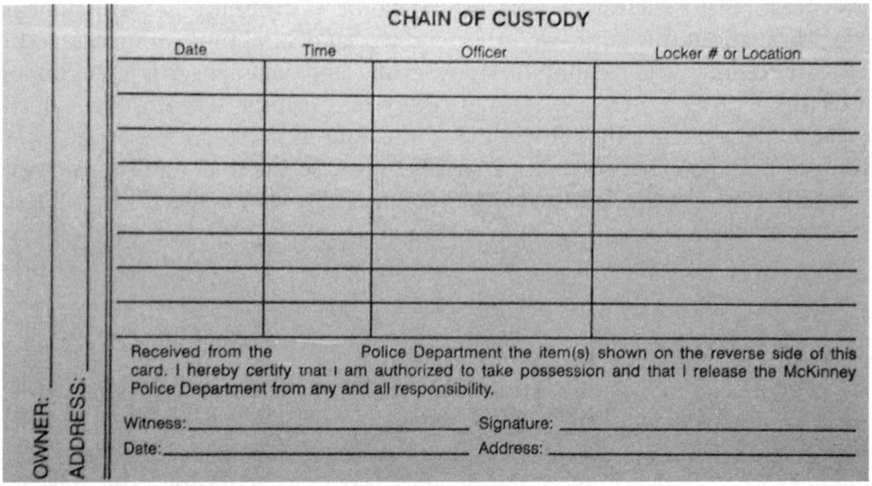

Date	Time	Officer	Locker # or Location

CHAIN OF CUSTODY

OWNER:
ADDRESS:

Received from the _____ Police Department the item(s) shown on the reverse side of this card. I hereby certify that I am authorized to take possession and that I release the McKinney Police Department from any and all responsibility.

Witness:_____ Signature: _____
Date:_____ Address: _____

Figure 2-1 Evidence tag

Normally, evidence is kept in a secure location, one with a lock and controlled access. Anytime the evidence is accessed, that access (including who, date, time, and what was done) is documented. The final transfer occurs when the evidence is taken to court.

NOTE It is important to keep in mind that a few jurisdictions have passed laws requiring that in order to extract the evidence, the investigator must be either a law enforcement officer or a licensed private investigator. This is a controversial law, given that normally, private investigator training and licensing do not include computer forensics training. You should check with specifics in your state, but in general, this does not preclude a computer forensics expert from analyzing the evidence; however, someone else might need to seize it. This immediately brings up the issue of chain of custody. The person seizing the evidence is not the examiner, and it is imperative that chain of custody be preserved.

Securing the Scene

In non-computer crimes, like burglary or even homicide, the crime scene is blocked off by police tape. This is to prevent people from contaminating the crime scene and to give the forensic team the opportunity to collect evidence. Such obvious physical barriers may also be present in some computer crime investigations, but not all. In the case of a computer crime scene, you must secure the computer, network, or target area of the attack. Usually, that will mean preventing access to the system. That will include disconnecting from the network and preventing people from accessing the system.

While a computer crime may seem quite different from a non-computer crime, many of the investigation principles are the same. For example, in a non-computer crime scene, you remove everyone from the scene who does not absolutely need to be there to conduct the investigation. The same principle applies to a computer crime investigation. The only people who should access the system(s) that are the subject of the investigation are those people with an actual need to perform some part of the investigation.

No one who does not absolutely need access to the evidence should have it. Hard drives should be locked in a safe or secure cabinet. Analysis should be done in a room with limited access.

Documentation

If you have never worked in any investigative capacity, the level of documentation may seem onerous to you. But the rule is simple: *Document everything*. It is really not possible to overdocument. It is likely that some cases will depend more on certain aspects of the documentation than others; however, you won't know what documentation is really important until the case is done. So err on the side of caution and document everything.

What do we really mean when we say document everything? Well, the documentation process begins at the crime scene itself, when you first encounter the crime scene. When you first discover a computer crime, you must document exactly what events occurred. Who was present and what where they doing? What devices were attached to the computer, and what connections did they have over the network/Internet? What hardware was being used and what operating system? All of these questions must be answered and must be documented.

Then when you begin your actual forensic investigation, you must document every step. Even before you begin your actual analysis, you will document the crime scene and the process of acquiring the evidence. You should also document how the evidence is transported to your forensic lab. From there, you continue documenting every step you take, starting with documenting the process you use to make a forensic copy. Then document every tool you use, every test you perform. You must be able to show in your documentation everything that was done. You can see a brief sample of a report in Figure 2-2.

Overview/Case Summary

1. On today's date, John Doe contacted my office in regards to imaging a report of harassing emails and is requesting a full forensic examination and report for possible criminal charges.
2. There is insufficient evidence at this time to request a warrant for the accused perpetrators computer.
3. The alleged victim has made his computer available for forensic examination.

Examination

1. On today's date I took possession of the alleged perpetrator's computer and victim's computer.
2. Using a sterile storage media (examination medium) that had been forensically wiped and verified by this examiner (MD5 hash value: ed6be165b631918f3cca01eccad378dd) using AccessData's Disk Imager. The MD5 hash value for the examination medium yielded the same MD5 hash value as previous forensic wipes to sterilize this media.
3. I then examined the emails received on the computer using Paraben's email analysis tool.

Findings

1. I discovered six emails that contained threatening or harassing messages (see screenshots below).
2. I tried the IP addresses of the email sender to a local ISP.
3. I subpoenaed the ISP's records and confirmed that the emails were sent from the alleged perpetrators IP address.

Figure 2-2   Sample report

You should note that this sample seen in Figure 2-2 is intentionally brief so that it fits well in an image. As mentioned, there really is no such thing as overdocumenting. More detail is always better. The SANS institute also gives some guidance on documenting a cyber forensic investigation at http://computer-forensics.sans.org/blog/2010/08/25/intro-report-writing-digital-forensics/. According to the Scientific Working Group on Digital Evidence (SWDGE),[2] a report should include the following:

> The report is to provide the reader with all the relevant information in a clear and concise manner using standardized terminology. The examiner is responsible for reporting the results of the examination.

Reports issued by the examiner must address the requestor's needs and contain the Identity of the reporting organization.

- Case identifier or submission number.

- Identity of the submitter.

- Date of receipt.

- Date of report.

- Descriptive list of items submitted for examination.

- Identity and signature of the examiner.

- Description of examination.

- Results/conclusions/derived items.

When documenting your analysis, the process should be documented with a level of detail that would allow any competent forensic examiner to take your documentation and be able to replicate your entire testing process. So it is not enough to simply say, for example, that you used AccessData to image a drive. Rather, you must give a step-by-step tutorial as to how you did the imaging.

 TIP It is also a good idea to use photographic and video documentation. Photographic documentation is usually done at the crime scene. The entire scene is photographed from multiple angles. Videotaping the crime scene is also possible, as well as using videotape to document the examination procedures.

Authority and Objectives

It is important that a forensic examiner be certain that he or she has the authority to investigate given evidence. Normally, these decisions will be made by lead investigators (law enforcement) or attorneys, but you do need to be aware of the issues.

One of the major issues is jurisdiction. In criminal cases, one of the first steps to decide is who has jurisdiction. Is this a federal, state, or local case? Or is it an intelligence matter and not a criminal one? In civil cases, the rules for that specific court (federal or state) must be adhered to.

Once you have established jurisdiction, the forensic examiner should at least be aware of whether or not there exists the authority to seize and examine the evidence. Was there a warrant or did the owner give consent? Was consent given in writing? If there was a warrant, did it specify this certain piece of equipment? If it did not, there should be some documentation/explanation as to why it was seized.

After you have determined that you have the authority to examine the evidence, you should establish some objectives. Forensic analysis is not a fishing expedition, hoping to find something juicy. You should have specific goals for your analysis.

Examination

Clearly, the examination is the most critical part of the forensic process. Of course, the seizing of evidence must be done according to accepted protocols. And the documentation of the procedures used is very important. However, all of those activities are in support of the actual examination.

According to the SWGDE Model Standard Operation Procedures for Computer Forensics,[3] there are four steps to an examination:

- **Visual Inspection** The purpose of this inspection is just to verify the type of evidence, its condition, and relevant information to conduct the examination. This is often done in the initial evidence seizure. For example, if a computer is being seized, you would want to document if the machine is running, its condition, and the general environment.

- **Forensic Duplication** This is the process of duplicating the media before examination. It is always preferred to work with a forensic copy and not the original.

- **Media Examination** This is the actual forensic testing of the application, which will take up a great deal of the rest of this book. By media, we mean hard drive, RAM, SIM card—any item that can contain digital data.

- **Evidence Return** Exhibit(s) are returned to the appropriate location, usually some locked or secured facility.

These steps cover the overall process. If any of these steps are omitted or performed incorrectly, the integrity of the investigation could be called into question.

 EXAM TIP The CCFP exam relies heavily on the SWGDE standards and documents. Anywhere in this book you see SWGDE cited, you should give that particular attention. It is also recommended that you visit their website and review any documents prior to taking the CCFP exam: www.swgde.org.

Code of Ethics

While there are legal requirements regarding forensic investigations, there are also ethical requirements, and these are just as important. As a forensic investigator, you need to keep two facts in mind. The first is that there are significant consequences resulting from your work. Whether you are working on a criminal case, a civil case, or simply doing administrative investigations, major decisions will be made based on your work. You have a heavy ethical obligation. It is also critical to remember that a part of your professional obligation will be testifying under oath at depositions and at trials. With any such testimony there will be opposing counsel who will be eager to bring up any issue that might impugn your character. Your ethics should be above reproach.

As you will see in this section, there is certainly overlap between ethics and legal requirements, but they are separate topics. One way of thinking about the difference between law and ethics is that ethical guidelines begin where the law ends.

(ISC)² Ethics

Before we begin an examination of the details of ethical requirements in forensic investigations, it is useful to first examine the (ISC)² ethical guidelines. Every person taking an (ISC)² certification test (CISSP, CSSLP, CCFP, etc.) agrees to abide by these ethical guidelines.[4] These guidelines are

- Protect society, the common good, necessary public trust and confidence, and the infrastructure.

- Act honorably, honestly, justly, responsibly, and legally.

- Provide diligent and competent service to principals.

- Advance and protect the profession.

Essentially, these ethical guidelines are general principles designed to provide a framework within which to practice the profession of cyber forensics. They are intentionally general, and one could say vague. My own policy is that when in doubt as to what the ethical course of action is, err on the side of caution. Put another way: If you believe something might be unethical but cannot decide, assume that it is unethical and act accordingly. You should note that the ethical guidelines published by the (ISC)² do not describe specific laws you must follow.

American Academy of Forensic Science Ethics

The American Academy of Forensic Science (AAFS) encompasses the entire breadth of forensics, not just cyber forensics. That includes fire forensics, medical forensics, financial forensics, etc. While the technical details of each type of investigation are quite diverse, the ethical challenges are remarkably similar. But due to the wide range of forensic subdisciplines, most of the AAFS ethical guidelines are necessarily broad. The actual ethical guidelines are listed here:[5]

a. Every member and affiliate of the Academy shall refrain from exercising professional or personal conduct adverse to the best interests and objectives of the Academy. The objectives stated in the Preamble to these bylaws include: promoting education for and research in the forensic sciences, encouraging the study, improving the practice, elevating the standards and advancing the cause of the forensic sciences.

b. No member or affiliate of the Academy shall materially misrepresent his or her education, training, experience, area of expertise, or membership status within the Academy.

   c. No member or affiliate of the Academy shall materially misrepresent data or scientific principles upon which his or her conclusion or professional opinion is based.

   d. No member or affiliate of the Academy shall issue public statements that appear to represent the position of the Academy without specific authority first obtained from the Board of Directors.

Item a is a generic admonition to behave in a way that does not embarrass the Academy and in fact improves its reputation. Item d is similar in that it directs members not to speak, or even appear to speak, on behalf of the AAFS.

Items b and c are of most interest to our discussion of ethics. Item b essentially says don't exaggerate. This is actually wonderful advice, though it may seem unnecessary. You might wonder if any expert would really exaggerate his or her credentials. The unfortunate answer is that yes, some would. In fact, I have personally encountered incidents of this sort of behavior. For example, someone might have a legitimate degree, even a master's degree, but to enhance his or her resume, they might get a doctorate degree from an unaccredited degree mill. Just as disconcerting is passing of self-published e-books as published works. When one publishes nonfiction, the publisher puts the book through a thorough vetting process, similar to peer review. Multiple editors, including a technical editor, review the book. In the case of certification guides, they are often checked against the certification objectives. A self-published work has no such verification process.

 NOTE Clearly, a few self-published works are very well written. However, self-published means it was not vetted by anyone other than the author. During a deposition or cross-examination at a trial, this issue will certainly come up.

Item c may seem even odder. The fact is that in many expert reports, there may be dozens of citations. The people reading the report, particularly a lengthy one, might not check carefully every citation. I have personally prepared expert reports that were close to 300 pages long with many scores of citations. It would certainly be possible to exaggerate or interpret the conclusions of one or more of those citations in order to enhance one's position.

Violating item b or c of the AAFS code of ethics can have extremely deleterious effects on your career. When you testify in court, whether it be specifically as an expert witness or simply as a forensic examiner (for example, for a law enforcement agency), your only real commodity is your reputation. Any hint or suggestion of exaggeration may, in fact, end your career. You can read the AAFS code of ethics at http://aafs.org/about/aafs-bylaws/article-ii-code-ethics-and-conduct.

ISO Code of Ethics

The ISO standards for ethics are much longer—currently, a 92-page document—and are concerned with forensic testing and forensic labs. It would be worthwhile for you to thoroughly review this document, particularly if you intend to establish a new forensic lab or manage an existing forensic lab. However, in this section, we will highlight some specific issues you are likely to be tested on in the CCFP test.

Lab Accreditation

For labs, there is a somewhat lengthy accreditation process. That process includes an introductory visit, assessment of your practice, and document review. After this, you are given some time to plan for the actual accreditation visit. The formal accreditation visit may be followed with recommendations for corrective action that must be reviewed prior to an accreditation decision being made.

The accreditation will be concerned with your handling of the chain of custody, security of the evidence, procedures in place, precautions, and policies. Policies must address routine handling and security of evidence, as well as how to handle incidents such as a breach in security protocol.

Digital Forensics

Section 30 of the ISO code of ethics refers specifically to digital forensics. One important issue dealt with in this section is the use of outside contractors. Specifically, the ethical standards state

> An agency may use the services of an outside party to perform aspects of digital and multimedia examination, but the agency must exercise caution in how the test results are reported so that accreditation is not incorrectly inferred for the tests in question.

This is very important. In any cyber forensics lab, you may encounter a case that requires forensic examination of some digital device with which you are not proficient. This may require the use of an outside contractor to examine that specific evidence. However, you are still responsible for ensuring that the outside contractor adheres to accepted forensic practices.

The ISO digital forensics ethical standards also address the issue of learning new skills. Specifically, the standards state that

> In circumstances where examiners attend classes, seminars or conferences to learn new analytical techniques, agencies shall take measures to assure themselves of the competency of the examiners prior to authorizing them to apply these techniques to case work.

This is also quite important. New technologies emerge, and new tools are developed. At some point, your forensic staff will need additional training. However, how much training is required to make them proficient in this new technology or technique? The lab must have some means of ensuring these forensic examiners are indeed proficient in the new skill set before allowing them to use it on an actual case. Related to this is the requirement that a forensic lab must have a protocol in place for evaluating new technologies and techniques before implementing them. So both the new technology and the examiner being trained in that new technology must be evaluated.

Ethical Conduct Outside the Investigation

As was mentioned earlier in this chapter, a part of your job as a forensic investigator involves testifying. To be effective at testifying, you must have impeccable character. It is guaranteed that opposing counsel will seek out any issues that might impugn your testimony. Obviously, this means a clean criminal record; however, other issues are also important.

Civil Matters

Have you ever been sued? If so, for what reason and did you win the case? Obviously, anyone can be sued, and being the object of a lawsuit does not mean you are untrustworthy. So if you have been sued, be prepared to answer a few questions.

First, was the lawsuit related to your professional work? This sort of lawsuit is one of the most damaging for a forensic investigator. As a cyber forensic investigator, if you have previously been sued—for example, due to allegations of incompetent network consulting—opposing counsel may use that to suggest you are not really competent in computer science and your investigation should not be considered reliable.

If the lawsuit was not related to your professional work but involved issues that might indicate unethical behavior on your part, such as dishonest business practices, this, too, can be used to impugn your testimony. It is very easy for opposing counsel to make the argument that if, for example, you were accused of being dishonest when you sold your house, you might also be dishonest when you conduct a cyber forensic investigation.

As mentioned, anyone can be the target of a lawsuit, and being a defendant in a lawsuit is not an automatic end to your forensic career. The first issue at hand is, Does the lawsuit involve issues that could impugn your character? Then the next obvious question is, Did you lose the lawsuit? However, again, my rule is to err on the side of caution. If you find yourself the target of lawsuits repeatedly, then you probably should take some time to seriously review your conduct to determine why you are being sued so often.

Criminal Matters

It should be fairly obvious that any history of criminal behavior will normally end your career in cyber forensics. But there are always exceptions. For example, if you had a misdemeanor charge when you were a youth and you are now middle aged, it is most likely you can explain that charge and move forward with your career. However, a general rule is that any sort of criminal charge, including reckless driving, misdemeanor assault, trespass, etc., is extremely detrimental to your career.

In general, criminal conduct is simply not acceptable. If there is any criminal charge in your background, even if it was a misdemeanor and was 20 years ago, you need to disclose this to the attorney you are working with or to senior investigators/supervisors. Someone in authority must be made aware of the details of the criminal act, including the outcome. This will allow that person or persons to determine if this prevents you from being an effective forensic investigator.

Other Issues

We live in an information age. Everything is public and it is very easy to find. You have to remember that cyber forensics is usually related to some court case, whether criminal or civil, and our legal system is adversarial. It is very likely that opposing counsel will perform a web search on your name in an attempt to find information that might be embarrassing. If you posted a picture to Facebook showing you inebriated at a New Year's Eve party, this is something that opposing counsel could use to embarrass you.

You should be very wary of anything you put on the Internet. It is okay to have a Facebook page (I have a personal Facebook page for friends and family and a public one for readers and fans), but the rule is simple: Do not post anything you would be embarrassed to see in a courtroom. Even political statements/opinions, if worded wrong, can be perceived as offensive.

Any professional opinion you make in public will come back to you. Something as simple as book reviews you write on Amazon.com can be used in a deposition or trial. For example, if you give a glowing review of a Linux book on Amazon.com, and the opposing expert is citing that book in his or her report, the opposing counsel will use your review to indicate that you must agree with their expert.

I am not saying that you cannot make public statements. Many experts do book reviews, write articles/books, and even speak at conferences. The key is to be very sure of what you write or say, being aware that it can come back to you in a later case.

Ethical Investigations

Ethics in your conduct of your investigation is critical. A number of issues may arise during an investigation that you need to be aware of. Before we begin a discussion of ethical investigations, it is important to differentiate between ethical and legal. Legal indicates that your investigation followed the letter of the law. Ethical indicates that you strove to maintain the highest standards and to avoid even the appearance of impropriety. The law does not require that you avoid even appearing to engage in misconduct. However, you must keep in mind that evidence is usually used in court proceedings, which, as mentioned, are adversarial in nature. This means that there will be opposing attorneys (and probably their own forensic expert) who will attempt to cast doubt on your investigation and your conclusions.

The Chinese Wall

There may be occasions when different members of the same firm are working on cases that could present a conflict of interest if those investigators shared information. This sometimes occurs with law firms. For example, one attorney represents company XYZ, Inc., and another represents ABC LLC.; however, at some point, XYZ files a lawsuit against ABC. Now the attorneys have a potentially serious problem of conflict of interest.

The Chinese Wall is a procedural barrier that prohibits two members of the same organization or team from sharing information related to a specific case or project. This can be more cumbersome than it sounds. The two people involved in a project or case that could lead to a conflict of interest must be prevented from communicating any information about that case, no matter how trivial. Furthermore, other people in the organization must also ensure they don't accidentally reveal inappropriate information to one of these two members.

 TIP The Chinese Wall concept is something that is part of the CCFP exam. It is rather simple, but make sure you can apply it to scenarios.

Relevant Regulations for Ethical Investigations

Clearly, if ethical conduct outside the investigation is important, then ethical conduct within the actual investigation is critical. Conducting an investigation in an ethical manner is just as important as following the legal guidelines. There are several issues to consider, as the following sections explain.

Authority to Acquire

Do you have the authority to acquire the evidence? This may seem like an odd question, but it is important. As mentioned previously, in many states, it is illegal for evidence to be seized by anyone who is not a law enforcement officer or a private investigator.

Provenance

Provenance is defined as the origin of something. For example, in art, the term refers to evidence showing that a given piece of art is actually the work of a specific artist. For example, was a Monet painting actually painted by Monet? In forensics, provenance has a very similar meaning. If it is alleged that a given file originated with a suspect's computer, can you show clearly that it was actually from that suspect's computer? If a child pornography website is accessed from a computer to which multiple people have access, for example, it will be more difficult to show that the suspect actually accessed the website.

Reliability

Is the evidence reliable? Is the evidence from a source that is reliable? For example, if someone brings evidence to the police, reliability is immediately a question. If evidence does not come from a reliable source, then it is not possible to base conclusions on that evidence.

Admissibility

Admissibility may seem similar to reliability and provenance, and they are related topics; however, they are not identical. This area of ethical consideration is far more related to legal guidelines in evidence. We discussed chain of custody at the beginning of this chapter, and you must keep that in mind throughout your investigation.

Fragility

The issue of evidence fragility is more related to how and when you collect evidence. In subsequent chapters as we discuss the gathering and processing of evidence, we will delve into this issue in more detail. An example would be spyware that is running on a live system. This is volatile evidence that might be lost if you turn off the computer without first recording the evidence. Yet another example involves active network connections to a suspect machine. These will definitely be lost when the machine is powered down; therefore, that evidence is considered fragile.

Authentication

Authentication is closely related to provenance and chain of custody. It refers to the ability to verify that the evidence is what it is claimed to be, was gathered in a reliable manner, and chain of custody was maintained. This will involve documentation of how the evidence was found, how it was seized, and the validation of drive images that are made for the investigation (something we will be discussing in detail).

The Evidence

When considering ethical guidelines for an investigation, the evidence itself can be an important guide to how to ethically handle the investigative process.

Criminal Investigations

Conducting a criminal investigation involves adhering to specific legal requirements. These legal requirements should also form the basis for ethical rules. The most obvious legal requirement in the United States is the Fourth Amendment to the U.S. Constitution. The Fourth Amendment states

> The right of the people to be secure in their persons, houses, papers, and effects, against unreasonable searches and seizures, shall not be violated, and no Warrants shall issue, but upon probable cause, supported by Oath or affirmation, and particularly describing the place to be searched, and the persons or things to be seized.

This seemingly simple statement is the basis for a great deal of case law regarding appropriate searches and the seizure of evidence. One question that has been the center of a great many court decisions is what constitutes an unreasonable search or seizure. U.S. courts have consistently held that for a search to be reasonable, either there must be a warrant issued by a court, or there must be some overriding circumstances to justify searching without a warrant.

Let's deal with the issue of warrants first. A warrant is essentially legal permission to seize evidence. This leads to the question of what constitutes a seizure. According to the Supreme Court, a "'seizure' of property occurs when there is some meaningful interference with an individual's possessory interests in that property," *United States v. Jacobsen*, 466 U.S. 109, 113 (1984), and the Court has also characterized the interception of intangible communications as a seizure. This is very important. A seizure occurs simply by preventing the suspect from being able to interact with his property. If you were, for example, to prevent the suspect from using his laptop computer, you have just legally seized that computer.

While there are exceptions to the requirement for a warrant, it is almost always best to get a warrant before seizing any evidence. There are two exceptions. The first is exigent circumstances, which usually does not apply to cybercrime. This refers to police entering a dwelling or seizing property to prevent imminent harm. For example, if an officer hears someone screaming "HELP" from an apartment, the officer does not need a warrant to enter the apartment. This would rarely apply to cybercrimes. However, the second exception might apply. The second exception is called plain sight. This means that if something is in plain sight, you don't need a warrant. For example, if a police officer is at a home responding to a noise complaint and can clearly see child pornography on a computer screen, the officer does not need a warrant.

Civil Investigations

Civil investigations center on lawsuits. A lawsuit involves the allegation of wrongdoing where the potential damages are financial rather than criminal. Civil litigation includes wrongful termination lawsuits, patent infringement suits, copyright infringement suits, and similar litigation. These cases will sometimes involve forensic examination of evidence.

For example, in the case of a sexual harassment lawsuit, it may be required to forensically extract and analyze e-mails. The process will be very much the same as it is with criminal investigations. The exact same issues with chain of custody and with documenting your process are involved. One major difference is that in a civil investigation, it is usually the case that a company owns the computer equipment and can provide permission to extract and analyze evidence; thus, warrants are unlikely to be needed.

Administrative Investigations

Administrative investigations are usually done strictly for informative purposes. These are not meant to support criminal or civil court proceedings. For example, if there is a system outage that causes significant disruption to business, management may want to have a forensic investigation performed in order to ascertain what caused the outage and how to avoid it in the future.

One might think that the normal processes used in criminal and civil investigations are not needed in this situation. And to some extent, this is true. Certainly, a warrant is not needed to seize evidence and examine it, provided the evidence belongs to the party requesting the investigation. For example, a company does not need a warrant to search company-owned computers. Furthermore, civilians cannot request search warrants. However, even if this is an internal forensic investigation for a company, it is still critical that you document every single step. There are two main reasons for this. The first is simply to accurately document the investigation in order to clarify and support any findings. The other reason is that it is possible an administrative investigation could lead to a criminal or civil investigation. For example, assume that you are investigating the reasons for an e-commerce server being offline for two days. In your investigation, you discover that the problem lies with a third-party company you use for application development. Management may wish to initiate civil litigation in order to recoup losses. This will not be possible if you have not followed sound forensic practices.

In other cases, evidence may reside on someone else's machine, but in a civil case, you do not get a search warrant. Instead, the attorney will file a motion to the court asking the court to order the other party to produce the evidence.

Intellectual Property Investigations

Under the topic of civil investigations, we mentioned patent lawsuits. Patent litigation and other intellectual property investigations are handled a bit differently than criminal investigations. To begin with, there is usually not a seizure of evidence. Instead, the court will order the defendant to produce the evidence to the plaintiff. The plaintiff will designate an expert to examine the evidence and reach some conclusion. The discovery process can be lengthy. It is common for defendants to take one of two approaches. The first is to produce as little as they believe will fulfill the court's order. This usually leads the plaintiff to make additional requests for discovery. The second tactic is to simply dump everything they have on the plaintiff, giving the plaintiff literally a mountain of evidence to sift through.

It is also often true that intellectual property investigations can be lengthy. One reason is that defendants often overproduce evidence. What I mean by this is that when the court orders the defendant to produce, for example, source code to a program, the defendant may produce all their source code, with no notes, no direction, and no indication of what it does. The expert then must take the time to first figure out what the code does and then determine if it violates the plaintiff's intellectual property rights.

NOTE   Normally, the defense will produce the required evidence in a secure room at their attorney's office. The plaintiff's expert then goes to that office and examines the evidence. This is often time consuming. On one particular case, I spent six months examining the code to make a determination. The defendant had produced over one terabyte of completely undocumented code.

An important part of patent litigation is the Markman hearing. In a patent infringement case, there is usually disagreement among the opposing attorneys as to what specific terms of a patent mean. This may sound like frivolous arguing, but it certainly is not. For example, what exactly constitutes an "applet"? Some programmers might say that an applet is a piece of self-contained Java code that executes within a web page. However, in a patent case, the terms have meaning based on what the inventor stated in the patent. The actual wording of the patent is called *intrinsic evidence*; supporting material from third-party sources is called *extrinsic evidence*. When the two parties disagree as to the definitions of words, each side prepares an argument for their position and submits it to the court. The court then has a Markman hearing to determine the definitions of the disputed terms. This is important for a forensic expert, as you must use the definitions the court has chosen even if they might be different from those commonly used in industry.

The Daubert Standard

One very important legal standard to keep in mind during any investigation is the Daubert standard. The Daubert standard essentially states that any scientific evidence presented in a trial has to have been reviewed and tested by the relevant scientific community. For a computer forensics investigator, that means that any tools, techniques, or processes you utilize in your investigation should be ones that are widely accepted in the computer forensics community. You cannot simply make up new tests or procedures. Harvard Law School[6] describes the Daubert standard as follows:

> The Supreme Court's decision in Daubert v. Merrell Dow Pharmaceuticals is often thought of as two separate holdings. (1) In the first, unanimous holding, the Supreme Court asserts that the long-standing Frye rule for the admissibility of expert testimony has been replaced by the more recently enacted Federal Rules of Evidence. (2) This holding has been generally well received and universally applied by the federal district courts. The second holding, however, has been a source of great confusion and controversy. In the second part of the Daubert decision, over the dissent of Justices Rehnquist and Stevens, Justice Blackmun writes that federal judges have a duty to ensure that 'an expert's testimony rests on a reliable foundation and is relevant to the task at hand.' (3) In addition, Justice Blackmun lays out a number of criteria by which the reliability of an expert's testimony may be judged. (4) While it is clear that the majority of the Court envisions a more active gatekeeping role for federal judges, it is not clear exactly what the limits and scope of that role should be. Perhaps most significantly, it is uncertain whether this more active judicial role applies only to determining the admissibility of 'hard' scientific evidence, or whether the Daubert decision is to be used to evaluate the admissibility of non-scientific and quasi-scientific expert testimony as well.

The Forensic Investigator as an Expert

As previously mentioned, forensic analysts/investigators will often serve as expert witnesses in trials. An expert witness is a bit different from a witness of fact. An expert witness is allowed to testify about things he or she did not see. However, the expert's testimony must be firmly grounded in accepted scientific methodology. In other words, the expert witness did not "witness" something occur, but rather forms opinions based on his or her expertise. Those opinions must be firmly grounded in scientific principles and evidence.

NOTE What is the difference between an expert witness and a forensic investigator? Sometimes, nothing. An expert witness is simply someone who has been hired to form opinions about a case and who has relevant expertise. We will discuss the qualities you may want in an expert, but there is no firm line. I have personally seen people with doctorate degrees and those with only bachelor's degrees serve as expert witnesses. A lot depends on the individual case and the totality of the person's expertise. Of course, the more qualifications one has, the better. Opposing counsel can file a motion with the court objecting to the expert, particularly if they believe the expert lacks appropriate expertise or has a conflict of interest.

Qualities of an Expert

If someone is going to testify at depositions or at trials, it is important that they have certain qualities. Not everyone who is an expert in a given field is appropriately used as an expert. Even qualified and credible experts might not be appropriate for every case. For this reason, there are specific qualities that should be considered:

- Clean background check
- Well trained
- Experienced
- Credibility
- No conflicts
- Personality

 TIP Remember that the opposing side in any trial, be it criminal or civil, will try and attack your expert witness's credibility. It is important that his or her professional qualifications be such that a jury will clearly accept their expertise.

Clean Background Check

It is absolutely critical that anyone working with computer crime investigations have a thorough background check. That may seem obvious, but there are plenty of companies that don't do any background checks on their employees. For law enforcement agencies and Department of Defense–related organizations, the background issue is already taken care of. However, when dealing with civilian employees and consultants, a criminal background check should be conducted and updated from time to time. It is probably best to make sure that any civilian consultant has the same level background check given to law enforcement and is held to the same standard.

You may think that anyone working in information security has had a background check. Unfortunately, this is not always the case. Sometimes, companies either do no background check or only a cursory one. I personally encountered an Internet Service Provider whose technical support manager had twice been in federal prison, and on both occasions had identity theft as one of his offenses. This means you cannot assume that an experienced professional has a clean criminal background.

Well Trained

Obviously, in order to be an expert in any field one must have significant training. That training can come from a variety of sources, including traditional academic degrees, job-related training, industry training, industry certifications, webinars, and continuing education.

Academic Training and Programs   If one is to serve as a testifying expert, it is best to have a graduate degree. It is certainly possible for one to have only a bachelor's degree, or even no degree, but a graduate degree is ideal. The degree should be in some related field such as computer science, computer information systems, or computer engineering. These academic programs ensure that the individual has a thorough baseline understanding of computer systems, operating systems, networks, programming, and related topics. It is certainly possible to have a degree in a different discipline, depending on other factors. For example, someone with a business degree might have taken a great many computer-related courses as part of their degree. Or someone with a degree in history might have combined that with extensive experience in the industry and industry training.

The nature of the academic training is also important. Obviously, you won't always be able to find an expert with a doctorate from a prestigious institution such as Harvard, Princeton, or Midland; it is not necessary. What you need is for the totality of that person's qualifications to make them clearly an expert on the topics that they need to testify about. It is important to make certain the institution the expert's degrees are from is regionally accredited. That may seem odd, but there has been a proliferation of spurious degrees, particularly online degrees. This is not to say that an online degree is illegitimate. Harvard, MIT, Stanford, Texas Tech, University of North Dakota, North Central University, Capella University, and American Military University all have fully accredited, recognized online programs. Whoever is hiring an expert should check the accreditation of any degree program.

It is also important that the expert be a learner. That means two different things. The first, of course, is that the expert must learn each new case, carefully studying all aspects of it and learning its nuances. This is the way the CCFP uses the term "expert as a learner." However, I would opine that it also means the expert must be continually learning. Even if one has a PhD in computer science from MIT, one should still refresh and expand one's learning from time to time. If you see an expert whose resume does not indicate any new learning in the past ten years, this should be cause for concern.

Certifications   Industry certifications are a significant part of the computer industry. Microsoft Certified Solutions Expert, Red Hat Certified Engineers, and Java Certified Programmers are all part of the IT profession. And the same is true with the security profession. There are a number of certifications relevant to IT security and forensics that might be of interest to you in selecting a consultant or expert witness. It should be noted that the (ISC)^2 certifications have gained wide respect in industry; thus, pursuing the Certified Cyber Forensics Professional certification from (ISC)^2 is definitely an indication of expertise. The ideal situation is when certifications are coupled with degrees and experience—then they make a powerful statement about the person's qualifications.

Experienced

Training and education are important, but frankly, experience is king. It is certainly valuable to have obtained training, but it is just as important to have actual experience. When someone is seeking a computer crime expert or consultant, they want someone who has real-world, hands-on experience. Now it may or may not be necessary to find someone who has investigated computer crimes. That may sound like an odd statement, and obviously, you would prefer someone with experience investigating computer crimes. However, someone with a strong understanding of investigation and forensics who has extensive experience in computer systems and networks can be a useful asset. That knowledge of operating systems and networks can be as important as, if not more important than, investigation experience. Of course, the ideal candidate will have both skill sets. But in no case should you use someone who has only academic training and has never functioned as a network administrator, security administrator, network consultant, or related job.

The obvious counterargument to this is that there is a first time for everything. Even the most experienced professional once had their first investigation. Ideally, however, that first investigation will involve assisting someone with more experience. You certainly do not want your case to be their first real-world attempt. If you are going to utilize an expert, it is important that they have experience, not just extensive training. And the more experience they have, the better.

Credibility

In most trials, both sides will have an expert witness, and most expert witnesses will have significant training and experience. Another issue that is important to keep in mind is credibility. This may be academic or professional credibility. How do you know if a particular individual has that credibility? To a layperson, simply having an advanced degree would seem to be evidence enough, but that is not the case. One needs to have contributed meaningfully to that particular academic discipline. That can mean any number of things. It is often evidenced by particular awards, such as endowed chairs at universities. It also can be evidenced by publications of both research papers and books.

A good indicator of expertise is how often other experts refer to their work. If you find no other researchers reference a person's work, that is a strong sign that their work is not considered credible or noteworthy by their professional peers. You can do a Google Scholar search on an author's name to see how often that person's works are cited by other experts in the field. However, even if an expert has not published books or research papers, they may still be a qualified expert. The expert is a technician in the specific field on which they are opining. This requires training and credibility.

No Conflicts

It is absolutely critical that your expert have no conflict of interest. When law firms are considering experts to use in a case, one of the first things they check for is a conflict of interest. This means the expert witness should have no prior business or personal relationship with any of the principal parties in the case. In civil litigation, this means the expert should have no prior relationship with the plaintiff or the defendant. In a criminal case, it usually just means the defendant, since the plaintiff is the state. What exactly constitutes a prior relationship? In most cases, this means no substantive contact, that the two parties do not know each other on a personal level or have business contacts. Some attorneys are even stricter and require that the expert to have never even met the involved parties and to have no direct communication with them outside of courtrooms and depositions. Remember that for better or worse, our legal system is adversarial. If there is any way the opposing counsel can construe the expert as being biased, they will do so. For this reason, it is best to avoid even the appearance of any relationship with any relevant parties.

Conflict of interest goes beyond direct relationships between the parties. It literally means that the expert has some interest in the outcome of the case. Ideally, an expert's only interest is in the truth. He or she should have no personal motive in seeing the case decided in favor of one party or the other. For example, an expert witness for the prosecution in a case involving child pornography might be considered to have a conflict of interest if someone close to them has been a victim of child pornography. Or an expert for the defense might be considered to have a conflict of interest if that expert is a member of the same fraternity, church, or social group as the defendant.

NOTE Remember the appearance of a conflict of interest can be enough to change the outcome of a trial. Therefore, one must carefully screen potential expert witnesses for conflicts of interest.

Personality

We have discussed the technical specifics to look for in an expert. But what issues are not found on a resume that might make a good (or bad) expert? These issues are important in any expert, but are most important in a testifying expert witness. Teaching ability is important. The expert witness will need to explain complex technical topics to a judge and jury. This requires someone who is skilled in communicating ideas. This is why lawyers often use professors as expert witnesses—they are comfortable teaching and speaking in front of groups. The expert is ultimately a teacher. Of course, you don't need to be a professor to be an expert witness, and many expert witnesses are not professors. But you do need to be able to teach.

A calm demeanor is also important. The fact is that a deposition or trial is bound to be stressful for the witness. In addition, some attorneys will endeavor to unsettle an expert witness, particularly during deposition. Remember that the other side's attorney is going to question the expert's credentials, methods, and findings. They may even question the expert's integrity. Someone who is easily upset will likely have a strongly negative reaction to this. The expert must be calm, confident, and not easily upset.

Another issue to be aware of with an expert is their history of testimony and expert reports. Have they previously testified to or made a public opinion that could reasonably be construed as contrary to the opinion they will be taking for you? For example, if an expert previously wrote an article stating that online sting operations to catch pedophiles are inherently unreliable, you cannot now use them to testify for you in support of evidence gathered in an online sting. Now this may seem obvious, and you may think that no expert would want to testify contrary to an opinion they previously espoused. However, it is an unfortunate fact that there are a few experts who indeed will say anything for a fee. So you (or the attorney handling the case) need to expressly inquire about this issue. It is important to note that the number of experts willing to say things they don't believe for a fee is far lower than some elements in the public perceive, particularly in technical subjects where the elements of the case are relatively concrete and less open to interpretation. The majority of experts will simply turn down a case if they don't agree with the conclusions that the client (in this case, you) wish them to support.

Related to past public opinions and testimony is the issue of honesty. Contrary to what you may have seen on television and movies, the vast majority of experts will not prevaricate in testimony or in their reports. Obviously, some issues are open to interpretation, even in technical disciplines, and some experts are more willing than others to take a more creative interpretation of the evidence. However, stating an outright falsehood, either through intentional lying or just being in error on the facts, is usually the end of an expert witness's ability to function in court cases.

Chapter Review

In this chapter, we have examined legal and ethical guidelines for conducting forensic investigation. We have looked at U.S. law regarding the search and seizure of evidence and standards for admissibility of evidence, as well as general ethical guidelines. As important as the examiner's ethical conduct during an investigation is the examiner's ethical conduct outside of the investigation. Furthermore, we have examined the differing ethical and legal requirements for various types of investigations, including criminal, civil, administrative, and intellectual property.

Questions

1. What term describes the route that evidence takes from the time you find it until the case is closed or goes to court?

    A. Law of probability

    B. Daubert path

    C. Chain of custody

    D. Separation of duties

2. If a police officer locks a door without a warrant so that a suspect cannot access his (the suspect's) own computer, what would be the most likely outcome?

   A. The evidence will be excluded because the officer seized it without a warrant.

   B. The evidence will be excluded because it does not meet the Daubert standard.

   C. The evidence will be admitted; this is not a warrantless seizure.

   D. The evidence will be admitted; the officer acted in good faith.

3. Which of the following is not part of the (ISC)^2 ethics guidelines?

   A. Obey the Daubert standard.

   B. Act honorably, honestly, justly, responsibly, and legally.

   C. Provide diligent and competent service to principals.

   D. Advance and protect the profession.

4. Which of the following is a guideline for admissibility of scientific evidence?

   A. The Daubert standard

   B. Warrants

   C. (ISC)^2 ethical guidelines

   D. The Fourth Amendment

5. According to the Scientific Working Group on Digital Evidence Model Standard Operation Procedures for Computer Forensics, which of the following is not required for chain of custody.

   A. Description of the evidence

   B. Documented history of each evidence transfer

   C. Documentation of how the evidence is stored

   D. Documentation of the suspect

6. What is the process whereby a court determines the meaning of disputed words in an intellectual property case?

   A. Deposition

   B. The Fourth Amendment

   C. The Markman hearing

   D. The Daubert test

7. Which of the following would allow a police officer to seize evidence without a warrant?

    A. If the suspect has a history of related crimes

    B. If the alleged crime is a felony

    C. If the evidence is in plain sight

    D. If the officer has a good tip

Answers

1. **C.** Chain of custody, which is a critical concept you must understand for the CCFP exam. Chain of custody is documenting every single step the evidence takes from seizure to trial.

2. **A.** Yes, any interference with a person's property is a seizure.

3. **A.** The Daubert standard is necessary, but is not part of the (ISC)² ethics.

4. **A.** The Daubert standard is the rule that governs the admissibility of scientific evidence. Essentially, it states that the techniques and tests used must be widely accepted in the scientific community.

5. **D.** Documentation of the suspect is not part of the chain of custody.

6. **C.** The Markman hearing determines the definition of disputed terms.

7. **C.** If the evidence is in plain sight.

References

1. The Scientific Working Group on Digital Evidence Model Standard Operation Procedures for Computer Forensics.

2. https://www.swgde.org/documents/Current%20Documents/SWGDE%20 QAM%20and%20SOP%20Manuals/2012-09-13%20SWGDE%20Model%20 SOP%20for%20Computer%20Forensics%20v3.

3. Section 7. https://www.swgde.org/documents/Archived%20Documents/ SWGDE%20SOP%20for%20Computer%20Forensics%20v2.

4. (ISC)² Code of Ethics. https://www.isc2.org/ethics/Default.aspx.

5. AAFS Section II code of ethics. http://aafs.org/about/aafs-bylaws/ article-ii-code-ethics-and-conduct.

6. http://cyber.law.harvard.edu/daubert/ch5.htm.

Evidence Management

In this chapter you will learn:

- Proper evidence collection techniques
- How to preserve and transport evidence
- Methods for tracking evidence
- Proper storage of evidence
- Evidence access control
- How to dispose of evidence after an investigation

Evidence management is a topic that covers the details of evidence collection, chain of custody, and managing the actual investigation. Some of these topics were briefly touched upon in Chapter 2 but will be covered in more depth in this chapter. The primary theme of this chapter is maintaining the chain of custody. Chain of custody is the cornerstone of any forensic investigation.

Evidence Collection

The first step in a forensic investigation should be the collection of evidence. As discussed briefly in Chapter 2, this will begin by documenting the location and environment where the evidence is being seized. When discussing documentation of the scene, several items should be included in that documentation.

Evidence Documentation

In order to make this point clear, let us walk through a hypothetical scenario together. Assume that you are at an apartment where police allege the laptop that is on the desk in the living room has been a source for child pornography. The first thing you should document is the condition of the computer in question. When you arrived, was it running or not? Does it appear to be damaged in any way? Once you have ascertained the condition and status of the target computer, are there any other devices connected to it? For example, a printer attached to that computer would be worth noting. You will also need to take note of all other computer equipment in the residence. This will include the router, cell phones, and other computing devices. Documentation of the scene must be at least done by writing down notes; however, photographs are often useful. Figures 3-1 and 3-2 provide two photographs of a possible cybercrime scene.

Figure 3-1   Suspect computer angle 1

Now if you examine these two images, you can see they document significant information. In Figure 3-1, you can see that there is a Sony Vaio laptop in a docking station. It has several USB devices connected to it, most importantly a Passport portable USB drive. This clearly shows that external USB devices are present at the crime scene and should be examined for possible evidence. In Figure 3-2, you readily notice the Epson

Figure 3-2
Suspect computer
angle 2

laser printer. More advanced printers often have permanent storage that can be examined to see what documents have been printed. However, you also see a second monitor and keyboard. This would indicate that at least at some point there has been a second computer present. It would then be necessary to search the location to see if the second computer is still on site. All of these facts are documented by taking two simple photographs of the crime scene. You should also write down a description of what is at the scene to go with the photographs taken.

 NOTE It is quite common for forensic investigators to document the scene using video recording. This is a good idea, with one caveat. If you are going to record video, it should be complete video. Do not stop the recording and then restart at a different angle or different portion of the crime scene. Doing so would allow the opposing counsel to question what occurred during the gap in recording. What was in the section you did not record? These questions can cast unnecessary doubt on a properly conducted investigation.

In some cases, sketching the scene may be helpful.[1] However, sketches should only be done if required to provide context for the evidence and if personnel capable of creating a readable and helpful sketch are available. In some physical crimes, such as homicide, sketching the scene can be invaluable. However, in cybercrimes, this is less often useful. You should determine the need for a crime scene sketch on a case-by-case basis.

Once the scene has been properly documented, you should also note any environmental conditions that might affect digital evidence, such as extreme moisture or temperature. You should also note all personnel who are present. This list might include the suspect (even if he or she is removed from the scene at some point during your investigation), any other forensic personnel, any law enforcement personnel, and anyone else at the scene. The documentation should include the person's name, role (i.e., a detective, the suspect, etc.), whether or not the person in question had access to the suspect equipment, the time they arrived, and when they left. In the case of the suspect, you should even document if they were in reach of the equipment in question.

The capture/point of transfer is generally when evidence is first seized.[2] It can, in some cases, be the point at which a disk is imaged; however, this is less likely. Most imaging today takes place at the forensic lab. In essence, documenting the scene is the process of documenting the capture point for the evidence.

Evidence Preservation

In addition to collecting evidence, the evidence must be preserved. When collecting evidence, the investigator must protect its integrity. This involves two related tasks. Make sure that nothing is added to the evidence and that nothing is destroyed. This process is called evidence preservation.

Preserving evidence is something that must be considered throughout the process of seizing evidence, analyzing evidence, and transferring evidence. One way this is accomplished is by always working with a copy of the evidence, not directly working with the evidence itself. This involves creating an image of any disk, drive, or other storage device. Earlier in this book we discussed how to image a hard drive manually with Linux commands. Most major forensics toolkits also provide imaging capabilities. Let us take a look at one of these tools.

 TIP The test won't ask you the specifics of how particular commercial tools such as EnCase and Forensic Toolkit work. However, in the field you will need to understand common forensic tools. Both EnCase and AccessData are popular with law enforcement agencies.

AccessData's Forensic Toolkit

AccessData produces the Forensic Toolkit.[3] They even provide the disk imager as a free utility you can download. Once you have installed it on your forensic computer, you begin by attaching the suspect drive and selecting Create Image from within the disk imager. This is shown in Figure 3-3.

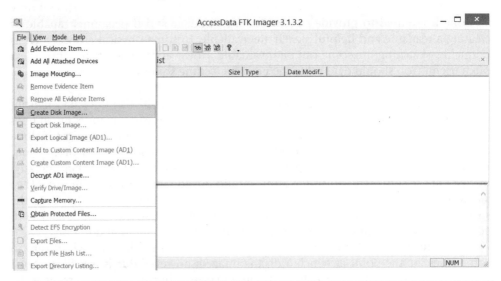

Figure 3-3 Choosing to create an image of a disk with Forensic Toolkit

The next step is to just follow the wizard, selecting which drive to image and where to put the image. Then AccessData Disk Imager does it for you. The process is shown in Figures 3-4 through 3-6.

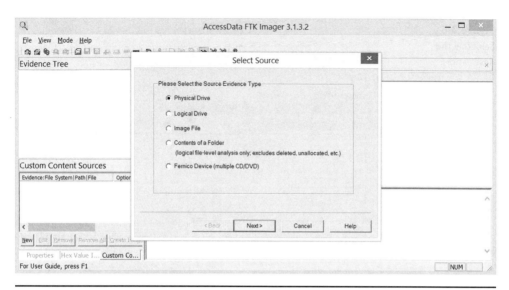

Figure 3-4 Select Source dialog box

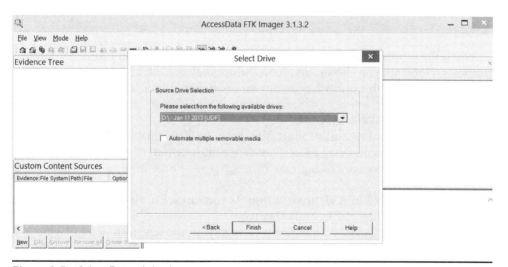

Figure 3-5 Select Drive dialog box

Figure 3-6
Selecting the
destination

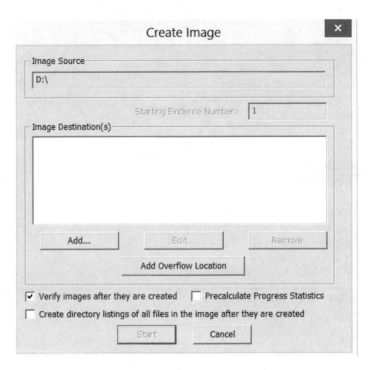

When the process is done, you will have an image that you can utilize for forensic purposes. Note that you should first hash the original and the image and compare the hashes; fortunately, this utility has an option to do that for you as well.

Guidance Software's EnCase

Guidance Software's EnCase[4] product also provides disk imaging capabilities. Their process is a bit different. Every piece of evidence must be part of a case file. So the first step is to either select an existing case or begin a new one. Beginning a new case is shown in Figure 3-7.

Then you select to add evidence to a case. As you can see in Figure 3-8, that can be a local disk, image, evidence file, and other types.

If you select a local disk, you will be presented with the screen shown in Figure 3-9. Notice that EnCase gives you the option of only working with write-protected disks. We will discuss disk write protection in detail, later in this chapter.

Figure 3-7   Starting a new case in EnCase

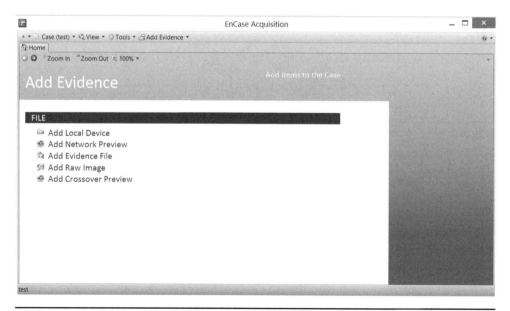

Figure 3-8   Adding evidence to the EnCase file

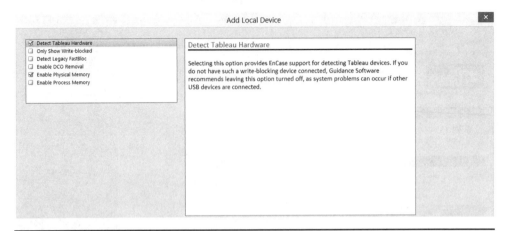

Figure 3-9   Selecting a write-protected disk in EnCase

After you have selected a disk, the rest is just walking through the wizard, similar to how it is done in AccessData. Your next screen will give you a list of disks connected to the machine you are running EnCase on. This is shown in Figure 3-10. Note that the drives in this figure are not write-protected.

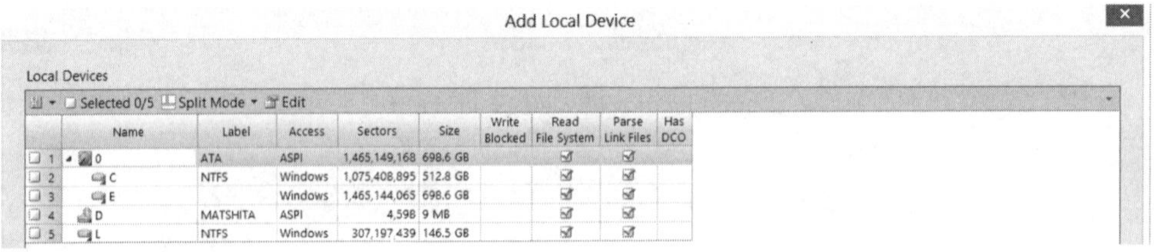

	Name	Label	Access	Sectors	Size	Write Blocked	Read File System	Parse Link Files	Has DCO
1	0	ATA	ASPI	1,465,149,168	698.6 GB		☑	☑	
2	C	NTFS	Windows	1,075,408,895	512.8 GB		☑	☑	
3	E		Windows	1,465,144,063	698.6 GB		☑	☑	
4	D	MATSHITA	ASPI	4,598	9 MB		☑	☑	
5	L	NTFS	Windows	307,197,439	146.5 GB		☑	☑	

Figure 3-10   Selecting a disk in EnCase

TIP   However you image the drive, remember to make two images, hash each image and the original, and then compare the hashes of the images to the original. They must match; if they don't, something went wrong during the copying process. Also remember that simply copying files is not adequate for forensic purposes. Complete disk imaging gets everything, bit by bit. File copying will skip hidden files, data hidden in slack space, and deleted data.

Write-Protected Storage Devices

Another of the most elementary aspects of evidence preservation is to use write-protected storage devices.[5] This means that the suspect drive should immediately be write protected before it is imaged. The media should also be labeled to include the following:

- Investigator's name

- The date the image was made

- Case name and number

This process is a critical step in securing evidence. Beyond the danger of simply accidentally writing some data to the drive, there is the issue of operating system writes. Many operating systems periodically write data to a drive. The NFTS file system may attempt to commit or roll back changes that occurred before the drive was seized. It is important that nothing be written to a drive that is used for evidence.

There are a variety of ways to write-protect a device. Most commonly used are write blockers that are made specifically to secure a drive for forensic purposes. These devices can be a hardware write blocker, or even a hard drive disk controller that is made specifically to disallow disk writing. These are often called forensic disk controllers, because forensic purposes are usually the only ones that require write protection. These forensic disk controllers simply interrupt any write commands sent from the operating system to prevent disk writing. Write-blocking devices are often classified by how they work: native or tailgate. A native device uses the same interface for both in and out. This is used when both ends are the same type of drive, such as SATA to SATA. A tailgate device uses one interface for one side and a different one for the other—for example, a USB to SATA write block. Some of the more widely used write blockers are listed in Table 3-1.

Table 3-1
Widely Used
Write Blockers

Name of Write Blocker	Type of Write Blocker
Tableau[6]	Hardware devices
WiebeTech[7]	Hardware devices
UltraWrite[8]	USB devices
ForensicSoft[9]	Software write blockers

There are also devices that have write-protection features on the drives themselves:

- The Kanguru[10] USB drive has a write-protect switch that can be turned on.

- Imation[11] also makes a USB drive with a write-protect switch.

Additional Evidence Preservation Considerations

While write-protecting the drive is a fundamental step in evidence preservation, other steps must be taken. One issue that must be addressed is preventing electronic static or other discharge from damaging or erasing data. Special evidence bags that are antistatic should be used to store digital devices. Preventing electrostatic discharge (ESD) and other electrical discharges from damaging the suspect drives is critical.

Cyber forensic labs should also block transmissions into or out of the lab. This is often done by constructing what is called a Faraday cage. The Faraday cage is named after the famous physicist Michael Faraday. A Faraday cage is a mesh of conducting material. This prevents electromagnetic energy from entering into or escaping from the cage. This prevents the device from sending data out, as well as prevents someone from the outside accessing the device via WiFi or cellular signals. There are portable bags that have a Faraday cage—these are called Faraday bags,[12] and in some cases, colloquially referred to as black hole bags.[13]

For mobile devices, such as smart phones, tablets, e-readers, and Google Glass, signal isolation is critical. As long as the device is remotely accessible, it is possible that someone could remotely wipe evidence. In fact, many smart phones have the option to remotely wipe them in case they are stolen. It is also possible that any device that can communicate over WiFi or cellular signal could be transmitting information. For example, if the device is infected with spyware, that spyware may continue to send information to an outside party. Whether it is electromagnetic interference (EMI) or radio frequency interference (RFI), blocking such signals is an important part of securing the evidence.

 NOTE It is becoming common for forensics labs to have terabytes of data they have trouble storing in a way that is easily accessible and searchable. One possible solution is WORM storage.[14] WORM stands for Write Once Read Many. It automatically write-protects data as soon as it is saved to the system. Large-scale WORM implementations allow for large amounts of data to be stored in a write-protected environment.

Evidence Transport

Once evidence is collected, it must be transported to the forensic lab. And it will again need to be transported to the courthouse for trial. It is critical that the chain of custody be maintained during this transport. Therefore, the first step in transport is to maintain possession of the evidence during this time. If a person takes evidence from a crime scene, he or she should proceed immediately to the forensic lab with no stops. Not even stops for meals. Then the evidence is checked in. When transporting evidence from the lab to the courthouse, the evidence is first checked out. The person who signs for the evidence should maintain custody of the evidence until it is checked back in.

During transport, it is often a good idea to first secure evidence in some container, such as a lockable briefcase or similar portable device, and then lock that container into the vehicle's trunk or other storage area. Even with the double locking, it is recommended that the person transporting evidence stay with the vehicle so that he or she can maintain custody of the evidence.

 NOTE While the popular television program *CSI* is fictional, and they do tend to exaggerate forensics, there was a specific episode that dealt with chain of custody that posed a realistic issue. The investigator gathered evidence from a crime scene, but it was the end of his shift, so on the way back to the police station, he stopped for breakfast. The evidence was in his locked vehicle for over 30 minutes, out of his sight while he ate and chatted with colleagues. Now in reality, this might or might not lead to the evidence being dismissed by a judge. It is not even certain that opposing counsel would be aware of the issue and challenge the chain of custody. However, it simply is not worth the risk. The proper thing to do is to go immediately to check in the evidence.

Evidence Tracking

In a forensic laboratory, you will have multiple cases going on simultaneously. It is virtually impossible to mentally track where all evidence is at a given time. As we have already discussed, the chain of custody is critical, and that includes tracking the evidence. There are a variety of means for tracking evidence. The specific method you utilize will depend on your agency's budget and case load. However, each major method is described here.

Logs

The most basic form of tracking is to maintain a log of evidence. This can be as simple as a document wherein each piece of evidence is tracked as it is removed from storage and returned. Figure 3-11 is a sample of such a log.

Case : CS 12991 **Item**: Dell Inspirion Laptop Serial Number 12345

Date Checked out	Time Checked out	Person Responsible	Reason	Time Checked in	Date Checked in
n/a	n/a	Det. Smith	Initial check of evidence	9:12 am	1/1/2014
1/3/2014	11:14 am	Analyst Juan Perez	Imaging of desk	2:11 pm	1/3/2014
1/3/2014	3:30 pm	Analyst Juan Perez	Initial scan of hard drive for evidence	5:45 pm	1/3/2014

Figure 3-11   Evidence tracking log

The log shown in Figure 3-11 is a sample—the specific formatting of the log your agency uses will probably vary somewhat from this image. However, this image shows several things that make a log useful. The first and most obvious is that the initial check-in date and time, along with who checked in that evidence, is clearly documented. Next, you should note that every time the evidence is removed from storage, the log clearly shows who removed the evidence, why they removed it, and exactly when it was checked out and when it was checked back in.

A well-maintained evidence log accomplishes two purposes. First and foremost, it aids in maintaining the chain of custody. With a complete log, you can easily show exactly where evidence was at any given time and who was accessing it. As we have discussed previously in this book, few things are more important in a forensic investigation than maintaining the chain of custody. However, the log accomplishes a second goal as well. If you should wish to examine evidence, you can go to the log and find out exactly where it is at that time. If it is currently checked out, you can talk to the person who has the evidence checked out and find out when they will be done with their testing. In addition to a log, it is common to find evidence is labeled (also discussed in this chapter), and when the investigation is complete and evidence is just waiting for trial, the evidence may be sealed.[15]

Software Tracking

A variety of software tracking packages can essentially take the place of a paper log. These packages simply make the maintaining and storing of logs more efficient. For example, these application-utilized databases will allow you to search for any item of interest, such as all entries related to a specific piece of evidence. Or perhaps you would like to know all items that have been checked out by a specific analyst in the past two weeks. You could even search for all activity in a given time frame. Several software applications are available for this purpose, including

- **Evidence Tracker** http://www.trackerproducts.com/evidencetracker/
- **ASAP systems** http://asapsystems.com/evidencetrac.php
- **Fusion RMS** http://fusionrms.tab.com/industry-solutions/ property-evidence-rms/

There are many others, and it should be noted that you will need to examine specific programs to see which one is a good fit for your agency.

 TIP I highly recommend using some sort of tracking software, though I don't recommend any specific product. If your agency's budget allows for the purchase of such software, it is much easier to manage than paper records.

Barcode

Another process for evidence tracking that is gaining popularity is barcode tracking. This is much like logging, but it is automated. System details can vary from implementation to implementation, but in general, the system works as follows. Each piece of evidence has a barcode attached to it or to its container (such as an evidence bag). Then, each analyst has their own barcode scanner. When a piece of evidence is accessed, its barcode is scanned. Then the system knows who accessed the evidence and when. It is also possible to use systems wherein the barcode scanners themselves also record their specific location, thus adding more detail to the record.

RFID

Radio frequency ID (RFID) chips can be utilized to track evidence. These systems are implemented in much the same way as a barcode. The RFID chip is attached to the evidence or the evidence container. Then, at any given time, the system knows the exact location of a given piece of evidence.

 TIP Remember that the log is the core of any evidence-tracking system. I would recommend that even if you use barcode or RFID, having each person actually sign for the evidence is a very good idea. An even better idea is to have a person responsible for the evidence, and each time it is checked out, the evidence handler and the investigator have to sign.

Evidence Storage

How and where to store evidence is an important topic. Proper storage of evidence is a significant part of maintaining the chain of custody and of evidence preservation. The evidence must be secured in a location that is safe from environmental hazards, inaccessible without proper authorization, and secure from electromagnetic interference. All of these issues must be addressed when selecting an evidence storage location.

Environmental Hazards

Environmental hazards include a variety of factors ranging from temperature control to fire suppression. Some threats from the environment include

- Fire and smoke contaminants
- Extreme cold or heat
- Utility loss (power, AC, heat)
- Water damage (broken pipes, flooding)

To protect against these environmental threats, several steps should be taken. The placement of the evidence room is a fundamental consideration. The room should be in a location not prone to flooding. It should also have adequate heat and air conditioning to prevent the temperatures from exceeding a range of approximately 50 degrees Fahrenheit to 85 degrees Fahrenheit. Colder temperatures are less likely to damage digital evidence, but some devices are susceptible to extreme heat.

 NOTE I am personally aware of a situation wherein a city (name withheld for confidentiality reasons) was storing servers, including those that had forensic evidence, in a basement room that had water pipes along the ceiling. Eventually, a pipe did break, destroying the servers in question and their data.

Fire is a common hazard that must be guarded against. All walls, the ceiling, and the door to the evidence room must have an acceptable fire rating. UL Labs have a three-volume set of parameters by which they rate the fire resistance of walls.[16]

It is also common practice to store data in a safe within the evidence room. Most safes also have a fire rating. The following is a list of common ratings:

- Class 100 is for safes that contain digital data.

- Class 150 is the rating for microfilm and similar media.

- Class 350 is the rating for paper documents.

If your evidence room is a fire-resistant room, with equivalent walls, ceiling, and door, and your evidence is in a fire-resistant safe within that room, you have a very good chance of the evidence being undamaged in case of a fire.

 EXAM TIP The CCFP does not ask details about fire ratings, fire extinguishers, or fire suppression. However, you will need this information in order to successfully set up a forensic lab. But you need not memorize these elements in order to take the CCFP. It should be noted that the (ISC)²'s Certified Information Systems Security Professional (CISSP) exam does ask about these specifics.

It is normal to have a fire extinguisher in or very near an evidence room. You should be aware that there are a variety of different types of fire extinguishers:

- **Carbon dioxide (CO_2)** CO_2 foam, inert gas, and dry powder extinguishers displace oxygen to suppress a fire. CO_2 is a risk to humans because of oxygen displacement.

- **Water extinguishers** Water suppresses the temperature required to sustain a fire.

- **Halon** This substance was banned under the 1987 Montreal Protocol on Substances That Deplete the Ozone Layer. FM200 is one replacement for Halon.

Fire extinguishers are also classified into four general classes based on what types of fires they can extinguish:

- **Class A**   Ordinary combustibles such as wood or paper
- **Class B**   Flammable liquids such as grease, oil, or gasoline
- **Class C**   Electrical equipment
- **Class D**   Flammable metals

The CCFP test is going to focus on the general concept of securing the evidence storage area from environmental dangers.

Unauthorized Access

For a room to be secure against unauthorized access takes more than simply having a good lock. To begin with, the walls must be sound. The walls must go all the way to the ceiling, rather than having a drop ceiling as many office buildings do. A drop ceiling would allow an intruder to enter an adjacent room and then simply come through the ceiling into the evidence room.

The door must be one that is not readily broken into. That indicates a door that resists forced entry and with hinges that are on the inside. A solid deadbolt lock is also necessary. Then, there should be some monitoring of who accesses the room. One way to control access is via a swipe card, with each authorized person having an individual card and the system recording who accesses the room and at what time. Ideally, such a system would have two-factor authentication, meaning that the swipe card is used in conjunction with a PIN number or password.

It is critical that the evidence room also be subjected to continuous video surveillance. That should include who enters the evidence room and the interior of the room itself. Remember that the cornerstone of evidence handling is the chain of custody. If you cannot prove that you have control of the evidence room, complete knowledge of who enters, when they enter, and what they do therein, then all of the evidence within the evidence room will be suspect.

Electromagnetic Interference

Previously in this chapter we have discussed electromagnetic interference and radio frequency interference. We also discussed evidence bags that function as Faraday cages. It is equally important that the evidence room that will contain electronic evidence also be a Faraday cage. That is usually accomplished during the initial construction of the room. A conductive mesh is added to the walls, floor, and ceiling, thus preventing RFI and EMI. There are electronic measuring tools that will indicate the efficacy of your Faraday cage. However, you can get a quick general indication with your cell phone. Attempt to use your phone outside the evidence room and then inside it. From inside the room, you should get no connectivity whatsoever. If you can get any connectivity, even intermittent and poor connection, this indicates your Faraday cage is not implemented properly. One common reason for that is incomplete coverage. For example, there may be some gap in the conductive mesh.

U.S. Army Digital Evidence Storage

The United States Army has specific guidelines on storing digital evidence:[17]

1. A person with digital media evidence should store such evidence in a dust-free, temperature- and humidity-controlled environment, whenever possible.

2. A person with digital media evidence will not store it near batteries, generators, electro-magnets, magnets, induction coils, unshielded microwave sources, or any material that generates static. NOTE: Vacuum cleaner motors generate small electromagnetic fields that may alter, erase, and/or destroy digital media such as tapes.

3. A person with digital media evidence should not store such evidence in the same container with electronic devices. Some electronic devices contain batteries with sufficient strength to erase digital data over extended periods.

4. The evidence custodian should make periodic checks of digital media evidence in the evidence room to determine battery life of the item(s). There is a very high risk that all evidence contained in digital storage could be lost. So you must connect the evidence with appropriate chargers that can remain connected to uninterrupted power.

5. Where possible, the evidence custodian should store digital media evidence in a fire safe designed to safeguard items in heat in excess of 120 degrees Fahrenheit.

6. Where possible, the evidence custodian should not store digital media or devices in areas with sprinkler fire protection systems. If this is not possible, the evidence custodian should cover the media with waterproof material. The media should not be completely wrapped in waterproof material, because condensation can build and destroy the evidence.

7. The evidence custodian should not store digital media and devices in the same confined area with caustic chemicals (for example, acids, solvents, industrial strength cleaners, flammables). Exposure to fumes from such materials may cause surface erosion of media and loss of data.

8. A person with items of evidence that are classified or that contain classified information or material will store such evidence in accordance with AR 380–5.

Note that items 1, 2, 5, 6, and 7 specifically deal with environmental threats. These are sound guidelines that can be used even outside the U.S. Army. Item 4 deals with the fact that digital evidence is fragile, and you must check to ensure it is still present and has not degraded. While these standards were designed for U.S. Army forensics labs, they are worth reviewing even by non-Army forensic analysts.

Evidence Access Control

You need to control who accesses evidence, when it is accessed, and how it is used. The first principle that one must bear in mind with evidence access control is who has a need to access this evidence. The principle is similar to one used in the intelligence community where they operate under the axiom of need to know. Need to know means that it does not matter how high your security clearance is or how trustworthy you are, if you do not have a need to know certain information, you are not granted access to it. A similar principle should guide access to forensic evidence. It does not matter how trustworthy the detective, agent, or technician is. It does not matter how thoroughly their background has been checked. If that person does not have an actual need to access evidence, then they should not be granted access to it.

Once you have established the principle of only providing access to those with a clear need, the next question becomes how you enforce this. We have previously discussed logs, card key access to the evidence room, and a person assigned to manage access. All of these methods can be useful in evidence access control.

Evidence Disposition

It might seem obvious that once a case is decided the evidence should be destroyed. However, it is not uncommon for cases to be appealed, thus requiring the evidence to be maintained. Furthermore, it is always possible that at some future date there will be a challenge to the outcome of the case, necessitating the review of the evidence. For this reason, it is strongly recommended that your laboratory utilize an archive system. Once a case has gone to trial or been settled, evidence is moved to archival storage.

Archival storage must meet all the security requirements that your normal evidence storage meets. That means issues of environmental security and personnel access are addressed. However, it should be easier to manage access to archival storage, given that it will be accessed with less frequency and by fewer people.

Many organizations do establish a final date by which time the evidence is actually destroyed. This is usually many years after the end of a case. It could easily be decades. Whatever your organization's policy on evidence destruction is, it is critical that all evidence be completely destroyed. In the case of disks, those disks should be broken and then burned. In the case of magnetic storage devices (like hard drives), the device should be magnetically wiped and then physically broken. It is imperative that the evidence not be recoverable from the destroyed media.

Chapter Review

In this chapter, you have learned how to properly seize, store, and transport evidence. Chain of custody, a critical concept, can only be maintained by properly documenting all phases of the investigation, beginning with the seizing of the evidence and moving on through the storage and transporting of the evidence.

Questions

1. Which of the following best describes the primary purpose of write-protecting a drive?

   A. To ensure evidence is not accidentally added to or destroyed.

   B. To ensure evidence is not accidentally destroyed.

   C. To keep the investigator from installing utilities on the drive.

   D. It is required by most forensic imaging techniques.

2. Which of the following are the two types of write protection?

   A. Fast and slow

   B. Windows and Linux

   C. Hardware and software

   D. Forensic and nonforensic

3. Which of the following best describes the term capture point?

   A. The time of the suspect's arrest

   B. The time the suspect is booked

   C. The time of entry into the facility to seize evidence

   D. The time when evidence is first seized

4. In which of the following cases would you log that evidence has transferred from one person to another?

   A. When checking evidence in initially

   B. When checking evidence out for court

   C. When evidence is checked out for analysis

   D. All of the above

5. What is RFI?

   A. Real-time forensic investigation

   B. Radio frequency interference

   C. Radio forensic investigation

   D. Real-time forensic initialization

6. What is EMI?

   A. Electromagnetic interference

   B. Emergency mobile investigation

   C. Electromagnetic investigation

   D. Emergency mandatory investigation

7. Which of the following is not an environmental danger to digital evidence?

   A. Fire

   B. Flood

   C. Extreme heat

   D. Loud noise

Answers

1. **A.** To ensure evidence is not changed in any way, whether added to or destroyed. Write-protecting keeps you from inadvertently adding or deleting data.

2. **C.** Hardware and software. In this chapter, you saw examples of hardware-based write protectors and software-based write protectors.

3. **D.** The time when evidence is first seized.

4. **D.** All of the above.

5. **B.** Radio frequency interference.

6. **A.** Electromagnetic interference.

7. **D.** Loud noise. It should be obvious that noise does not disturb digital media.

References

1. Evidence E-Zine.http://www.evidencemagazine.com/index.php?option=com_content&task=view&id=184.

2. http://revealmedia.com/wp-content/uploads/2013/09/storage.pdf.

3. http://www.accessdata.com/products/digital-forensics/ftk.

4. http://www.guidancesoftware.com/products/Pages/encase-forensic/overview.aspx.

5. FBI Evidence Preservation. http://www.fbi.gov/stats-services/publications/law-enforcement-bulletin/august-2011/digital-evidence.

6. http://www.tableau.com/index.php?pageid=products.

7. http://www.cru-inc.com/products/wiebetech/.

8. http://www.digitalintelligence.com/products/usb_write_blocker/.

9. https://www.forensicsoft.com/.

10. http://www.kanguru.com/storage-accessories/kanguru-ss3.shtml.

11. https://support.imation.com/app/answers/detail/a_id/1583.

12. http://www.faradaybag.com/.

13. http://www.amazon.com/Black-Hole-Faraday-Bag-Isolation/dp/B0091WILY0.

14. http://revealmedia.com/wp-content/uploads/2013/09/storage.pdf.

15. http://inece.org/conference/8/proceedings/44_Lubieniecki.pdf.

16. UL Labs. http://www.ul.com/global/eng/pages/offerings/services/architectural/faq/.

17. http://www.apd.army.mil/pdffiles/r195_5.pdf.

PART II

Forensic Science

■ **Chapter 4**   Principles and Methods
■ **Chapter 5**   Forensic Analysis

Principles and Methods

In this chapter you will learn to:
- Understand and apply Locard's principle of transference
- Understand the Inman-Rudin paradigm
- Identify cyber evidence
- Classify cyber evidence
- Reconstruct cyber evidence

Learning to properly seize evidence is critical for cyber forensics. The first step is to formulate a scientific approach to evidence collection, one that is based on sound forensic principles. Then, it is critical to be able to clearly identify what is evidence and what is not. After identifying and classifying potential evidence, you have to be able to collect it. This may involve reconstructing data from damaged files.

Scientific Approach to Forensics

It is important to keep in mind that forensics is a scientific process. It is not an art. That may seem like a somewhat obvious, or even unnecessary, statement; however, it is an important fact to keep in mind. There are well-established scientific principles that have been utilized in forensics, and particularly in cyber forensics. It is important that you understand these principles.

The Scientific Method

First let us examine how science works. One always begins with a hypothesis. Contrary to popular misconception, a hypothesis is not a guess. It is a question that is testable. If a question cannot be tested, then it has no place in science whatsoever. Once one has tested a hypothesis, one has a fact. For example, if I suspect that confidential documents were on your computer and subsequently moved to a USB device and deleted (my hypothesis), I can conduct a forensic examination of your computer (my test). If that examination finds that a USB drive was connected to the computer, and an undelete program recovers the deleted documents, I now have a fact.

The next step is to build a theory of the crime based on multiple facts. The fact that confidential documents were on your computer, while very interesting evidence, is not, in and of itself, enough. Is it possible someone else used your computer? Yes, it is. Is it possible that you accidentally had confidential information (i.e., you mistakenly took home documents you should not have) and then immediately deleted them? Yes, it is. So we must find additional facts. For example, we would want to know if your username was the one logged in when the files were deleted. Once we recover the deleted files, we would want to know when they were last accessed and modified (this might tell us if you were using the files). We might also want to check your e-mail to see if there is any communication with a third party that might have an interest in these documents.

Once you have collected enough facts, there must be some explanation of the facts. In science, that explanation is called a theory.[1] To be a good theory, it must account for all the available facts. For example, my theory of the crime might be that you stole the confidential documents with the intent to sell them to a competitor. I would need to check all the facts and see if they all match my theory. This process of forming a hypothesis, testing the hypothesis, and synthesizing facts into a cogent theory is the scientific method.

The Philosophy of Science

A forensic examiner must also be well acquainted with the philosophy of science. The philosophy of science is based upon two principles: verification and falsifiability. We have already touched upon the idea of verification. Verification is done by testing. No matter how strongly you feel about a given hypothesis, it must be tested. And you must accept that the testing may actually refute your hypothesis.

Karl Popper was a philosopher who articulated the basic philosophy of science. He argued that the central property of science is falsifiability. Falsifiability means that it is possible to disprove something. The best way to understand this concept is to contemplate a counterexample. So let's consider something that is not falsifiable. For example, I tell you that I did not place the incriminating files on my computer; someone else did. However, that someone else is invisible; does not emanate any heat; cannot be touched, felt, or sensed; and logs in with my username. There is absolutely no way to test that. It is, therefore, not falsifiable. Ideas that are not falsifiable have no place in science.

How do you apply the philosophy of science to cyber forensics? The first step is to approach your investigation with a scientific mindset. First and foremost, this means dispassionately. Some crimes will naturally outrage anyone, including a forensic analyst. Crimes such as child pornography can make it more difficult to be dispassionate. However, it is critical that, no matter the crime, you let the evidence guide your conclusions. The philosophy of science also means that if you have a belief about some aspect of a crime that you first formulate a testable hypothesis and conduct that test.

Peer Review

Peer review is another important issue in the scientific community. Peer review means that other professionals in that field have reviewed the work and found it to be valid. For example, if you wish to publish a paper on some forensic technique and you submit that paper to a peer-reviewed journal, the first thing that happens is the editor sends your paper (without your name on it) to three experts in the field to review. These experts don't have to agree with your conclusions, but they must agree that the paper is valid, the processes appropriate, and the methodology viable. This occurs before the paper is even published.

The paper must describe what you did, with sufficient detail to allow anyone who wishes to repeat your work and test your findings. Once your paper is published, any reader of that journal is free to test your findings and to write to the journal should they have issues with your conclusions or your methodology.

The idea behind peer review is that an idea is subjected to multiple stages of review: first by the reviewers that determine if the paper is even of sufficient quality for publication and then by the readers, who tend to be professionals in that field. If an idea withstands such scrutiny, this is still no guarantee that it is completely accurate, but it is certainly a much higher level of reliability than any other method we have. For this reason, peer-reviewed sources are usually considered more reliable than nonpeer-reviewed sources.

 NOTE It is not the case that nonpeer-reviewed sources are unreliable. It is simply that peer review gives a higher likelihood of reliability. Another way to test the reliability of a publication or an author is to do a Google Scholar[2] search. This searches scholarly sources to see if other people in the field cite that work. Obviously, a new work would not have any citations. But if a publication has been around for a few years and it is reliable, one would expect it to have citations. For example, my first computer security–related book was a textbook with the title *Computer Security Fundamentals* (Prentice Hall, 2005). A Google Scholar search finds 31 citations to that book. This is an indication that at least some experts in the field of computer security found that work to be reliable and worthy of citing.

The question becomes how do you apply the peer review concept to cyber forensics? The answer, which we will discuss later, is primarily about having a peer review your work. In the context of sources you may cite in your report, some experts advocate only using sources that are peer reviewed. I personally disagree with that. There are other reliable sources that you can use. However, at least some of your sources should be peer reviewed.

Locard's Principle of Transference

Dr. Edmond Locard was a forensic scientist who formulated what has become known as Locard's exchange principle or Locard's principle of transference. This principle was first applied to physical forensics, and it essentially states that one cannot interact in any environment without leaving something behind.[3] For example, someone cannot break into a house and not leave something behind. That something could be a fingerprint, a hair, a footprint, etc. Now a careful criminal will cover up some of this—for example, using gloves to keep from leaving fingerprints—but something will be left behind.

NOTE Edmond Locard was a French medical doctor and forensic researcher born in 1877. He was sometimes referred to as the "Sherlock Holmes of France." In addition to his medical training, he passed the bar in 1907. He did a great deal of study on fingerprints and opined that a 12-point match should be considered sufficient for a positive identification.[4]

Normally, Locard's principle is applied to trace evidence. Trace evidence occurs when two objects come into contact with each other. Some trace is left. The most obvious example would be that when a human hand comes in contact with an object, a trace—namely the fingerprint—is left behind.

Locard's principle is important for two reasons. The first reason is that this principle tells us that if a suspect interacted with a computer system or digital device, there should be some evidence to indicate that interaction. The evidence might be only trace evidence, and it might be difficult to find. And the more skilled the perpetrator is, the more difficult it will be to find evidence, but the evidence is there. The second reason this principle is important is that it highlights the reason why you should only work with a copy of the suspect storage media, not the original, and why you should write-protect media. You as a forensic investigator are interacting with the evidence, and you could inadvertently introduce trace evidence.

 EXAM TIP Locard's principle is important for another reason: The CCFP examination does ask you about it. It is critical that you be very familiar with it and its application. Obviously, I cannot tell you specific questions you may be asked, but I do advise that you make certain you understand and can apply Locard's principle.

When an investigator inadvertently introduces trace evidence, this is referred to as contamination. In any forensic investigation, you must be very careful to avoid contamination. For cyber forensics, this is done with techniques we discussed in Chapter 3.

As mentioned, while Locard's principle has traditionally been associated with physical forensics, it also applies to cyber forensics. It is impossible to interact with a system and not leave some trace. This includes intruders, malware, and anything else that interacts with a computer system. Now it may be that the trace is difficult to locate, but it will be there.

 NOTE Locard's principle is another reason why we work with copies of drives rather than the original drive. Just as it is impossible for malware, for example, to be on a machine and leave absolutely no trace, it is impossible for a forensic analyst to work with a drive and leave no trace.

Inman-Rudin Paradigm

Inman and Rudin published a paper entitled "The Origin of Evidence"[5] that describes the Inman-Rudin paradigm. In that paper, the authors commented that traditionally five concepts have been applied to forensic analysis: transfer, identification, individualization, association between source and target, and reconstruction.[6] The authors suggested a sixth idea be added to that: the idea that matter must divide before it can be transferred. The authors used the term matter because they were thinking of traditional forensics involving tangible objects. It might be better today to talk about evidence dividing.

Let's look at the first five concepts. Those five concepts, as applied to cyber forensics, are

- **Transfer (Locard's exchange principle)**   This principle was explored previously in this chapter under the section "Locard's Principle of Transference."

- **Identification (placing objects in a class)**   This is about the first stage in classifying evidence. What is it? In the case of cybercrimes, is the evidence a server log, a recovered file, network traffic analysis, or some other sort of evidence?

- **Individualization (narrowing the class to one)**   This is about taking the identification step to another level. In the case of cybercrimes, this is not always possible. For example, a piece of malware could be a Trojan horse as well as a virus and spyware.

- **Association (linking a person with a crime scene)**   How do you associate a piece of evidence with a specific person? For cybercrimes, if you have a virus, can you show that it was created by the suspect? What evidence might you need? For example, finding the source code for the virus on the suspect's personal computer would be one piece of evidence.

- **Reconstruction (understanding the sequence of past events)**   This is the process of determining what happened. It is not always possible to do this as completely as we might like. But, for example, if you believe a virus was created by a suspect, can you show first that it was created by the suspect? Then you would need to show that the suspect released it, perhaps by uploading it to some file server. Then you would want to show at least one victim downloading the virus from that file server. Essentially, you want to reconstruct exactly what happened.

Inman-Rudin added a sixth principle. They stated that evidence must divide before it can transfer. This is related to Locard's principle of transference. Since it is a fragment that is transferred, the original evidence must divide before a fragment can be left. This is obvious with things such as DNA, blood, and other physical evidence. It is a bit more complex with cyber forensics. Clearly, a virus can copy itself rather than divide. It is also possible that a cybercrime might add some evidence to the registry without first dividing. Even web traffic will add cookies, browser history, or other evidence. While not actually "dividing" as Inman-Rudin envisioned it, it is the same concept. The item in question (virus, website visited) leaves some trace of itself.

Identify and Classify Evidence

As you collect evidence, you will need to identify what is evidence, what is not, and classify the evidence. Identifying evidence means to determine what is and is not evidence. In general, evidence is information that has probative value. Probative value means this is information that might prove something at a trial.[7] In other words, it is data that is relevant to the case at hand. For example, if someone is accused of stealing intellectual property, when searching their computer, if you find that the person also visits legal pornographic websites, this has no probative value and is not evidence.

There have been multiple perspectives on how to classify digital evidence. One commonly used perspective, published in the *International Journal of Computer Science and Information Technology,*[8] is to divide digital evidence into four categories:

- **Database** Evidence from a data repository. This could be a relational database management system such as Microsoft SQL Server or Oracle, or it could be file storage such as XML. For readers not familiar with it, XML is a file format for storing data in a manner that resembles HTML.

- **Computer** Evidence found on a computer, including browser history, deleted files, Windows registry settings, computer logs, etc.

- **Network** Network traffic evidence, often found by using a network protocol analyzer or packet sniffer, such as Wireshark.

- **Mobile** Evidence from a mobile device.

This classification approach is about determining where the data came from. It is a good place to start when acquiring new evidence. It may also be useful to classify the evidence based on the following factors:[9]

- **Source** Where did the evidence come from? This would include three of the four classifications (computer, network, and mobile device) previously mentioned.

- **Format** What format is the data in? Various formats include data stored normally on a storage device, archived data (such as backup media), deleted data that has been recovered, volatile data such as the contents of memory or the SWAP file (discussed in detail later in this book).

- **Type** This includes video, pictures, cookies, bookmarks, trace evidence, etc. This may be the most common classification in cyber forensics. What is the evidence? It could be a server log, evidence from the Windows Index.dat file, Windows registry evidence, call history from a cell phone, etc.

It is important to correctly classify evidence and to document that classification.

Locations Where Evidence May Reside

Evidence can be found in many diverse locations. The most obvious would be hard drives or permanent storage. However, data can be retrieved from live connections, network traffic, memory, and many other locations.

Storage Media

While cyber forensics now encompasses a wide variety of devices, a great deal of your investigations will involve storage media of some type. Therefore, it is critical to understand the basics of these storage media types. Also note that some information in this section, as well as file systems, will be information we covered in Chapter 1. We are covering it again here in more detail. The fact that it is covered twice is indicative of just how important this information is. You simply cannot effectively function in cyber forensics without a good understanding of these topics.

Hard Drives

The first hard drive was created by IBM in 1956. Now it is hard to imagine a computer without one. There are a myriad of different types of storage. However, the basic hard drive is still the most common place to search for evidence. Computer servers, workstations, laptops, and tablets all have hard drives, so an understanding of how hard drives function is important.

While there are now solid-state drives (which we will discuss later in this section), our first item to discuss is the magnetic hard drive. The data is stored by arranging bits magnetically, and the data is organized by sectors and clusters, which are in turn organized in tracks around the platter. A typical sector is 512 bytes, and a cluster can be from 1 to 128 sectors. The first thing to be wary of with magnetic storage is electromagnetic interference. Magnetic storage drives can be damaged or destroyed by electromagnetic energy. This is why we put such devices in special evidence bags that are "antistatic" (i.e., reduce electromagnetic static).

These drive types were discussed in Chapter 1; a brief summary is provided here:

- **IDE (Integrated Drive Electronics)** This is an older standard but one that was commonly used on PCs for many years.

- **EIDE (Extended Integrated Drive Electronics)** This is an extension/enhancement to IDE. Both IDE and EIDE use a 40-pin connector that can be seen in Figure 4-1.

Figure 4-1
IDE/EIDE
connector

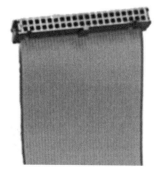

PART II

- **PATA (Parallel Advanced Technology Attachment)** This type of connection looks much like IDE and has a 40-pin connector just like IDE (http://pcsupport .about.com/od/termsp/g/parallelata.htm). It has been supplanted by SATA.

- **SATA (Serial Advanced Technology Attachment)** This is the most common hard drive connector as of 2014, and unlike IDE or EIDE drives, this type of drive has no jumpers to set the drive. You can see the connector in Figure 4-2.

Figure 4-2
SATA connector

SATA has gone through progressive versions. The first, 1.0, communicated at a maximum of 1.5 gigabits of information per second. Sata 3.0 was released in 2009 and achieved 6 gigabits of information per second. Version 3.1 was released in 2011 and added many possibilities such as zero power optical drives. As of this writing, SATA 3.2 is the most recent version with a bandwidth of up to 16 gigabits per second. It also includes a mode called DevSleep that is low power consumption.

- **SCSI (Small Computer System Interface)** This is far more common in high-end servers. You can see the connector in Figure 4-3. Serial SCSI is an enhancement to SCSI. It supports up to 65,537 devices and does not require termination. Fibre Channel is a successor to parallel SCSI. It is usually used with Fibre Channel Arbitrated loops.

Figure 4-3
SCSI connector

All of these drive types are magnetic storage. The different types define the connectivity, transfer rate, and maximum storage capacity of each drive. All of these are susceptible to electromagnetic interference, but they also have moving parts, so they are also susceptible to physical damage. Dropping a drive can damage it and make it quite difficult to retrieve the data.

In addition to magnetic storage drive, there are solid-state drives (SSDs). These drives use microchips that retain data in nonvolatile memory chips and contain no moving parts. Since about 2010, most SSDs use NAND (Negated AND gate)–based flash memory, which retains memory even without power. These drives usually require one-half to one-third of the power that magnetic drives do, making them popular. They also have much faster startup times, making them an excellent choice for tablets.

 NOTE Solid-state drives are faster and use less power than magnetic drives. So why are they not the only drive used today? The answer is that they don't last as long and are a bit more expensive. So for large-scale storage, as in a server, they are not an appropriate choice as of the time of this writing.

External hard drives are becoming far more common. They usually connect via USB to the host computer. The size is usually 2.5 or 3.5 inches. As of this writing, 2 terabyte is most common, but you can find external drives up to 6 terabytes in size. Forensically these are very important because of their portability. You will see later in this book that one can read the Windows Registry and see all that USB devices that have been connected to a given machine. This can give you an indication that you should be seeking external drives.

Both magnetic and solid-state drives include features that are specifically significant to cyberforensics:

- **Master boot record** The master boot record (MBR) requires only a single sector, leaving 62 empty sectors of MBR space for hiding data.

- **Unallocated space** An operating system can't access any unallocated space in a partition. That space can contain hidden data.

- **File slack** This is the unused space that is created between the end of the file and the end of the cluster. This can definitely hold hidden data.

- **Host-protected area** The host-protected area (HPA) was designed as an area where computer vendors could store data that is protected from user activities and operating system utilities, such as delete and format. To hide data in the HPA, a person would need to write a program to access the HPA and then write the data.

Regardless of what type of hard drive you are using, you will follow some common procedures:

1. Document all the data you can about the hard drive in question. That includes model, type, size, etc.

2. You may want to take digital photos, particularly if the drive has any visible damages.

3. As we mentioned previously, create an image of the drive and work with the image.

Partitions and Disk Geometry

Hard disk drives (HDDs) record data by magnetizing ferromagnetic material directionally to represent either a 0 or a 1 binary digit. The magnetic data is stored on platters, and the platters are organized on a spindle, with a read/write head reading and writing data to and from the platters. The data is organized as follows:

- A sector is the basic unit of data storage on a hard disk, usually 512 bytes. It should be noted that while hard drives have 512 byte sectors, CDs and DVDs use 2048 bit sectors. The sector itself is actually made up of parts, usually three. There is a sector header, the actual data, and the error correcting code. The header has information that the drive and driver controller will use. There is a new technology called Advanced Format that uses 4096 byte sectors.

- A cluster is a logical grouping of sectors. Clusters can be 1 sector in size to 128 sectors. That means a cluster could be anywhere from 512 bytes up to 64KB. The minimum size a file can use is one cluster. If the file is less than the size of a cluster, the remaining space is simply unused. So if the cluster is 64KB and the file is only 10KB, there is 54KB of unused space, called slack space.

- Drive geometry refers to the number of cylinders on a disk, the number of tracks per cylinder, the number of sectors per track, and the size of each sector.

That is a basic description of most hard drives (with the exception of solid-state drives). Drives must be formatted before use. There are basically two types of formatting. There is the low-level format, which actually sets up the structure of sectors, tracks, and clusters. The high-level format just sets up an empty file system on the target drive.

- Digital audio tape (DAT) drives are still in use today. Most people are now using more modern media to store backups, but some tape backups still exist. DAT was (and is) the most common sort of tape backup. It looks a lot like an audio tape. Digital linear tape (DLT) and super DLT are two other types of tape storage that specifically involve a magnetic tape. It is still a backup tape and will, therefore, contain archived data.

- Optical media (CD, DVD, and Blu-Ray) are more common today. Optical media depend on a laser to detect the distance light has traveled, and the disks have pits—an area with a pit equals a 0 and no pit equals a 1. Due to these pits, a scratch can damage data on an optical disk. CDs, or compact discs, typically hold 600 megabytes to 1 gigabyte of data. The DVD (digital video disk) can hold 4.7 gigabytes of data, or double that (9.4 gigabytes) for a double-sided DVD. DVD uses a smaller wavelength (about 650 nm) than does a CD (about 780 nm). This allows the DVD to use smaller pits, thus increasing storage.

- The latest incarnation of optical media, as of this writing, is the Blu-Ray Disk. They store 25 gigabytes of data per layer, so a dual-layer Blu-Ray Disk can store 50 gigabytes. There are also triple- and quadruple-layer disks, such as the Blu-Ray Disk XL that allows up to 150 gigabytes of storage.

Hardware Interfaces

Since storage devices are connected to a computer via a hardware interface, it is important to have some knowledge of such interfaces. Computers frequently have devices attached to them such as printers, scanners, web cameras, etc. The manner in which these devices are connected is important for any forensic investigation.

USB

USB, or universal serial bus, was developed in the mid-1990s and has become the de facto standard. Keyboards, mice, printers, and more all connect with USB cables now. USB has three major versions (1.0, 2.0, and 3.0), with variations of each. They are all backward compatible with the previous version. The difference is mostly about speed. For example, USB 3.0 achieves speeds of 5 gigabytes per second, and 3.1 reaches speeds of 10 gigabits per second. You can see the USB connector in Figure 4-4.

Figure 4-4
USB interface

Serial

Serial ports communicate data one bit at a time. Actually, Ethernet, FireWire, and USB are all variations of serial communications. When we talk of serial ports, however, we usually mean the standard DE9 (9-pin) connecter shown in Figure 4-5. It should be noted that the original standard had more pins.

Figure 4-5
Serial interface

Parallel

Parallel ports send multiple bits simultaneously. They are the default ports for printers, and usually have a 25-pin connector, as shown in Figure 4-6.

Figure 4-6
Parallel
connector

Video

Monitors/video have a number of different connections that can be used. The most common is VGA (Video Graphics Array). These are 15-pin connectors, as shown in Figure 4-7.

Figure 4-7
VGA connector

A variety of screen resolutions are available with the different variations of the VGA interface, but the connectors are interoperable.

DVI (Digital Visual Interface) is designed to maximize video quality. These devices are used on Macintosh computers. You can see a DVI connector in Figure 4-8.

Figure 4-8
DVI connector

One problem with the DVI connectors is shown in this image. Note the horizontal connection next to the pins. With DVI, there are a variety of different ways the connector pins can be arranged. This makes it difficult for end users to be sure they have the correct DVI connector.

HDMI (High-Definition Multimedia Interface) is also becoming more common. These devices look much like the HDMI connectors one might find on a television, Blu-Ray player, or similar device.

An older technology that one might still find is the s-video connector. These connectors were popular in the late 1990s for video editing work. It allowed one to connect a video camera to a computer in order to download and then digitally edit video.

Other Interfaces

SCSI was already discussed in reference to hard drives; it can also be used to connect peripheral devices. This is not as common as USB, or even serial or parallel. Two outdated technologies are PS2 and FireWire. PS2 is a small, round plug and was used for keyboards, although that has not been the case for many years. FireWire was a rival to USB, but has gradually faded in use. At one time, Macintosh strongly supported FireWire, but began phasing it out in 2012.

File Systems

Like the information on hard drives, file systems were introduced briefly in Chapter 1. However, it is covered here in more detail as this is significant information for the exam. It is that important that you understand these concepts fully. Computer drives organize information by clusters according to a specific file system. There are a few commonly used file systems that you are likely to encounter, and they are discussed here.

FAT (File Allocation Table) is an older system that was popular with Microsoft operating systems for many years. FAT was first implemented in Microsoft Stand-alone Disk BASIC.FAT stores file locations by sector in a file called, eponymously, the File Allocation Table. This table contains information about which clusters are being used by what particular files and which clusters are free to be used. The various extensions of FAT (FAT16, FAT32) differ in the number of bits available for filenames. For example, FAT16 only supports 16-bit filenames, whereas FAT32 supports 32-bit filenames. Note that floppy disks use FAT12.

Microsoft eventually introduced a new file system to replace FAT. This file system is called New Technology File System (NTFS). This is the file system used by Windows NT 4, 2000, XP, Vista, 7, Server 2003, and Server 2008. One major improvement of NTFS over FAT was the increased volume sizes NTFS could support. The maximum NTFS volume size is $2^{64}-1$ clusters. As of this writing, no version of Windows currently supports volumes that large.

Extended File System (EXT) was the first file system created specifically for Linux. There have been many versions of EXT—the current version is 4. The EXT 4 file system can support volumes with sizes up to 1 exabyte (10^{18} bytes, or 1 billion gigabytes) and files with sizes up to 16 terabytes. This is, frankly, a huge file and volume size, and no current hard drives come even close to that. For an administrator, one of the most exciting features of EXT 4 is that it is backward compatible with EXT 2 and EXT 3, making it possible to mount drives that use those earlier versions of EXT.

The Reiser File System is a popular journaling file system used primarily with Linux. Reiser was the first file system to be included with the standard Linux kernel, and first appeared in kernel version 2.4.1. Unlike some file systems, Reiser supported journaling from its inception, whereas EXT did not support journaling until version 3. The Reiser File System is open source and was invented by Hans Reiser.

The Berkeley Fast File System is also known as the Unix File System. As its names suggest, it was developed at Berkeley specifically for Unix. Like many file systems, Berkeley uses a bitmap to track free clusters, indicating which clusters are available and which are not. Like EXT, Berkeley also includes the fsck utility. These utilities will be described in detail later in this book when we explore Linux-based forensics.

Files are organized on the computer based on the file system. There are many file systems, but they can be divided into two primary categories. Journaling is the process whereby the file system keeps a record of what file transactions take place so that in the event of a hard drive crash, the files can be recovered. Journaling file systems are fault tolerant because the file system will log all changes to files, directories, or file structures. The log in which changes are recorded is referred to as the file system's journal, thus the term journaling file systems.

There are actually two types of journaling: physical and logical. With physical journaling, the system logs a copy of every block that is about to be written to the storage device before it is written. The log also includes a checksum of those blocks to make sure there is no error in writing it. With logical journaling, only changes to file metadata are stored in the journal.

File Format

What is a file? Well, you probably are aware that everything on a computer is stored as bits: 1's and 0's. But a disk is not simply an amorphous collection of 1's and 0's; there is structure. And, more importantly, there are boundaries between one set of bits and another. When bits form a cohesive unit, with a clear starting point and end point, you have a file. You are probably familiar with thinking of word documents, text files, and spreadsheets as files. But pretty much everything on your computer is a file. Executables are files; images are files. All files start with a file header and end with a file footer.

It is a very easy thing to change the extension of a file so it looks like some other type of file. However, that will not change the file structure itself. The file header will contain information on exactly what the file is, regardless of the file extension. The file header will give you an accurate understanding of the file, whether or not the extension has been changed. A few basic facts about files:

- File headers start at the first byte of a file. This is perhaps the most important part of the file from a forensic point of view. It is easy to change a file's extension, but that won't actually change the file or the file header.

- In graphics file formats, the header might give information about an image's size, resolution, number of colors, and the like.

- The Executable and Linkable Format (ELF, formerly called Extensible Linking Format) is a common standard file format for executables, object code, and shared libraries for Unix-based systems. If the suspect drive you are analyzing uses Unix or Linux, this is the file format that executables and libraries will be in. That is important to keep in mind as you examine file headers.

- Portable Executable (PE) is used in Windows for executables and DLLs. PE files are derived from the earlier Common Object File Format (COFF) found on VAX/VMS. This is for Windows what ELF is for Unix.

- Area density refers to data per area of disk. Basically, this is an indication of how much data is stored on the disk compared to disk size.

- Windows Office files have a Globally Unique ID (GUID) to identify them. This allows you to differentiate between two documents even if they have the same name (but are, obviously, in different folders).

File Types

You may encounter a great many different files on a target computer. In fact, much of your evidence gathering will involve files. There are many different file types—the more common are described here. It is impossible to list all the files one might encounter in the space of this chapter. It is also not necessary. We will cover the most common ones, and you can get a more comprehensive list online in many places, including http://filext.com.[10]

- **JPEG (Joint Photographic Experts Group)**   This file type takes its name from the group who created the standard for these digital image files. The maximum image size is 65,535 × 65,535.[11]

- **GIF (Graphics Interchange Format)**   Supports 8 bits per pixel, with a palette of up to 256 colors.[12]

- **TIFF (Tagged Image File Format)**   Used for raster graphics. Widely used in graphic design and publishing.[13]

- **EXIF (Exchangeable Image File Format)**   This is actually a format for images and sound. The standard was originally defined by the Japan Electronic Industries Development Association and includes a number of metadata tags. The structure is based on TIFF files. It can be applied to a variety of file types, including JPEG.[14]

- **PNG (Portable Network Graphics)**   This is an image file format that uses 24-bit RGB (Red Green Blue) pallets or 32-bit RGB (Red Green Blue) pallets. It does not support CMYK (cyan, magenta, yellow, and key [black]).[15]

- **The Advanced Forensic Format**[16]   This file format was invented by Basis Technology. It is an open file standard with three variations: AFF, AFD (AFF Multiple File),[17] and AFM (AFF with External Metadata). The AFF version stores all data and metadata in a single file. The AFM variation stores the data and the metadata in separate files. The AFD variation stores the data and metadata in multiple small files. The AFF file format is part of the AFF Library and Toolkit, which is a set of open-source computer forensics programs. Sleuth Kit and Autopsy both support this file format. AFF files are sometimes broken into several smaller AFD files.

- **EnCase format**   This is a closed format defined by Guidance Software for use in their EnCase tool to store hard drive images and individual files. It includes a hash of the file to ensure nothing was changed when it was copied from the source.

- **GfZIP (Generic Forensic Zip)** This is an open-source file format used to store evidence from a forensic examination. It is based on the open-source gzip compression utility. There are a variety of zip formats and each uses a slightly different algorithm to handle compression.

- **Compressed files** There are a variety of file compression utilities, each with its own file extension. You have probably seen .zip files (WinZip or PKZip). There is also .7z (7-Zip files), tar (common in Unix/Linux), and RAR (RAR archive), to name a few.

- **ISO** This is the format for most optical media such as CDs and DVDs.

- **DLL** This stands for Dynamic Linked Library and is a Windows file format. It is essentially a functionality without user interface. Programmers use DLL to accomplish some functions.

- **EXE** This is an executable file, a program a user can execute.

- **Data files** There are many different data file types. Some of the more common are .dat (data file), .db (SQLite), .mdb (Microsoft Access), .mdf (Microsoft SQL Server), and .nsf (Lotus notes). These file types are obviously quite interesting to a forensic investigation.

These are just a few of the file types you are likely to encounter in a forensic investigation. All of these can be analyzed by examining their file headers for detailed metadata.

Header Analysis

The information that describes the file type is stored in the header of a file. Such information is called the signature of the file, or file signature, and is often unique to one another. In other words, the file extension and the file signature of each file should match. If they do not, that is an indication the file has been altered in some fashion. Sometimes, the file extension is all that has been changed. This is done to hide the file from a cursory examination.

Every file has a file header and footer that contain information on the format of the content stored in the file. Files of a particular type can be searched for using the information stored in the file header alone. Such information can be easily obtained by opening files using a hex editor such as HexEdit. Such tools allow users to see and edit the raw and exact contents stored in a file.

Executables (regardless of the operating system they are designed for) have a header that describes the base address of its code section, data section, the list of functions that can be exported from the executable, etc. When the file is executed, the OS simply reads this header information first and then loads the binary data from the file in the appropriate manner indicated by the file header information.

This information is interesting, but only useful if you can actually view the headers of a file. We will look at a few basic file header viewers. Let's start with PE Explorer,[18] which is used to view the file headers of executables in Windows. First, I loaded an installation executable into PE Explorer. You can see the results in Figure 4-9.

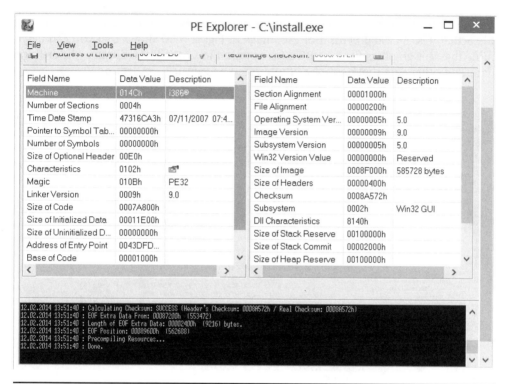

Figure 4-9 PE Explorer

As you can see, this gives you information on the file creation date, the size of the file, and a host of technical details. Depending on the computer crime being investigated, this may or may not be good evidence. For example, if you suspect malware, compare the file size shown in a file header viewer (such as PE Explorer) versus the file header size shown in Windows Explorer. If the latter is bigger than the former, it might indicate the presence of a Trojan horse.

There are a number of hex editors (i.e., software that shows you the content of some file in hexadecimal format). Most are pretty similar in functionality. Let's take a look at one, MiTeC Hexadecimal Editor.[19] I opened an old PNG graphics file on my Windows 8 laptop. The results are shown in Figure 4-10.

Now you may not be used to reading data in hexadecimal format and might be thinking that tools like this are not that helpful. First, notice on the right side that at least some data can easily be translated into characters you probably are used to seeing. For example, the very first part of this file indicates it is a PNG file. This is one very useful function of hex editor tools: Regardless of the file extension, you can see what the file actually is. A casual perusal of the image in Figure 4-10 shows that you can determine that this graphics file uses RGB (as opposed to CMYK), the file size, the creation date, and other data that might be of interest in a forensic investigation.

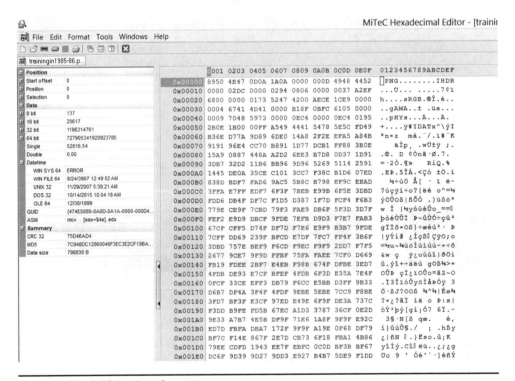

Figure 4-10 PNG header information

NOTE There is a term in computer files called the magic number.[20] That refers to a number in the header file that tells you what that file is (i.e., a text file, JPEG, GIF, DOC, etc.).

Recovering Data

There are two scenarios in which you will be recovering data. The first is when the media is physically damaged, and the second is when there is logical damage, such as the file is corrupt. We will discuss specific techniques (such as file carving), but some general principles apply to each situation.

Physical Damage

A hard drive can fail for a number of reasons. It can be dropped and broken, simply wear out over time, or be damaged through some type of electromagnetic problem, such as a power surge. It is important to keep in mind that you may not be able to recover data. But to attempt to recover data, try the following steps:

1. Remove the drive from the system it is in and connect it to a known functioning test system. It should be connected as a secondary drive.

2. Boot the test system either to its primary drive, or even a boot disk, such as a Linux live CD.

3. Determine whether the failed drive is recognized and can be installed as an additional disk on the test system. If the drive installs, copy all directories and files to a hard drive on the test system. If a drive fails on one system but installs on another, the drive may be usable.

4. If the hard drive is not spinning or the test system does not recognize it, perform limited repair. You may be able to get the hard drive to start and be recognized by the test system.

Logical Damage

This can occur much more readily than physical damage. Corrupted files, improper shutdowns, and power outage at key moments can all cause logical damage. Even turning off a machine while it is booting or shutting down can lead to logical damage. Errors in hardware controllers and drivers can also lead to logical damage. In all these situations, the media is physically intact and functioning, but the data itself has been damaged.

Most operating systems provide a basic repair tool for their native file systems. Microsoft Windows has chkdsk utility that can be used to identify and, in some cases, repair bad clusters. Linux comes with the fsck utility (file system check). Mac OS X provides Disk Utility. A number of companies have developed third-party products that can resolve logical file system errors. The Sleuth Kit (www.sleuthkit.org) has a suite of tools, including file system repair utilities. TestDisk is another example (www.cgsecurity.org/wiki/TestDisk). TestDisk can recover lost partitions and corrupted partition tables.

File and Metadata Carving

Data carving is the process of attempting to extract data from some larger set of data. A specific example of data carving is file carving. File carving is often used to recover data from a disk where there has been some damage or where the file itself is corrupt. This is a common method of data recovery, particularly when the file metadata has been damaged. Sometimes, this is just called "carving." In the case of file carving, you are trying to extract the data from a single file from the larger set of data—that is, the entire disk or partition.

Most file-carving utilities operate by looking for file headers and/or footers and then pulling out the data that is found between these two boundaries.[21] There are a number of tools for file carving—one that is quite easy to use and is free is carver-recovery, so we will look at it.

Carver-Recovery

This utility is a free download[22] that also includes the source code for you to modify if you wish. It contains several utilities. The carver recovery.exe, shown in Figure 4-11, simply allows you to select a drive image, and it will attempt to recover files. This is a broad-based tool for attempting to recover from an entire drive or partition.

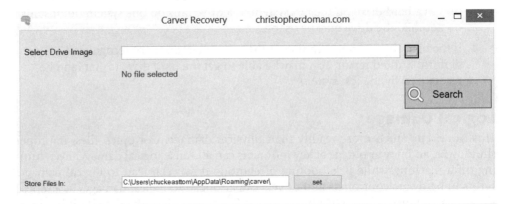

Figure 4-11   carver-recovery

There is also a command-line tool named Scalpel that is included in the download. This tool has a number of flags you can use to manage how the file carving is done. The flags are shown in Figure 4-12.

Figure 4-12 Scalpel in action

Metadata

Metadata is literally "data about data."[23] In the context of computer files, this means data about the file. This can include when a file was created, modified, and even when it was last accessed. For documents, it can even include the username who last saved the document. Clearly, this can be of interest in a forensic investigation. Many tools will help you analyze metadata. One of the most widely used forensic tools is the Sleuth Kit,[24] and it is free. It comes with a suite of command-line tools, but there is also a free graphical interface for it called Autopsy.

Using Autopsy, I loaded a JPEG file that contained an image of an Aston Martin (see Figure 4-13).

Once the image is loaded, some metadata immediately appears in Autopsy, such as creation, modification, and last accessed times. You can see this in Figure 4-14.

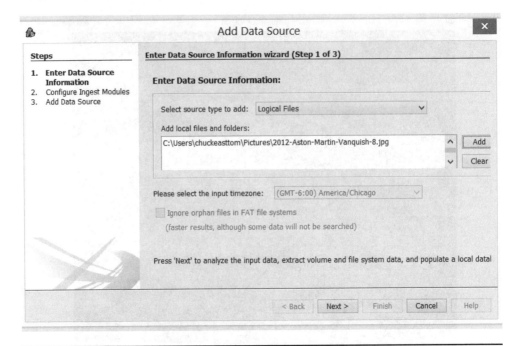

Figure 4-13 Loading an image in Autopsy

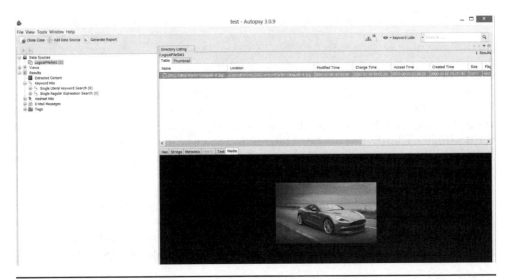

Figure 4-14 Autopsy image data

You can then choose to view the image metadata, hex format, or text data. This is shown in Figure 4-15.

```
Hex  Strings  Metadata  Results  Text  Media
Page:   1   of 4       Page  ← →   Go to Page:

0x00000000: FF D8 FF E0  00 10 4A 46   49 46 00 01  01 00 00 01   ......JFIF......
0x00000010: 00 01 00 00  FF DB 00 43   00 1B 12 14  17 14 11 1B   ........C........
0x00000020: 17 16 17 1E  1C 1B 20 28   42 2B 28 25  25 28 51 3A   ...... (B+(%%(Q:
0x00000030: 3D 30 42 60  55 65 64 5F   55 5D 5B 6A  78 99 81 6A   =0B`Ued_U][jx..j
0x00000040: 71 90 73 5B  5D 85 B5 86   90 9E A3 AB  AD AB 67 80   q.s[]..........g.
0x00000050: BC C9 BA A6  C7 99 A8 AB   A4 FF DB 00  43 01 1C 1E   ............C..
0x00000060: 1E 28 23 28  4E 2B 2B 4E   A4 6E 5D 6E  A4 A4 A4 A4   .(#(N++N.n]n....
0x00000070: A4 A4 A4 A4  A4 A4 A4 A4   A4 A4 A4 A4  A4 A4 A4 A4   ................
0x00000080: A4 A4 A4 A4  A4 A4 A4 A4   A4 A4 A4 A4  A4 A4 A4 A4   ................
0x00000090: A4 A4 A4 A4  A4 A4 A4 A4   A4 A4 A4 A4  A4 A4 FF C0   ................
0x000000a0: 00 11 08 02  F1 05 00 03   01 22 00 02  11 01 03 11   .........".......
0x000000b0: 01 FF C4 00  1A 00 00 03   01 01 01 01  00 00 00 00   ................
0x000000c0: 00 00 00 00  00 00 00 01   02 03 04 05  06 FF C4 00   ................
0x000000d0: 46 10 00 02  02 01 03 03   02 04 05 02  05 01 07 03   F...............
0x000000e0: 00 0B 00 01  02 11 21 03   12 31 04 41  51 22 61 13   ......!..1.AQ"a.
0x000000f0: 71 81 91 05  32 42 52 A1   14 B1 23 33  62 C1 D1 53   q...2BR...#3b..S
0x00000100: 24 43 72 82  E1 F0 F1 06   15 34 55 63  92 35 64 A2   $Cr......4Uc.5d.
0x00000110: 44 54 83 93  B2 FF C4 00   17 01 01 01  01 01 00 00   DT..............
0x00000120: 00 00 00 00  00 00 00 00   00 00 00 01  02 03 FF C4   ................
0x00000130: 00 1C 11 01  01 01 01 00   03 01 01 00  00 00 00 00   ................
0x00000140: 00 00 00 00  11 01 02 12   21 41 31 51  FF DA 00 0C   ........!A1Q....
0x00000150: 03 01 00 02  11 03 11 00   3F 00 F1 00  00 20 18 00   ........?.... ..
0x00000160: 00 00 C0 00  00 00 7D 84   3E C0 03 10  C0 06 21 80   ......}.>.....!.
0x00000170: C0 00 06 00  01 4C 00 10   14 B8 00 18  00 00 C0 10   .....L..........
0x00000180: C4 30 01 88  60 03 42 19   03 00 18 08  45 31 50 08   .0..`.B.....E1P.
0x00000190: 28 60 80 00  00 00 43 02   84 03 00 00  0A 00 04 86   (`....C.........
0x000001a0: 00 00 00 00  03 01 00 C0   01 00 D0 E8  10 00 50 21   ............P!
```

Figure 4-15 Autopsy image hex data

As you can see, it is relatively easy to load a file in Autopsy and view the metadata for that file. While an image was used in this example, the same can be done with any computer file.

Known File Filtering

Known file filtering (KFF) is the process of filtering out files that are known. For example, if you know a computer contains a number of innocuous spreadsheets, you might wish to filter those out of the searchers in order to allow you to search for files that might constitute evidence.[25]

 NOTE We have examined means to recover data from damaged media. Recovering data from an encrypted drive is a nontrivial task. We will be discussing this in detail in Chapter 7 when we cover more details on cryptography and steganography.

Media File Forensic Steps

At some point, you will need to power down a device and transport it back to the forensic lab. Many people think that the first step in acquiring forensic evidence is to shut down the computer. At one time, this was in fact recommended by many sources.

However, it has become clear that doing so will actually erase information. What about malware currently running on the suspect machine? Evidence in memory? Or someone currently connected to the machine? All of this evidence will be lost. Therefore, it is necessary to record such evidence before shutdown. Remember that you want to be careful and make certain you don't inadvertently alter or add data to the computer when performing these steps.

There is no specific order required by law or by forensic standards, so you may perform these steps in any order you see fit. The following is just the steps in the order I normally take them.

Running Processes

In Windows (all versions) you press the CTRL, ALT, and DELETE keys at the same time and then select Task Manager. This will give you a tabbed display. Select Processes. The Windows 8 version of this is shown in Figure 14-16.

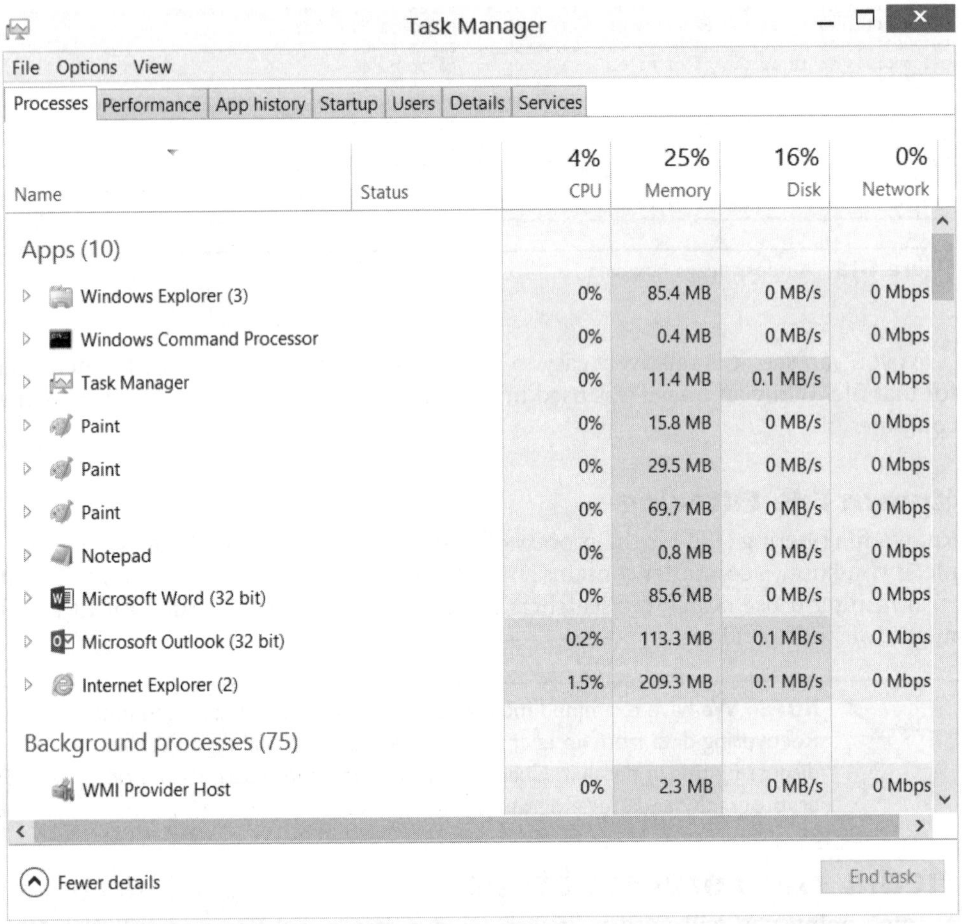
Task Manager
File Options View
Processes Performance App history Startup Users Details Services
Name Status 4% CPU 25% Memory 16% Disk 0% Network
Apps (10)
Windows Explorer (3) 0% 85.4 MB 0 MB/s 0 Mbps
Windows Command Processor 0% 0.4 MB 0 MB/s 0 Mbps
Task Manager 0% 11.4 MB 0.1 MB/s 0 Mbps
Paint 0% 15.8 MB 0 MB/s 0 Mbps
Paint 0% 29.5 MB 0 MB/s 0 Mbps
Paint 0% 69.7 MB 0 MB/s 0 Mbps
Notepad 0% 0.8 MB 0 MB/s 0 Mbps
Microsoft Word (32 bit) 0% 85.6 MB 0 MB/s 0 Mbps
Microsoft Outlook (32 bit) 0.2% 113.3 MB 0.1 MB/s 0 Mbps
Internet Explorer (2) 1.5% 209.3 MB 0.1 MB/s 0 Mbps
Background processes (75)
WMI Provider Host 0% 2.3 MB 0 MB/s 0 Mbps
Fewer details
End task

Figure 4-16 Running processes in Windows

You should now take a screen shot of this and save it. It will be important to document what processes were running. In some cases, this might reveal malware, though not in all cases. It also could indicate programs running in the background. Most importantly, it is a built-in utility in Windows and does not make any changes to the system.

Netstat

The netstat command shows network statistics and any current connections. You will always see some connections running, even for a machine that is connected to a small home network. The basic netstat command is shown in Figure 14-17.

Figure 4-17 netstat

This command is in Windows and Unix/Linux, so it is a built-in utility that does not require any changes to the system. There are also a number of command flags that can be used with netstat to provide more specific information.[26] Some of these are described here:

- netstat -a shows all active TCP connections and the ports they use.

- netstat -p shows connections for a specific protocol such as TCP, ICMP, etc.

- netstat -o will show the process ID for each connection.

- netstat -r shows the contents of the routing table.

You can use these flags in combination, such as netstat -a -o.

Net Sessions

This is similar to netstat, but can be more meaningful. Netstat will even show meaningless connections, such as your computer opening a web browser. Net sessions only shows established network communication sessions, such as someone logging on to that system. This requires that the command be run as administrator (unlike netstat).

Openfiles

Openfiles lists currently open shared files. It also must be run as administrator. This is likely to only yield information if someone else is currently accessing the suspect machine. However, such information can be quite valuable if you suspect an outside party of breaking into the system and they are still connected.

Make sure you run each of these commands and take a screen shot of the results. This will allow you to document the status of the computer when you discovered it. Only then should you power down the machine.

Chapter Review

In this chapter, we started by discussing two very important principles of forensics: Locard's principle of transference and the Inman-Rudin paradigm. Both of these are critical for the CCFP exam. We also discussed how to identify and classify evidence. You learned the essentials of storage media and locating evidence, as well as how to examine file metadata and even to reconstruct damaged files. We also covered how to properly gather information from the suspect system prior to shutting it down.

Questions

1. Which of the following most accurately describes Locard's principle of transference?

   A. Computer viruses will always leave a trace.

   B. When two objects come in contact, some trace is left behind.

   C. The forensic examiner will always accidentally alter the evidence in some way.

   D. You must transfer evidence to the lab in a forensically sound manner.

2. When a forensic examiner accidentally alters or introduces evidence, it is referred to as:

   A. Locard's principle of transference

   B. Transfer

   C. Contamination

   D. File carving

3. Which of the following was added by the Inman-Rudin paradigm?

A. Transfer

B. Individualization

C. Association between source and target

D. Evidence must divide before it can be transferred

4. What best describes metadata?

A. Data that is important to the investigation

B. Data about data

C. Data that is hidden

D. Operating system data

5. File carving is best described as:

A. Breaking a file into smaller pieces for analysis

B. Finding the header and footer of a file and assembling the blocks in between

C. Removing infected files

D. Using a different OS to analyze files

Answers

1. **B.** Locard's principle tells us that when two objects come in contact, they leave some sort of trace.

2. **C.** Locard's principle also tells us that anytime a forensic investigator interacts with evidence, there is a chance of contamination.

3. **D.** The Inman-Rudin paradigm suggests that evidence must divide before it can leave a trace.

4. **B.** Metadata is simply data about data.

5. **B.** File carving consists of identifying the header and footer and carving out what is in between.

References

1. http://www.scientificamerican.com/article/just-a-theory-7-misused-science-words/.

2. http://scholar.google.com/.

3. http://www.forensichandbook.com/locards-exchange-principle/.

4. http://forensicsciencecentral.co.uk/edmondlocard.shtml.

PART II

5. http://www.forensicdna.com/~Media/The_Origin_of_Evidence.pdf.

6. http://www.ncbi.nlm.nih.gov/pubmed/11955825.

7. http://dictionary.law.com/Default.aspx?selected=1623.

8. http://www.vsrdjournals.com/CSIT/Issue/2011_5_May/ 10_Seema_Yadav_Policy_Paper_May_2011.pdf.

9. http://eprints.qut.edu.au/28073/1/c28073.pdf.

10. http://filext.com/alphalist.php?extstart=%5EA.

11. http://www.jpeg.org/public/jfif.pdf.

12. http://www.w3.org/Graphics/GIF/spec-gif87.txt.

13. http://www.iso.org/iso/iso_catalogue/catalogue_ics/ catalogue_detail_ics.htm?csnumber=2181.

14. http://www.media.mit.edu/pia/Research/deepview/exif.html.

15. http://www.iso.org/iso/catalogue_detail.htm?csnumber=29581.

16. http://cs.harvard.edu/malan/publications/aff.pdf.

17. https://media.readthedocs.org/pdf/sift/latest/sift.pdf.

18. http://www.heaventools.com/download-pe-explorer.htm.

19. http://www.techsupportalert.com/best-free-hex-editor.htm#hxd.

20. *Computer Science Handbook*, Second Edition, edited by Allen B. Tucker. CRC Press, 2004.

21. http://www.sans.org/reading-room/whitepapers/forensics/ data-carving-concepts-32969.

22. http://code.google.com/p/carver-recovery/downloads/ detail?name=Portable_Executable.zip&can=2&q=.

23. http://nij.gov/topics/forensics/evidence/digital/analysis/Pages/metadata.aspx.

24. http://www.sleuthkit.org/sleuthkit/download.php.

25. http://www.nsrl.nist.gov/Documents/aafs2005/aafs2005.pdf.

26. http://technet.microsoft.com/en-us/library/ff961504.aspx.

Forensic Analysis

In this chapter you will learn how to:
- Properly plan a cyber forensic investigation
- Prepare case notes and reports
- Understand quality control procedures
- Implement lab and individual case quality control procedures

Planning and quality control are two critical aspects of any forensic investigation. Proper documentation and reporting are also essential skills any forensic analyst needs. You may wonder why we are covering these topics before delving into the specifics of how to conduct forensic examinations. The answer is simple. These principles should guide everything else you do in cyber forensics. If you master every technique in this book but don't have proper documentation or quality control, your forensics investigations will be unsuccessful.

Planning

Prior to conducting a cyber forensics investigation, it is important that you plan the investigation. This can be one of the most important parts of your investigation. Your plan should include how to collect the evidence, safeguard the evidence, and analyze the evidence. It is completely inappropriate to simply decide these elements as the case progresses.

Collecting the Evidence

The first question to ask is usually how you will acquire the evidence. This may seem like an odd question, but there are different approaches to seizing evidence, depending on the nature of the evidence and the conditions where it is located.

If this is a cell phone or laptop, you may be able to simply transport the suspect equipment to your lab and work with it there. Of course, it must be transported in a manner that not only preserves the chain of custody, but also ensures that there is no contamination of the evidence. For example, a cell phone should be transported in a container that blocks any signals.

In the case of an e-commerce server that is perhaps part of an identity theft investigation, it may not be possible to just take the server offline. That would disrupt normal business for the e-commerce site. In that case, you have two options. The best is to switch over to a backup server and then image the suspect server on the site. If there is no backup server, you will have to temporarily take the server down, just long enough to image the server, and then put it back in operation.

There are also cases where remote gathering of evidence will be required. This is not the preferred method and should only be used if there simply is no other choice. One example might be a case involving military personnel stationed overseas or perhaps employees of an embassy. It would take time to get to the scene and to extract the evidence. It may be necessary to remotely image the suspect drive in order to preserve evidence. Keep in mind that this is the least preferred method and should be used only when there is no other viable option.

Analyze the Evidence

As you probably suspect, much of this book is focused on specific techniques for analyzing evidence, and you will see several such techniques in subsequent chapters. However, there are general guidelines for evidence analysis that should be part of your standard operating procedure. Each is discussed in the sections that follow.

Validation of Findings

It is always important to validate whatever findings you have. There are two major reasons for this. The first reason is that you are a human and capable of making mistakes. Given the possibility of error, validation allows you to lessen the chance of this happening and to catch errors when they do occur. Another reason is that if a case does go to court, it is likely that the opposing counsel will hire a forensic expert who will question your findings. If you validate all findings, that will help address any questions.

 NOTE My experience in court cases is that opposing counsel and their expert will disagree with virtually everything you state. They will find some nuance, some technicality, on which to base their disagreement. So I make it a policy to back up everything I say with not only multiple tests where appropriate, but multiple references. For example, if I state in my report a certain fact about how NTFS operates, I like a minimum of two reputable sources to support my view.

So how do you validate your findings? The answer is actually simple. Repeat the test with a different tool. For example, if you use Disk Digger to find deleted files, also see if another tool such as NTFS Undelete will find the same files. It may be possible for someone to claim the tool was in error or you made a mistake with one test. But if two tests, done with two different tools, find the same results, it would be very difficult for anyone to claim error.

It is important that your forensic lab make a standard practice of validating all evidence, or at least the most key pieces of evidence. It is also best, when possible, that a different investigator validate the evidence. Having two different tests, using two different tools, conducted by two different investigators yield the same results makes it almost ridiculous for opposing counsel to claim a mistake was made.

Proper Evidence Handling

In the first four chapters of this book, we discussed how to transport, store, and secure evidence. This is what we mean by proper evidence handling. However, the specific techniques and procedures used in your lab should be documented in your standard operating procedure and then adhered to in each and every investigation.

One concept you will see throughout this chapter is the documentation of procedures, the codifying of good forensic practices, as standard operating procedures (SOPs). One cannot assume that all forensic analysts will have the same level of skill and knowledge. Therefore, it is important to have very clear and detailed standard operating procedures that tell every investigator exactly what to do in any given situation. These SOPs also provide a benchmark for quality control measures, which we will discuss later in this chapter.

Completeness of Investigation

We have discussed previously in this book at some length the problem with improper evidence handling. It can lead to evidence being excluded. But an equally problematic issue is that of incomplete investigations. Too often, forensic investigators have a very large caseload, and as soon as evidence of the accused crime is found, they stop the investigation. This is wrong for multiple reasons.

The first reason is that you must acquire all relevant evidence related to an incident. If you stop at the first piece of evidence you find, what happens if opposing counsel is able to get that evidence dismissed, or to at least address it at trial and cast doubt on the case? It is important to have all the evidence possible.

The second issue involves getting an incomplete picture. A common claim by those accused of child pornography is that some virus or other malware must have put that on their computer. If you simply stop investigating when child pornography is discovered, you will have difficulty countering this claim. However, if you continue your investigation, you will determine how often the images were accessed, when they were downloaded, any websites visited, if there was malware on the machine, if the malware is capable of surreptitiously downloading images, etc. All of these facts will lead to a complete picture that will either clearly demonstrate the suspect's guilt or exonerate him or her.

NOTE   In my entire career, I have not yet encountered a virus that downloads child pornography. I can certainly envision one being created—it would not be overly difficult. But the lack of one existing in the wild makes these claims by accused child pornographers very doubtful.

Legal Compliance

Legal issues have already been addressed in this book too and need not be revisited in detail here. However, it should be pointed out that your standard operating procedure must address all relevant legal issues. These may include federal and state laws, standards for a specific industry, or standards set by a government agency.

The critical issue is to ensure that your SOP addresses all relevant guidelines. So ensure that you consult all laws and regulations applicable to your industry and geographical area. It is also important to monitor changes in these laws to ensure you continue to comply.

Case Notes and Reports

Obviously, case notes and reports are related. In fact, the case notes should lead to the creation of the report. However, they are still two separate items, each of which should be handled differently. Both are discussed in this section.

Case Notes

Case notes are a bit more informal than expert reports. They are your own notes as you progress through a case. However, saying they are a bit more informal does not mean these are personal notes with no structure or standards. These notes can be subpoenaed for court. They are certainly subject to review by other analysts in your lab as part of the normal quality control procedure. However, they are not a formal report of findings. Case notes are thorough and should be created as you conduct your examination. The U.S. Department of Justice defines what should be found in case notes[1]:

> Documentation should be contemporaneous with the examination, and retention of notes should be consistent with departmental policies. The following is a list of general considerations that may assist the examiner throughout the documentation process.

- Take notes when consulting with the case investigator and/or prosecutor.
- Maintain a copy of the search authority with the case notes.
- Maintain the initial request for assistance with the case file.
- Maintain a copy of chain of custody documentation.
- Take notes detailed enough to allow complete duplication of actions.
- Include in the notes dates, times, and descriptions and results of actions taken.
- Document irregularities encountered and any actions taken regarding the irregularities during the examination.

- Include additional information, such as network topology, list of authorized users, user agreements, and/or passwords.

- Document changes made to the system or network by or at the direction of law enforcement or the examiner.

- Document the operating system and relevant software version and current, installed patches.

- Document information obtained at the scene regarding remote storage, remote user access, and offsite backups.

I believe this list can be summarized a bit more briefly as follows:

- Take notes of any conversation you have.

- Keep copies of all relevant documents, including warrants, requests to investigate, etc., along with the notes.

- Everything you do should be documented, including the method, tool, date, time, results, and any irregularities.

- Document as much information as you can about the target system, including hardware, operating system, etc.

The notes should be clear enough that any competent forensic analyst could take your notes and re-create your entire examination. This is important for court, and important for quality control. Thorough notes would allow another examiner to check your process for any irregularities or errors. I find it useful to think of case notes as a diary of your progress through the case. It is also helpful to conceive of case notes as lab notes. If you ever took chemistry courses in college, you will recall that your lab notes had to detail all the steps of your experiment in such detail that anyone else could take those notes and repeat the experiment. This is a good guide for writing case notes, too.

Reports

A forensic report is a formal document that represents the tests performed and the results obtained. In some cases, particularly civil trials, there may be a specific expert report that is filed with the court. Let's address each of these separately.

The Forensic Report

In most cases, forensic labs require you to create a report of your forensic process. This report will detail what tests you conducted and the results. If you took adequate and complete case notes, you should be able to use those as the basis for your forensic report. Your forensic report is essentially a summary of the case notes. The SANS Institute recommends three sections in your report[2]:

Overview/Case Summary: This is a general summary of what the case is about and what the goal of the investigation is.

Forensic Acquisition and Exam: In this section, you will discuss what you did, starting with acquiring the forensic evidence and then your actual tests.

Findings and Report: This section has your conclusions.

The popular forensic tool EnCase actually has forensic report templates and will generate a basic report for you. This is shown in Figure 5-1.

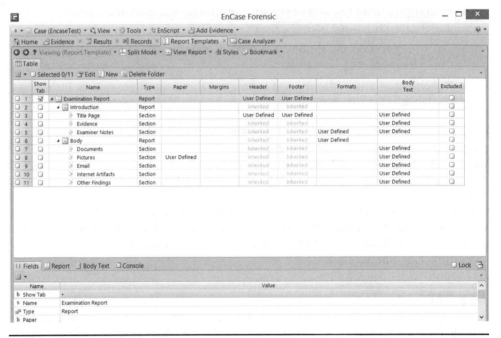

Figure 5-1   EnCase reports

Notice the body of the report is broken down into sections covering e-mail evidence, documents found, etc.

AccessData's Forensic Toolkit (FTK) asks you to input case information when acquiring a drive image, shown in Figure 5-2. This information will be used to create the report header, preloaded with case information, including the investigator's name.

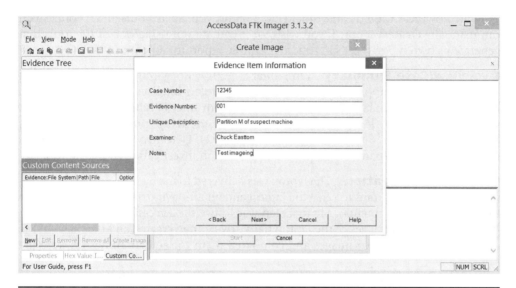

Figure 5-2 FTK case information

The free forensic tool Autopsy also generates reports. In Figure 5-3, a report for an unprocessed case is shown. You can see even without processing evidence that this report gives you basic case information.

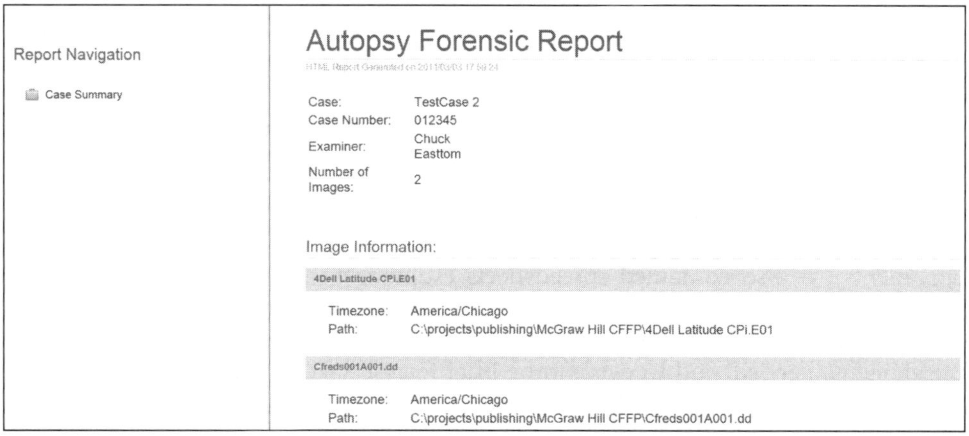

Figure 5-3 Autopsy report

All the major forensics tools provide some level of reporting. However, automated reports can only document what tests you conducted with a given tool. They cannot document what you may have done with other tools or the processes you used prior to using this tool, for example, in acquiring the evidence. I recommend you use the reports generated by these tools as attachments to a report you create yourself. Of course, you can manually create a report if you wish, or if you are not using one of the tools that generate its own reports. Let's look at an example report for a fictitious case.

Overview/Case Summary   On January 2, 2014, I began the process of imaging and processing a laptop suspected of containing stolen intellectual property. I began by photographing the laptop (Dell Inspiron 17 with Intel Pentium Processor 2127U, 4 gigabytes of RAM [Single Channel DDR3L 1600MHz], running the Windows 8.1 operating system, Serial number SN 292929292). Detective Racheal Smith of the Metropolis Police Department requested I perform an investigation of this laptop.

Forensic Investigation   The laptop was delivered to me by Detective Smith along with copies of the warrant to seize the laptop and an affidavit detailing how she seized the laptop (see attachments). My first step was to use the AccessData Forensic Toolkit Image to create two images of the laptop hard drive. I then created an MD5 hash of the original disk and the two images and compared them to see that all hashes were the same.

At that point, I placed the original disk and one of the images in our forensic safe and began my examination of one of the images. My first step was to search for all PDFs, Word documents, or Excel spreadsheets to determine if any were related to the stolen intellectual property. I found two PDFs that were company documents, marked confidential, and contained details of the intellectual property (those e-mails are printed and attached to this report). I then used the Disk Digger tool to search for deleted files. I discovered two additional files, both Excel spreadsheets, and they appeared to contain data relating to the value of the intellectual property. Those files are printed and attached to this report.

Next, I searched the machine for all e-mail files (i.e., Outlook .pst files). I found a .pst file marked private.pst located in C:\IllegalStuff\ that was not attached to the running copy of Microsoft Outlook. Upon examining that file, I found four e-mails discussing the sale of the intellectual property to various third parties (those e-mails are printed and attached to this report).

Findings and Report   Conclusions: My examination demonstrated that the suspect laptop contained the intellectual property that had been stolen (i.e., the PDF documents). It also contained spreadsheets estimating the value of the intellectual property and e-mails discussing the sale of this property to third parties.

Consider our report for this fictitious case. Although it is a bit brief, it contains all the elements needed, and we wish to be brief for the sake of including the report in this book. Notice in the introduction we provide the basic allegation in the case, the specifics of what we are examining, and who asked us to examine it. Also notice that throughout the report we reference attachments. We attach the warrant, the request to

PART II

investigate, and later we attached printouts of what we found. This allows anyone reading the report to immediately understand what was done and why.

In the next section, we tell what we did, beginning with the imaging of the drive and the validation of that image. We also tell what tests we conducted, tools used, and results of those tests. Again, we reference attachments showing what we found. Finally, in the conclusions we summarize what we found. Notice we did not make an assessment of guilt or innocence. We simply summarized what we found. A forensic report is not an assessment of guilt or innocence; it is an unbiased examination of the facts that we can find as a result of applying forensic science. Simply factual conclusions, not opinions.

Scientific accuracy is also critical in your forensic report. Every conclusion you document should be well supported by accepted forensic and computer science. I find it useful to cite standards that support my conclusions.

The Expert Report

An expert report is a bit different from a forensic report. Usually, civil cases use this format. To begin with, an expert report will have the same data and the same exhibits/attachments as a forensic report, but will be much more detailed. Expert reports generally start with the expert's qualifications. This should be a complete curriculum vitae (CV) detailing education, work history, and publications. This needs to be as thorough as possible. List all education, work experience, publications, etc. In many cases, one also lists past expert witness work.

 NOTE   Many professionals have worked their entire career under the belief that a resume should be kept as brief as possible. Some even recommend keeping it to a single page. That may be appropriate for a job hunting resume, but for your CV, you need to put everything in. If you would like to see an example, my own CV is posted on my website: www.ChuckEasttom.com. As of this writing, it is already 15 pages long.

After the CV, you move into the topic at hand. It is much like the forensic report; however, you should include every single detail. There is no such thing as too much detail. I also personally make it a practice to use numerous citations from various sources to support even basic factual assertions. For example, if I make the statement that undeleting from a FAT-based system simply removes the item from the File Allocation Table, I will cite at least one or two reputable sources. Yes, this is a commonly known fact, and any computer professional would know that (or at least should), but it is always a good idea to support your assertions.

If you did a validation of your tests, particularly with another round of testing, detail that as well. Note that we will be discussing validating results in detail later in this chapter. If you have any additional evidence, including documents produced, statements from the accused, officer statements, deposition transcripts, anything at all, it should go into this report. You want as many lines of evidence as you can. Evidence from sources outside the case is called extrinsic evidence; evidence from the case itself is called intrinsic evidence.

The next issue with an expert report is its completeness. The report must cover every item the expert wishes to opine on, and in detail. Nothing can be assumed. In some jurisdictions, if an item is not in the expert report, then the expert is not allowed to opine on it during testimony. Whether or not that is the case in your jurisdiction, it is imperative that the expert report be very thorough and complete. And, of course, it must be error free. Even the smallest error can give opposing counsel an opportunity to impugn the accuracy of the entire report and the expert's entire testimony. This document should be carefully proofread by the expert and by the attorney retaining the expert. Of course, an expert report is inclusive of all exhibits/attachments. One such exhibit should be a list of all items you considered in forming your opinions.

Finally, an expert report is not a neutral document. You have formed an opinion and your report should clearly state what it is. For example, if you believe the accused did steal intellectual property, your report should first demonstrate that via evidence and then clearly state your conclusion. Whereas a forensic report has conclusions only, the expert report will also have your expert opinions.

As you can see, an expert report can quickly become a rather long document. Even small cases often involve expert reports that are in excess of 30 pages. In more complex cases, expert reports that are 200 or more pages long are not unusual. The largest I have personally seen was over 600 pages, not counting attachments/exhibits. However, this is not meant to indicate that one should be unnecessarily verbose in a report. Quite the contrary. Be as concise and clear as possible. However, the necessity of explaining all the testing and analysis done and defining terms is likely to increase the size of the report.

 NOTE One critical factor in case notes, forensic reports, and expert reports is clarity in your writing. It is important that anyone reading your report knows exactly what you are trying to document. Avoid ambiguities, colloquial phrasing, unnecessary abbreviations, or anything that is not completely clear to anyone reading the document.

Quality Control

It should be obvious that maintaining quality in forensics investigations is necessary and, in fact, critical. This means the lab maintains quality in equipment and processes, the individual examiners maintain quality in their skillset, and each examination and analysis maintains a level of quality.

Lab Quality

Obviously part of quality control is the quality of the lab itself. Beyond the skill of the individual examiners and what skill is used in a specific forensic test, the lab itself must maintain quality. Fortunately there are some standards to guide you on this issue.

FBI RCFL

RCFL, or Regional Computer Forensics Laboratory,[3] is a "one stop, full service forensics laboratory and training center devoted entirely to the examination of digital evidence in support of criminal investigations." This means a lab that is involved in forensics and training. These labs offer a great deal of training options, including continuing education courses[4] such as

- Case Agent Investigative Review
- Image Scan Training
- Social Media Evidence
- Capturing a Running Computer System
- Mobile Forensics

These labs provide an excellent source for continuing education. They also provide a model for how a forensic lab should ideally be set up. If your laboratory meets the standards,[5] you can apply to enter into a Memorandum of Understanding with the FBI to become a participating agency in the RCFL.

American Society of Crime Laboratory Directors

The American Society of Crime Laboratory Directors (ASCLD)[6] provides guidelines for forensics labs of all types, not just cyber forensics. It also provides standards for certifying forensics labs. ASCLD offers voluntary accreditation to public and private crime laboratories in the United States and around the world. The ASCLD/LAB certification regulates how to organize and manage crime labs. Achieving ASCLD accreditation is a rigorous process, and there are literally a few hundred criteria that must be met. This can often take more than two years to fully prepare for accreditation. The lab spends this time developing policies, procedures, document controls, analysis validations, and so on. Then, the lab needs another year to go through the process. The ASCLD does have courses to help prepare one for lab accreditation.[7] This course is described as follows:

> This course has been designed to assist crime laboratory personnel to prepare for ASCLD/LAB–International. ISO 17025:2005 and ASCLD/LAB–International Supplemental Requirements for Testing Labs will be reviewed and preparation exercises will be provided. This program will serve to provide the attendees with a better understanding of the types of planning and activities which may be considered in order to prepare for the formal application and external assessment process. This program is designed to supplement internal management practices which a laboratory should have in place to support ASCLD/LAB–International preparation activities. Attendees familiar with the ASCLD/LAB Legacy program will be provided with opportunities to compare internal laboratory activities involved with each program. An attendance certificate will be mailed to the student.[8]

PART II

The assessment team begins by reviewing the application and documentation showing the lab's policies and procedures. This is done before they actually visit the lab to conduct the assessment. The assessment takes about a week. Typically, the assessment team generates 5 to 15 findings that require corrective action. The lab requires several months to make corrections to the satisfaction of the lead assessor. Once the facility has made all corrections, the lead assessor recommends the lab to the board of directors for accreditation. Finally, the ASCLD/LAB board of directors votes on whether to accredit the lab.

The ASCLD/LAB program also provides for periodic audits to ensure that forensic specialists are performing lab procedures correctly and consistently for all casework. The society performs these audits in computer forensics labs to maintain quality and integrity. Pursuing ASCLD accreditation is a very good way to ensure the lab maintains quality standards.

 TIP The standard ISO/IEC 17025:2005 covers "requirements for the competence of testing and calibration laboratories." This standard is common to all forensics labs, not just cyber forensics. The test will simply ask you to identify what the standard is, not details about the requirements.

Tool Quality Control

It is also important to ensure your tools are up to standard. This begins with selecting only tools that have been widely used and accepted in the cyber forensic community. But it is maintained by testing tools. There are two primary ways to test a given tool.

The first method is to conduct a test on a known item with preset properties. In other words, if you are testing a tool that searches for images with certain characteristics, you set up a drive image that has some specific type of image on it. For testing purposes, you might use anything, such as images with elephants. Then run the tool and test how many of those images it was able to find. Since you put the images there, you know exactly how many should be discovered.

The second method is to test against a known good tool. For example, if you are evaluating the use of an undelete tool you have not previously used, compare that tool's results against those of one or two tools you have used and that you know to be quality tools.

Both of these methodologies allow you calibrate your forensic tools and ensure they meet quality standards. It is impossible to perform quality forensic investigations without quality tools. It is also important that you document the testing and calibration of these tools. Furthermore, you should periodically recalibrate any and all tools you use. A common challenge to any forensic examination is for opposing counsel to inquire if the tools have been calibrated.

Investigator Quality Control

Just as the laboratory must maintain quality, you have to maintain the quality of your individual analysts and investigators. Quality of forensics personnel includes ensuring they have the appropriate training and education. It also involves ensuring that they have a clean background.

PART II

Training and Education

Obviously, you need to ensure that all investigators are properly trained, but what exactly does that mean? Unfortunately, the field of cyber forensics is not as clearly defined as other fields, for example, medicine. If you are seeking a registered nurse, there is a state licensing requirement that clearly defines the qualifications and even mandates continuing education requirements. That is not the case for forensic personnel. So there is some ambiguity as to what is required. In this section, we will discuss various training, educational, and certification qualifications one might seek in a cyber forensic analyst. However, the analyst does not need to have all of these. You should look for a combination of factors that indicate competence.

The first issue is college education. Until recently, there were no college majors for cyber forensics. Now, many universities have such degrees.[9,10,11,12] Obviously, having such a degree would be a good sign that the analyst was competent. However, there are a few issues with such degrees. The first is that there are so few accredited universities offering such degrees and they are so new, that it is unlikely many of your prospective analysts will have one. The second is that since these programs are so new, it is difficult to tell which ones are of the best quality.

 NOTE Cyber security and cyber forensics are hot topics. This has led to a number of unaccredited institutions offering related degrees. In the United States, regional accreditation is the accreditation that is needed for any school. Claims of national or international accreditation are of little use. I cannot recommend acquiring a degree from any school that is not regionally accredited.

Usually, a computer-related degree or a degree with a significant amount of computer-related courses is desired. For example, it is common for business majors to take a number of computer courses. You may also find someone who has majored in criminal justice but also took computer science courses.

In addition to degrees, the computer industry is replete with certifications. This book is designed to help one study for the (ISC)²'s Certified Cyber Forensic Professional exam. Obviously, that is one certification that is desirable in a cyber forensic specialist. But there are others. It would be impossible to discuss all relevant certifications here, so we will only mention the most widely recognized.

- **CISSP** The Certified Information Systems Security Professional, also from the (ISC)², is one of the oldest and most widely recognized security-related certifications. It is a general certification and is not specific to forensics.

- **CompTIA Security+/CASP** The Computer Technology Industry Association has their Security+ certification. Many experts regard this as CISSP Lite. It covers the same domains as CISSP, but with less depth. It is appropriate for those with about two years of experience. They have also added their Advanced Security Practitioner (CASP) certification test, which is very thorough.

- **EC Council Certifications** The EC Council has two relevant certifications. The first is their Certified Ethical Hacker certification. This teaches the basics of hacking. If a forensic investigation involves allegations of hacking, it is always good if the investigator has a working knowledge of hacking techniques. They also have their Certified Hacking Forensic Investigator certification, which is a general forensic certification.

- **Vendor Certification**   If an investigation involves a specific product, it is never a bad thing to have training in that product. For example, if you are certified in Microsoft Windows Server 2012, that knowledge would be useful when investigating a Windows Server. Similarly, if an investigation involves a Cisco router, then having some level of training in Cisco products is desirable.

- **EnCase Certified Examiner Certification**   Guidance Software, the creator of the EnCase software, sponsors the EnCase Certified Examiner (EnCE) certification program. This certification is open to the public and private sectors. It focuses on the use and mastery of system forensics analysis using EnCase. For more information on EnCE certification requirements, visit www.guidancesoftware.com.

- **AccessData Certified Examiner**   AccessData is the creator of Forensic Toolkit (FTK) software. This company sponsors the AccessData Certified Examiner (ACE) certification program. ACE certification is open to the public and private sectors. This certification is specific to use and mastery of FTK. Requirements for taking the ACE exam include completing the AccessData boot camp and Windows forensic courses. For more information on ACE certification, visit www.accessdata.com.

In addition to industry certifications, there are professional development and continuing education courses. We already mentioned the ASCLD continuing education courses. Most colleges and universities offer some continuing education or professional development short courses in a variety of computer science–related topics. The popular online site EdX offers online courses from major universities such as MIT and Harvard. Many of these courses are related to computer science, engineering, and even law. Clearly, such courses should also be considered when evaluating a potential investigator.

Also, many organizations provide training to their staff. I have on more than one occasion conducted such courses for government agencies such as the U.S. Secret Service. These courses are not college courses, or even certification courses, but do serve to increase the knowledge and skillset of the students. Similarly, many vendors such as Microsoft, AccessData, etc., provide training in their specific products.

So who is the ideal forensic investigator? Obviously, one who combines all of these elements. However, that is unrealistic. For example, you might have an investigator with an unrelated degree, or even no degree, but who has had extensive professional training and has multiple certifications, including CISSP and CCFP. This person should at least be considered for the position of forensic analyst. What you are seeking is a clear indication that the individual possesses two things:

- A working basic knowledge of relevant computer science topics such as operating systems, networking, hardware, etc. This could be demonstrated by a computer science–related degree or a related minor. It could also be demonstrated by industry certification or years of experience in a related job such as technical support.

- A solid understanding of cyber forensics. This can also be demonstrated by appropriate college courses, corporate training, or certifications such as the CCFP.

Background Checks

When your forensic analysts are law enforcement personnel, the issue of a background check is a moot point. However, there are more and more civilian labs. It is important you conduct the same level of scrutiny that would be conducted by either a military clearance, such as a secret clearance, or a law enforcement background check.

Obviously, you would prefer someone with no issues in their past. And any felonies, any computer-related crimes, and any financial crimes should be automatic disqualifiers. But are there "gray areas"? Yes, there are. For example, simple possession offenses, trespassing, etc., may be something you can accept, provided

- The incident was several years ago
- It was a misdemeanor charge
- There have been no other crimes

Some organizations also perform a credit check. It is not necessary that a forensic analyst have perfect credit. The theory behind the check is twofold. First, someone in extremely dire financial problems might be susceptible to bribery. In addition, someone with habitual credit issues might be irresponsible. Whether or not you agree with those two statements, credit checks are often part of background checks.

The other issue involves updating the background check. Just because someone had a clear background when you hired them ten years ago does not mean their background is still clear. The federal government uses the following standard for background checks on personnel with security clearances:[13]

> An individual is normally subject to periodic reinvestigation at a minimum of every 5 years for a Top Secret level clearance and every 10 years for a Secret level clearance.

This is a good model to follow. Periodic rechecks, whether it be every five years or every ten, can help avoid difficult situations.

You may wonder why a background check is so important. The answer involves two reasons. First, someone who has committed serious crimes should not be trusted to investigate crimes. That should be fairly obvious. Another reason is that any issues in your analyst's background can be used by opposing counsel to damage that investigator's credibility.

Depending on how thorough a background check you need, you have a number of options when conducting one. Usually, a private investigator is hired to do a background check, and the person you are checking signs a release authorizing the investigator to gather criminal and other records. Any reputable private investigator in your area can do this for you. You can even conduct one yourself:

- Most counties now have court records online. Run the analyst's name through all the counties they state they lived in on their resume.

- Check using search engines such as Google, as well as social media like Facebook.

- Call all references, past jobs, colleges, etc.

 NOTE From time to time, I work with law firms as an expert witness in computer-related cases. When a law firm is considering hiring me, one of the first steps is to ask about my background, including criminal, drug, mental health, etc. They want to know that their witness is credible and won't be made to look untrustworthy on the stand. If you want to work in forensics, it is important that your conduct be above reproach.

Examination Quality Control

If the laboratory has maintained quality standards and the investigator is a competent, qualified person with a clean background, does this automatically mean the individual examination is of sufficient quality? The answer is no. Anyone can make an error. This is why you also need to apply quality standards to each and every investigation your lab performs.

We already mentioned the best way to ensure quality of individual examinations, and that is to repeat the examination. Ideally, the re-examination would be by a different examiner using different tools, completely repeating the entire examination. However, in the real world, most labs are backlogged with cases and cannot do this. There must be a balance between the need for quality control and the need to process evidence expeditiously. Usually, a compromise is made that consists of three parts.

Supervisor Review

For every examination, a supervisor should review the case notes and forensic report to ensure that the process documented matches the lab's standard operating procedure and that no anomalies are present. If a supervisor is the one doing the initial examination, then someone else in the lab should review that supervisor's notes and report. This type of quality control is efficient yet can be effective. These reviews are also often called administrative review.

 EXAM TIP The test also discusses peer review. This is similar to a supervisor review or a spot check. It simply is done by one of your colleagues rather than a supervisor or administrator. It is never a bad idea to have a colleague check your results and your methodology.

Spot Checking

In addition to supervisor review, individual tests from individual cases should be periodically retested by a colleague or supervisor. If these spot checks consistently yield the same results as the initial examination, that is a strong indicator that proper procedures are being adhered to and quality is being maintained. Any deviation would necessitate that entire case being reprocessed.

Major Case Re-examination

When a case is of preeminent importance, it may be necessary to have a complete re-examination. This could be a situation where the case is one in which mistakes, even the most trivial, are simply not acceptable. Ideally, all cases would be treated in this way, but that is usually impractical. So your lab manager may determine specific cases that are of such critical importance that a complete re-exam is required.

In all cases of examination quality control, the results should be documented. It is important for a lab to know just how effective the quality control measures are. For example, supervisor reviews might show 99.9 percent quality examinations, but spot checks show 98 percent. That could indicate some deviation between the actual examinations and the reviews, or it could simply indicate that the specific cases selected for spot check had a greater-than-average number of errors. Whatever the cause, it should be investigated.

Chapter Review

In this chapter, we discussed the importance of planning your investigation. It cannot be overstated that cyber forensic investigations need to be planned and properly executed. This is a science, not an art. We also discussed the details of case notes, forensic reports, and expert reports. While the CCFP exam does not place a great deal of emphasis on the differences between those documents, these issues will be of critical importance in your career.

We also discussed quality control standards for cyber forensics. This is a critical topic for the CCFP exam and for your career. It is important that we maintain quality in the lab, with the individual investigators, and during each and every examination.

Questions

1. Which of the following does not need to be in the forensic investigation plan?

    A. How to collect the evidence

    B. Who to submit the report to

    C. How to safeguard the evidence

    D. The procedures for analyzing the evidence

2. Which type of exam validation primarily tests to see if the case notes/ report match SOP?

   A. Supervisor review

   B. Spot check

   C. Document review

   D. Intrinsic review

3. What does it mean to validate your findings?

   A. To ensure they meet Daubert standards

   B. To ask a colleague if they agree with your findings

   C. To repeat the test

   D. To re-read your notes to see if you followed SOP

4. The ASCLD is primarily concerned with:

   A. Standards for forensic investigators

   B. Standards for forensic training

   C. Standards for forensic testing

   D. Standards for forensic labs

5. Which of the following would be least likely to disqualify a forensic investigator?

   A. A misdemeanor charge for hacking into a computer in college

   B. A felony charge for check fraud

   C. A misdemeanor charge for trespass while in college

   D. Multiple recent credit issues, including repossessions and foreclosures

Answers

1. **B.** The plan should include how to collect the evidence, safeguard the evidence, and analyze the evidence.

2. **A.** The supervisor review involves reviewing all case notes and the report to see if they are in compliance with SOP.

3. **C.** So how do you validate your findings? The answer is actually simple. Repeat the test, preferably with a different tool.

4. **D.** The ASCLD is for certifying forensic labs.

5. **C.** A is not the right answer because any computer crime is a concern for a cyber forensics investigator. **B** is a felony, and these automatically disqualify forensic investigators. **D** involves recent and repeated financial problems, and this was specifically discussed in the chapter.

References

1. https://www.ncjrs.gov/pdffiles1/nij/199408.pdf.

2. http://digital-forensics.sans.org/blog/2010/08/25/intro-report-writing-digital-forensics/.

3. http://www.rcfl.gov/.

4. http://www.rcfl.gov/DSP_T_CoursesLE.cfm.

5. http://www.rcfl.gov/Downloads/Documents/Benefits_of_Participation.pdf.

6. http://www.evidencemagazine.com/index.php?option=com_content&task=view&id=1159&Itemid=217.

7. http://www.ascld-lab.org/training/.

8. http://www.ascld-lab.org/preparation-course-for-testing-labs/.

9. http://www.umuc.edu/academic-programs/masters-degrees/digital-forensics-and-cyber-investigations.cfm.

10. http://www.amu.apus.edu/academic/programs/degree/1409/graduate-certificate-in-digital-forensics.

11. http://www.shsu.edu/programs/master-of-science-in-digital-forensics/.

12. http://www.mssu.edu/academics/programs/computer-forensics.php.

13. http://www.state.gov/m/ds/clearances/c10977.htm#14.

PART III

Digital Forensics

- **Chapter 6**   Hardware Forensics
- **Chapter 7**   Hidden Files and Antiforensics
- **Chapter 8**   Network Forensics
- **Chapter 9**   Virtual Systems
- **Chapter 10**   Mobile Forensics

Hardware Forensics

In this chapter you will learn:
- Hard drive details
- How data is stored on a hard drive
- How to recover data from damaged hard drives
- How to recover deleted files
- More details on operating system concepts

Previously in this book you have seen some general facts about hard drives and operating systems. In this chapter, we will go into more depth. It cannot be overemphasized that the more you know about hardware and operating systems, the more effective you will be as a cyber forensic analyst. In this chapter, you will also see how to recover deleted files in both Windows and Linux.

Hard Drive Specifications

In previous chapters, we discussed the specifications of hard drives in a general manner. In this chapter, we will get a bit more specific. It is important to understand how the hard drive is functioning in order to effectively perform a forensic analysis.

General Hard Drive Facts

Hard drives (with the exception of solid-state hard drives) are literally platters that are stacked up like plates on a spindle. A read/write head is used to read the data from the platters or to write data to the platters. This is shown in Figure 6-1.

Figure 6-1
Hard drive
structure

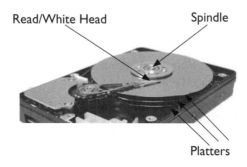

Read/White Head   Spindle

Platters

The platters are made of a ferromagnetic material. It is usually a bad idea to open a hard drive, as the one in Figure 6-1 is opened. Any dust that gets between the read/write head and the platters or any scratches on the platters can create problems when attempting to read or write data.

The data on the platters is divided into sectors (we discussed this in previous chapters) that are usually 512 bytes in size. Those sectors are arranged in circles around the platter called tracks. The data itself is in clusters that comprise anywhere from 1 to 128 sectors. Data is recorded by magnetizing the material of the platter to represent either a 0 or 1 (binary numbers).

The platters inside a hard disk drive are usually made of glass or aluminum. It is the polished magnetic material on the surface that makes the platter appear shiny like a mirror. You can see the track/cluster structure in Figure 6-2.

Figure 6-2
Hard drive data structure

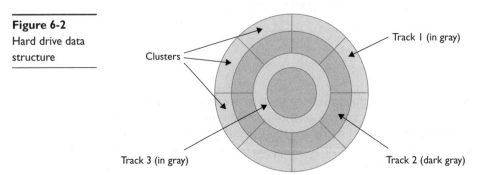

Clusters

Track 1 (in gray)

Track 3 (in gray)

Track 2 (dark gray)

Partitions

A computer could have one or more hard drives, often called physical drives. The reason they are termed "physical drives" is because it is possible to divide a single physical drive into multiple logical drives. Think of a large office being divided into four cubicles. Physically, there is just one room, but there are four logical offices. This is essentially what partitioning your drive does. There are four types of partitions:

- **Primary partition**   This type of partition has an operating system and is bootable. You must have at least one primary partition to boot up the system, but you can have as many as four. For example, you might have one partition for Windows 8 and another for Ubuntu Linux.

- **Active partition**   Simply put, this is the particular primary partition you have currently booted up. For example, if you have two primary partitions (one for Windows 8 and one for Ubuntu Linux), then when you boot into Windows 8, that primary partition is the active one. If you reboot the machine into Ubuntu Linux, then the Linux partition is now the active partition. You can only have one for each machine.

- **Extended partition**   You can only have one per physical disk. This is essentially the space on your hard drive that you have chosen to divide into subspaces for use.

- **Logical partitions**   These are the aforementioned subspaces. When you divide a physical disk into C drive, D drive, etc., these are logical partitions. The various partitions on my own laptop are shown in Figure 6-3 as they appear in Windows 8.

Figure 6-3   Windows 8 partitions

These four partition types are the standard partitions found on modern computers. You might find a few other nonstandard partitions:

- **Encrypted partitions**   A variety of tools allow you to encrypt either the entire disk or just a partition. TrueCrypt[1] is one such tool. There are many others. We will discuss encrypted drives in detail later in this chapter.

- **Hidden partitions**   When dividing a physical disk into partitions, it is possible to have a partition that is not visible to most users. Hidden partitions are of interest in forensic investigations because they provide an excellent way for someone to hide data. There are several ways to determine if a hidden partition exists. The most obvious is to see if there is a difference between the actual specified disk size and the total size of visible partitions. If you see a difference, this could indicate a hidden partition. There are also tools such as Raw Disk Viewer[2] that will show hidden partitions.

- **Unallocated space**   This is an area of a hard drive that is not allocated for a specific partition. It is often called free space. This is not the same as a hidden partition because there has been no attempt to hide it—it simply is not allocated for use. This may not seem interesting forensically, but it is possible that currently unallocated space was previously part of a partition. If that is the case, there could still be data fragments there.

- **Slack space**   This is space between the data and the cluster size.[3] For example, if the cluster size is 10 sectors, that means a cluster size of 5,120 bytes, and if you save a file that is 2,000 bytes in size, there are 3,120 bytes of unused space in that cluster that cannot be used by any other file. This is slack space, and it is a great place to look for hidden data. The tool Autopsy from SleuthKit that you have seen previously in this book can detect data in slack space.[4] Autopsy uses the strings and grep tools:

  "Strings is first run on the image and the data is passed to grep to do the actual search. This process will find ASCII and UNICODE strings that are consecutive anywhere in the file. This is frequently referred to as the physical layout. For example, it will find strings in the middle of an allocated sector, in an unallocated sector, in slack space, and in meta data structures. This will find a string that crosses sectors, which is good if the two sectors are for the same file."[5]

Finding Data

The next issue to discuss is how the hard drive finds data. Essentially, the read/write head is moved over the correct track and then the disk spins until the correct sector is right under the head. There are a few terms that are important here. The first is seek time. This is the time it takes for the head to be positioned over the track. Then we have the term latency period. That defines how long it takes for the desired sector to be moved under the head. Access time is equal to the seek time plus latency time.

Once data has been located, there is still the issue of transferring the data from the hard drive to the CPU and RAM so it can be utilized. This is usually measured in the amount of data one can transfer in one second. There are actually two transfer rates that are combined into what is normally called "the transfer rate." The first is the internal data transfer rate. That is the speed at which the hard disk can physically read or write data to or from the surface of the hard drive platter and then transfer it to the internal read buffer/cache. The external transfer rate is how fast the data can be communicated from that read buffer/cache to system memory (RAM).

RAID

Many readers may already understand RAID, but in case you don't, let's begin with a brief description. RAID is an acronym for Redundant Array of Independent Disks. The concept is simple. We all know that hard drives fail, but what if you had a backup hard drive in the machine, with a complete duplicate of all the information on the main drive? Then, if the main drive fails, the system could just switch over to the backup drive and keep going. This is actually one of the most common RAID implementations. The common RAID levels are listed here:

- **RAID 0**, also called disk striping, distributes data across multiple disks in a way that gives improved speed for data retrieval. This doesn't do much for backup, but since the data is stored in multiple drives, it can be retrieved faster. Imagine you had a large book, perhaps the complete works of William Shakespeare, and you needed to search for a specific quote. If that book was spread across three drives and each was searching simultaneously, the search would be much faster. This is the idea behind RAID 0.

- **RAID 1** mirrors the contents of the disks. The disk is completely mirrored so there is an identical copy of the drive running on the machine. Essentially, your computer is using one drive, but everything that happens on that drive (saving data, moving data, deleting data, etc.) is simultaneously executed on the backup drive. This provides a good failsafe should the primary drive fail. Of course, you can perform mirroring with more than one drive—you just need an equal number of backup drives. So if you have three drives you actually use, you need three drives of at least the same size to mirror them.

- **RAID 3 or 4** (striped disks with dedicated parity) combines three or more disks in a way that protects data against loss of any one disk. Fault tolerance is achieved by adding an extra disk to the array and dedicating it to storing parity information. The storage capacity of the array is reduced by one disk, the parity disk. That dedicated disk has information that would help you reconstruct the data (yes, for you hardware engineers, this is a simplification of the process!). So if you took the complete works of William Shakespeare and divided it among three drives (drives C, D, and E) and then one drive (drive D) fails, you still have two-thirds of the data. The parity bits on the parity drive will allow the system to rebuild the missing third.

- **RAID 5** (striped disks with distributed parity) also combines three or more disks in a way that protects data against the loss of any one disk. It is similar to RAID 3, but the parity is not stored on one dedicated drive. Instead, parity information is interspersed across the drive array. For example, what if one of the drives fails AND the parity drive fails? That would be a disaster for RAID 3 or 4. So RAID 5 also distributes the parity drive.

- **RAID 6** (striped disks with dual parity) combines four or more disks in a way that protects data against loss of any two disks. It is basically RAID 5 expanded.

- **RAID 1+0** (or 10) is a mirrored data set (RAID 1) that is then striped (RAID 0)—hence, the "1+0" name. A RAID 1+0 array requires a minimum of four drives: two mirrored drives to hold half of the striped data, plus another two mirrored for the other half of the data.

These are the essentials of RAID. There are a few other types of RAID; however, the most common you will see are levels 1, 1+0, and 5. Acquiring a RAID for forensics

PART III

purposes has some challenges that are not encountered when acquiring a single drive. Some people recommend acquiring each disk separately. This will work just fine for RAID 1 or 1+0—simply image each disk as if it were a single disk. However, with RAID 0, 3, 4, 5, and 6 there is data striping. The data is striped across multiple disks. In these situations, acquiring the disks separately is not recommended. The recommended way to handle this is to image the entire RAID array. Now that means your target forensic drive is either an equal size (or greater) RAID or a very large drive!

Both Forensic Toolkit (FTK)[6] and EnCase provide built-in tools for acquiring RAID arrays. For example, in EnCase the steps are as follows:

1. Open the case of the suspect computer and document the RAID setup. Leave the cover open because you will need access to the hard drives later on.

2. Download and create a network boot disk (because it contains many popular SCSI drivers and also supports parallel port and network crossover acquisitions).

3. Unplug the power and data connectors to each hard drive (noting where they were connected because we will need to reconnect later).

4. Boot the suspect computer and configure the BIOS to boot to floppy only.

5. Save the settings and power down the computer.

6. Reconnect the hard drives in the same way that they were connected in step 4.

7. If performing a DOS drive to drive acquisition, connect your partitioned and FAT-32 formatted storage drive to a spare hard drive connector on the suspect computer. If there are no more connectors, you may use one from the CD-ROM drive, or connect it to an add-on IDE controller card and insert the controller card into a free PCI slot on the motherboard.

8. Now insert your boot floppy and boot the computer using it. If you are working with a SCSI RAID array, choose the options to Auto Detect and load the SCSI drivers using the network boot disk. If you intend to perform a network crossover acquisition, allow the computer to detect and load drivers for the network card.

9. Launch EnCase for DOS. Remember, the BIOS sees the RAID as one drive, so you will only see one large physical drive in EnCase.

10. Acquire the RAID array as you would acquire a single IDE hard drive.

11. When the acquisition is finished, the RAID array will appear as one physical disk in EnCase.[7]

Recovering from Damaged Media

What happens when your forensic investigation involves damaged media? I am sure you have seen hard drives that were dropped, CDs that were scratched, and other similar problems. In a forensic investigation, this is even more likely. It is not uncommon for a suspect, if he or she has the opportunity, to purposefully attempt to destroy evidence. This means you are probably going to encounter damaged media at some point in your career.

It is a nontrivial task to repair physical damage. It usually requires specialized tools and expertise. However, for forensic purposes, you don't need to fix the broken media—you just need to recover as much data from it as you can. It is possible that the drive is even operable and can be booted. So we have a few steps you should take.

1. The first step is to just remove the drive from the system it is in and connect it to a test system. The damaged drive should be configured as a secondary drive so the system boots to its own drive.

2. Attempt to connect to the drive. It is possible that the system will recognize the drive; then you can image the drive as you normally would.

3. If the test system recognizes the drive but cannot read from it, you can try open-source tools such as DCFLdd (an enhanced version of the dd utility) to try to image it.

4. If the test system does not recognize the drive, check to see if the hard drive is even spinning. If it is not spinning and all previous measures have failed, you will need to send it to a specialist to repair.

 NOTE This poses an issue for chain of custody. You will need to work with a vendor that specializes in forensic hard drive recovery and who understands the issues of chain of custody. You cannot simply mail a drive to any repair person. If you do, any evidence you collect will be inadmissible in court.

Aside from physical damage, there can be logical damage. This means that the drive itself is intact and functioning, but something is making the data unrecoverable. For example, a sudden power outage can damage the file system. Most operating systems provide a basic repair tool for their own file systems. Microsoft Windows has chkdsk, Linux comes with the fsck utility, and Mac OS X provides Disk Utility. You should first attempt one of these utilities to see if it can repair the file system. If that fails, you may need to seek out third-party file system repair software.

In some desperate situations where you have already tried everything else, you can simply do a high-level format and then try to recover data using undelete tools (we will be discussing these later in this chapter). This is a last resort, as you will undoubtedly lose some data. But it is possible to recover some data in this fashion.

CMOS/BIOS

By now, you are well aware of hard drives and have a basic understanding of operating systems (we will get into more depth on operating systems later in this chapter). But we have not discussed BIOS/CMOS yet. Consider this: If a computer is off, there is a boot process that starts up the machine and eventually loads the operating system. What process gives the computer instructions between the time power is turned on until the operating system is loaded? That process is the Basic Input Output System, or BIOS. BIOS is what is called firmware. That means software that is embedded in a chip.

CMOS is closely related. CMOS is an acronym for Complementary Metal-Oxide Semiconductor. The chip stores information such as the system time and date and the system hardware settings for your computer that are used during startup. CMOS is responsible for the quick power on self test (often termed POST).

There have been innovations designed to replace BIOS. The Advanced Configuration and Power Interface (ACPI) specification provides an open standard for replacing BIOS. ACPI, first released in December 1996, defines platform-independent interfaces for discovering what hardware is in a machine, configuration, power management, and monitoring. The specification is central to Operating System–directed configuration and Power Management (OSPM). ACPI and OSPM are improvements to the BIOS concept. Where BIOS has to be programmed with what hardware a computer has, however, ACPI will automatically discover it.

 EXAM TIP The CCFP won't ask you deep details about BIOS, CMOS, ACPI, or OSPM. However, this information will be useful to you when examining a suspect PC or laptop.

The Swap File

You have probably heard the term swap file or virtual memory before. Some operating systems, such as Windows, utilize a sort of temporary memory to augment RAM. The basic premise is that there is a finite amount of RAM and we need to maximize its usage. Consider a user who has several programs open at one time (Firefox web browser, Outlook e-mail, Microsoft Word, and Adobe Photoshop). While all of these are open, the user is probably only interacting with one or two at any given time. So operating system moves the program that has the longest time since the user interacted with it to the swap file. The least used program is "swapped" in and out of the swap file and RAM. This allows the system to make more efficient use of RAM.

The size of swap files is usually about 1.5 times the size of the physical RAM in the machine. Swap files contain remnants of whatever programs the user has been working with. In other words, the user might have been working with an Excel spreadsheet and not saved it, but part of it is still in the swap file. This brings up an important forensic fact. Swap files are not erased when the system shuts down. They work on a queue system, which means data is not erased until that space is needed again. This means it is very likely you will be able to find data in the swap file.

On Windows machines before XP, the swap file had an .swp extension (for swap). From XP on, the file has been named pagefile.sys. You can examine this file's contents with any standard hex editor. Some forensic analysts like to use a favorite general-purpose tool, such as Scalpel (which you saw earlier in this book).

NOTE You should also be aware that there are a number of tools available on the Internet for wiping the swap file. If you find the swap file has no content at all, this would be an indication of two things. The first is that someone took care to wipe evidence from this computer. The second is that the perpetrator has a significant level of computer skill.

Operating System Specifics

The computer hardware is obviously important, but the bulk of your forensic analysis will involve examining the operating system for evidence. Usually, most users don't interact directly with the hardware; they interact with the operating system. In previous chapters, you saw brief descriptions of major operating systems and file systems. In this section, we will delve deeper into operating system concepts.

Operating System Essentials

Let's begin by defining what an operating system is. The operating system is a program that is responsible for basic computer functionality. Operating systems perform basic tasks, such as processing input from the keyboard or mouse, managing memory, sending output to the display screen, maintaining and accessing files, and controlling external devices such as printers and scanners.

Operating systems also provide the framework that applications interact with. A word processor does not need to know how to process input from the keyboard or how to send data to the printer. It simply needs to know what operating system functions to call. This is one reason why a program written for Windows won't run on Linux. The operating system calls that a program depends on are different from one operating system to another. It should be clear that the operating system is the most important program on any given computer. As you might suspect, operating systems come in various types. They can be broadly classified as seen in Table 6-1.

Type	Description
Multiuser	This type of operating system allows simultaneous users to run programs. That does not mean two or more users struggling to use the same keyboard. It refers to multiple users, usually networking into the same server.
Multiprocessing	This type of operating systems allows the computer to effectively utilize more than one CPU.
Multitasking	This type of operating system allows more than one program to run concurrently. If you have a single-core CPU, this involves switching between programs in such a way that the user sees the programs as running concurrently.
Multithreading	This type of operating system allows a program to have different threads running separately. For example, a word processor has a thread that displays the typing on the screen and another thread that periodically auto-saves.

Table 6-1 Operating System Types

An operating system might actually fit into multiple categories. For example, Windows, Unix, and Linux all support multiprocessing and multithreading, but only Unix (and Unix variants) support multiple users.

The Kernel

The core of all operating systems is the kernel. Some experts might even argue that the kernel actually is the operating system and other associated utilities are just supporting programs. I don't take quite such an extreme view.

Users don't interact directly with the kernel. Most of the programs you interact with and may think of as the operating system are simply additional programs being run by the operating system. For example, the shell in Linux or the command window in Windows are both utilities and are not part of the operating system kernel. The kernel is responsible for basic functionality like low-level input/output, hardware interfacing, and memory management. One of the primary tasks of the kernel is to facilitate the execution of applications and provide those applications with features such as hardware access and process management.

 NOTE A process defines which memory portions the application can access. In short, a process is a separate space in memory.

One of the most important functions of the kernel is memory management. Unlike most other programs on the computer, the kernel has full and unfettered access to the memory. So one of the kernel's functions is to allow processes to access memory in a safe way. Modern operating systems allocate a portion of memory as "protected" and don't allow programs other than the operating system to access them. One way this can be accomplished is with techniques such as virtual addressing. Virtual addressing allows the kernel to make a given physical address appear to be another address— the virtual address. Virtual address spaces may be different for different processes; the memory that one process accesses at a particular (virtual) address may be different memory from what another process accesses at the same address. This allows every program to behave as if it is the only one (apart from the kernel) running, and thus prevents applications from crashing each other.

There are two types of kernels: monolithic and micro-kernel. In micro-kernel architecture, the kernel provides basic services such as communication, I/O, and memory and process management. Other functions are provided by utilities associated with the kernel, but not actually part of it. In a monolithic architecture, all of these services are included as part of the kernel itself.

EXAM TIP The CCFP won't delve into details about the kernel. We are discussing just a basic overview here so that your understanding of operating systems is more complete. I actually recommend that you, at a minimum, read at least one good operating system book. There is a chapter excerpt from a very good introduction to operating systems book you can read online: http://highered .mcgraw-hill.com/sites/dl/free/0073518174/910027/Chapter01_final.pdf.

The GUI

The graphical user interface, or GUI, is not the operating system. That simple fact escapes many users. It is more obvious with operating systems like Linux, where one can select from a number of GUIs. In Windows systems, the separation may not seem so clear. But in essence, the GUI is a user-friendly interface that allows the end user to interact with the operating system more easily.

Quite a few programs come with any modern operating system that is not actually part of the operating system. For example, if you purchase Windows 8, you also get a web browser, an e-mail client, a paint program, games, etc. These are simply applications that the vendor is shipping with the operating system. Even items like network utilities, shells, and general utilities are not part of the kernel, but are instead additional applications that have been included in the operating system. Think about it this way: If the system could run effectively without it, then it is not part of the operating system.

Interrupts

Interrupts are an important part of an operating system. The various hardware devices or programs can communicate with the operating system by these pathways. A more technical definition would be that an interrupt is an asynchronous signal indicating the need for attention. Hardware devices and programs can both access interrupts in order to request the attention of the operating system. When a hardware device triggers an interrupt, the operating system's kernel decides how to deal with this event. This is usually accomplished by the operating system executing some code designed to process input from that hardware. For example, if there is input from the keyboard, that interrupt will cause a specific operating system utility to function in order to process the incoming keyboard signals. An application can also trigger an interrupt to the operating system. For example, if an application needs to access hardware, it will send an interrupt to the operating system's kernel.

Device drivers are simply programs that provide an interface between the operating system and some hardware, such as a printer. These can be quite important from a forensic point of view. One reason these drivers can be interesting is that the presence of nonstandard drivers for equipment you don't see when the computer is seized may indicate there is additional equipment that needs to be found and examined. Normally, operating systems ship with a number of device drivers. It is also common practice for hardware vendors to include drivers as part of their installation programs. So, for example, if you find a Windows machine with drivers for a printer and those drivers don't normally ship with Windows, that is an indication a printer was once attached to that computer.

API

All operating systems must also provide some sort of application programming interface (API) whereby programs can interact with the operating system. Without an API, programs would not be able to communicate with the operating system. These are the core functions of any operating system. However, just these functions would make a very bare-bones operating system with limited usefulness. Microsoft heavily documents the Windows API.[8] The Windows API will not be useful to you in all forensic cases. In fact, it is most useful in cases involving malware. The better you understand the API, the more likely you are to understand what sophisticated malware might be capable of.

Extracting Deleted Files

One very important thing to remember is that deleting files does not really destroy them. They are recoverable. This is important, because criminals are likely to delete incriminating files if they get a chance. So understanding how you can recover those files is important. In this section, we will first examine the theory behind recovering deleted files and then look at some specific tools.

Windows

We will start with Windows because it is the most common operating system, and you will undoubtedly encounter it routinely. It is also very easy to recover deleted files in Windows. Let's explore a way.

Microsoft Windows will use one of two file systems. Older versions use FAT (either FAT16 or FAT32) and newer versions (since Windows 2000) use primarily NTFS. Both file systems were introduced briefly earlier in this book, so you should have some basic understanding of how they function. In both file systems, a table is used to map files to specific clusters where they are stored.

FAT

In FAT16 and FAT32, the table used to store cluster/file information is the File Allocation Table—thus the name of the file system. The File Allocation Table (FAT) is just a list of entries that map to each cluster on the partition. Each entry records one of five things:

- The cluster number of the next cluster for this file. If the file occupies more than one cluster, it is important to know where the next cluster is.

- If this cluster is the end of a chain of clusters in a file, it must be marked with an end of chain (EOC) character.

- Bad clusters are marked in FAT so they don't get used.

- Reserved clusters have a special entry in the File Allocation Table.

- Finally, any clusters that are open and available are marked.

When a file is deleted, the data is not actually removed from the drive. The bits are still there on the disk. All that happens is that the File Allocation Table is updated to reflect that those clusters are now available for use. If new information is saved to the drive, it may be saved to those clusters, or it may not. It also is possible that the old, deleted file occupied more clusters than the new file; thus, the deleted file was only partially overwritten, and a fragment remains. For forensic analysis, this means that the more recently a file was deleted, the more likely you will be to recover the file. Over time, it becomes more likely that those clusters have had other data saved in them and less likely that you will be able to recover data. In fact, the cluster may have been deleted and saved over several times.

NTFS

Starting with Windows 2000 through the current (as of this writing) Windows 8 and Windows Server 2012, NTFS is the preferred file system for Windows operating systems. NFTS is an acronym for New Technology File System. Two files in NTFS are related to locating files/clusters. These are the MFT (Master File Table; some sources call it the Meta File Table) file and the cluster bitmap. The MFT describes all files on the disk, including filenames, timestamps, security identifiers, and file attributes such as "read only," "compressed," "encrypted," etc. There is one record in the MFT for each file or folder on the drive. The MFT is analogous to the File Allocation Table in FAT and FAT32. The cluster bitmap file is a map of all the clusters on the hard drive. This is an array of bit entries, where each bit indicates whether its corresponding cluster is allocated/used or free/unused.

When files are deleted from an NTFS system, the process is similar to what occurs in FAT. However, there is one difference. Before the cluster is marked as available, it is first marked as deleted, which effectively moves it to the Recycle Bin. Before Windows Vista, the Recycle Bin resided in a hidden directory called RECYCLER. In Vista and beyond, the name of the directory has changed to $Recycle.bin. Only when you empty the Recycle Bin is the cluster marked as fully available.

 EXAM TIP The test won't ask you about what tools to use; we discuss those later for your practical use. However, the test will ask you why files can be recovered, and the preceding section is critical information in that regard.

Windows Tools

A number of tools are available to recover deleted files from Windows computers. In this section, you will be introduced to several of these tools. Most are easy to use and either free or very low cost. You can also simply do a web search on "Windows undelete" and find a number of tools that way.

DiskDigger

DiskDigger is a widely used tool that is quite easy to use. It's available at http://diskdigger .org/. It can be downloaded for free and is fully functional. When recovering files with the free version, you will have to recover one at a time; the commercial version allows you to recover multiple files at once. When you launch the program, you will see a screen like the one shown in Figure 6-4.

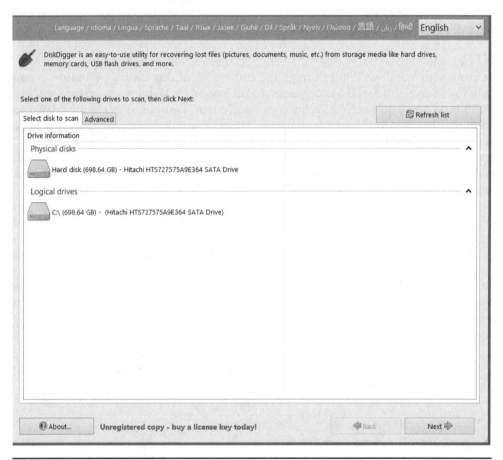

Figure 6-4 DiskDigger main screen

You just select the drive or partition you wish to recover deleted files from and select Dig Deep or Dig Deeper, as shown in Figure 6-5. The difference is that Dig Deeper takes longer, but does a more thorough job of file recovery.

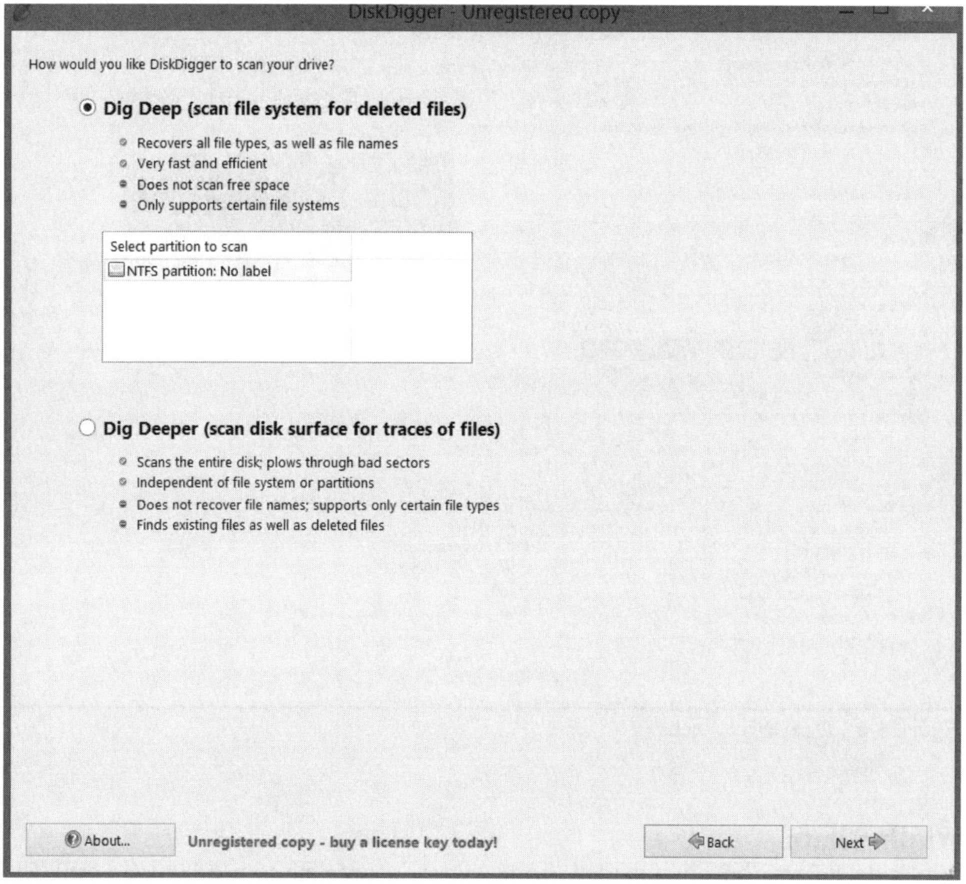

Figure 6-5   DiskDigger – Dig Deeper

Once the file recovery process is complete, DiskDigger presents you with a list of files it found, as shown in Figure 6-6. You then select the file(s) you wish to recover.

Once recovery is done, you will see a screen like the one shown in Figure 6-6. You can select any file and recover it. The files are color coded. A green dot by a file means the file can be recovered in its entirety, red means there is a problem (you likely won't recover any of the file), and gray indicates a partial recovery is possible. As you can see, this is a very easy-to-use tool.

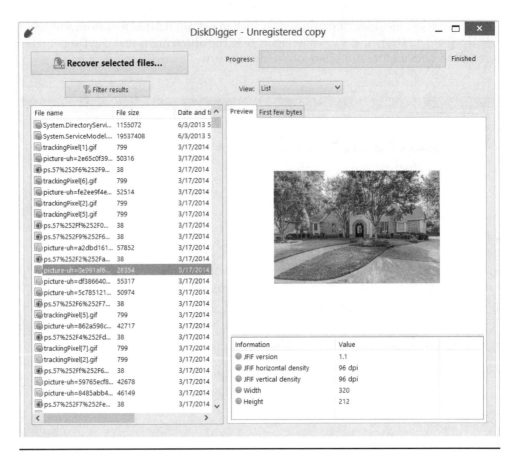

Figure 6-6   DiskDigger results

WinUndelete

WinUndelete can be downloaded from www.winundelete.com/download.asp. The program begins by launching a wizard that will guide you through file recovery. Step 1 is shown in Figure 6-7.

One of the things I like best about this tool can be seen in Step 2, shown in Figure 6-8. In Step 2, you can direct WinUndelete to simply scan for certain file types. This can speed up the search, particularly if you know what you are looking for.

When it has finished running the recovery process, the files will be placed in a folder for you to view.

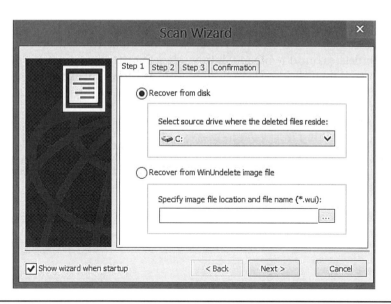

Figure 6-7 WinUndelete Step 1

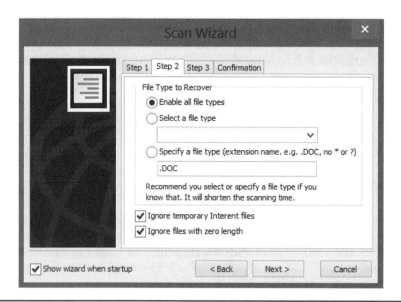

Figure 6-8 WinUndelete Step 2

NTFS Undelete

This is another easy-to-use tool for Windows undeletion. You can download it from http://ntfsundelete.com/download. Simply select the partition you wish to run NTFS Undelete on and then click the Start Scan button, as shown in Figure 6-9.

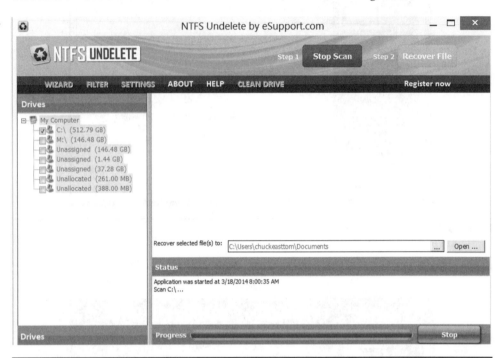

Figure 6-9   NFTS Undelete

When the scan is done, NTFS Undelete will present its results, as shown in Figure 6-10. You simply select the file you want to recover, and click the Recover File button.

Scrubbing Files

Many people believe the Department of Defense recommends overwriting data seven times to ensure it is completely deleted. The actual standard is DOD 5220.22-M. However, the DoD standard does not have a set recommendation of seven passes to securely delete. Instead, the DoD recommends a matrix of how to sanitize different types of media.[9] If one follows this matrix, the data will be unrecoverable by undelete techniques. The seven times rule is, however, a good rule of thumb.

Figure 6-10 NTFS Undelete results

Linux

Files can be undeleted in Linux, just like in Windows. The file storage is a bit different. First, consider how Linux stores files. The content of files is stored in contiguous blocks. The exact size of these blocks depends on the parameters used when the partition was created. The blocks are analogous to clusters in Windows and normally have sizes of 1,024, 2,048, or 4,096 bytes. You can think of these blocks as something similar to the clusters in NTFS, though they are not exactly the same thing, just a related concept. The specific block size is stored in the superblock. The entire partition is divided into an integral number of blocks, starting at zero.

The blocks are divided into groups. Each group uses one block as a bitmap to keep track of which block inside that group is allocated (used). So the group has a block for tracking other blocks' status. Another block is used as a bitmap for the number of allocated inodes. An inode is a data structure in the file system that stores information about a file—for example, file size, location, last time accessed, etc.

An inode can refer to a file or a folder/directory. In either case, the inode is really a link to the file. This is important because there are basically two types of links. The first type is the *hard link*. A hard link is an inode that links directly to a specific file. The operating system keeps a count of references to this link. When the reference count reaches zero, the file is deleted. In other words, you can have any number of names referencing a file, but if that number of references reaches zero (i.e., there is *no* name that references that file), then the file is deleted.

The second type of file link is called a *soft link* or *symbolic link*. In this case, the link is not actually a file itself, but rather a pointer to another file or directory. You can think of this as the same thing as a shortcut, such as you might find in Windows.

Unlike Windows, Linux also has some built-in commands that can be used to undelete files, and there are also some tools that can be used. We will examine both. Remember that Linux can run on multiple file systems, including EXT, ReiserFS, FAT, and others, but EXT—specifically EXT3 and EXT 4—are the most common.

Manual

You can use some commands built into Linux to recover files. Unfortunately, some of these may vary from one Linux distribution to another, but the steps given here will work on a wide variety of Linux distributions.

The first step is to move the system to single-user mode using the init command:

```
init 1
```

Linux Run Levels

If you are not familiar with the init command, Linux uses this to initialize different run levels. A run level determines what level the operating system is running, as shown in this table:

Mode	Run Level Description
0	Halt
1	Single-user mode
2	Not used (user-definable)
3	Full multiuser mode without GUI
4	Not used (user-definable)
5	Full multiuser mode with GUI
6	Reboot

The Linux/Unix command grep can be used to search for files, and even the contents of files. The grep command is very popular, and frankly, if you are working with Linux at all, you are probably already familiar with it. Here is a generic example of searching for a file on a partition:

```
grep -b 'search-text' /dev/partition >somepic.jpg
```

NOTE A few grep flags of use in these searches:
-i: Ignore case.
-B: Print number lines/size of leading context before matching lines.
-A: Print number lines/size of trailing context after matching lines.

To recover a text file starting with the word "mypic"on /dev/sda1, you can try the following command:

```
# grep -i -a -B10 -A100 'mypic' /dev/sda2>output.txt
```

What is happening in this command is that grep is searching for this phrase, ignoring case (thus, the -i), looking through binary files, even if they are deleted, and finding any with the name "mypic" anywhere in them. If found, they are sent to output.txt.

ExtUndelete

This tool works with both EXT3 and EXT4 partitions. You can download it from http://extundelete.sourceforge.net/. This product uses some rather simple shell commands. For example, if you want to restore all deleted files from the sda1 partition, use this command:

```
extundelete /dev/sda4 --restore-all
```

The website documents all the various options you can utilize with this tool.

Macintosh

With the advent of OS X, Macintosh is actually based on FreeBSD, which is a Unix clone, much like Linux. In fact, if you go to a terminal window in Mac OSX, what you see is a shell where you can run Unix commands. This means that some of the techniques that work for Linux will also work with Macintosh. Again, some tools will help automate this process for you.

MacKeeper

This is a Macintosh file recovery tool available from http://mackeeper.zeobit.com/recover-deleted-files-on-mac. There is a free, fully functional trial version, and it is relatively easy to use. Open MacKeeper and select the volume you want to search for deleted files on; then select Scan. Then select Undelete. That's all there is to it.

Certainly, other tools can recover deleted Macintosh files as well. You should experiment with various tools and find the one(s) that are most useful for you. As always, you should be comfortable with a given operating system before attempting forensic analysis of it.

Encrypted Files

Many tools can be used to encrypt files and hard drives. Windows has the Encrypting File System that started with the use of NTFS with Windows 2000.[10] We will dive into the details of how cryptography works, including actual algorithms used, later in this book, but in this section, you will be introduced to some file and drive encryption tools.

EFS

Since Windows 2000, Microsoft has implemented the Encrypting File System (EFS) as part of the NTFS file system. This provides a simple way to encrypt and decrypt files or folders. Simply right-click a file, choose Properties, then choose Advanced, and select Encrypt, as shown in Figure 6-11.

Figure 6-11
EFS

The file or folder will now appear in green lettering in Windows Explorer. The key is tied to the user name and password, so when that user logs in, the file or folder will open normally, but will not open for other uses.

If your hard drive crashes and you restore a backup with EFS-encrypted files to a new drive, even if you create the exact same user name and password, the EFS files won't open. This is why you need to back up your EFS key and store it in a safe place. The steps are simple:[11]

- In the search box, type **Command Prompt**, and then, in the list of results, click Command Prompt.

- Insert the removable media that you're using to store your certificate.

- Navigate to the directory on the removable media drive where you want to store the recovery certificate by typing the drive letter and then pressing ENTER.

- Type **cipher /r:file name** (where "file name" is the name that you want to give to the recovery certificate), and then press ENTER. If you're prompted for an administrator password or confirmation, type the password or provide confirmation.

To restore the key:

- Insert the removable media that contains your recovery certificate.

- Click the Start button. In the search box, type **secpol.msc**, and then press ENTER. If you're prompted for an administrator password or confirmation, type the password or provide confirmation.

- In the left pane, double-click Public Key Policies, right-click Encrypting File System, and then click Add Data Recovery Agent. This opens the Add Recovery Agent wizard.

- Click Next, and then navigate to your recovery certificate.

- Click the certificate, and then click Open.

- When you are asked if you want to install the certificate, click Yes, click Next, and then click Finish.

- Open the Command Prompt window by clicking the Start button. In the search box, type **Command Prompt**, and then, in the list of results, click Command Prompt.

- At the command prompt, type **gpupdate**, and then press ENTER.

TrueCrypt

TrueCrypt is a free, open-source product that is available for Windows, Linux, or Macintosh and utilizes 256-bit AES encryption.[12] It allows you to encrypt volumes, partitions, or entire disks. When you first install the program, it will prompt you to view a tutorial. The interface is reasonably simple, and can be seen in Figure 6-12.

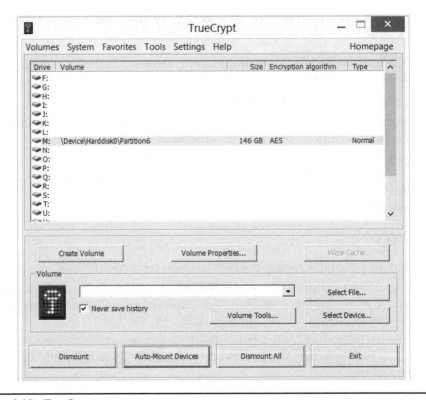

Figure 6-12 TrueCrypt

How to Deal with Encrypted Drives and Files

Later in this book, we will discuss cryptography in some depth, including cryptanalysis. The fact is that, unlike what you see in television dramas, it is very difficult to "break" the cryptography of a drive, file, or partition. You may be able to guess the passcode, but if it is encrypted properly, you simply won't break the encryption. It is also a good idea to learn as much as you can about the person who encrypted the drive or file. There may be a passphrase that is related to them. For example, a fan of *Star Trek* might use NCC 1701 as a passcode. Another avenue is to see if you can retrieve any other passwords the user has, for example an email password. People frequently reuse the same password in different environments. If none of these work, you can attempt to use the cryptanalysis techniques we discuss in Chapter 7, but as you will see their efficacy is not always practical to use.

Chapter Review

In this chapter, we have discussed the details of hard drives and operating systems. These concepts are key to forensics. The CCFP exam will only touch on these topics briefly, but you will use them throughout your career. We delved a bit deeper into operating system specifics, and you learned about swap files, hidden files, and slack space, all of which are covered on the CCFP exam. We also discussed how to recover deleted files. You will need to understand these principles for the CCFP, although specific tools won't be covered.

Questions

1. When a Windows 8 machine is shut down, what happens to the data in the swap file?

    A. It is lost when the power supply ends.

    B. It is on the hard drive and can be viewed with a hex editor.

    C. It is automatically deleted.

    D. It is stored in the registry.

2. What happens when a file is sent to the Recycle Bin in NTFS?

    A. The file is deleted.

    B. The file is removed from the File Allocation Table.

    C. The cluster is marked as deleted in the MFT.

    D. The cluster is marked as available.

3. When a file is saved to an NTFS partition and it occupies less than an entire cluster, what is done with the remaining space?

    A. It is unused.

    B. It is available for other files.

    C. It is reclaimed by the operating system.

    D. It is treated as used.

4. Which RAID level uses disk striping with distributed parity?

    A. 1

    B. 2

    C. 3

    D. 5

5. How many times should you overwrite a cluster to ensure the file(s) are truly deleted?

   A. 3

   B. 7

   C. 10

   D. 43

Answers

1. **B.** The swap file is literally a file on the hard drive (modern Windows systems have it as pagefile.sys) and can be viewed with a hex editor.

2. **C.** The cluster is marked as deleted in the MFT. When the Recycle Bin is emptied, the cluster will be marked as available.

3. **A.** If a file takes up less than the full cluster, the remaining space cannot be used by other files.

4. **D.** RAID 5 is disk striping with distributed parity. RAID 3 is disk striping with dedicated parity. RAID 1 is disk mirroring.

5. **B.** A good rule of thumb is to overwrite seven times.

References

1. http://www.truecrypt.org/.

2. http://www.osforensics.com/faqs-and-tutorials/hidden-partitions-drive.html.

3. http://www.pcmag.com/encyclopedia/term/56995/slack-space.

4. http://www.giac.org/paper/gsec/3133/introduction-hiding-finding-data-linux/105105.

5. http://www.sleuthkit.org/autopsy/help/grep_lim.html.

6. http://digital-forensics.sans.org/blog/2009/06/18/forensics-101-acquiring-an-image-with-ftk-imager/.

7. http://encasefinal.blogspot.com/2010/12/how-to-acquire-raids-encase.html.

8. http://msdn.microsoft.com/en-us/library/ff818516(v=vs.85).aspx.

9. http://recycleyourmedia.com/webuytape/compliance/d-o-d-data-sanitization-matrix/.

10. http://windows.microsoft.com/en-us/windows/what-is-encrypting-file-system.

11. http://windows.microsoft.com/en-us/windows/back-up-efs-certificate#1TC=windows-7.

12. http://www.truecrypt.org/.

Hidden Files and Antiforensics

In this chapter you will learn:

- Cryptography
- Steganography
- Cryptanalysis
- Log tampering
- Other techniques

It should be no surprise to you that criminals wish to hide evidence. There are several ways they can do this. One of the more obvious methods involves encrypting data, photos, or other evidence. There are also techniques for hiding evidence in other files (steganography) and simply altering logs to hide the evidence of a breach in security. Some criminals will even opt to completely wipe the suspect drive to prevent evidence from being gathered. It is important for any forensic analyst to have a good understanding of these methods.

Cryptography

The first thing to learn about cryptography is the terminology. Many people mistakenly use terms like cryptography and cryptology interchangeably. Cryptography is the study of methods for encrypting and decrypting a message. Cryptanalysis is the study of methods to break cryptography. Cryptology includes both cryptography and cryptanalysis.

An algorithm is the process or steps needed to accomplish some task. In cryptography, another term for a cryptographic algorithm is a cipher. The text you wish to encrypt is called plain text; the numeric input needed to make the cipher work is called the key. And finally, the output of a cryptographic algorithm is called cipher text.

Many people avoid studying cryptography, believing it is too hard…too much math. Well, yes, there is some math. And if you want to become a cryptologist, then yes, you will need to have a very good understanding of number theory, discrete math, and a few other mathematical disciplines. However, it does not take very much math at all to gain a fundamental understanding of how cryptography works. I have found the best way to teach cryptography is to begin with historical methods that are simple to grasp. That is how we will start here.

The History of Encryption

Secure communication is not a new concept. From ancient generals to conspirators in the Middle Ages, people have had a need to communicate in such a way that others could not read what they wrote. While in modern times, cryptography means mathematics, and usually computers, in ancient times, the methods were simpler.

Before we begin exploring a few of these methods, keep a few facts in mind. First of all, in ancient times, a significant portion of the population was illiterate. Simply writing something down kept it from most people. The second fact to keep in mind, which is related to that first fact, is that historical methods are not secure today. You cannot use these methods in modern times. A computer would crack any of these within seconds. However, these methods contain the elements of cryptography and make an excellent place to begin our study of cryptography.

The Caesar Cipher

One of the oldest recorded ciphers is the Caesar cipher. This is also one of the most widely known ancient ciphers. It is featured in a number of security-related certifications. Historians claim this was used by Julius Caesar. The method is simple: You choose some number by which to shift each letter of a text. For example, if the text is

A cat

And you choose to shift by three letters, then the message becomes

D gdw

Or, if you choose to shift by one letter to the left, it becomes

Z bzs

In this example, you can choose any shifting pattern you wish. You can shift either to the right or left by any number of spaces you like. Because this is a very simple method to understand, it makes a good place to start our study of encryption. It is, however, extremely easy to crack. You see, any language has a certain letter and word frequency, meaning that some letters are used more frequently than others. In the English language, the most common single-letter word is *a*, with *I* a close second. The most common three-letter word is *the*, with *and* being a close second. The most common two-letter combinations are *oo* and *ll*. Those three rules alone could help you decrypt a Caesar cipher. For example, if you saw a string of seemingly nonsense letters and noticed that a three-letter word was frequently repeated in the message, you might easily surmise that this word was *the*, and use that to begin decrypting the message.

Furthermore, if you frequently noticed a single-letter word in the text, it is most likely the letter *a*. You now have found the substitution scheme for *a, t, h*, and *e*. You can now either translate all of those letters in the message and attempt to surmise the rest or simply analyze the substitute letters used for *a, t, h,* and *e* and derive the substitution cipher that was used for this message. Decrypting a message of this type does not even require a computer. It could be done in less than ten minutes using pen and paper by someone with no background in cryptography.

NOTE When I teach cryptography or security classes in person, I actually have the class do exactly that. Create a message, encrypt it with a Caesar cipher, and then pass it to a classmate to see how long it takes them to break it. Usually, about half the class breaks the cipher in about ten minutes.

Caesar ciphers belong to a class of ciphers known as substitution ciphers. The name simply means that each letter of the plain text is substituted for one letter in the cipher text. The particular substitution scheme used (*a* becomes *c, b* becomes *d*, etc.) is called a substitution alphabet. Because one letter always substitutes for one other letter, the Caesar cipher is sometimes called a monoalphabet substitution method, meaning that it uses a single substitution for the encryption.

ROT 13

This is another single-alphabet substitution cipher. It is very much like the Caesar cipher, except it has a fixed shift. All characters are rotated 13 characters through the alphabet.

The phrase

A CAT

Becomes

N PNG

ROT 13 is a single-substitution cipher.

Scytale

This was a cylinder used by ancient Greeks, particularly the Spartans. You would wrap a leather strap around a cylinder and create the message. The recipient needed to have a cylinder of the exact same diameter to read the message.

Atbash Cipher

This cipher was used by ancient Hebrew scholars. It involves substituting the first letter of the alphabet for the last and the second letter for the second to the last, etc. It simply reverses the alphabet. While they used Hebrew, we can see how this would work in English:

A becomes Z, B becomes Y, C becomes X, etc.

This is a single-substitution cipher, just like ROT 13 and Caesar.

Multialphabet Substitution

Eventually, an improvement in single-substitution ciphers was developed, called multialphabet substitution. In this scheme, you select multiple numbers by which to shift letters (i.e., multiple substitution alphabets). For example, if you select three substitution alphabets ($+1, -1, +2$), this means you shift the first letter right one, the second letter left one, then the third letter right two, and then repeat. The fourth letter is shifted right one, the fifth left one, and the sixth shifted right by two. Thus

A CAT

becomes

B BCU

Notice that this disrupts the letter and word frequency. At one point in our short message, A becomes B; in another, it becomes C; and since we have three substitution alphabets, it could, in a longer message, become Z. This makes it more difficult to decipher the underlying text.

Vigenere Cipher

One of the most widely known multialphabet ciphers was the Vigenere cipher. This cipher was invented in 1553 by Giovan Battista Bellaso. It is a method of encrypting text by using a series of different monoalphabet ciphers selected based on the letters of a keyword. This algorithm was later misattributed to Blaise de Vigenère, and so it is now known as the "Vigenère cipher," even though Vigenère did not really invent it.

You use the table shown in Figure 7-1, along with a keyword you have selected. Match the letter of your keyword on the top with the letter of your plain text on the left to find the cipher text. For example if the plain text letter is E and the keyword letter is F, the cipher text will be J, as shown in Figure 7-1.

Figure 7-1 The Vigenere cipher

```
  A B C D E F G H I J K L M N O P Q R S T U V W X Y Z
A A B C D E F G H I J K L M N O P Q R S T U V W X Y Z
B B C D E F G H I J K L M N O P Q R S T U V W X Y Z A
C C D E F G H I J K L M N O P Q R S T U V W X Y Z A B
D D E F G H I J K L M N O P Q R S T U V W X Y Z A B C D
E E F G H I J K L M N O P Q R S T U V W X Y Z A B C D
F F G H I J K L M N O P Q R S T U V W X Y Z A B C D E
G G H I J K L M N O P Q R S T U V W X Y Z A B C D E F
H H I J K L M N O P Q R S T U V W X Y Z A B C D E F G
I I J K L M N O P Q R S T U V W X Y Z A B C D E F G H
J J K L M N O P Q R S T U V W X Y Z A B C D E F G H I
K K L M N O P Q R S T U V W X Y Z A B C D E F G H I J
L L M N O P Q R S T U V W X Y Z A B C D E F G H I J K
M M N O P Q R S T U V W X Y Z A B C D E F G H I J K L
N N O P Q R S T U V W X Y Z A B C D E F G H I J K L M
O O P Q R S T U V W X Y Z A B C D E F G H I J K L M N
P P Q R S T U V W X Y Z A B C D E F G H I J K L M N O
Q Q R S T U V W X Y Z A B C D E F G H I J K L M N O P
R R S T U V W X Y Z A B C D E F G H I J K L M N O P Q
S S T U V W X Y Z A B C D E F G H I J K L M N O P Q R
T T U V W X Y Z A B C D E F G H I J K L M N O P Q R S
U U V W X Y Z A B C D E F G H I J K L M N O P Q R S T
V V W X Y Z A B C D E F G H I J K L M N O P Q R S T U V
W W X Y Z A B C D E F G H I J K L M N O P Q R S T U V
X X Y Z A B C D E F G H I J K L M N O P Q R S T U V W
Y Y Z A B C D E F G H I J K L M N O P Q R S T U V W X
Z Z A B C D E F G H I J K L M N O P Q R S T U V W X Y
```

Using the previous chart, if you are encrypting the word "cat" and your keyword is "horse," then the cipher text is "jok."

Some sources view the Vigenere cipher as just a series of Caesar ciphers, and that is a reasonably accurate view.

 EXAM TIP The CCFP (as well as many other security certification tests) is most likely to ask you about Caesar and Vigenere, if you get any questions about historical ciphers. So make sure you fully understand these two.

Transposition Ciphers

In addition to substituting, one can use transposition. With transposition, you simply move the text around. For example, you might decide to take every three-letter block and switch it with the next block. So the phrase "I like single malt scotch" becomes

Kes ili gle sin tso mal tch

The most widely known transposition cipher was the rail fence cipher. With this cipher, you would write out your plain text on two lines, then combine the lines to make the cipher text. For example, the plain text message "attack at dawn" is written out on two rows

```
A    t    c    a    d    w
   T    a    k    t    a    n
```

And the cipher text becomes

Atcadwtaktan

Enigma Machine

Most readers have heard of this machine. It was a polyalphabet cipher typewriter. It had 26 different substitution alphabets, and each time a user typed a key, the machine would rotate to the next alphabet. This was the height of cryptographic technology during World War II.

 NOTE There are many more historical ciphers, and more to learn about cryptology in general, than we can cover in this book. If you are fascinated by this topic, you might find www.CryptoCorner.com to be a good place to start.

Modern Cryptography

After reading the first portion of this chapter, you should have a pretty good understanding of historical cryptography. It is now time for us to move on to discuss modern cryptography. Modern cryptography is split into two main branches: symmetric and asymmetric. Symmetric cryptography means that the same key is used to decrypt a message as was used to encrypt it. With asymmetric cryptography, the key used to encrypt a message cannot decrypt it; you need a second key.

Symmetric cryptography can be further broken down into two subgroups block ciphers and stream ciphers. With block ciphers, the plain text is divided into blocks (usually 64 or 128 bits) and each block is encrypted. With stream ciphers, the plain text is encrypted in a stream, one bit at a time. All modern block ciphers include binary operations.

Binary Operations

If you have a background in computer science, particularly programming, you should be familiar with binary numbers and binary operations. But for those readers not familiar with them, a brief explanation follows.

First, a binary number is just a number written in base 2. You are familiar with base 10 numbers. In base 10, you don't really have a number 10—you have 0 through 9. After 9, the next number is really saying "a 1 in the tens place and a 0 in the ones place." The same is true with base 2. You don't really have a number 2. Instead, 10 means "a one in the twos place and a 0 in the ones place." This chart might clarify that a bit:

Base 10 (decimal)	Base 2 (binary)
0	0
1	1
2	10
3	11
4	100
5	101

When working with binary numbers, there are three operations not found in normal math: AND, OR, and XOR operations. Each is illustrated next:

- **AND**   To perform the AND operation, you take two binary numbers and compare them one place at a time. If both numbers have a 1 in both places, then the resultant number is a 1. If not, then the resultant number is a 0, as you see here:

```
1 1 0 1
1 0 0 1
-------
1 0 0 1
```

- **OR**   The OR operation checks to see whether there is a 1 in either or both numbers in a given place. If so, then the resultant number is 1. If not, the resultant number is 0, as you see here:

```
1 1 0 1
1 0 0 1
-------
1 1 0 1
```

- **XOR** The XOR operation affects your study of encryption the most. It checks to see whether there is a 1 in a number in a given place, but not in both numbers at that place. If it is in one number but not the other, then the resultant number is 1. If not, the resultant number is 0, as you see here:

```
1 1 0 1
1 0 0 1
-------
0 1 0 0
```

XORing has a very interesting property in that it is reversible. If you XOR the resultant number with the second number, you get back the first number. And if you XOR the resultant number with the first number, you get the second number.

```
0 1 0 0
1 0 0 1
-------
1 1 0 1
```

The fact that the XOR operation is reversible makes it useful in cryptography. One could argue that simply converting text to binary format (first converting it to ASCII codes and then the binary equivalents) and XORing it with a random stream of bits would constitute encryption, and technically, that would be correct. However, that XOR alone would be very weak. But it is actually a part of many modern symmetric ciphers.

Symmetric Encryption

As we mentioned previously, symmetric encryption refers to those methods where the same key is used to encrypt and decrypt the plain text.

Data Encryption Standard

Data Encryption Standard (DES) was developed by IBM in the early 1970s. DES uses a symmetric key system. Recall from our earlier discussion that this means the same key is used to encrypt and decrypt the message. DES uses short keys and relies on complex procedures to protect its information. The actual algorithm is quite complex. The basic concept, however, is as follows (Federal Information Processing Standards, 1993):

1. The data is divided into 64-bit blocks, and those blocks are then transposed.

2. Transposed data is then manipulated by 16 separate steps of encryption, involving substitutions, bit-shifting, and logical operations using a 56-bit key.

3. The data is then further scrambled using a swapping algorithm.

4. Finally, the data is transposed one last time.

More information about DES is available at the Federal Information Processing Standards website at www.itl.nist.gov/fipspubs/fip46-2.htm.

DES is no longer considered secure due to the short key. A computer can attempt a brute-force attack, which means simply trying every possible key. With a 56-bit key, that means 2^56 possible keys. That means 72,057,594,037,927,936 possible keys. That may seem impossible, but remember that computers can attempt a lot of keys, very fast, and it is unlikely you will have to try all of them before you get a match. But assuming you do, and assuming the computer trying to break DES can try 1 billion keys a second, it would take 2.2 years to try all the possible keys. There is a principle in cryptography based on the Birthday paradox. The math behind this is a bit more than we can cover here, but put simply, the Birthday paradox asks how many people would need to be in a room to have a strong likelihood (not a guarantee, just a strong probability) of two of those people having the same birth month/day (but not year). You might think that it would take 365, and for a guaranteed match, you would be right. But just to have a good chance of a match, you would only need 23, or the square root of 365. Applying that to DES, you have a good chance of having a match on the key after trying only 84,886,744 random keys. And as you can see, if our computer can try 1 billion keys a second, then it is likely to get a match in only one second!

One variation of DES is called triple-DES or 3-DES. In 3-DES, you get three separate keys and encrypt the plain text three times with DES, each time using a different key. First you encrypt the plain text with key 1, then encrypt that result with key 2, and then encrypt that result with key 3. There are variations of 3-DES that actually use only two keys.

EXAM TIP   Though DES is outdated, CCFP and other security certifications like to ask questions about it.

Feistel Ciphers

DES is part of a class of ciphers called Feistel ciphers. This function is named after its inventor, the German-born physicist and cryptographer Horst Feistel.

At the heart of many block ciphers is a Feistel function. This makes it one of the most influential developments in symmetric block ciphers. It is also known as a Feistel network. Figure 7-2 shows how it works.

Figure 7-2   The Feistel cipher

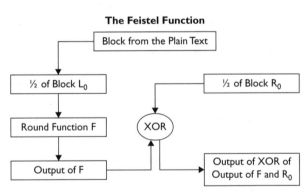

1. This function starts by splitting the block of plain text data (often 64 bits) into two parts (traditionally termed L_0 and R_0).

2. The round function F is applied to one of the halves. The term "round function" simply means a function performed with each iteration, or round, of the Feistel cipher. The details of the round function F can vary with different implementations. Usually, these are relatively simple functions to allow for increased speed of the algorithm.

3. The output of each round function F is then XORed with the other half. What this means is that, for example, you take L_0, pass it through the round function F, then take the result and XOR it with R_0.

4. Then the halves are transposed. L_0 is moved to the right and R_0 is moved to the left.

5. This process is repeated a given number of times. The main difference between cryptography algorithms is the exact nature of the round function F and the number of iterations.

NOTE Many symmetric ciphers, including DES, GOST, and AES, use what is called an s-box. That is short for "substitution box." Basically, a certain number of bits are input into the box and substituted for something else. So, for example, 1101 might come into the box and the output be 0110. There are many variations of the s-box, such as p-boxes (or permutation boxes).

Blowfish

Blowfish is a symmetric block cipher. This means that it uses a single key to both encrypt and decrypt the message and works on "blocks" of the message at a time. It uses a variable-length key ranging from 32 to 448 bits. Blowfish was designed in 1993 by Bruce Schneier. It has been analyzed extensively by the cryptography community and has gained wide acceptance. It is also a noncommercial (i.e., free of charge) product, thus making it attractive to budget-conscious organizations.

AES

AES stands for Advanced Encryption Standard. This standard uses the Rijndael algorithm. This algorithm was part of a contest seeking a replacement for DES. Fifteen different algorithms made it to the second-to-last round, then five in the last round, and ultimately, Rijndael won out.

The AES specifies three key sizes: 128, 192, and 256 bits. By comparison, DES keys are 56 bits long, and Blowfish allows varying lengths up to 448 bits. AES uses a block cipher. Interested readers can find detailed specifications for this algorithm, including a detailed discussion of the mathematics, at http://csrc.nist.gov/archive/aes/rijndael/Rijndael-ammended.pdf.

This algorithm is widely used and is considered very secure, and therefore, is a good choice for many encryption scenarios.

IDEA Encryption

IDEA is another block cipher. The acronym IDEA stands for International Data Encryption Algorithm. This particular algorithm works with 64-bit blocks of data, two at a time, and uses a 128-bit key. The procedure is fairly complicated and uses subkeys generated from the key to carry out a series of modular arithmetic and XOR operations on segments of the 64-bit plain text block. The encryption scheme uses a total of 52 16-bit subkeys. These are generated from the 128-bit subkey with the following procedure:

1. The 128-bit key is split into eight 16-bit keys, which are the first eight subkeys.

2. The digits of the 128-bit key are shifted 25 bits to the left to make a new key, which is then split into the next eight 16-bit subkeys.

3. The second step is repeated until the 52 subkeys have been generated. The encryption consists of eight rounds.

GOST

GOST is a DES-like algorithm developed by the Soviets in the 1970s. It was originally classified, but was released to the public in 1994. It uses a 64-bit block and a key of 256 bits. It is a 32-round Feistel cipher.

The round function is as follows:

1. Add the subkey modulo 2.

2. Put the result through s-boxes.

3. Rotate the result 11 bits.

The key schedule involves the following:

1. Divide the 256-bit key into eight 32-bit subkeys.

2. Each subkey is used four times.

This cipher uses s-boxes that take in 4 bits and output 4 bits.

Serpent

Serpent has a block size of 128 bits and can have a key size of 128, 192, or 256 bits, much like AES. The algorithm is also a substitution-permutation network like AES. It uses 32 rounds working with a block of four 32-bit words. Each round applies one of eight 4-bit to 4-bit c-boxes 32 times in parallel. Serpent was designed so that all operations can be executed in parallel.

Skipjack

This algorithm was developed by the National Security Agency (NSA) and was designed for the clipper chip. It was originally classified. The clipper chip was a chip with built-in encryption; however, the decryption key would be kept in a key escrow in case law enforcement needed to decrypt data without the computer owner's cooperation. This feature made the process highly controversial. Skipjack uses an 80-bit key to encrypt or decrypt 64-bit data blocks. It is an unbalanced Feistel network with 32 rounds.

Unbalanced Feistel simply means a Feistel cipher wherein the two halves of plain text for each block are not the same size. For example, a 64-bit block might be divided into a 48-bit half and a 16-bit half rather than two 32-bit halves.

RC 4

Ron Rivest created this algorithm in 1987. The RC stands for Ron's Cipher. It is the most widely used software stream cipher. The algorithm is used identically for encryption and decryption, as the data stream is simply XORed with the key.

RC 4 uses a variable-length key, from 1 to 256 bytes. That key constitutes a state table that is used for subsequent generation of pseudo-random bytes and then to generate a pseudo-random stream, which is XORed with the plain text to produce the cipher text.

The permutation is initialized with a variable-length key, typically between 40 and 256 bits, using the key-scheduling algorithm (KSA). Once this has been completed, the stream of bits is generated using the pseudo-random generation algorithm (PRGA).

Asymmetric Cryptography

Asymmetric cryptography (also called public key cryptography) is essentially the opposite of single-key encryption. With any public key encryption algorithm, one key (called the public key) is used to encrypt a message and another (called the private key) is used to decrypt the message. You can freely distribute your public key so that anyone can encrypt a message to send to you, but only you have the private key and only you can decrypt the message. This is why asymmetric cryptography is sometimes called public key cryptography.

For some reason, all security books and cryptography books like to use the fictitious characters Alice, Bob, and Eve to explain how asymmetric cryptography works, and I will continue that tradition.

Let's assume Alice would like to send Bob a message. But Alice is concerned that Eve might eavesdrop (thus her name!) on the communication. With public key/asymmetric cryptography, Alice will get Bob's public key and use that to encrypt the message she sends to Bob. Now should Eve intercept the message and have access to Bob's public key, it is okay. That key won't decrypt the message. Only Bob's private key will, and this he safeguards. You can see this in Figure 7-3.

Figure 7-3
Alice and Bob
use asymmetric
crypto

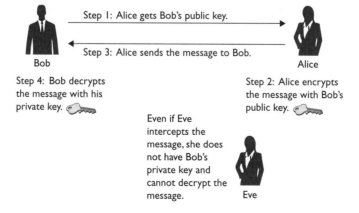

Step 1: Alice gets Bob's public key.

Step 3: Alice sends the message to Bob.

Bob

Alice

Step 4: Bob decrypts
the message with his
private key.

Step 2: Alice encrypts
the message with Bob's
public key.

Even if Eve
intercepts the
message, she does
not have Bob's
private key and
cannot decrypt the
message.

Eve

EXAM TIP Expect questions regarding what key Alice or Bob will need to use to encrypt a message and to decrypt it. This is also true for many other certification tests, such as the CISSP.

RSA

The RSA is perhaps the most widely known asymmetric algorithm. This is a public key method developed in 1977 by three mathematicians: Ron Rivest, Adi Shamir, and Len Adleman. The name RSA is derived from the first letter of each mathematician's last name. The algorithm is based on prime numbers and the difficulty of factoring a large number into its prime factors.

 EXAM TIP The CCFP and other security certifications will definitely ask you about RSA. However, you just need to know the basic facts already listed. You don't need to know the details of the algorithm. In fact, no certification test asks about the details of any of the cryptography algorithms.

While not critical for the CCFP exam, it might help your understanding to look at the RSA algorithm. First, to create the key, you start by generating two large random primes, p and q, of approximately equal size. Now you need to pick two numbers that, when multiplied together, create a product that is the size you want (i.e., 2048 bits, 4096 bits, etc.)

Now multiply p and q to get n.

Let $n = pq$.

The next step is to multiply Euler's totient for each of these primes. Now you are probably asking, what is Euler's totient? Don't let the name scare you—the concept is pretty simple. First, let's define the term co-prime. Two numbers are considered co-prime if they have no common factors. For example, if the original number is 8, then 8 and 9 would be co-prime. 8's factors are 2 and 4; 9's factors are 3—there is nothing in common (1 is not considered). Well, the famous mathematician Euler (pronounced "oiler") asked a simple question: Given a number X, how many numbers smaller than X are co-prime to X? We call that number Euler's totient, or just the totient. It just so happens that for prime numbers, this is always the number minus 1. For example, 7 has 6 numbers that are co-prime to it.

When you multiply two primes together, you get a composite number, and there is no easy way to determine the Euler's totient of a composite number. Euler noticed something else interesting. If you multiply any two prime numbers together, the Euler's totient of that product is the Euler's totient of each prime multiplied together. So our next step is:

Let $m = (p - 1)(q - 1)$.

So basically, *m* is the Euler's totient of *n*.

Now we are going to select another number—we will call this number *e*. We want to pick *e* so that it is co-prime to *m*.

We are almost done generating a key. Now we just find a number *d* that, when multiplied by *e* and modulo *m*, would yield a 1 (Note: Modulo means to divide two numbers and return the remainder. For example, 8 modulo 3 would be 2). In other words:

Find *d*, such that de % $m = 1$.

Now you will publish *e* and *n* as the public key and keep *d* and *n* as the secret key. To encrypt, you simply take your message raised to the *e* power and modulo *n*:

$$= M^e \% n$$

To decrypt, you take the cipher text and raise it to the *d* power modulo *n*:

$$P = C^d \% n$$

Now don't panic. Most people without a background in number theory have to study this for some time before they are comfortable with it. And you don't need to know the RSA algorithm in depth to pass the CCFP. I presented it here so you would understand how public key/asymmetric cryptography works.

Let's look at an example that might help you understand. Of course, RSA would be done with very large integers. To make the math easy to follow, we will use small integers in this example, which is from Wikipedia[1]:

1. Choose two distinct prime numbers, such as $p = 61$ and $q = 53$.

2. Compute $n = pq$ giving $n = 61 \times 53 = 3233$.

3. Compute the totient of the product as $\varphi(n) = (p - 1)(q - 1)$ giving $\varphi(3233) = (61 - 1)(53 - 1) = 3120$.

4. Choose any number $1 < e < 3120$ that is co-prime to 3120. Choosing a prime number for *e* leaves us only to check that *e* is not a divisor of 3120. Let $e = 17$.

5. Compute *d*, the modular multiplicative inverse of yielding $d = 2753$.

    The *public key* is ($n = 3233$, $e = 17$). For a padded plain text message *m*, the encryption function is m^{17} (mod 3233).

    The *private key* is ($n = 3233$, $d = 2753$). For an encrypted cipher text *c*, the decryption function is c^{2753} (mod 3233).

PART III

RSA is based on large prime numbers. Now you might think, couldn't someone take the public key and use factoring to derive the private key? Well, hypothetically, yes. However, it turns out that factoring really large numbers into their prime factors is pretty difficult. There is no efficient algorithm for doing it. And when we say large numbers, RSA can use 1024-, 2048-, 4096-bit, and larger keys. Those make for some huge numbers. Of course, should anyone ever invent an efficient algorithm that will factor a large number into its prime factors, RSA will be dead.

Diffie-Hellman

Diffie-Hellman, which was the first publicly described asymmetric algorithm, is a cryptographic protocol that allows two parties to establish a shared key over an insecure channel. In other words, Diffie-Hellman is often used to allow parties to exchange a symmetric key through some unsecure medium, such as the Internet. It was developed by Whitfield Diffie and Martin Hellman in 1976.

One problem with working in cryptology is that much of the work is classified. You could labor away and create something wonderful that you cannot tell anyone about. Then, to make matters worse, years later, someone else might develop something similar and release it, getting all the credit. This is exactly the situation with Diffie-Hellman. It turns out that a similar method had been developed a few years earlier by Malcolm J. Williamson of the British Intelligence Service, but it was classified.

 EXAM TIP CCFP, like so many security certifications, has a few algorithms it focuses on. If you get public key/asymmetric questions on your test, there is a good chance they will be about RSA or Diffie-Hellman.

DSA

Digital Signature Algorithm (DSA) is a patented algorithm (U.S. Patent 5,231,668) invented by David W. Kravitz. It was adopted by the U.S. government in 1993, with FIPS (Federal Information Processing Standard) 186 as the preferred standard for digital signatures. While any asymmetric algorithm can be used for digital signatures, this algorithm was designed specifically for that purpose. This, of course, begs the question of what is a digital signature.

Remember that cryptographic algorithms are about protecting confidentiality, ensuring that only the intended recipient can read the message. Well, digital signatures take asymmetric cryptography and reverse it so that they can protect integrity. Put another way, assume your boss sends you an e-mail telling you that you have done such a great job, he thinks you should take the next week off with pay. It would probably be a good thing to verify that this is legitimate e-mail, really sent from him, and not a prank. What a digital signature does is take the sender's private key and encrypt either the entire message or a portion of it (like the signature block). Now anyone with the sender's public key can decrypt that. So let us return to Alice and Bob to see how this works.

Bob wants to send Alice a message and make certain she knows it's from him. So he signs it with his private key. When Alice uses Bob's public key, the message decrypts and she can read it. Now suppose that Bob did not really send this. Instead, Eve sent it, pretending to be Bob. Since Eve does not have Bob's private key, she had to use some other key to sign this message. When Alice tries to decrypt it (i.e., verify the signature) with Bob's public key, she will get back gibberish, nonsense. This is shown in Figure 7-4.

Figure 7-4
Digital signatures

Step 1: Bob signs the message with his private key.

Step 2: Bob sends the message with signature.

Bob

Alice

Step 3: Alice verifies the signature using Bob's public key.

Elliptic Curve

This algorithm was first described in 1985 by Victor Miller (IBM) and Neal Koblitz (University of Washington). Elliptic curve cryptography (ECC) is based on the fact that finding the discrete logarithm of a random elliptic curve element with respect to a publicly known base point is difficult to the point of being impractical to do. There are a number of variations, such as ECC-DH (ECC Diffie-Hellman) and ECC-DSA (ECC Digital Signature Algorithm). The real strength of ECC base systems is that you can get just as much security with a smaller key than with other systems, like RSA. For example, a 384-bit ECC key is as strong as a 2048-bit RSA key.

Cryptographic Hash

A cryptographic hash function has three properties. The first is that it is one-way. That means it cannot be "unhashed." The second is that a variable-length input produces a fixed-length output. That means that no matter what size of input you have, you will get the same size output. Finally, there should be few or no collisions. That means if you hash two different inputs, you should not get the same output.

In previous chapters, we have discussed hashing an image of a drive to ensure that nothing was missed or altered when imaging the original drive. This is where the "variable-length input produces fixed-length output" and "few or no collisions" comes in. If you have a terabyte drive and you image it, you want to make sure your image is an exact copy. If you make a hash of the original and the image and compare them, you can verify that everything is copied exactly into the image. If it were not the case that a variable-length input produced a fixed-length output, then you would have hashes that were humongous and took forever to compute. Also, if two different inputs could produce the same output, then you could not verify the image was an exact copy.

MD5

This is a 128-bit hash that is specified by RFC 1321. It was designed by Ron Rivest in 1991 to replace an earlier hash function, MD4. MD5 produces a 128-bit hash or digest. It has been found to not be as collision resistant as SHA.

SHA

The Secure Hash Algorithm (SHA) is perhaps the most widely used hash algorithm today. There are now several versions of it, all of which are considered secure and collision free:

- **SHA-1** This is a 160-bit hash function that resembles the earlier MD5 algorithm. This was designed by the NSA to be part of the DSA.

- **SHA-2** This is actually two similar hash functions, with different block sizes, known as SHA-256 and SHA-512. They differ in the word size: SHA-256 uses 32-byte (256-bit) words, whereas SHA-512 uses 64-byte (512-bit) words. There are also truncated versions of each standardized known as SHA-224 and SHA-384. These were also designed by the NSA.

- **SHA-3** This is the latest version of SHA. It was adopted in October 2012.

RipeMD

RACE Integrity Primitives Evaluation Message Digest (RipeMD) is a 160-bit hash algorithm developed by Hans Dobbertin, Antoon Bosselaers, and Bart Preneel. There exist 128-, 256- and 320-bit versions of this algorithm, called RIPEMD-128, RIPEMD-256, and RIPEMD-320, respectively. These all replace the original RIPEMD, which was found to have collision issues. The larger bit sizes make this far more secure than MD5 or RipeMD.

GOST

This hash algorithm was initially defined in the Russian national standard GOST R 34.11-94 Information Technology–Cryptographic Information Security–Hash Function. It produces a fixed-length output of 256 bits. The input message is broken up into chunks of 256-bit blocks. If a block is less than 256 bits, then the message is padded by appending as many zeros to it as are required to bring the length of the message up to 256 bits. The remaining bits are filled up with a 256-bit integer arithmetic sum of all previously hashed blocks, and then a 256-bit integer representing the length of the original message, in bits, is produced. It is based on the GOST block cipher.

Windows Passwords

Verifying images of drives is not the only purpose for hashes. Hashing is how Windows stores passwords. For example, if your password is "password," then Windows will first hash it, producing something like:

0BD181063899C9239016320B50D3E896693A96DF

It will then store that in the Security Accounts Manager (SAM) file in the Windows System directory. When you log on, Windows cannot "unhash" your password, so what Windows does is take whatever password you type in, hash it, and then compare the result with what is in the SAM file. If they match exactly, then you can log in.

Getting Around Windows Passwords

Now how does this relate to forensics? Well, knowledge of hashing provides a means to circumvent Windows passwords. You may encounter a Windows machine that is suspected of having evidence, and the suspect will not reveal the password. Once you have obtained a warrant to search the drive, you can use the method described here to circumvent the password.

In 1980, Martin Hellman described a cryptanalytic technique that reduces the time of cryptanalysis by using precalculated data stored in memory. This technique was improved by Rivest before 1982. Basically, these types of password crackers are working with precalculated hashes of all passwords available within a certain character space, be that a–z or a–zA–z or a–zA–Z0–9, etc. This is called a rainbow table. If you search a rainbow table for a given hash, whatever plain text you find must be the text that was input into the hashing algorithm to produce that specific hash.

Now this still does not solve the issue of cracking Windows passwords. When Windows boots up, it seizes the SAM file and you cannot copy it off the machine. (Besides, you would need to log in to get the SAM file.) Tools like OphCrack can be used to boot to Linux, grab the SAM file, and take the hashes from that file. Then they search their rainbow tables to see if they can find a match. If a match is found, that must be the user's password.

Salt

In terms of hashing, salt refers to random bits that are used as one of the inputs to the hash. Essentially, the salt is intermixed with the message that is to be hashed. Salt data makes rainbow tables harder to implement. The rainbow table must account for the salting algorithm as well as the hashing algorithm. Thus, the method is effective against rainbow table attacks.

Steganography

Steganography is the art and science of writing hidden messages in such a way that no one, apart from the sender and intended recipient, suspects the existence of the message—a form of security through obscurity. Often, the message is hidden in some other file, such as a digital picture or audio file, so as to defy detection.

The advantage of steganography over cryptography alone is that messages do not attract attention to themselves. If no one is aware the message is even there, then they won't even try to decipher it. In many cases, messages are encrypted and hidden via steganography.

There are some basic steganography terms you should know:

- *Payload* is the data to be covertly communicated. In other words, it is the message you wish to hide.

- The *carrier* is the signal, stream, or data file into which the payload is hidden.

- The *channel* is the type of medium used. This may be still photos, video, or sound files.

The most common way steganography is accomplished today is via least significant bits (LSB). In every file, there are a certain number of bits per unit. For example, an image file in Windows is 24 bits per pixel. If you change the least significant of those bits, then the change is not noticeable with the naked eye. And one can hide information in the LSB of an image file. With LSB replacement, certain bits in the carrier file are replaced.

Historical Steganography

In modern times, steganography means digital manipulation of files to hide messages. However, the concept of hiding messages is not new. As with cryptography, many methods have been used throughout history:

- The ancient Chinese wrapped notes in wax and swallowed them for transport. This was a crude but effective method of hiding messages.

- In ancient Greece, a messenger's head might be shaved, a message written on his head, and then his hair was allowed to grow back. Obviously, this method required some time to be available.

- In 1518, Johannes Trithemius wrote a book on cryptography and described a technique where a message was hidden by having each letter taken as a word from a specific column.

- During WWII, the French Resistance sent messages written on the backs of couriers using invisible ink.

- Microdots are images/undeveloped film the size of a typewriter period embedded in innocuous documents. Spies supposedly used these during the Cold War.

- Also during the Cold War, the U.S. Central intelligence Agency used various devices to hide messages. For example, they developed a tobacco pipe that had a small space to hide microfilm, but could still be smoked.

Methods and Tools

Steganophony is a term for hiding messages in sound files. This can be done with the LSB method or other methods, such as echo hiding. This method adds extra sound to an echo inside an audio file, and the extra sound conceals information.

Information can also be hidden in video files. There are various methods to accomplish this. Discrete cosine transform is often used for video steganography. This method alters values of certain parts of the individual frames. The usual method is to round up the values.

A number of tools are available for implementing steganography. Many are free or at least have a free trial version. A few of these tools are listed here. Two are discussed in detail in the sections that follow.

- **QuickStego**   Very easy to use, but very limited.
- **Invisible Secrets**   Much more robust, with both a free and commercial version.
- **MP3Stego**   Specifically for hiding payload in MP3 files.
- **Stealth Files 4**   This works with sound files, video files, and image files.
- **Snow**   Hides data in whitespace.
- **StegVideo**   Hides data in a video sequence.

Invisible Secrets

Invisible Secrets is a popular tool for steganography. It is important that a forensic examiner be familiar with the more widely known forensic tools and be able to utilize them. You can download Invisible Secrets from www.invisiblesecrets.com/download .html. Let's walk through the process of hiding a message using this tool. First, select an image—anything you like. I am going to use an image of the cover of this book. Then take a text editor, such as Notepad, and put some text in it. Now we will hide that message in the image file.

First select Hide/Unhide Files. This is shown in Figure 7-5 with the option you should select circled.

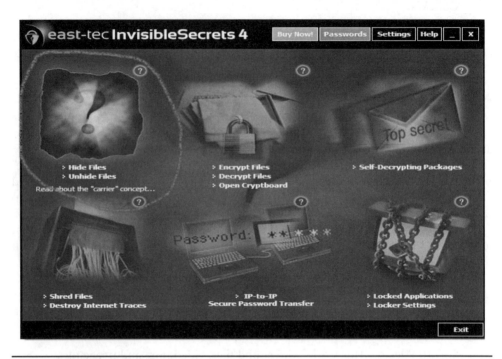

Figure 7-5   Invisible Secrets Hide/Unhide

Then hide the text file you created (I named mine "stegtest.txt") as shown in Figure 7-6.

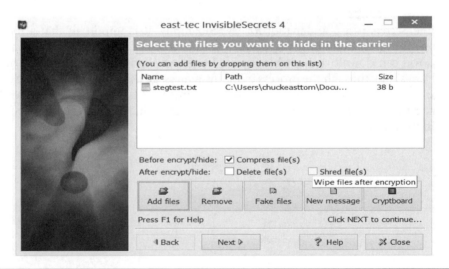

Figure 7-6   Hiding a test file in Invisible Secrets

Now select the image file in which you wish to hide this text. This is shown in Figure 7-7.

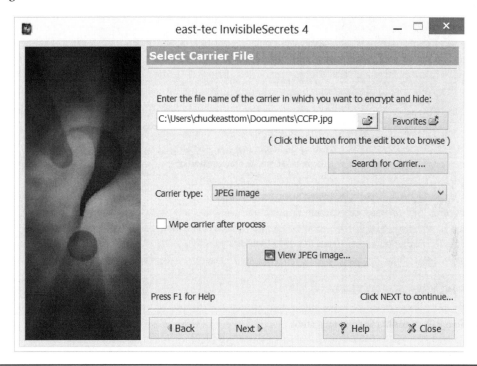

Figure 7-7 Choosing the carrier file in Invisible Secrets

Incidentally, the current version of Invisible Secrets allows you to hide data in .wav files as well as images. This is shown in Figure 7-8.

Figure 7-8
Invisible Secrets
different carrier
types

JPEG image	⌄
JPEG image	
BMP image	
HTML page	
PNG image	
WAV sound	

The next screen has you select a password for this hidden data, and has you (optionally) encrypt the data as well. For this demonstration, we will leave it unencrypted and use a trivial password. You can see this in Figure 7-9.

In the final step, you simply pick a location and name for the output file. This will include your hidden message (the payload) and the file you wish to hide it in (the carrier file). You can see this step in Figure 7-10.

The resulting image, shown in Figure 7-11, is indistinguishable from the original carrier file. You can enlarge it with Photoshop, examine it carefully, and you won't be able to see that it contains hidden information.

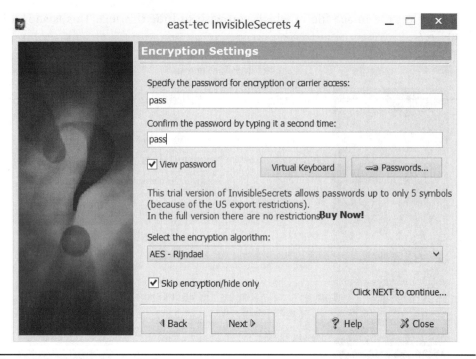

Figure 7-9   Invisible Secrets final steps

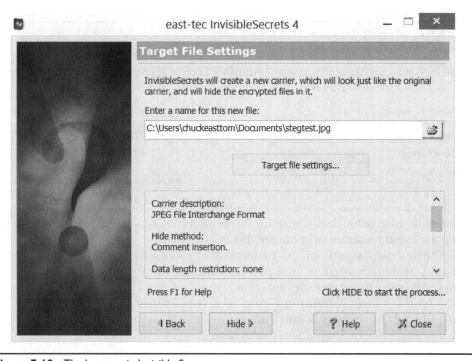

Figure 7-10   The last step in Invisible Secrets

Figure 7-11
The resulting
image in Invisible
Secrets

MP3Stego

This is another tool, one you can download for free from www.petitcolas.net/fabien/ steganography/mp3stego. This tool is used to hide data in MP3 files. From the MP3 Stego readme file are these instructions:

> *encode -E data.txt -P pass sound.wav sound.mp3*
> compresses sound.wav and hides data.txt. This produces the output called sound.mp3. The text in data.txt is encrypted using "pass".
> *decode -X -P pass sound.mp3*
> uncompresses sound.mp3 into sound.mp3.pcm and attempts to extract hidden information. The hidden message is decrypted, uncompressed and saved into sound.mp3.

You can see this is a very simple program to use.

Steganalysis

If you can hide data in images or other carrier files, there must be some way to detect it, right? One of the most common methods is to analyze close color pairs. By analyzing changes in an image's close color pairs, the steganalyst can determine if LSB substitution was used. Close color pairs consist of two colors whose binary values differ only in the LSB. You would expect a certain number of pixels to vary only in the LSB, but if the number of such pixels is greater than one would expect, that might indicate steganographically hidden data.

There are several methods for analyzing an image to detect hidden messages. The Raw Quick Pair (RQP) method is one. The RQP method is essentially an implementation of the close color pair concept. This method is based on statistics of the numbers of unique colors and close color pairs in a 24-bit image. RQP analyzes the pairs of colors created by LSB embedding.

Another option uses the chi-squared method from statistics. Chi-square analysis calculates the average LSB and builds a table of frequencies and pairs of values. Then it performs a chi-square test on these two tables. Essentially, it measures the theoretical versus calculated population difference.

 NOTE Steganography is an important concept in forensic analysis. Technically sophisticated child pornographers frequently hide their illicit images in innocuous images. It is also a popular technique with terrorists. During the raid on Osama bin Laden's compound, which resulted in his death, a number of computer hard drives were found. It was discovered that Osama bin Laden was communicating with Al-Qaeda members using messages hidden in pornographic images.

Cryptanalysis

Cryptanalysis is a daunting task. It is essentially the search for some means to break through some encryption. And, unlike what you see in the movies, it is a very time-consuming task that frequently leads to only partial success. Cryptanalysis involves using any method to decrypt the message that is more efficient than simple brute-force attempts. (Remember that brute force is simply trying every possible key.)

A cryptanalysis success is not necessarily breaking the target cipher. In fact, finding any information about the target cipher or key is considered a success. There are several types of cryptographic success:

- **Total break**   The attacker deduces the secret key.
- **Global deduction**   The attacker discovers a functionally equivalent algorithm for encryption and decryption, but without learning the key.
- **Instance (local) deduction**   The attacker discovers additional plain texts (or cipher texts) not previously known.
- **Information deduction**   The attacker gains some Shannon information about plain texts (or cipher texts) not previously known.
- **Distinguishing algorithm**   The attacker can distinguish the cipher from a random permutation.

In this section, we will look at some common methods for cryptanalysis.

Frequency Analysis

This is the basic tool for breaking most classical ciphers—it is not useful against modern symmetric or asymmetric cryptography. It is based on the fact that some letters and letter combinations are more common than others. In all languages, certain letters of the alphabet appear more frequently than others. By examining those frequencies, you can derive some information about the key that was used. Remember in English the words *the* and *and* are the two most common three-letter words. The most common single-letter words are *I* and *a*. If you see two of the same letters together in a word, it is most likely *ee* or *oo*.

Kasiski

Kasiski examination was developed by Friedrich Kasiski in 1863. It is a method of attacking polyalphabetic substitution ciphers such as the Vigenère cipher. The idea is to first examine the cipher text (or, even better, multiple cipher texts) just to see if you can determine how long the keyword is. Once the length of the keyword is discovered, you line up the cipher text in columns, with the number of columns being equal to the length of the keyword. Then, each column can be treated as a monoalphabetic substitution cipher. Then, each column can be cracked with simple frequency analysis. The method simply involves looking for repeated strings in the cipher text. The longer the cipher text, the more effective this method will be. This is sometimes also called Kasiski's test or Kasiski's method.

Modern Methods

As mentioned, the level of success when cracking modern cryptographic methods depends on a combination of resources. Those resources are computational power, time, and data. If you had an infinite amount of any of these, you could crack any modern cipher. But you won't have an infinite amount.

Known Plain Text Attack

This method is based on having a sample of known plain texts and their resulting cipher texts. Then you use this information to try to ascertain something about the key used. It is easier to obtain known plain text samples than you might think. Consider e-mail. Many people, myself included, use a standard signature block. If you have ever received an e-mail from me, you know what my signature block is. Then, if you intercept encrypted e-mails I send, you can compare the known signature block to the end of the encrypted e-mail. You would then have a known plain text and the matching cipher text to work with. However, this requires many thousands of known plain text samples to be successful.

Chosen Plain Text Attack

This is closely related to the known plain text attack, with the difference being that the attacker has found a method to get the target to encrypt messages the attacker chooses. This can allow the attacker to attempt to derive the key used and thus decrypt other messages encrypted with that key. This can be difficult, but is not impossible. Again, this requires many thousands of chosen plain text samples to be successful.

Cipher Text Only

The attacker only has access to a collection of cipher texts. This is much more likely than known plain text, but also the most difficult. The attack is completely successful if the corresponding plain texts can be deduced, or even better, the key. The ability to obtain any information at all about the underlying plain text is still considered a success.

Related-Key Attack

This is like a chosen plain text attack, except the attacker can obtain cipher texts encrypted under two different keys. This is actually a very useful attack if you can obtain the plain text and matching cipher text.

These are the basic approaches used to attack block ciphers. There are other methods that are beyond the scope of this book and that the CCFP won't mention, but I will give you a brief overview here.

Differential Cryptanalysis

Differential cryptanalysis is a form of cryptanalysis applicable to symmetric key algorithms. This was invented by Eli Biham and Adi Shamir. Essentially, it is the examination of differences in an input and how that affects the resultant difference in the output. It originally worked only with chosen plain text. There is a pretty good tutorial on this method at www.theamazingking.com/crypto-diff.php.

Linear Cryptanalysis

Linear cryptanalysis is based on finding affine approximations to the action of a cipher. Note that an affine function is a specific mathematical function that uses some linear function and some constant. The details on the mathematics are beyond the scope of this book. It is commonly used on block ciphers. This technique was invented by Mitsuru Matsui. It is a known plain text attack and uses a linear approximation to describe the behavior of the block cipher. Given enough pairs of plain text and corresponding cipher text, bits of information about the key can be obtained. Obviously, the more pairs of plain text and cipher text one has, the greater the chance of success. There is a pretty good tutorial on this method at http://www.theamazing king.com/crypto-linear.php.

Log Tampering

In addition to technically advanced techniques such as steganography and cryptography, there are simpler methods for an attacker to hide their tracks. The most obvious is log tampering. In any system that an attacker is interacting with, there is likely to be some logging of events. These will leave evidence of the attack. The savvy attacker will want to eliminate such evidence.

Log Deletion

One can easily delete any log, in Windows or in Linux. However, it will then be obvious that someone tampered with the logs. If you are examining the logs for a database server and see that all log entries prior to 2:30 A.M. are gone, that is a good indication that someone deleted the log. You may not know what they did, since the log is now gone, but you will know something happened.

Auditpol

This is a Windows tool[2] that is a bit more subtle. It will allow the attacker to turn off auditing, do whatever they intend to do, then turn auditing back on again. However, a savvy forensic analyst can still find evidence that this was done. If you see a server log that has entries approximately every 2 minutes, but there is a gap of 15 minutes with no entries, that could indicate someone used Auditpol.

Winzapper

This tool[3] is the attacker's friend. It allows the attacker to simply delete, or zap, specific log entries. It is difficult, if not impossible, to detect. You need to have local administrator privileges to use Winzapper.

Other Techniques

There are a variety of techniques an attacker can use to hide his or her tracks. Some of these involve masking or removing evidence that a crime has occurred; others involve making it difficult to track the criminal.

Onion Routing

Onion routing was originally developed by the U.S. Department of the Navy. The concept is this: Each packet is encrypted and a header is put on it. That header has the destination address of the next onion router in the network and the source address of the next onion router in the network. At each router, the packet is decrypted, but only showing the next "hop" in the destination. Until the final destination is reached, the packet is not fully decrypted. This means that if the packet is intercepted en route, you cannot tell its origin or ultimate destination. You can see this in Figure 7-12.

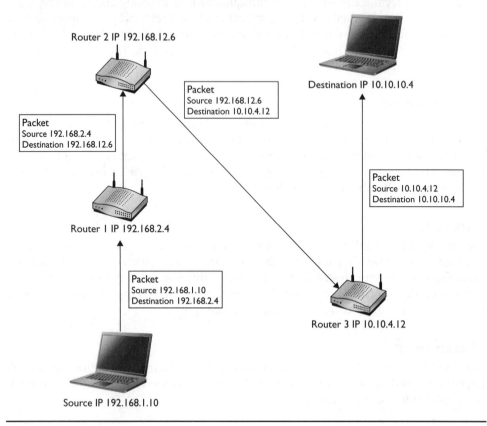

Router 2 IP 192.168.12.6

Packet
Source 192.168.12.6
Destination 10.10.4.12

Destination IP 10.10.10.4

Packet
Source 192.168.2.4
Destination 192.168.12.6

Packet
Source 10.10.4.12
Destination 10.10.10.4

Router 1 IP 192.168.2.4

Packet
Source 192.168.1.10
Destination 192.168.2.4

Router 3 IP 10.10.4.12

Source IP 192.168.1.10

Figure 7-12   Onion routing

The concept has been modified by civilians into what are called Tor networks. A Tor network uses a series of servers, each functioning like an onion router.

Spoofing

When a criminal is remotely accessing the victim, they frequently don't want to be traced to their actual computer. There are two primary ways to prevent this. The first is IP spoofing, which mean simply using a different IP address. There are tools to do this, and it can be done manually.

Another technique is MAC spoofing. The MAC address of a network card is set at the factory and cannot be changed. But you can trick your machine into broadcasting a different MAC address than the one actually on the network card. Techniques like this are difficult for a forensic analysis to counter.

Wiping

The ultimate in evidence hiding is to wipe the drive. As we mentioned previously in this book, the U.S. Department of Defense recommends overwriting data seven times to truly wipe it. So there is a good chance that a criminal who simply formatted a drive has still left some evidence. However, a technically skilled criminal might employ methods that are more thorough:

- **dd**   If you recall from earlier chapters, the Linux command dd can be used to truly forensically wipe a drive.

- **Degaussing**   Recall that a hard drive stores data magnetically. Thus, exposing a hard drive to a strong magnetic force can permanently wipe the data.

Tunneling

Another technique that can be used to hide data is tunneling. Tunneling is the process of encrypting network traffic. This is done for many legitimate reasons. For example, when you log in to your bank account online, the traffic is encrypted. When you connect to your workplace network from a remote site, the traffic is encrypted. Sometimes attackers will use a VPN (Virtual Private Network) to encrypt their traffic to keep it from being analyzed by packet sniffers, intrusion detection systems, or other security measures.

Chapter Review

In this chapter we have examined a variety of ways that one can hide evidence. These antiforensic techniques are likely to be employed by technically skilled criminals. For the CCFP exam, the most important ciphers to know are Caesar, Vigenere, DES, AES, Blowfish, RSA, and Diffie-Hellman. The concepts of hashing and rainbow tables are also important. If you would like to learn more about cryptography, steganography, and hashing, visit www.CryptoCorner.com.

We also discussed steganography and even used a widely available tool to hide data in an image. Remember the most common modern steganographic technique is the LSB method. Also keep in mind that there are a variety of ways an attacker can tamper with logs or simply wipe the drive of all evidence on it.

Questions

1. Which of the following is the oldest known encryption method?

   A. PGP

   B. Multialphabet

   C. Caesar cipher

   D. Cryptic cipher

PART III

2. What type of encryption uses a different key to encrypt the message than it uses to decrypt the message?

   A. Private key

   B. Asymmetric

   C. Symmetric

   D. Secure

3. Which of the following encryption algorithms uses three key ciphers in a block system and uses the Rijndael algorithm?

   A. DES

   B. RSA

   C. AES

   D. NSA

4. The most common way steganography is accomplished is via _____.

   A. MSB

   B. ASB

   C. RSB

   D. LSB

5. Hiding data in sound files is called _____.

   A. Steganography

   B. Steganohiding

   C. Cryptography

   D. Steganophony

Answers

1. C. The Caesar cipher is the oldest known cipher and is purported to have been used by Julius Caesar.

2. B. Asymmetric or public key cryptography uses two different keys. RSA is the most widely used asymmetric cipher today.

3. C. AES uses 128-, 192-, and 256-bit keys.

4. D. The most common way to hide data is called least significant bit (LSB).

5. D. Steganophony is essentially steganography done with sound files.

References

1. http://en.wikipedia.org/wiki/RSA_(cryptosystem).

2. http://technet.microsoft.com/en-us/library/cc731451.aspx.

3. http://ntsecurity.nu/toolbox/winzapper/.

Network Forensics

In this chapter you will learn to:
- Understand network traffic and packets
- Capture and analyze traffic
- Analyze web traffic

A great many cybercrimes occur over networks and often the Internet. Viruses, spyware, and Trojan horses are frequently spread over networks. Crimes such as denial of service (DoS) attacks and cyber stalking depend almost exclusively on network communications. There are other examples, ranging from someone hacking into a database to cyber terrorism. Clearly, network forensics is critical. In this chapter, you will learn the basics of network forensics.

Network Packet Analysis

The first, most fundamental thing to learn about network forensics is packet analysis. If you don't understand network packets and how to analyze them, you won't be effective at network forensics.

What Is a Packet?

You are aware, I am sure, that data is ultimately represented in a computer by 1's and 0's, then sent over some wire as voltages that represent 1's and 0's. When data is sent, it is divided into chunks, called packets. In addition to the data carried in a packet, the packet must have the following three things:

- Some information to route the packet to its destination.
- Some boundaries—where does the packet begin and end
- Some means to detect errors in transmission

Packets are divided into three sections: header, data, and footer. The header will contain information about how to address the packet (i.e., where it is going). The data portion is obviously the information you want to send. The footer serves both to show where the packet ends and to provide error detection.

There are many different types of packets. One major way to distinguish between them is packets that have a fixed length size and those that don't. Fixed-length-size packets are often called cells or frames. An example is Asynchronous Transfer Mode (ATM), a high-speed connection technology that uses fixed-length, 53-byte packets called cells. These still have a header, a data portion, and a footer.

While these terms get used interchangeably, there actually are technical definitions. Anything sent at layer 2 of the Open Systems Interconnection (OSI) model is called a frame. Anything at layer 4 is called a segment or datagram. Packet is a general term that can apply to any of them.

In practice, datagram usually denotes a packet sent using an unreliable, or "connectionless," protocol. Reliable, or "connection-oriented," protocols verify that each packet is received. Unreliable protocols simply make a connection and then start sending packets, hoping they all arrive at the destination. This may seem a bit odd, but consider that it takes significant bandwidth to verify each packet is received. With high-bandwidth applications, such as video, this would be a problem. Also keep in mind that with video transmission or audio, a single lost packet from time to time will not be noticeable to the user. Contrast that to e-mail, for example. E-mail does not use a lot of bandwidth. A single lost packet (or even a single lost word) could change the entire message. In general, reliable protocols are used when every single packet must be received.

 NOTE The terms reliable and unreliable are far more accurate and widely used today. But in the past, the terms connection oriented and connectionless were used, so they are included here.

Packet Header

The first place to begin is the packet header. This is a great place to start gathering forensic information. For example, where the packet came from, what protocol it was, and other useful information can be found in a header. There can actually be three headers. In normal communications, there is usually an Ethernet header, a TCP header, and an IP header. Each contains different information. Combined, they have several pieces of information that will be interesting to forensic investigations.

Let's begin with the TCP header. It contains information related to the transport layer of the OSI model. It will contain the source and destination port for communications. It will also have the packet number, such as packet 10 of 21. It will also have control bits that are used to establish, reset, and terminate communications. The most common control bits are

- **URG (1 bit)** Packet is marked as urgent.
- **ACK (1 bit)** Acknowledges the attempt to synchronize communications.
- **RST (1 bit)** This is used when something goes wrong and the connection must be reset.
- **SYN (1 bit)** Synchronizes sequence numbers. Only the first packet sent from each end should have this flag set. Some other flags change meaning

based on this flag, and some are only valid for when it is set, and others when it is clear.

- **FIN (1 bit)** The communication is done and the connection can be dropped.

A detailed diagram of the TCP header is given in Figure 8-1.

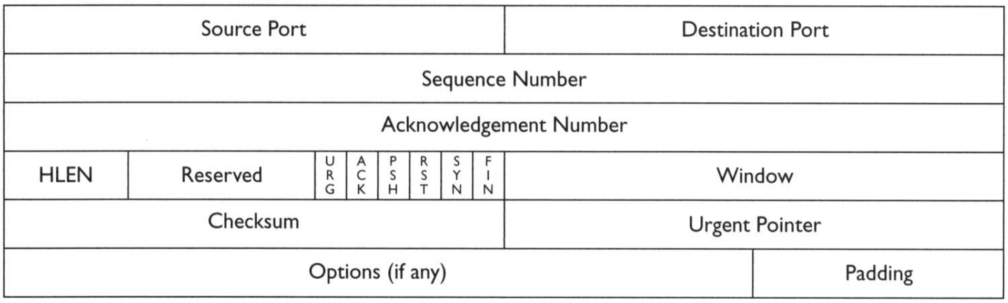

Source Port								Destination Port	
Sequence Number									
Acknowledgement Number									
HLEN	Reserved	URG	ACK	PSH	RST	SYN	FIN	Window	
Checksum								Urgent Pointer	
Options (if any)								Padding	

Figure 8-1 TCP header

The IP header usually gets the most attention. The most obvious useful pieces of information in it are source and destination addresses. The IP header has the source IP address, the destination IP address, and the protocol. It also has a version number, showing if this is a version 4.0 or 6.0 IP packet. The size variable describes how large the data segment is. Two other interesting fields are TTL, or time to live, and protocol. TTL is a field that tells the IP packets how many "hops" to go forward until giving up on reaching the destination. In other words, at what point should the packet give up hopping around the Internet before it reaches the destination. The protocol indicates what network protocol this packet is transmitting. In Chapter 1, we discussed several protocols. A comprehensive list of all 1024 well-known ports and protocols is beyond the scope of this book, but when you see traffic with a given protocol, it is important to find out what that protocol does. It can be very informative. A detailed diagram of the IP header is given in Figure 8-2.

Figure 8-2
IP header

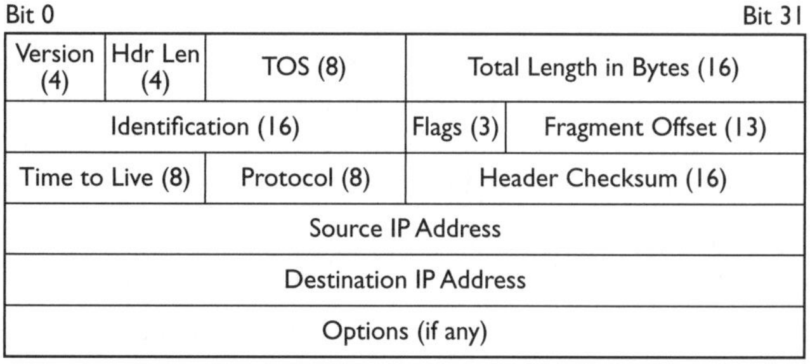

Version (4)	Hdr Len (4)	TOS (8)	Total Length in Bytes (16)	
Identification (16)			Flags (3)	Fragment Offset (13)
Time to Live (8)		Protocol (8)	Header Checksum (16)	
Source IP Address				
Destination IP Address				
Options (if any)				

Bit 0 … Bit 31

Basic Communications

A normal network conversation starts with one side sending a packet with the SYN bit turned on. The target responds with both SYN and ACK bits turned on. Then the sender responds with just the ACK bit turned on. Then communication commences. After a time, the original sender terminates the communication by sending a packet with the FIN bit turned on.

Some attacks depend on sending malformed packets. For example, with the common DoS attack, the SYN flood is based on flooding the target with SYN packets but never responding to the SYN/ACK that is sent back. Some session hijacking attacks use the RST command to help hijack communications.

The Ethernet header contains source and destination MAC addresses. Of course, a destination MAC address is only present if this is (1) traffic on a segment of the network using a single switch or (2) traffic that has reached the final network segment of its destination.

Payload

This is the actual data that is being transmitted. The importance of the payload is obvious. Of course, if traffic is encrypted, you may not be able to read the contents of the packet's data. However, as you have already seen, the header can be quite informative.

Trailer

The trailer, also referred to as the footer, first and foremost indicates the end of a packet. It usually also has error checking. The most common error checking used in packets is cyclic redundancy check (CRC). CRC is pretty neat. Here is how it works in certain computer networks: It takes the sum of all the 1's in the payload and adds them together. The result is stored as a hexadecimal value in the trailer. The receiving device adds up the 1's in the payload and compares the result to the value stored in the trailer. If the values match, the packet is good. But if the values do not match, the receiving device sends a request to the originating device to resend the packet.

Ports

You are probably already aware that a port is very much like a channel upon which communication can occur. We discussed ports in Chapter 1 and briefly mentioned them earlier in this chapter. Recall that ports are much like channels on TV that allow you to "tune in" to certain types of communication, such as port 80 for Hypertext Transfer Protocol, or web traffic. Let's first look at common ports and then discuss how this is forensically important.

- **20 and 21 - FTP (File Transfer Protocol)**   For transferring files between computers. Port 20 is for data, and port 21 is for control. FTP is about uploading or downloading files. You may be using a link on a web page to upload or download, but it is FTP doing the uploading or downloading.

- **22 - SSH and Secure FTP**   Basically, 22 is for either encrypted FTP or an encrypted protocol named Secure Shell (SSH) that is very much like Telnet.

- **23 - Telnet**   Used to remotely log on to a system. You can then use a command prompt or shell to execute commands on that system. Popular with network administrators. Unlike SSH, it is not encrypted.

- **25 - SMTP (Simple Mail Transfer Protocol)**   This protocol is used just to send e-mail.

- **43 - WhoIS**   A command that queries a target IP address for information.

- **53 - DNS (Domain Name Service)**   Translates URLs into IP addresses, or as many textbooks so colorfully put it: names to numbers.

- **69 - TFTP (Trivial FTP)**   Trivial FTP is just like FTP except it does not confirm packet delivery. Once a connection is made, it just sends the packet and hopes for the best. It also does not allow you to create new directories on the target.

- **80 - HTTP (Hypertext Transfer Protocol)**   This is used to communicate with a web server and to display websites.

- **88**   Authenticates to a Kerberos server.

- **110 - POP3 (Post Office Protocol Version 3)**   This protocol is used to retrieve e-mails.

- **137, 138, and 139 - NetBIOS**   NetBIOS was an older Microsoft network protocol. It is still used in tools like SAMBA that allow Linux machines to share data with Windows machines.

- **161 and 162 - SNMP (Simple Network Management Protocol)**   Simple Network Management Protocol is used to manage and administer networks.

- **179 - BGP (Border Gateway Protocol)**   Border Gateway Protocol is how gateway routers exchange routing information.

- **194 - IRC (Internet Relay Chat)**   Chat rooms.

- **220 - IMAP (Internet Message Access Protocol)**   Internet Message Access Protocol is a protocol for receiving e-mails and it is more advanced than POP3.

- **389 - LDAP (Lightweight Directory Access Protocol)**   Lightweight Directory Access Protocol is essentially a directory or phone book of everything on your network, including workstations, servers, and printers.

- **443 - HTTPS (Hypertext Transfer Protocol Secure)**   This is just HTTP encrypted with SSL (Secure Sockets Layer) or TLS (Transport Layer Security).

- **445 - Active Directory**   Windows, since Windows 2000 uses Active Directory.

- **464 - Kerberos change password**

- **465 - SMTP over SSL**   This is basically encrypted SMTP.

- **54320/54321 - B02K port**   Back Orifice 2K is a widely known back door program.

- **6666 - Beast port**   This is another piece of malware.

- **43188 - Reachout port**   This is a remote application program used by hackers to gain control of the target system.

- **407 - Timbuktu port**   Timbuktu is an open-source remote control program that works much like PC Anywhere or Windows Desktop. It is also popular with hackers who use it to take control of victims' systems.

- **3389 - Windows Remote Desktop**

It is not necessary that you memorize all of these ports and protocols, but it is important to be aware of the most critical ones. It is also important to know what ports/protocols represent a likely attack. For example, finding a back door program like Timbuktu on a computer should be significant to you.

Network Traffic Analysis

Analyzing network traffic is key. Once you have a working knowledge of network packets and protocols, you are ready to start analyzing packets. The place to start is with a packet sniffer. A packet sniffer is software that intercepts network traffic and allows you to view the packets. These are also sometimes referred to as network sniffers.

Network monitoring or analysis involves capturing network traffic. This begins with running some network packet sniffer in promiscuous mode. Promiscuous mode simply means that the network card looks at any packet that it sees on the network, even if that packet is not addressed to that network card.

Wireshark is one of the most common packet sniffers, so let's start with it. It is a free tool you can download from www.wireshark.org and is available for several operating systems. Perhaps one of the things I like most about it is how easy it is to use. The user simply selects an interface (network card) and then starts the process.

So first you select the network card you want to use, as shown in Figure 8-3.

Figure 8-3   Selecting a network card in Wireshark

Then you simply click Start. You can alternatively set the options for that network card and filter out some traffic. I recommend you capture all traffic and then just filter what you view. You will then see all the packets as shown in Figure 8-4.

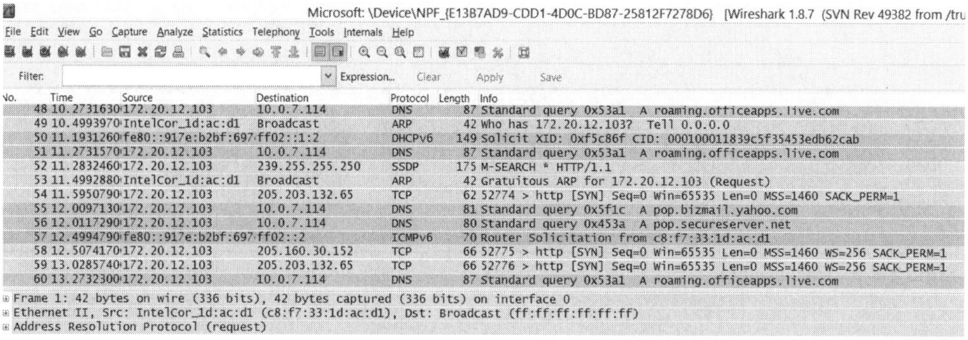
Microsoft: \Device\NPF_{E13B7AD9-CDD1-4D0C-BD87-25812F7278D6} [Wireshark 1.8.7 (SVN Rev 49382 from /tru
File Edit View Go Capture Analyze Statistics Telephony Tools Internals Help
Filter: Expression... Clear Apply Save
No. Time Source Destination Protocol Length Info
48 10.2731630 172.20.12.103 10.0.7.114 DNS 87 Standard query 0x53a1 A roaming.officeapps.live.com
49 10.4993970 IntelCor_1d:ac:d1 Broadcast ARP 42 Who has 172.20.12.103? Tell 0.0.0.0
50 11.1931260 fe80::917e:b2bf:697 ff02::1:2 DHCPv6 149 Solicit XID: 0xf5c86f CID: 000100011839c5f35453edb62cab
51 11.2731570 172.20.12.103 10.0.7.114 DNS 87 Standard query 0x53a1 A roaming.officeapps.live.com
52 11.2832460 172.20.12.103 239.255.255.250 SSDP 175 M-SEARCH * HTTP/1.1
53 11.4992880 IntelCor_1d:ac:d1 Broadcast ARP 42 Gratuitous ARP for 172.20.12.103 (Request)
54 11.5950790 172.20.12.103 205.203.132.65 TCP 62 52774 > http [SYN] Seq=0 Win=65535 Len=0 MSS=1460 SACK_PERM=1
55 12.0097130 172.20.12.103 10.0.7.114 DNS 81 Standard query 0x5f1c A pop.bizmail.yahoo.com
56 12.0117290 172.20.12.103 10.0.7.114 DNS 80 Standard query 0x453a A pop.secureserver.net
57 12.4994790 fe80::917e:b2bf:697 ff02::2 ICMPv6 70 Router Solicitation from c8:f7:33:1d:ac:d1
58 12.5074170 172.20.12.103 205.160.30.152 TCP 66 52775 > http [SYN] Seq=0 Win=65535 Len=0 MSS=1460 WS=256 SACK_PERM=1
59 13.0285740 172.20.12.103 205.203.132.65 TCP 66 52776 > http [SYN] Seq=0 Win=65535 Len=0 MSS=1460 WS=256 SACK_PERM=1
60 13.2732300 172.20.12.103 10.0.7.114 DNS 87 Standard query 0x53a1 A roaming.officeapps.live.com
Frame 1: 42 bytes on wire (336 bits), 42 bytes captured (336 bits) on interface 0
Ethernet II, Src: IntelCor_1d:ac:d1 (c8:f7:33:1d:ac:d1), Dst: Broadcast (ff:ff:ff:ff:ff:ff)
Address Resolution Protocol (request)

Figure 8-4 Viewing packets

As you can see, for each packet, you can view the source address, destination address, and the protocol used. This is shown in Figure 8-5.

Figure 8-5 Packet address and protocol

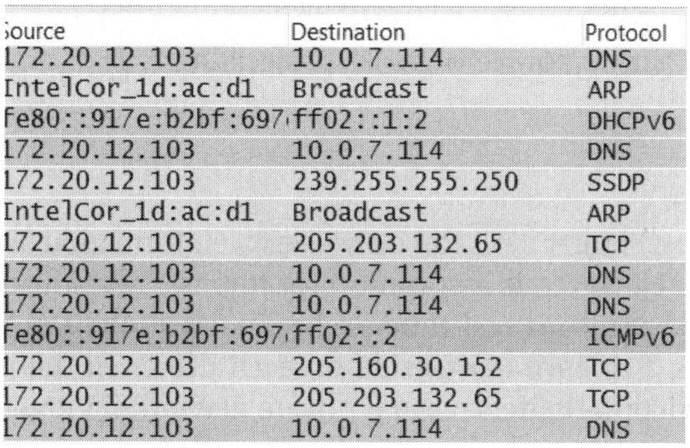
Source Destination Protocol
172.20.12.103 10.0.7.114 DNS
IntelCor_1d:ac:d1 Broadcast ARP
fe80::917e:b2bf:697 ff02::1:2 DHCPv6
172.20.12.103 10.0.7.114 DNS
172.20.12.103 239.255.255.250 SSDP
IntelCor_1d:ac:d1 Broadcast ARP
172.20.12.103 205.203.132.65 TCP
172.20.12.103 10.0.7.114 DNS
172.20.12.103 10.0.7.114 DNS
fe80::917e:b2bf:697 ff02::2 ICMPv6
172.20.12.103 205.160.30.152 TCP
172.20.12.103 205.203.132.65 TCP
172.20.12.103 10.0.7.114 DNS

If you double-click a packet, you can see both the data content and the header, as shown in Figure 8-6. Notice that all three packet headers are shown, including the TCP, IP, and Ethernet headers mentioned earlier in this chapter.

With almost no study, it is easy to get useful information from Wireshark. We have examined some basic information here. There are also tutorials on the Internet; a few are included here:

- http://www.wireshark.org/docs/wsug_html_chunked/
- https://www.youtube.com/watch?v=Lu05owzpSb8
- http://cs.gmu.edu/~astavrou/courses/ISA_674_F12/Wireshark-Tutorial.pdf

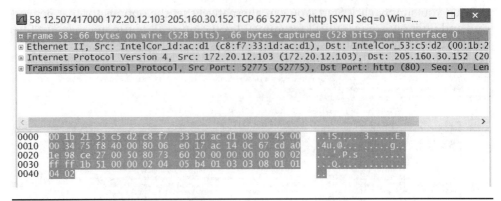

Figure 8-6   Packet details

The following are some other popular tools for network analysis:

- NetIntercept (http://www.sandstorm.net/products/netintercept/)
- CommView (http://www.tamos.com/products/commview/)
- Softperfect Network Protocol Analyzer (http://www.softperfect.com)
- HTTP Sniffer (http://www.effetech.com/sniffer/)
- ngrep (http://sourceforge.net/projects/ngrep/)

Log Files

Wireshark and similar tools can only give you information about things that are occurring in real time. However, it is common for forensic investigations to take place long after the attack. That means real-time packet analysis might not be possible. It is then time to view logs. Evidence may reside on each device in the path from the attacking system to the victim. Routers, virtual private networks (VPNs), and other devices produce logs. Network security devices, such as firewalls and intrusion detection systems (IDSs), also generate logs. An IDS is software that automates the process of monitoring events occurring in a computer system or network and analyzing them for signs of possible incidents and attempting to stop them.

A device's log files contain the primary records of a person's activities on a system or network. For example, authentication logs show accounts related to a particular event and the authenticated user's IP address. They contain date and timestamps, as well as the username and IP address of the request. Application logs record the time, date, and application identifier. When someone uses an application, it produces a text file on the desktop system containing the application identifier, the date and time the user started the application, and how long that person used the application.

Operating systems log certain events, such as the use of devices, errors, and reboots. You can analyze operating system logs to identify patterns of activity and unusual events.

Network device logs, such as firewall and router logs, provide information about the activities that take place on the network. You can also use them to support logs provided by other systems.

Examine log files to discover attacks. For example, a firewall log may show access attempts that the firewall blocked. These attempts may indicate an attack. Log files can show how an attacker entered a network. They can also help find the source of illicit activities. For example, log files from servers and Windows security event logs on domain controllers can attribute activities to a specific user account. This may lead you to the person responsible.

IDSs record events that match known attack signatures, such as buffer overflows or malicious code execution. Configure an IDS to capture all network traffic associated with a specific event. In this way, you can discover what commands an attacker ran and what files he or she accessed. You can also determine what files the criminal uploaded, such as malicious code.

You bump into a few problems when using log files, however. One is that logs change rapidly, and getting permission to collect evidence from some sources, such as Internet service providers (ISPs), takes time. In addition, volatile evidence is easily lost. Finally, hackers can easily alter logs to include false information.

Web Traffic

Many attacks are based on websites. For example, SQL injection is a common attack on websites. Other attacks include cross-site scripting. Let's look at some of these attacks and how to analyze them.

SQL Injection

SQL (Structured Query Language) is the language used for communicating with relational databases. It is a relatively simple-to-understand query language with terms that look like basic English, such as SELECT, UPDATE, WHERE, INSERT, etc.

EXAM TIP   The CCFP exam will ask you in a general way what SQL injection is, but it will not go into the level of detail provided in this section. I am providing extra detail because this is a very common attack and you should be intimately familiar with it so you can effectively investigate such crimes.

SQL injection works by the user entering an SQL statement rather than the text the website asked you to enter. There are a number of variations on this attack, but the most common is to enter an SQL statement into the username and password text fields of a login screen such that the SQL statement is always true.

SQL is used to communicate with a database, so it is common to have SQL statements executed when someone clicks a logon button. For example, the SQL statements take the username and password entered and query the database to see if they are correct. The problem begins with the way websites are written. They are written in some scripting, markup, or programming language such as HTML, PHP (Hypertext Preprocessor), ASP (Active Server Pages), etc. These languages don't understand SQL, so the SQL is usually put in a string and whatever the user inputs in the username and password boxes is appended to the string. Here is an example:

```
"SELECT * FROM tblUSERS WHERE UserName ='" + txtUserName + "'"AND Password =
'"+password +"'"
```

Notice the single quotes are inserted into the text so that whatever the user types into the username and password text fields is enclosed in quotes within the SQL query string, like this:

```
SELECT * FROM tblUSERS WHERE UserName ='admin' AND Password = 'password'';
```

The most basic version of SQL injection involves the attacker putting an SQL statement that is always true into the username and password fields, like this:

```
' or '1' ='1
```

This results in an SQL query like this:

```
'SELECT * FROM tblUSERS WHERE UserName ='' or '1' ='1' AND Password = '' or
'1' ='1''
```

So now it says to get all entries from table = tblUsers if the username is " (blank) OR IF 1 =1. And if password = " (blank) OR IF 1=1! And since 1 always equals 1, the user is logged in. Now the 1=1 is just one possible true statement; there are a great many others—for example, a=a, 7=7, etc.

This basic introduction to the simplest form of SQL injection is as far as some sources go. But given that you will likely have to investigate attacks such as this, we will delve a bit deeper.

Once the attacker has been able to log in using SQL injection, he or she may wish to enumerate the other accounts. Let's assume the user name that the attacker logged in as was jsmith. The following would provide the attacker with the next user:

```
' or '1' ='1 and username <> 'jsmith
```

or try

```
' or '1' ='1 and not username = 'jsmith
```

Obviously, "username" may not be a name of a column in that database. The attacker might have to try various permutations to get one that works—for example, user_name, u_name, etc. Also, remember that Microsoft Access and SQL Server allow multiword column names with brackets (i.e., [User name]) but MySQL and PostGres do not accept brackets.

The real disconcerting issue with SQL injection is that there are far more damaging things the attacker can do other than just log in. For example, something like this entered

```
x'; DROP TABLE members; --
```

rather than ' or '1' ='1 deletes the entire table!

Or perhaps the attacker would like the server to e-mail you the password. Many database servers have built-in e-mail addresses:

```
x'; UPDATE members SET email = 'me@somewhere.net' WHERE email = 'somebody@
example.com
```

As you can see, SQL injection is a very powerful tool for hackers. The only limitations on the attacker are

- The attacker's knowledge of SQL
- The attacker's knowledge of the various databases
- The attacker's patience

If the attacker is patient and has a good knowledge of SQL and of various major database systems, then if the site is vulnerable to SQL injection, the attacker will have a wide range of things that he or she can do.

As a forensic examiner, you will need to search the logs (database, web server, and firewall) for evidence of SQL injection. The most obvious evidence would be seeing `' or '1' = '1` logged as a command sent from the client's computer to the server.

 NOTE The way to defend against this attack is to always filter input. That means the website code should check to see if certain characters are in the text fields and, if so, to reject that input. For example, a programmer could write a simple function to read through all the characters typed into a text field and reject the input if it contains common SQL injection characters.

Parameter Tampering

Parameter tampering is a form of web-based hacking in which certain parameters in a URL are changed. This is often done to alter the behavior of a web application. You may not have noticed, but some websites store information in the URL. Some will put in the session ID, user name, or even account number. By altering those fields, an attacker may be able to login as a different person.

Cross-Site Scripting

In this attack, the perpetrator finds some place on a website where users can interact with each other. A product review section is a good example of such a location. Rather than put a comment into the input text field, the attacker types in some script, such as JavaScript. The next time a user visits that section of the website, the script is executed. That script can be anything the attacker wants. It might redirect the user to a phishing site, prompt the user for information, or read the user's browsing history.

All of these web attacks will show up in logs you can review. For example, the web server log or even the firewall log could show the actual commands the user typed, thus providing evidence of the attack.

HTTP Sniffer

This product is easy to use, much like Wireshark, and it has a free trial version. It is used specifically to capture web traffic. You can think of it as a packet sniffer that details the HTTP protocol. You can see all the HTTP commands going to the server and the responses from the server. It is shown in Figure 8-7. Note that the actual address of the website being analyzed has been redacted.

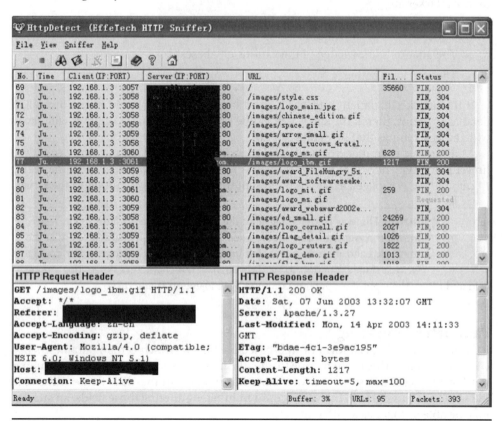

Figure 8-7 HTTP Sniffer

Web Traffic

To really analyze web traffic, regardless of the tool used, you will need to have a good understanding of how web traffic works. In this section, we will explore the basics of web communication.

Web traffic uses HTTP. That protocol normally operates on port 80. The primary means of communication is via messages. Table 8-1 gives you a summary of the basic HTTP messages a web page might send.

The most common messages are GET, HEAD, PUT, and POST. In fact, you might see only those four during most of your analysis of web traffic. LINK and UNLINK are a lot

Table 8-1	GET	Request to read a web page
HTTP Commands	HEAD	Request to read a web page
	PUT	Request to write a web page
	POST	Request to append to a page
	DELETE	Remove the web page
	LINK	Connects two existing resources
	UNLINK	Breaks an existing connection between two resources

less common. You should know that the GET command actually is the server getting information, so it is very much like the POST command. The differences between the two are

- GET requests can be cached. POST requests are never cached.
- GET requests remain in the browser history. POST requests do not remain in the browser history.
- GET requests can be bookmarked. POST requests cannot be bookmarked.
- GET requests should never be used when dealing with sensitive data.
- GET requests have length restrictions. POST requests have no restrictions on data length.

The response codes are just as important. You have probably seen Error 404 File Not Found. But you may not be aware that there are a host of messages going back and forth, most of which you don't see. The messages are shown in Table 8-2.

Message Range	Meaning
100–199	These are just informational. The server is telling your browser some information, most of which will never be displayed to the user. For example, when you switch from HTTP to HTTPS, a 101 message goes to the browser telling it that the protocol is changing.
200–299	These are basically "okay" messages, meaning that whatever the browser requested, the server successfully processed. Your basic HTTP messages like POST, GET, HEAD, etc., should, if everything is working properly, get a 200 code in response.
300–399	These are redirect messages telling the browser to go to another URL. For example, 301 means that the requested resource has permanently moved to a new URL; message code 307 indicates the move is temporary.
400–499	These are client errors, and the ones most often shown to the end user. This might seem odd since, for example, 403 File Not Found means that the server could not find the file you asked for. However, the issue is that the server functioned properly, just that file does not exist. Therefore, the client request was in error.
500–599	These are server-side errors. For example, 503 means the service requested is down, possibly overloaded. You will see this error frequently in DoS attacks.

Table 8-2 HTTP Response Messages

These error messages can be important for forensics. Some of the reasons are shown in the table. For example, multiple 503 errors could indicate a DoS attack. Error code 305 is also forensically interesting. It states that the requested source is only available via a proxy. That gives information about the architecture of that web server. Message 407 is related, but it states that authentication with the proxy is required.

Nmap

Nmap may be the most popular port scanner available. I highly recommend it. Network administrators, and even hackers, use it to scan networks. However, it can be an invaluable tool in network forensics. If you suspect a backdoor has been installed on a given network, running Nmap on the range of IP addresses will tell you if a common backdoor port is operating (like 31337 for Back Orifice or 407 for Timbuktu). Nmap started as a command-line-only tool, but there is a free graphical version of it for Windows. This tool is shown in Figure 8-8.

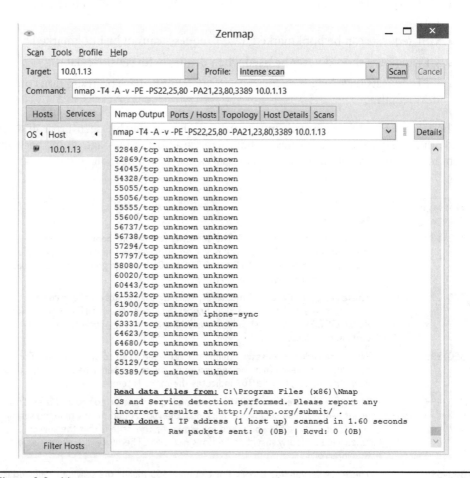

Figure 8-8   Nmap

While this is a graphical tool, it can be modified using flags. Note the flag window shown in Figure 8-9.

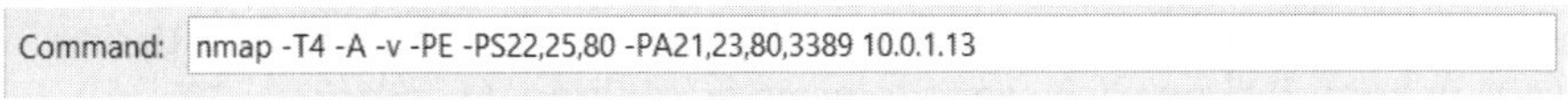

Command: `nmap -T4 -A -v -PE -PS22,25,80 -PA21,23,80,3389 10.0.1.13`

Figure 8-9 Nmap flag window

As you select options, the flags that alter Nmap's functionality are entered for you. There are many others you can enter yourself, if you wish.

Snort

Snort is primarily used as an open-source IDS, but it can also function as a robust packet sniffer with a lot of configuration options. For full installation instructions, visit www .snort.org. They also offer a free manual at www.snort.org/assets/82/snort_manual .pdf. For network analysis, you want to run Snort as a packet sniffer and configure it to log verbose data. It should be noted that while Snort has been ported to Windows, it was designed for Linux. It runs flawlessly in Linux, but requires some extensive configuration to run in Windows.

Snort works in one of three modes: sniffer, packet logger, and network intrusion-detection:

- **Sniffer** In packet sniffer mode, the console (shell or command prompt) displays a continuous stream of the contents of all packets coming across that machine. This can be a very useful tool for a network administrator. Finding out what traffic is traversing a network can be the best way to determine where potential problems lie. It is also a good way to check whether transmissions are encrypted.

- **Packet logger** Packet logger mode is similar to sniffer mode. The difference is that the packet contents are written to a text file log rather than displayed in the console. This can be more useful for administrators who are scanning a large number of packets for specific items. Once the data is in a text file, users can scan for specific information using a word processor's search capability.

- **Network intrusion-detection** In network intrusion-detection mode, Snort uses a heuristic approach to detecting anomalous traffic. This means it is rules based and it learns from experience. A set of rules initially governs a process. Over time, Snort combines what it finds with the settings to optimize performance. It then logs that traffic and can alert the network administrator. This mode requires the most configuration because the user can determine the rules she wishes to implement for the scanning of packets.

Snort works primarily from the command line (shell in Unix/Linux; command prompt in Windows). Configuring Snort is mostly a matter of knowing the correct commands to enter and understanding their output. Anyone with even moderate

PART III

experience with either Linux shell commands or DOS commands can quickly master the Snort configuration commands. Perhaps Snort's greatest advantage is its price: It is a free download. For any organization to not be using some IDS is inexcusable when a free product is available. Snort is a good tool when used in conjunction with host-based firewalls or as an IDS on each server to provide additional security.

Wireless

Wireless networks are everywhere. Just a few years ago, this was not the case. But now, not only can one find a wireless network in virtually any home, office, hotel, or coffee shop, but some newer cars are coming with WiFi. Chances are that at some point in your forensic career, you will investigate a crime involving WiFi. So let's begin by ensuring you have a good understanding of it:

- **802.11a** This was the first widely used WiFi standard. It operated at 5 GHz and was relatively slow.

- **802.11b** This standard operated at 2.4 GHz and had an indoor range of 125 ft with a bandwidth of 11 Mbps (megabits per second).

- **802.11g** There are still many of these wireless networks in operation, but you can no longer purchase new WiFi access points that use 802.11g. This standard includes backward compatibility with 802.11b. 802.11g has an indoor range of 125 ft feet and a bandwidth of 54 Mbps.

- **802.11n** This standard was a tremendous improvement over preceding wireless networks. It obtained a bandwidth of 100 to 140 Mbps. It operates at frequencies of 2.4 or 5.0 GHz and has an indoor range of up to 230 ft.

- **IEEE 802.11n-2009** This technology has a bandwidth of up to 600 Mbps with the use of four spatial streams at a channel width of 40 MHz. It uses multiple-input multiple-output (MIMO), which uses multiple antennas to coherently resolve more information than is possible using a single antenna.

It is not uncommon for a cybercriminal to attempt to infiltrate a target network via that network's wireless connection. Some attackers have a specific target in mind; others seek targets of opportunity. Basically, these attackers are looking for networks that appear as if they would be relatively easy to break into. There are two major ways to find such networks:

- **War driving** This means the attacker and a partner drive around scanning for networks. When they find a wireless network that has security that is weak enough they believe they can crack it, they part and start to crack that network.

- **War flying** This is fairly new. It basically is war driving done with a small model airplane, similar to military drone surveillance.

Several tools are available just for discovering wireless networks. Some of the more popular tools include

- NetStumbler (www.NetStumbler.com)
- MacStumbler (www.MacStumbler.com)
- iStumbler (www.iStumber.net)

There are even apps available for both iPhone and Android that can scan for wireless networks. So WiFi scanning can be accomplished with relative ease. If a hacker discovers a poorly secured wireless network, one thing he may try is to access the wireless access point's administrative screen. Unfortunately, too many people turn on these devices and don't think to change the default settings. There are websites that store default passwords that anyone can look up. One very popular website is www .routerpasswords.com.

Network-Related Cybercrimes

Certain computer attacks actually strike at the network itself rather than a specific machine. Even if they are targeting a given machine, the impact of the attack may be felt throughout the network. A few of those attacks are discussed here.

Denial of Service

This is the classic example of a network attack. A DoS attack can be targeted at a given server, but usually, the increased traffic will affect the rest of the target network. In a DoS attack, the attacker uses one of three approaches. The attacker can damage the router's ability to operate, overflow the router with too many open connections at the same time, or use up the bandwidth of the router's network. In a DoS attack, the attacker usually floods the network with malicious packets, preventing legitimate network traffic from passing. The following sections discuss specific types of DoS attacks.

Ping of Death Attack   In a ping of death attack, an attacker sends an Internet Control Message Protocol (ICMP) echo packet of a larger size than the IP protocol can accept. At one time, this form of attack caused many operating systems to lock or crash, until vendors released patches to deal with the ping attacks. Firewalls can be configured to block incoming ICMP packets.

Related to the ping of death is the ping flood. The ping flood simply sends a tremendous number of ICMP packets to the target, hoping to overwhelm it. This attack is ineffective against modern servers. It is just not possible to overwhelm a server, or even most workstations, with enough pings to render the target unresponsive.

Teardrop Attack   In a teardrop attack, the attacker sends fragments of packets with bad values in them that cause the target system to crash when it tries to reassemble the fragments. Like the ping of death attack, the teardrop attack has been around long enough for vendors to have released patches to avoid it.

SYN Flood Attacks   In a SYN flood attack, the attacker sends unlimited SYN packets to the host system. The SYN packets, which are requests to initiate communication, are supposed to be responded to by the client. Essentially, the client sends the server a packet with the SYN bit turned on. The server sets up some resources to handle the connection and responds to the client with both the SYN and ACK bits turned on, acknowledging the synchronization request. The client is supposed to respond with a packet that has the ACK bit turned on. In this attack, the client just floods the server with SYN packets, never responding. This can overwhelm the target system with phantom connection requests and render it unable to respond to legitimate requests.

Most modern firewalls can block this attack. This is because most modern firewalls look at the entire "conversation" between client and server, not just each individual packet. They can recognize that while a single packet with the SYN bit turned on from a specific client is normal traffic, 10,000 such packets in under five minutes is not, and will be blocked.

Smurf Attacks   A smurf attack generates a large number of ICMP echo requests from a single request, acting like an amplifier. This causes a traffic jam in the target network. Worse still, if the routing device on the target network accepts the requests, hosts on that network will reply to each echo, increasing the traffic jam.

These are a few ways an attacker can execute a DoS attack. In analyzing such attacks, the first evidence will be in the logs of the firewall and the target server. Then you need to analyze the packets sent and see where they came from. Document as much information as you can about the offending network traffic.

Router Forensics

Using network forensics, you can determine the type of attack over a network. In some cases, you can also trace the path back to the attacker. A router is a hardware or software device that forwards data packets across a network to a destination network. The destination network could be multiple networks away. A router may contain read-only memory with power on self test code, flash memory containing the router's operating system, nonvolatile random access memory (RAM) containing configuration information, volatile RAM containing the routing tables, and log information.

Router Basics

The basic networking hardware devices are

- Network card
- Hub
- Switch
- Router

A network interface card (NIC) is an expansion board you insert into a computer so the computer can be connected to a network. A NIC handles many things:

- Signal encoding and decoding
- Data buffering and transmission
- Media access control
- Data encapsulation (building the frame around the data)

These are relatively simple devices, and they don't store information that you can examine.

A hub is used to connect computers on an Ethernet network. A hub does not do anything to see that packets get to their proper destination. Instead, the hub will take any packet it receives and simply send a copy out every port it has. This is based on the theory that the packet is going somewhere, so it should be sent out all available avenues. This causes a lot of excess network traffic, however, and hubs are no longer used.

A switch prevents traffic jams by ensuring that data goes straight from its origin to its proper destination, with no wandering in between. It remembers the address of every node on the network and anticipates where data needs to go. A switch only operates with the computers on the same local area network (LAN). That is because a switch operates based on the MAC address in a packet, and that is not routable. It cannot send data out to the Internet or across a wide area network (WAN). These functions require a router.

A router is similar to a switch, but it can also connect different logical networks or subnets and enable traffic that is destined for the networks on the other side of the router to pass through. Routers can connect networks that use dissimilar protocols. They also typically provide improved security functions over a switch. Routers utilize the IP address, which is routable, to determine the path of outgoing packets. They work at the network layer of the OSI model.

The routers determine where to send information from one computer to another. In a sense, routers are specialized computers that send your messages and those of every other Internet user speeding to their destinations along thousands of pathways. Routers maintain a routing table to keep track of routes—which connections are to be used for different networks. Some of these routes are programmed in manually, but the router "learns" many of them automatically. This is done by examining incoming packets, and if one comes from an IP address the router has not seen before, it adds that address to its routing table. Modern routers also inform each other about both new routes and those that are no longer working to make this as efficient as possible.

Modern routers are complex devices. They handle packets, often have firewall and Dynamic Host Configuration Protocol (DHCP) capabilities, are programmable, and maintain logs. The gold standard in routers is Cisco, and it is worthwhile to become familiar with at least the basics of working with a Cisco router.

For a good overview of Cisco routers, this document will be a great help to you: http://www.cisco.com/c/en/us/td/docs/switches/datacenter/sw/5_x/nx-os/unicast/configuration/guide/l3_cli_nxos/l3_overview.html.

PART III

Types of Router Attacks

Routers can be vulnerable to several types of attacks, including router table poisoning. This is one of the most common and effective attacks. To carry out this type of attack, an attacker alters the routing data update packets that the routing protocols need. This results in incorrect entries in the routing table. This, in turn, can result in artificial congestion, overwhelm the router, and allow an attacker access to data in the compromised network.

Getting Evidence from the Router

Network crimes will obviously involve network routers. And even if the network router is not the actual target of the crime, it will be an intermediary device between the attacker and the target. However, in some cases, the router is used to help perform the attack. The previously mentioned smurf attack is a good example of this.

Getting evidence from a router is quite different from getting evidence from a PC, laptop, or server. The first major difference is that with a router, you do not shut down the device and image it. The reason is that once you shut it down, you will have potentially lost valuable evidence. For this reason, router forensics requires a great deal of care. You absolutely must make certain that you are careful not to alter anything, and you must be meticulous in documenting your process.

The first step is to connect with the router so you can run certain commands. Hyper-Terminal is a free tool that can be used to connect to and interact with your routers. Since this is a live router, it is important to record everything you do. Fortunately, Hyper-Terminal makes this easy. You can see HyperTerminal in Figure 8-10.

Figure 8-10   HyperTerminal

Several commands are important to router forensics. The most important and commonly used commands are described here:

- The show version command provides a significant amount of hardware and software about the router. It will display the platform, operating system version, system image file, any interfaces, how much RAM the router has, and how many network and voice interfaces.

- The show running-config command will show you the currently executing configuration.

- The showstartup-config command will show you the system's startup configurations. Differences between startup config and running config can be indicative of a hacker having altered the system.

- The show ip route command will show the routing table. Manipulating that routing table is one primary reason hackers infiltrate routers.

These are a few commands you will probably find useful in your forensics examination. However, there are many others you may find useful, including

- show clock detail
- show version
- show running-config
- show startup-config
- show reload
- show ip route
- show ip arp
- show users
- show logging
- show ip interface
- show interfaces
- show tcp brief all
- show ip sockets
- show ip nat translations verbose
- show ip cache flow
- show ip cef
- show snmp user
- show snmp group

The release of version 11.2 of Cisco IOS (operating system) introduced the new command show tech-support. This has allowed for the collection of multiple sources of information concerning the router in a single command. This one command will output the same thing as running all of the following commands:

- show version
- show running-config
- show stacks
- show interface
- show controller
- show process cpu
- show process memory
- show buffers

Obviously, this is just an introduction to router forensics. Ideally, you will have a good working knowledge of routers, roughly equivalent to a Cisco Certified Network Associate. If you are not familiar with Cisco routers, it is best to get a colleague or outside consultant who is skilled in routers to perform the forensic analysis.

Firewall Forensics

Firewalls are the primary barrier between your network and the outside world. For this reason, virtually any intrusion from the outside will leave some trace in the firewall. A basic understanding of firewalls is essential for the forensic analyst.

Firewall Basics

Before you delve too deep into firewall forensics, you should ensure you have a basic, working understanding of them. There are several ways to categorize firewalls, but there are two that are more basic than the rest.

Packet Filter

This is the most basic type of firewall. It simply filters incoming packets and either allows or denies them entrance based on a set of rules that were put into its configuration. This is also referred to as a screened firewall. It can filter packets based on size, protocol used, source IP address, etc. Many routers offer this type of firewall option in addition to their normal routing functions.

Stateful Packet Inspection

The stateful packet inspection (SPI) firewall will examine each and every packet, denying or permitting based on not only the current packet, but also previous packets in the conversation. This means that the firewall is aware of the context in which a specific packet was sent. This makes these firewalls far less susceptible to ping floods and SYN floods, as well as being less susceptible to spoofing.

Earlier in this chapter, you learned a list of ports to be aware of. You should absolutely check the firewall logs for any sort of connections or attempted connections on those ports. You also learned about packet flags that might indicate a port scan. If your firewall logs such details, you will want to scan the log for any packets that might indicate a scan.

Using protocol analysis may help you determine who the attacker is. For example, you can ping each of the systems and match up the TTL fields in those responses with the connection attempts. The TTLs should match; if they don't, they are being spoofed by an attacker. One drawback is that scanners may randomize the attacker's own TTL, making it difficult to pinpoint the source.

What to Look For

Analyze the firewall logs in depth to look for signs of an attack. Different attacks will leave different evidence traces in the firewall log. Many DoS attacks will be obvious—a flood of packets from the same source IP address, the volume of which greatly exceeds normal network traffic.

Even a scan can be detected in the firewall logs. If you see a series of packets going through each of the ports in order, that is obviously a port scan. If you see a variety of packets coming through the firewall from the same source IP address but with varying TTL values, that is called firewalking. Someone is basically lobbing packets past your firewall at different "distances" to see how your network responds. This is a popular type of scan with skilled hackers.

Logs to Examine

Operating systems, IDSs, servers, and many other devices have logs. It is important to check these logs for possible forensic evidence. Obviously, we cannot cover every known log in the space of this small section, but we can cover some basic logs you should be aware of.

Windows Logs

Let's start with Windows 7/8/2008/2012. With all of these versions of Windows, you find the logs by clicking the Start button in the lower-left corner of the desktop and then clicking the Control Panel. You then will click Administrative Tools and the Event Viewer. Here are the logs you would check for (note that not all appear in every version of Windows):

 NOTE With all of these, you have to turn the logging on; otherwise, there will be nothing in these logs.

- **Security log**   This is probably the most important log from a forensics point of view. It has both successful and unsuccessful login events.

- **Application log**   This log contains various events logged by applications or programs. Many applications will record their errors here in the application log.

- **System log**   The System log contains events logged by Windows system components. This includes events like driver failures. This particular log is not as interesting from a forensics perspective as the other logs are.

- **ForwardedEvents log**   The ForwardedEvents log is used to store events collected from remote computers. This will only have data in it if event forwarding has been configured.

- **Applications and Services log**   This log is used to store events from a single application or component rather than events that might have system-wide impact.

The same logs can be found in both Windows client systems and Windows Server systems. It is also possible that the attacker cleared the logs before leaving the system. There are tools that will allow one to wipe out a log. It is also possible to simply turn off logging before an attack and turn it back on when you are done. One such tool is auditpol.exe. Using `auditpol \\ipaddress /disable` turns off logging. Then, when the criminal exits, they can use `auditpol \\ipaddress /enable` to turn it back on. There are also tools like WinZapper that allow one to selectively remove certain items from event logs in Windows. WinZapper is shown in Figure 8-11.[2]

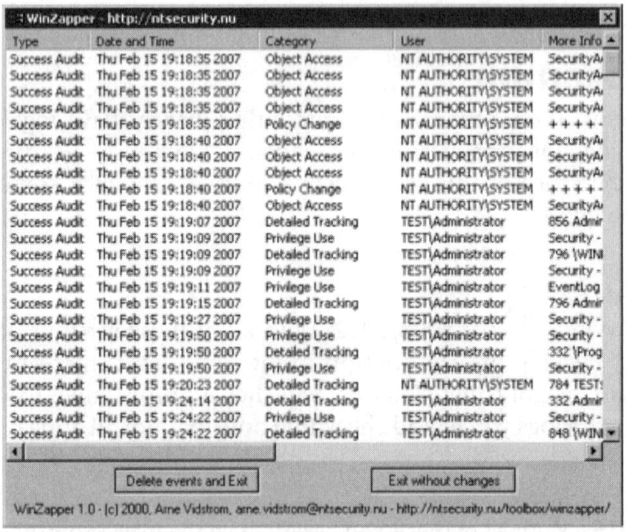

Figure 8-11   WinZapper

Linux Logs

Obviously, Linux also has logs you can check. Depending on your Linux distribution and what services you have running on it (like MySQL), some of these logs may not be present on a particular machine:

- **/var/log/faillog** This log file contains failed user logins. This can be very important when tracking attempts to crack into the system.

- **/var/log/kern.log** This log file is used for messages from the operating system's kernel. This is not likely to be pertinent to most computer crime investigations.

- **/var/log/lpr.log** This is the printer log, and it can give you a record of any items that have been printed from this machine. That can be useful in corporate espionage cases.

- **/var/log/mail.*** This is the mail server log, and it can be very useful in any computer crime investigation. E-mail can be a component in any computer crime, and even in some noncomputer crimes such as fraud.

- **/var/log/mysql.*** This log records activities related to the MySQL database server and will usually be of less interest to a computer crime investigation.

- **/var/log/apache2/*** If this machine is running the Apache web server, then this log will show related activity. This can be very useful in tracking attempts to hack into the web server.

- **/var/log/lighttpd/*** If this machine is running the Lighttpd web server, then this log will show related activity. This can be very useful in tracking attempts to hack into the web server.

- **/var/log/apport.log** This records application crashes. Sometimes, these can reveal attempts to compromise the system or indicate the presence of a virus or spyware.

- **var/log/user.log** These contain user activity logs and can be very important to a criminal investigation.

Operating System Utilities

There are a number of utilities built into the operating system that can be useful in gathering some forensic data. Given that Windows is the most commonly used operating system, we will focus on those utilities that work from the Windows command line. However, one of the key issues in conducting forensics work is to be very familiar with the target operating system. You should also note that many of these commands are most useful on a live running system to catch attacks in progress.

Netstat

This command is used to detect ongoing attacks. It lists all current network connections—not just inbound, but outbound as well. You can see this utility in Figure 8-12.

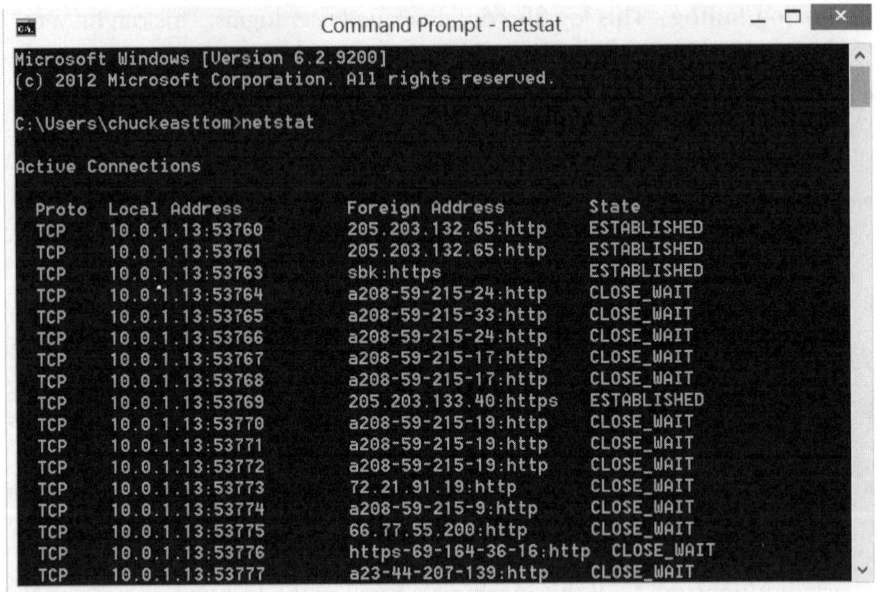

Figure 8-12 within the image:

```
Command Prompt - netstat                          _ □ ×

Microsoft Windows [Version 6.2.9200]
(c) 2012 Microsoft Corporation. All rights reserved.

C:\Users\chuckeasttom>netstat

Active Connections

  Proto  Local Address          Foreign Address        State
  TCP    10.0.1.13:53760        205.203.132.65:http    ESTABLISHED
  TCP    10.0.1.13:53761        205.203.132.65:http    ESTABLISHED
  TCP    10.0.1.13:53763        sbk:https              ESTABLISHED
  TCP    10.0.1.13:53764        a208-59-215-24:http    CLOSE_WAIT
  TCP    10.0.1.13:53765        a208-59-215-33:http    CLOSE_WAIT
  TCP    10.0.1.13:53766        a208-59-215-24:http    CLOSE_WAIT
  TCP    10.0.1.13:53767        a208-59-215-17:http    CLOSE_WAIT
  TCP    10.0.1.13:53768        a208-59-215-17:http    CLOSE_WAIT
  TCP    10.0.1.13:53769        205.203.133.40:https   ESTABLISHED
  TCP    10.0.1.13:53770        a208-59-215-19:http    CLOSE_WAIT
  TCP    10.0.1.13:53771        a208-59-215-19:http    CLOSE_WAIT
  TCP    10.0.1.13:53772        a208-59-215-19:http    CLOSE_WAIT
  TCP    10.0.1.13:53773        72.21.91.19:http       CLOSE_WAIT
  TCP    10.0.1.13:53774        a208-59-215-9:http     CLOSE_WAIT
  TCP    10.0.1.13:53775        66.77.55.200:http      CLOSE_WAIT
  TCP    10.0.1.13:53776        https-69-164-36-16:http  CLOSE_WAIT
  TCP    10.0.1.13:53777        a23-44-207-139:http    CLOSE_WAIT
```

Figure 8-12 Netstat

This command is one I recommend a forensic analyst run before shutting down and imaging a suspect computer. This will let you know if there are active connections with that computer. Such active connections could indicate spyware, a backdoor program (like Timbuktu or Back Orifice), or a virus.

Net sessions

This command lists any active sessions connected to the computer you run it on. This can be very important if you think an attack is live and ongoing. If there are no active sessions, the utility will report that, as shown in Figure 8-13.

This command is more refined than netstat. Netstat shows all communication, even ordinary network traffic, such as a Windows 7 or Windows 8 machine communicating with other machines in the same Home Group. Net sessions will only show active connections, apart from normal network traffic.

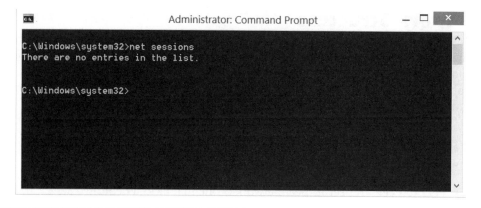

Figure 8-13   Net sessions

Openfiles

This is another command useful for finding live ongoing attacks. This command will list any shared files that are currently open. You can see this utility in Figure 8-14.

 NOTE   I also teach penetration testing classes, and one of the first things I teach students to do is to access shares. If an attacker has attempted to breach this computer, it is likely that evidence will be found in the computer's shares.

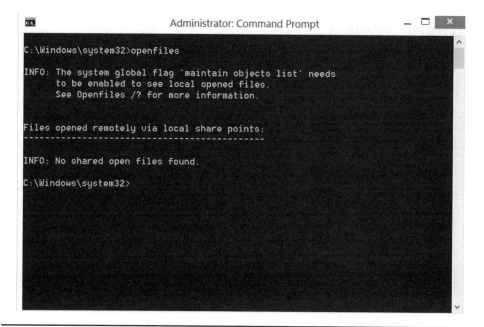

Figure 8-14   The Openfiles command

Network Structure

While performing forensic analysis on networks, it is important to understand how networks are constructed. Earlier in this chapter, we discussed protocols and packets, which gives you a good understanding of how network traffic is constructed. In Chapter 1, we discussed IPv4 and IPv6, giving you a working knowledge of how networks communicate. Now we will examine how the network is designed.

Types of Networks

Networks can be classified into four basic types, each of which is described here:

- **Peer to Peer**   A peer-to-peer network is one that lacks a dedicated server; thus, every computer acts as both a client and a server. This is a good networking solution when there are ten or fewer users that are in close proximity to each other. A peer-to-peer network always has less security.

- **Client/Server**   This type of network is designed to support a large number of users and utilizes a dedicated server(s) to accomplish this. Clients log in to the server(s) in order to run applications or obtain files. Security and permissions can be managed by one or more administrators, which means better security.

- **Centralized**   This is also a client/server-based model that is most often seen in mainframe environments, but the clients are "dumb terminals." From some perspectives, this is not a true network, since each terminal only has direct access to the centralized server and not to each other.

- **Mixed Mode**   A mixture of two or more of the preceding networks.

Network Topology

Network topology refers to how the network is physically or logically wired:

- **Bus**   This topology is an old one and essentially has each of the computers on the network daisy-chained to each other. This is shown in Figure 8-15.

Figure 8-15
Bus topology

- **Star**   The star topology uses twisted-pair (10baseT or 100baseT) cabling and requires that all devices be connected to a hub. This is shown in Figure 8-16.

Figure 8-16
Star topology

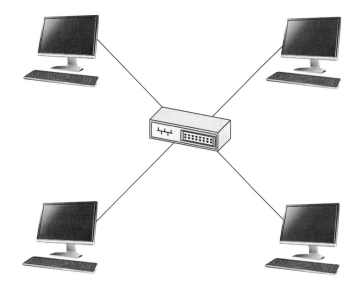

- **Mesh** In a true mesh topology, every node has a connection to every other node in the network. A full mesh network can be expensive, but it provides redundancy in case of a failure between links. This is shown in Figure 8-17.

Figure 8-17
Mesh topology

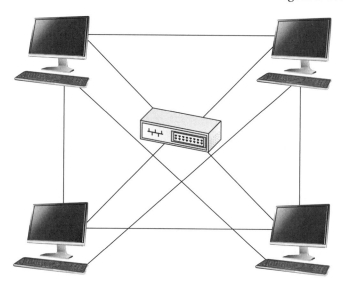

- **Point to Point** In this topology, one point is connected to another. Remote offices connected to each other via a VPN are a good example. This is shown in Figure 8-18.

PART III

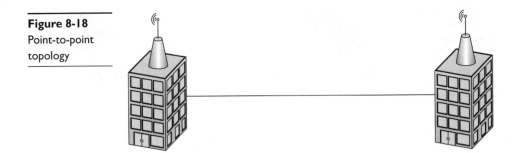

Figure 8-18
Point-to-point
topology

- **Point to Multipoint**   With point to multipoint, a single central location is connected to branches. This can be a central office connected to multiple remote offices. This is shown in Figure 8-19.

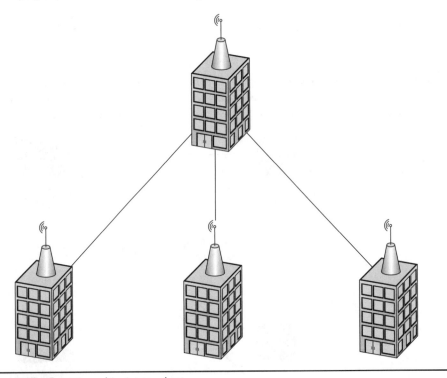

Figure 8-19   Point-to-multipoint topology

- **Tree**   The tree topology literally connects the computers (or networks) in a tree-like fashion. This is shown in Figure 8-20.

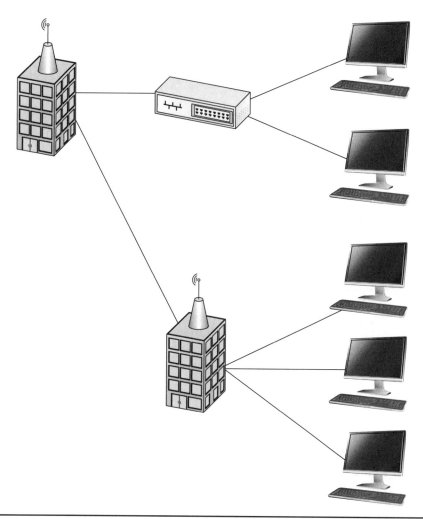

Figure 8-20 Tree topology

Knowing the network topology will give you insight into the various points of inter-est, usually connecting switches and routers, as well as the pathway through which network traffic must travel.

Shares

Previously in this chapter, we mentioned computer shares. A network share is the same thing, only shared throughout the network. It is often a place for colleagues to deposit common documents for reference or collaboration. This is also a common point of access for an intruder or a place that an insider will look to find valuable information. It is important that part of your network forensic analysis involve examining network shares and any records of who accessed them and when.

Services

Network services are programs that operate at the network application layer and above in the OSI model. Web servers usually run as web services and operate at the network level. E-mail services, FTP services, SNMP—these are all network services. Depending on the nature of the attack, one or more of these services may have been compromised.

P2P Networks and Proxies

The term proxy has been previously mentioned in this chapter. It simply means something that stands in for something else. In the world of network proxies, it is a service that is an intermediary between users and the outside world (i.e., the Internet). To access the Internet, users must go through a proxy service. Proxy logs will reveal all user activity on the Internet, including blocked activity. Examining the proxy logs can provide a wealth of forensic information.

In peer-to-peer (P2P) networks, each person connecting is simply an individual computer that wishes to communicate with other computers on the network. There is no centralization to these networks. These have become quite popular with file sharing and related activities. If copyright violation is one of the crimes being investigated, then you definitely want to look into any P2P networks the suspect machine may have connected to.

SANS

Storage area networks (SANs) are typically set up just for massive storage. They are connected to the main organizational network and appear to users as a single storage device. A typical SAN will include servers, network storage devices, and high-speed routers connected together with fiber-optic connections. These can store many terabytes of data and have redundancy so that a single server in the SAN going down will have no impact on the end users' ability to access data. Any crime that can involve a network can obviously also involve a SAN.

Social Networks

Social networks can provide a wealth of forensic data, even in non-cybercrimes. Social media includes any sort of Internet site that allows users to share personal information. Facebook, Twitter, YouTube and LinkedIn are all examples. These constitute different types of social networks. Facebook allows users to have a profile and to post their activities, opinions, etc. YouTube videos are yet another type of social network that allows people to post videos.

Obviously, there can be crimes directly involving these networks, but more frequently, they provide evidence of other crimes. For example, here is an interesting hacker tool called Firesheep designed specifically to hack into Facebook. I believe Facebook has since corrected the problem, but here is how it worked: When a user logged into Facebook, once they were authenticated, a cookie was downloaded onto their machine indicating that they were logged in as a particular username. Since Facebook is encrypted, it would be very impractical to break the encryption. What Firesheep does is scan the network for any of these cookies being downloaded and grab a copy. Then the person using Firesheep can connect to Facebook as that specific user. Facebook will just read their cookie and assume that is who is connecting.

I am frequently amazed at how much people will disclose on social media, including evidence of their own criminal activity. In one case, a criminal failed to show up for court. The police checked his Facebook page, where he was routinely updating his status, including location.[3] In another case, a robber made a YouTube video bragging about their crimes…and not disguising their identity.[4]

There are two serious issues with collecting evidence from social media. The first is jurisdiction. Obviously, social media might be hosted anywhere, and the user might connect from anywhere. Thus, the laws regarding collection of evidence could vary. The second issue is the terms of service for the specific social media in question. Usually, those terms of service allow the vendor and law enforcement to collect anything posted, but it is a good idea to verify that before collecting evidence.

Chapter Review

In this chapter you have learned the fundamentals of network forensics. First, you learned the details of packets, headers, and what information could be gathered from the packet headers. We then looked at some tools such as Wireshark and Snort. Later in the chapter, we examined the basics of firewall and router forensics.

Questions

1. Which Windows log will tell you if software has been uninstalled?

   A. Install

   B. Application

   C. Security

   D. User

2. What does a 500 HTTP response indicate?

   A. Client error

   B. OK

   C. Redirect

   D. Server error

3. Why would you not turn off a router before examining it for evidence?

    A. You may destroy evidence.

    B. You would turn it off.

    C. It will lose its routing tables when powered off.

    D. It violates FBI forensic guidelines.

4. What does a router use to determine the path to send packets on?

    A. MAC address

    B. IP address

    C. Protocol used

    D. Next available port

5. Which header would have the sender's port number?

    A. TCP

    B. IP

    C. Ethernet

    D. None

Answers

1. **B.** The application log will show installation and removal of files.

2. **D.** 500 series are server errors; 400 series are client errors.

3. **A.** When a router shuts down, all running config files are wiped, so evidence could be destroyed.

4. **B.** IP addresses, or layer 3 addresses, are used by routers. MAC addresses, or layer 2 addresses, are used by switches.

5. **A.** TCP will have port, Ethernet will have MAC, and IP will have the IP address.

References

1. http://www.w3schools.com/tags/ref_httpmethods.asp.

2. http://www.thefullwiki.org/Winzapper.

3. http://mashable.com/2012/12/12/crime-social-media/.

4. http://theweek.com/article/index/227257/7-suspected-criminals-who-got-themselves-caught-via-facebook.

Virtual Systems

In this chapter you will learn
- Types of clouds
- Types of virtual systems
- How these systems affect forensics
- Where to find evidence in a virtual environment

Virtual systems of all types are becoming ubiquitous. Many businesses host terabytes of data in clouds; individuals use virtual machines to give them access to a variety of platforms on a single desktop. Virtualization is a major component of modern IT systems, and therefore, has a significant impact on many forensic investigations.

Types of Virtual Systems

Virtual systems encompass a broad range of disparate technologies—everything from the virtual machine you might install on your local system to the clouds used by so many organizations today.

Virtualization is a broad term that encompasses many technologies. It is a way to provide various IT resources that is independent of the physical machinery of the user. Virtualization enables a logical IT resource that can operate independently of the end user's operating system as well as hardware.

Virtual Machines

A virtual machine (VM) is an interesting concept, and was the precursor of the more broad-based virtual systems that we will discuss later in this chapter. A virtual machine essentially sets aside a certain portion of a computer's hard drive and RAM (when executing) to run in complete isolation from the rest of the operating system. It is as if you are running an entirely separate computer—it simply shares the resources of the host computer. It is, quite simply, a virtual computer, thus the name.

Virtual machines are a popular way to host multiple operating systems on a single computer. For example, a computer forensic analyst who is comfortable with Windows might have a laptop running Windows 8 and decide to install a virtual machine that runs Linux in order to learn more about Linux. A more formal definition of a virtual machine would be that it is a software-based emulation of a computer. It is a virtual computer. There are actually two types of virtual machines. A system virtual machine is emulating an entire functioning system with a complete operating system. This is the type discussed in our aforementioned scenario. The second type is a process virtual machine. This type simply runs a single application. This is often done to isolate that application from the rest of the operating system.

Later in this chapter, we will review the basic components of a virtual system from which you are likely to get evidence. However, we will cover some basic VM architecture here. First, the physical machine upon which the virtual machine is running is called the host machine. That machine's operating system is referred to as the host operating system. The virtual machine is also called the guest machine. The hypervisor is a basic element of all VMs that provides the guest machine with a virtual operating platform. It also manages the execution of the guest operating systems.

The hypervisor is the most important part of the VM architecture. It is software that is installed on the host machine (often as part of a software package) that initiates, manages, and controls the virtual machines.

A VM requires some virtualizing software that interfaces between the VM and the hardware. Essentially, the VM is using this software to interact with the hardware, rather than interacting via the host operating system. The virtualization process includes mapping resources such as the virtual hard disk and virtual memory to actual hardware resources. The virtualization software also has to use real machine instructions to carry out the VM's virtual instructions.

Several virtual machine applications are available to you. Each allows you to install the virtual machine software and then install any operating system you wish within the virtual machine. Oracle VirtualBox is one popular VM.[1] You can see VirtualBox in Figure 9-1.

Microsoft also has a virtual machine product called Microsoft Virtual PC. It was specifically designed to allow a Windows user to run multiple operating systems on a single computer.[2] When you launch Virtual PC, you will basically have a window that is actually an entirely different operating system (much as Oracle VirtualBox works), as seen in Figure 9-2.

Oracle VirtualBox is popular in part because it is free and available for multiple operating systems. You can install VirtualBox on a Windows, Linux, or Macintosh system.

Another popular virtual machine product is VMware (www.vmware.com). Like the previously mentioned products, this allows you to host a variety of operating systems on a single host computer. You can see this in Figure 9-3.

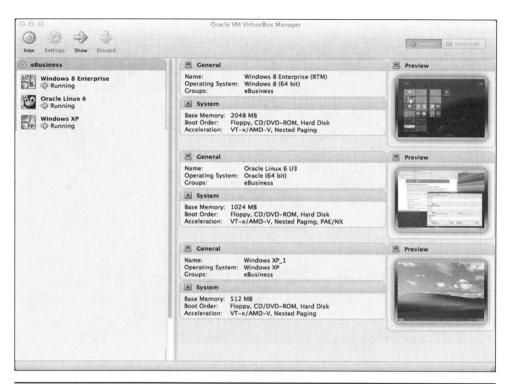

Figure 9-1   Oracle VirtualBox

Figure 9-2   Microsoft Virtual PC

PART III

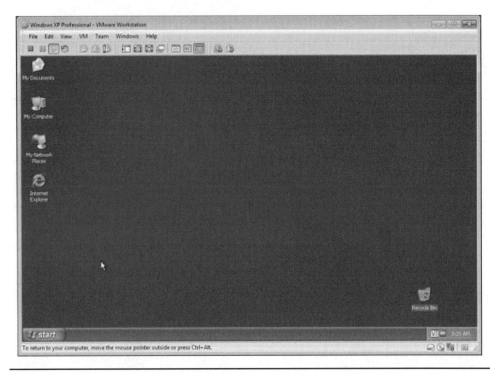

Figure 9-3 VMware

Service-Based Systems

In addition to a virtual computer, there are a variety of virtual services that can be run on your computer. With any of the service-based systems, a given company provides a specific item, possibly a software product, or an operating system, or even an entire infrastructure. The subscriber pays for access to this item/service via virtualization. This means their computer uses something quite similar to a virtual machine to access the service. Often, these service-based systems are provided through the cloud, which we will discuss in more detail later in this chapter.

Software as a Service

Traditionally, one thinks of software as something to install on a computer. For example, I am typing this chapter using Microsoft Word, which is installed on my computer. And if you visit my website (www.ChuckEasttom.com), you will do so using your favorite browser (Chrome, Firefox, Safari, Internet Explorer, Opera, etc.), which is also software installed on your computer. From the advent of personal computers, purchasing software and installing it on one's machine was the way software was implemented. However, software as a service (SaaS) provides a different model.

With software as a service, the application you need is provided to you as a service, often via some web interface. For example, Microsoft Office is offered as a service via the Web. The advantages to this model are numerous, the first being that there is no need for installation. Your IT team does not install or maintain the software—it is accessed as a service. Another advantage is that updates to the software are handled by the service provider. And yet another advantage is that there are no issues regarding software compatibility since it is not actually installed on your system.

The issues with software as a service and its implications for forensics fall primarily into two areas. The first concerns the actual location of the data. If the software in question involves a database, then the data likely resides with the service provider. This is common with database systems such as SQL Server and Oracle if they are provided in a software as a service model. It is also common with medical records software.

The second issue when forensically examining SaaS is the location of metadata. Even if the software being offered via a service vendor does not contain a database, it most likely has some files. For example, using a word processor provided as a service begs the question of where the metadata regarding those files is stored. Clearly, at least some metadata will be stored with the individual documents. But finding all metadata can be tricky.

 NOTE Some industries have embraced software as a service more than others. For example, engineering software is usually installed locally on the computer, but medical billing and electronic medical records software is often implemented as a service.

Platform as a Service

Platform as a service (PaaS) is a system where the entire operating system (i.e., the platform) is provided via virtual means. Often, this is popular with programmers who must create software that can function on multiple different operating systems. For that reason, PaaS systems often include a programming development environment, a database, and even a web server.

Platform as a service presents some forensic challenges too. The first is how to recover deleted files. This may be more challenging since those files will reside with the hardware the service provider is using to provide the operating system. A related issue has to do with examining slack space for evidence. Since slack space depends on clusters on the hard drive, it may not be accessible via a virtualized operating system, depending on how the virtualized system is implemented. For PaaS-related forensic investigations, you will likely need to coordinate with the service provider. If they are uncooperative, a subpoena or warrant may be required.

Infrastructure as a Service

Infrastructure as a service (IaaS) is a method whereby the entire infrastructure is provided as a service. The servers are virtual servers, the clients are virtual machines, etc. Obviously, there has to be some network connectivity that is either wireless or cabled, but the rest of the infrastructure is provided via virtual systems.

The IaaS implementation is challenging forensically. It has all the challenges of platform as a service, but with additional issues. For example, where are log files stored? If the network has virtualized components (such as the NIC), how will you access it?

I would suggest that it will be extremely difficult to conduct an effective investigation involving IaaS without data from the service provider. However, there is a silver lining to this cloud. Most service providers for IaaS also have their own logging of activity for performance-related reasons. You may be able to get additional information that might not normally be available in a nonvirtualized environment. For example, in a physical environment, unless you are capturing network traffic, then it is ephemeral and you won't be able to examine it later. However, in an IaaS environment, it is possible that the service provider would be logging that information.

The Cloud

A cloud has been defined by the NIST (National Institute of Standards and Technology) as "a pool of virtualized computer resources."[3]

The basic functionality of services in the cloud is handled by a few specific servers that handle scheduling and routing. As stated in the book *Distributed and Cloud Computing: From Parallel Processing to the Internet of Things* (Morgan Kaufmann, 2001), "A few control nodes are used to manage and monitor the cloud activities. The scheduling of user jobs requires the cloud to assign the work to various virtual clusters. The gateway nodes provide the access points of the service from the outside world."[4]

If the server selected cannot process the request for data, an application, etc., then another server is found in the cloud that can. The authors state: "If a backend datacenter cannot serve the client, it sends a message to the domain datacenter to select a closer backend that has a copy of the application that [meets] the response time constraints."[5]

So the picture we have is one of a number of diverse servers, many duplicating the capabilities of other servers, thus providing robust failover as well as load balancing. The entire process is completely transparent to the user, who neither knows nor cares where exactly his or her data resides. However, this presents significant issues for a forensic investigator. The lack of localization of data is a forensic challenge. Ultimately, one needs to locate data for forensic investigations. However, in the cloud, not only is the data not on the suspect's or victim's computer, but it is not on a specific single server. Rather, it is on multiple servers in the cloud.

Cloud Basics

A cloud system depends on several parts. Each of these could be a location for evidence.

- **Virtual storage**   The virtual servers are hosted on one or more actual physical servers. The hard drive space and RAM of those physical servers are partitioned for the various virtual servers' usage.

- **Audit monitor**   There is usually an audit monitor that monitors usage of the resource pool. This monitor will also ensure that one virtual server does not or cannot access another virtual server's data.

- **Hypervisor**   The hypervisor mechanism is the process that provides the virtual servers with access to resources.

- **Logical network perimeter**   Since the cloud consists of virtual servers, not physical ones, there is a need for a logical network and a logical network perimeter. This perimeter isolates resource pools from each other.

Individual cloud implementations might have additional utilities, such as administration consoles that allow a network administrator to monitor, configure, and administer the cloud.

Cloud Types

People often speak of the cloud as if there were only one cloud, or at least one type of cloud. This impression is inaccurate. There are multiple clouds and multiple types of clouds. Any organization with the appropriate resources can establish a cloud, and they may establish it for diverse reasons, leading to different types of clouds.

- Public clouds are defined by the NIST as simply clouds that offer their infrastructure or services to either the general public or at least a large industry group.[6]

- Private clouds are those clouds used specifically by a single organization without offering the services to an outside party. There are, of course, hybrid clouds, which combine the elements of a private and public cloud. These are essentially private clouds that have some limited public access.

- Community clouds are a midway point between private and public. These are systems wherein several organizations share a cloud for specific community needs. For example, several computer companies might join to create a cloud devoted to common security issues.

EXAM TIP You should know the types of cloud for the test, as you are likely to be asked about them.

Beyond these types of clouds, what is a cloud fundamentally? In short, it is network redundancy taken to a new level. In order to address disaster recovery, it is imperative for a robust network to have multiple redundant servers. So should a disaster of any type (even a hard drive failure) cause one server to fail, the organization simply uses the other server. In the simplest configuration, the two servers are connected. They are complete mirrors of each other. Should one server fail for any reason, then all traffic is diverted to the other server.

This situation works great in environments where there are only a few severs and the primary concern is hardware failure. But what if you have much larger needs? For example, what if you need to store far more data than any server can? Well, that led to the next step in the evolution of network redundancy—the storage area network. In a SAN, there are multiple servers and storage devices all connected in a high-speed small network. This network is separate from the main network used by the organization. When a user on the main network wishes to access data from the SAN, it appears to the user as a single storage device. The user need not even be aware a SAN exists—from their perspective, it is just a server. This not only provides increased storage capacity, but also provides redundancy. The SAN has multiple servers—should one of them fail, the others will continue operating, and the end user will not even realize a failure occurred. You can see an example of a SAN in Figure 9-4.

Figure 9-4
SAN example

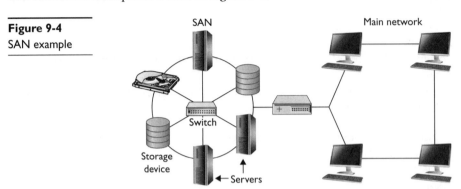

The SAN, however, is not adequate for some needs. It is a finite storage network with finite storage resources. Thus, the second issue is the comparative failsafe nature of a SAN versus the cloud. A hard drive failure, accidental data deletion, or similar small-scale incident will not prevent a redundant network server or SAN from continuing to provide data and services to end users. But what about an earthquake, flood, or fire that destroys the entire building that hosts the SAN? The SAN does not have adequate fault tolerance for this situation, but the cloud does.

It is not inaccurate to think of a cloud as the logical next step after a SAN. When a company hosts a cloud, they establish multiple servers in diverse geographic areas, with data being redundantly stored in several severs. There may be a server in New York, another in San Francisco, and another in London. The end user simply accesses "the cloud" without even knowing where the data actually is. It is hard to imagine a scenario wherein the entire cloud would be destroyed. The basic architecture of a cloud is shown in Figure 9-5.

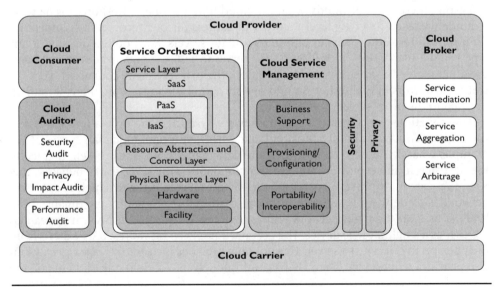

Figure 9-5 General cloud architecture (Source: NIST Cloud Computing Special Publication 500-292)

As you can see, the data and services are distributed widely. The cloud broker is responsible for finding the appropriate services, virtual environments, and other services the user might need.

Forensic Issues

Any of the virtual environments we have discussed in this chapter will present certain forensic challenges. Extracting evidence from a stand-alone computer is not the same as extracting the same evidence from a cloud or virtual machine. There are two main issues. The first are technical issues. These involve how we go about identifying and collecting the data. The second set of issues involves legal and procedural issues. What laws, policies, and agreements related to cloud computing and other virtual environments might affect our forensic analysis?

Technical Issues

The first problem is that the "machine" is likely not one that can be confiscated. With the exception of a simple virtual machine on a single computer, virtualized systems, particularly those using virtualized servers, are not residing on a specific computer you can seize and image.[7] Unlike many of the situations we have described in this book, in cloud forensics, you probably won't have full access to the entire system (i.e., the actual hardware). You won't be able to create a physical image of that disk. That means you may be working with a logical copy.

The first step in any forensic process involving virtualized systems is to identify what is virtualized. For example, with a cloud, you will have limited, or no, access to the hardware involved. With virtual machines, you probably have access to the host computer. In that case, you can image that drive and then look for key evidence relevant to the VM.

 NOTE Some sources suggest you can just image the virtual machine, without imaging the host system.[8] However, the host system will contain files such as the backup of the VM's swap file. That is why I recommend you image the entire host, including the virtual machine.

Evidence from any virtualized environment can include the files in it (database files, registry files, etc.), as well as files that describe the cloud. Essentially, virtualized environments have added dimensions not encountered in a standard cyber forensics investigation. In both stand-alone computers and virtualized systems, you want to seize evidence found on the computer system itself; but with virtualized systems, you will also need to collect evidence about the virtual system itself.

VMware

Let's first examine VMware virtual machines. Certain files are key to VMware systems. You will find these files on the host system:

- **.log files**   Simply a log of activity for a virtual machine.
- **.vmdk**   This is the actual virtual hard drive for the virtual guest operating system. Virtual hard drives can be fixed or dynamic. Fixed virtual hard drives remain the same size. Dynamic virtual hard drives expand as needed.
- **.vmem**   A backup of the virtual machine's paging file/swap file. This can be very important to a forensic investigation.
- **.vmsn**   These are VMware snapshot files, named by the name of the snapshot. A VMSN file stores the state of the virtual machine when the snapshot was created.
- **.vmsd**   A VMSD file contains the metadata about the snapshot.
- **.nvram**   This is the file that stores the BIOS information for the virtual machine. This should be noted in your forensic report, even if it does not contain critical information for the case.
- **.vmx**   This is the configuration file for a virtual machine, such as the operating system and disk information. It is just a text file, so it is easy to analyze.
- **.vmss**   This file stores the state of a suspended virtual machine.

Each of these files should be examined when performing a forensic analysis of a VMware virtual machine.

VirtualBox

There are, of course, similar files with Oracle VirtualBox. VirtualBox stores its files in the user's home folder. In Windows, it will look something like C:\Documents and Settings\Username\. In Linux, the location will be something similar to /home/username, and in Mac systems, it will be /Users/username.

- **.vdi**   These are VirtualBox disk images called virtual disk images.
- **/.config/VirtualBox**   This is a hidden file that contains configuration data.
- **.vbox**   This is the machine settings file extension. Prior to version 4.0, it was .xml.

VirtualBox also allows you to create a core dump that will dump the contents in volatile memory, as well as metadata about the system. There are step-by-step instructions for creating a core dump at www.virtualbox.org/wiki/Core_dump/.

Virtual PC

And, of course, Microsoft Virtual PC has related files that you will need to examine forensically. The key files are described here:

- **.vhx**   These are the actual virtual hard disks. These are obviously quite important to a forensic examination.

- **.bin files**   These contain the memory of the virtual machine, so these absolutely must be examined.

- **.xml files**   These files contain the virtual machine configuration details. There is one of these for each virtual machine and for each snapshot of a virtual machine. These files are always named with the GUID used to internally identify the virtual machine in question.

Regardless of the virtual machine you are working with, these files could contain evidence and thus must be collected and analyzed.

The Cloud

The cloud is even more difficult to extract forensic data from than a virtual machine. It is unlikely that you will have any access to the hardware or be able to make a bit-by-bit copy of the hard disk. Instead, you will have to make a logical copy of the relevant virtual system that includes the virtualized application, service, or operating system. As you already know, a logical copy might miss some forensic evidence (such as slack space or deleted files). However, you can still acquire the virtualized environment and extract what evidence you can.

Legal/Procedural Issues

Clouds are, by definition, distributed computing systems. This brings into question jurisdiction. Where is the data actually located and what laws apply as a result? Some cloud systems, particularly private clouds, are entirely within a given country. This situation greatly simplifies jurisdictional issues. However, a cloud could be distributed across national boundaries, making the jurisdiction a significant concern. Certainly, some clouds are entirely contained within a single country such as the United States, or at least a loose federation such as the European Union. But you may encounter cloud services that are hosted across multiple national boundaries.

Therefore, assume you are performing an investigation based in the United States. The investigation involves a cloud service. Before you seize data, you may need to ascertain where that cloud provider geographically locates their servers. For example, if they have servers in the United States as well as Europe, your U.S. warrant may not be adequate.

It may be necessary to contact law enforcement officials in the countries where the cloud servers are located. Since data is likely to be replicated across multiple servers, you may need to contact several nations. The degree of cooperation you receive will depend on multiple factors, the first being the political climate at the time. As I write this chapter, tensions are quite high between Western Europe and North America, on the one hand, and Russia, on the other. If your cloud investigation required access to servers in both Germany and Russia for an investigation based in the United States, you may not receive full cooperation.

Another issue is the nature of the investigation. Certain crimes tend to engender law enforcement cooperation across national boundaries. Crimes such as terrorism and child exploitation are likely to get some level of cooperation, even from countries that may not be politically aligned with your own. On the other hand, identity theft involving small amounts of money, theft of intellectual property, and other similar nonviolent crimes may not generate a sense of urgency in the host nation's law enforcement community.

 NOTE While jurisdictional issues can be significant, there is the option of simply requesting data from the cloud provider. If you do not suspect the provider of actually being involved in the crime, and a reputable law enforcement agency requests data, and the request is specific (i.e., not a broad fishing expedition), there is at least a chance of the cloud provider simply giving you the data you need.

European Union Privacy Laws

The European Union (EU) has strict privacy laws. They have seven principles regarding personal data (these will be discussed in detail later in this book). That has an impact on cloud forensics. If you are performing an analysis of a cloud that includes servers in the European Union, then the privacy laws will apply to your collection of data.

HIPAA

In the United States, health-related records are protected by HIPAA (Health Insurance Portability and Accountability Act), which has strict requirements for the safeguarding of health-related data and notifying patients should their data be disclosed.

HIPAA regulates how various healthcare-related entities (clinics, insurance companies, medical service providers, hospitals, etc.) deal with patient information that is designated as protected health information. The law requires that such data be held securely and privately and not be disclosed to third parties without written permission from the patient or a legal compulsion, such as a warrant or subpoena.

PHI (protected health information) is defined as the patient's name, all geographic identifiers smaller than the state (i.e., address/city), phone number, e-mail, Social Security number, medical record numbers, certificate/license numbers, health insurance beneficiary numbers, vehicle numbers, URLS, IP address, biometric data (including fingerprint, voiceprint, or retinal scan), full-face photographs, or "any other unique identifying number, characteristic, or code."

Even if your investigation does not involve the types of records covered under these laws, the fact remains that the cloud is a distributed network of servers. If you are seizing evidence off a given server in the cloud, it is entirely possible that other customers' applications, data, and entire virtual servers are also running on the same server(s).

Credit Card Laws

If your cloud service hosts an e-commerce site, then you probably are engaged in credit card processing. Credit card processing is covered by PCI (Payment Card Industry) security standards. These standards define how to deal with credit card data. The following list is not comprehensive, but covers the main issues of PCI standards:

- All transmission of cardholder data across any open network must be encrypted.
- No default passwords are to be used on related systems.
- Cardholder data must be protected by a firewall.
- Access to cardholder data must be restricted on a need-to-know basis.
- All access to cardholder data must be tracked and monitored.
- Physical access to the systems and data must be restricted.
- You must maintain security policies.
- You must develop and maintain secure systems and applications.
- The system must include regularly updates to antivirus software.

Even if the cloud vendor advertises that it is PCI compliant, that is not enough. You should perform due diligence and get details on exactly what the vendor does to maintain such compliance. Some states have embraced enhanced versions of PCI. For example, the state of Minnesota passed a law in 2007 that prohibits retention of payment card data. So after a customer's credit card is processed, the credit card information must be deleted.

Chapter Review

We have seen myriad issues in this chapter that involved extracting evidence from virtual environments and from the cloud. We have also examined the different types of virtual environments you are likely to encounter. It is important that you have at least a working knowledge of each of these in order to conduct forensic examinations.

You also learned about the challenges you will face when forensically analyzing virtual environments. You learned about the difficulty in extracting evidence when you may not have access to the system's hardware. You also learned about legal and regulatory challenges.

Questions

1. What part of a cloud implementation provides the virtual servers with access to resources?

   A. Hypervisor

   B. Resource monitor

   C. Resource auditor

   D. Virtual manager

2. What is the file extension for a VMware virtual hard drive?

   A. .vdi

   B. .vmdk

   C. .vhx

   D. .vmi

3. What is the file extension for a Virtual PC virtual hard drive?

   A. .vdi

   B. .vmdk

   C. .vhx

   D. .VMI

4. In the HIPAA law, what is PHI?

   A. Personal health information

   B. Protected health information

   C. Private health information

   D. Proscribed health information

5. A cloud that is shared by multiple organizations is called what?

   A. A public cloud

   B. A combined cloud

   C. A shared cloud

   D. A community cloud

Answers

1. **A.** The hypervisor provides the virtual servers with access to resource pools.

2. **B.** With VMware, the virtual hard disks end with a .vmdk extension.

3. **C.** With Virtual PC, the virtual hard disks end with a .vhx extension.

4. **B.** PHI is protected health information.

5. **D.** When multiple organizations share a cloud for some common purpose, it is called a community cloud.

References

1. https://www.virtualbox.org/.

2. http://www.microsoft.com/en-us/download/details.aspx?id=3702.

3. http://www.ijcit.com/archives/volume1/issue2/Paper010225.pdf.

4. Chapter 7, *Cloud Architecture and Datacenter in Distributed Computing: Clusters, Grids and Clouds*, by Kai Hwang, Geoffrey Fox, and Jack Dongarra, May 2, 2010.

5. *Cloud Tree: A Hierarchical Organization as a Platform for Cloud Computing*, by Khaled A. Nagaty, p. 1, Cloud Computing Using Hierarchical Organization.

6. http://www.ijarcsse.com/docs/papers/Volume_3/3_March2013/V3I3-0320.pdf.

7. http://www.crosstalkonline.org/storage/issue-archives/2013/201309/201309-Zawoad.pdf.

8. http://www.forensicfocus.com/downloads/virtual-machines-forensics-analysis.pdf.

PART III

Mobile Forensics

In this chapter you will learn:
- How to gather data from mobile devices
- About mobile device operating systems
- To apply forensics to embedded devices
- How to identify types of mobile data

Cell phones and mobile devices are ubiquitous in our modern world. It is, in fact, quite uncommon to see someone who does not have one or more such devices. I personally use a tablet and a smartphone, and even my grandson uses a tablet regularly. The nearly universal nature of these devices makes then interesting forensically.

Most of cyber forensics deals with cybercrimes. It is certainly possible to find supporting evidence against a drug dealer on their computer, but you really have no case without physically finding narcotics. However, mobile devices are different. While they can certainly contain evidence of cybercrimes, they are also frequently used in non-cyber cases. There have been numerous cases where evidence from a phone has been of assistance in a murder case, an assault, a theft, or many other non-cybercrimes.

However, mobile devices present a host of issues not found in other computer devices. Thus, it is also important to fully understand the hardware and operating systems used in mobile devices. In this chapter, we will fully explore these issues.

Cellular Device Concepts

Before you can begin studying the forensic analysis of mobile devices, you need to have a good working understanding of how they function. In this section, you will learn the essential concepts and technologies used in mobile devices. I suspect most, if not all, readers of this book regularly use cell phones, tablets, and other devices. But you may not have considered the nature of how these devices work.

In this section, we will begin with terminology and then move into cellular networks, and then the individual operating systems used on various mobile devices. Obviously, entire books could be written, and indeed have been written, on this topic. The purpose in this section is to give you the basic working knowledge necessary to be effective as a cyber forensics analyst.

The Basics

You need to know some basic devices and terminology before we delve into cell phones. Some of these, such as SIM, are probably at least somewhat familiar to you. The purpose of this section is to provide a foundation for the rest of this book.

Subscriber Identity Module (SIM)

This SIM is the heart of the phone. It is a circuit, usually a removable chip. The SIM is how you identify a phone. If you change the SIM in a phone, you change the phone's identity. The SIM stores the International Mobile Subscriber Identity (IMSI). The IMSI, which we will discuss in detail in just a moment, uniquely identifies a phone. So if you change the SIM, you effectively change the IMSI, and thus change the phone's identity. This SIM will also usually have network information, services the user has access to, and two passwords. Those passwords are the personal identification number (PIN) and the personal unblocking code (PUK). A SIM card is shown in Figure 10-1.

Figure 10-1
SIM card

International Mobile Subscriber Identity (IMSI)

The IMSI is usually a 15-digit number, but can be shorter in some cases (some countries use a shorter number). As mentioned, it is used to uniquely identify a phone. The first three digits are a mobile country code (MCC); the next digits represent the mobile network code. In North America, that is three digits; in Europe, it is two digits. The remaining digits are the mobile subscription identifier number (MSIN) that identifies the phone within a given network. To prevent tracking and cloning, the IMSI is only sent rarely. Instead, a temporary value or TMSI is generated and sent.

Integrated Circuit Card Identification (ICCID)

While the IMSI is used to identify the phone, the SIM chip itself is identified by the ICCID. The ICCID is engraved on the SIM during manufacturing, so it cannot be removed. The first seven digits identify the country and issuer, and are called the Issuer Identification Number (IIN). After that is a variable-length number that identifies this chip/SIM and then a check digit.

Electronic Serial Number (ESN)

ESNs are only used in CDMA phones (those are discussed later in this chapter). More modern phones use the International Mobile Equipment Identity (IMEI) number. The first 8 bits of the ESN identify the manufacturer, and the subsequent 24 bits uniquely identify the phone. The IMEI is used with GSM and LTE as well as other types of phones.

International Mobile Equipment Identity (IMEI)

This is a unique number used to identify GSM, UMTS, LTE, and satellite phones. It is printed on the phone, often inside the battery compartment. You can display it on most phones by entering #06# on the dial pad. Using this number, a phone can be "black-listed" or prevented from connecting to a network. This works even if the user changes the SIM card.

Personal Unlock Number (PUK)

This is a code used to reset a forgotten PIN. However, using the code wipes the phone and resets it to its factory state, thus destroying any forensic evidence. If the code is entered incorrectly ten times in a row, the device becomes permanently blocked and unrecoverable.

Public Switched Telephone Network (PSTN)

This is a term you will encounter a lot. It simply refers to the normal telephone network, the land line. Another common term for this is POTS (literally this means "plain old telephone service").

Mobile Switching Center (MSC)

This term refers to the switching network for cell phones, particularly in 3G or in GSM networks. The MSC processes all the connections from both mobile devices and land-line calls. It is also responsible for routing calls between base stations and the PSTN.

Base Transceiver Station (BTS)

This is part of the cell network. The BTS is responsible for communications between the phone and the network switching system (MSC). It consists of a base transceiver station and a base station controller. The base station system comprises radio transceiver equipment that communicates with cellular devices. It is a central controller coordinating the other pieces of the BSS.

Home Location Register (HLR)

The database used by the MSC for subscriber data and service information. It is related to the Visitor Location Register (VLR), which is used for roaming phones.

Visitor Location Register (VLR)

The VLR is a database that contains information about the subscribers roaming within an MSC's location area. Basically, the HLR is a list of subscribers in their home area, and the VLR is a list of those phones that are roaming.

Short Message Service (SMS)

SMS is what people commonly refer to as "texting." It functions using the Mobile Application Part (MAP) of the SS7 protocol. The maximum size of messages depends on how the subscriber configured the phone. Common message size maximums are 160, 140, and 70 characters. There is an extension to SMS called Multimedia Messaging Services (MMS) that allows other media types, such as pictures.

Networks

In addition to understanding the cell phones themselves, it is necessary to understand the networks. All cell phone networks are based on radio towers. The strength of that radio signal is purposefully regulated to limit its range. Each cell tower base station consists of an antenna and radio equipment. What follows is a brief description of the different types of networks.

Global System for Mobile Communications (GSM)

This is an older technology, what is commonly called 2G. This is a standard developed by the European Telecommunications Standards Institute (ETSI). Originally, GSM was developed just for digital voice, but was expanded to include data. It operates at many different frequencies, but the most common are 900 MHz and 1800 MHz. In Europe, most 3G networks use the 2100 MHz frequency.

NOTE The G simply means generation, so 2G is second generation, 3G third generation, etc.

Enhanced Data Rates for GSM Evolution (EDGE)

Many consider this intermediate level between 2G and 3G. It is technically considered pre-3G but was an improvement on GSM (2G). It was specifically designed to deliver media such as television over the cellular network.

Universal Mobile Telecommunications Systems (UMTS)

This is 3G and is essentially an upgrade to GSM (2G). It provides text, voice, video, and multimedia at data rates up to and possibly higher than 2 megabits per second.

Long-Term Evolution (LTE)

LTE is what is commonly called 4G. It provides broadband Internet, multimedia, and voice. LTE is based on the GSM/EDGE technology. Theoretically, it can support speeds of 300 megabits per second (Mbps). Unlike GSM and GSM-based networks, LTE is based in IP, just like a typical computer network.

WiFi

All cellular phones and other mobile devices today are able to connect to WiFi networks. Wireless networking has become the norm, and free WiFi hot spots can be found in restaurants, coffee shops, and hotels.

Integrated Digitally Enhanced Network (iDEN)

iDEN is a GSM-based architecture that combines a cell phone, two-way radio, pager, and modem into a single network. It operates on 800 MHz, 900 MHz, or 1.5 GHz frequencies and was devised by Motorola.

Understanding the networks that cell phones work on is important to understanding cell phone forensics. Today, you are most likely encountering LTE, though 3G networks/phones still exist.

Operating Systems

It is important to remember that a modern cell phone or tablet is actually a computer. A few short years ago, this was not the case. However, modern mobile devices are, in every respect, full-fledged computers. This means they have hardware, operating systems, and applications (often called apps). It is important to have at least a working knowledge of the operating systems used on mobile devices in order to successfully perform forensic analysis.

iOS

Apple's iPhone, iPod, and iPad are very common, and all run on the same operating system: iOS. The iOS operating system was originally released for the iPhone and iPod in 2007, and later expanded to include the iPad. It is based on a touch interface, wherein the user will perform gestures such as swiping, dragging, pinching, tapping, etc., on the screen. The iOS is based on the OS X for Macintosh but is heavily modified.

The iOS is divided into four layers. The first is the Core OS layer, and this is the heart of the operating system. This is a layer that users and applications don't directly interact with. Instead, applications interact with the Core Services layer, the second layer. The third layer, or Media layer, is responsible for music, video, etc. Finally, there is the Cocoa Touch layer, which responds to user gestures. You can see an iPhone in Figure 10-2.

Figure 10-2
The iPhone

The iOS uses the HFS+ file system. HFS+ was created by Apple as a replacement for the Hierarchical File System (HFS), and is used in both iOS and OSX. iOS can use FAT32 when communicating with Windows machines, such as when synchronizing an iPhone with a Windows PC.

The iOS divides its data partition as follows:

- Calendar entries
- Contact entries
- Note entries
- iPod_control directory (this directory is hidden)
- iTunes configuration
- iTunes music

Clearly, the calendar and contact entries can be of interest in any forensic investigation. However, some of the data hidden in the iPod_control directory is also important. Of particular interest to forensics investigation is the folder iPod_control\device\sysinfo. This folder contains two very important pieces of information:

- iPod model number
- iPod serial number

 NOTE   Contacts are always interesting in an investigation. Certainly, I am not advocating guilt by association. I am certain that if, for example, you are analyzing a drug dealer's phone that several of his contacts have nothing to do with drug trafficking. They could be simply relatives, neighbors, friends, etc. However, it seems very likely that at least some of his contacts will either be suppliers or customers. So analyzing the contacts list and message history in any phone is going to be an important part of any forensic analysis.

 NOTE   Jailbreaking is the process of taking an iPhone (or similar device) and bypassing the vendor limitations so that you can modify the phone's performance. Often, this is done to run unauthorized software. However, this can negatively affect the security of the phone. A similar process exists for Android phones and is referred to as "rooting." The term root comes from the fact that Android is Linux based, and the term for an administrator in Linux is "root."

Apple products have a recovery mode that can be used by forensic analysts. It bypasses the operating system and boots into what is called iBoot, Apple's stage 2 boot loader. This will prevent synchronizing with a computer or any running apps while you are imaging the phone.

To enter recovery mode, power off the device, then hold down the home button, and connect to a computer via USB while continuing to press the home button. Continue holding the home button until "Connect to iTunes" appears and then release.

Android

The Android is the most popular alternative to the Apple iOS. While there are other smartphone operating systems, iOS and Android account for the overwhelming majority. The Android operating system is based on Linux—in fact, it is a modified Linux distribution, and it is open source. That means that if you have the programming and operating system knowledge to follow it, you can download and read the Android source code for yourself (see http://source.android.com/). It should be noted that proprietary Android phones often make their own modifications or additions to the open-source Android source code.

The Android operating system was first released in 2003 and was subsequently acquired by Google in 2005. The versions of Android have been named after desserts/sweets:

- Version 1.5 Cupcake, released April 2009

- Version 1.6 Donut, released September 2009

- Version 2.0 - 2.1 Éclair, released October 2009

- Version 2.2 Froyo, released May 2010

- Version 2.3 Gingerbread, released December 2010

- Version 3.1 - 3.2 Honeycomb, released February 2011

- Version 4.0 Ice Cream Sandwich, released October 2011

- Version 4.1 - 4.2 Jelly Bean, released June 2012

- Version 4.4 KitKat, released September 2013

The differences from version to version usually involve adding new features and are not a dramatic alteration of the operating system. All versions are all Linux based, and the core functionality, even from Cupcake to KitKat, is remarkably similar. This means that if you are comfortable with any version of Android, you should be able to perform a forensic analysis with all versions of Android. You can see an Android phone in Figure 10-3.

 NOTE The Android phone allows anyone to add any app at any time, unlike the iPhone, which requires a user to install only approved apps from the iTunes store. This is both an advantage and a security issue. The advantage is the flexibility that Android users enjoy. The problem is that this leads to far more malware for Android than for iPhone. While writing this chapter, I read an article indicating that 97 percent of mobile malware is found on the Android.[1] This does mean that as a forensic analyst, you are very likely to encounter Android phones.

Figure 10-3
Android phone

In 2010, Google launched its Nexus series of devices. This series of devices includes smartphones and tables that all run the same Android operating system. This makes the smartphone and tablet identical in function and features.

Windows

Microsoft has produced several variations of Windows aimed at the mobile market. The company's first foray into the mobile operating system market was *Windows CE*. That operating system was also released as the *Pocket PC 2000*, which was based on Windows CE version 3. In 2008, Windows Phone was released. It had a major drawback in that it was not compatible with many of the previous Windows Mobile apps. In 2010, Microsoft released *Windows Phone 7*.

With the advent of Windows 8, Microsoft is moving all of its devices to the same operating system. This means that PCs, phones, and tablets will all use the same Windows, namely Windows 8. This simplifies forensic analysis. The Windows 8 phone is shown in Figure 10-4.

PART III

Figure 10-4
Windows 8
phone

BlackBerry

Some readers may think the BlackBerry is a thing of the past, but they are still in use, albeit with a reduced market share. While writing this chapter, I had lunch with a friend whose company issues BlackBerrys to its staff, so this phone is still relevant to forensic examiners. The first BlackBerry device was not even a phone, but rather a pager capable of receiving e-mail pages, and it was released in 1999. BlackBerry uses its own proprietary operating system: BlackBerry 10. It is based on the QNX operating system. BlackBerry supports the major features that other mobile phones support, such as drag and drop, gestures, etc. A BlackBerry phone is shown in Figure 10-5.

Kindle

The Kindle Fire is a lot more than just a book reader. It is a fully functional operating system that allows the user to get on the Internet as well as install and use apps. Therefore, it is very important forensically. Fortunately, however, the Kindle Fire runs a specialized version of Android, so if you are comfortable with Android, then you should be able to forensically analyze Kindle Fire. The first version of Kindle Fire used a customized Android 2.3.3 Gingerbread OS; later versions of the Kindle use more recent versions of Android, but they are still customized to meet Kindle's specific needs. You can see the Kindle Fire in Figure 10-6.

Figure 10-5
The BlackBerry
phone

Figure 10-6
Kindle Fire

Apps

Clearing the operating systems for mobile devices can provide some interesting forensic evidence, but don't forget the apps they run. For example, mobile apps often have GPS components, and some store history. Communications apps might have a history of texts, e-mails, and messages. And, of course, the camera app could contain photos or videos that are relevant to the investigation.

EXAM TIP There are also apps that allow the owner to remotely wipe a phone. This is one reason you place the phone in an evidence bag that blocks transmissions. This is also why the forensics lab should be a Faraday cage and block transmissions.

NOTE You may have heard the term "burner phone." This can be any type of phone—iPhone, Android, Windows—but it is one that is paid for with cash and has prepaid minutes on it, so it is not traceable to a particular owner. If you encounter a burner phone in forensics, it won't trace back to a specific individual. However, you may be able to trace it to the store where it was sold. Then, law enforcement officers may be able to subpoena security video from that store and discover who purchased the phone.

What Evidence Can You Get from a Mobile Device?

We discussed earlier in this chapter that cell phones (and other mobile devices) can have a wealth of evidence, even in noncomputer crimes. We mentioned that contact lists can be useful. However, one can derive many other pieces of evidence from a mobile device.

Cell Phone Records

Obviously, the records of actual calls are important forensically. Who did the person call? How frequently? How long did they speak? These are all important to an investigation. For example, if the crime in question is drug trafficking, and the phone is used to call the same number at about the same time/day each week, this could be a supplier or customer.

Photos and Videos

Rather than simply tell you that certain items on a phone are forensically valuable, let's look at some actual cases. In our first case, the cell phone was accidently dropped near the scene and was used to identify the alleged perpetrator. In 2013, cell phone pictures led to an arrest in a burglary of a Jared jewelry store. The alleged thief discarded clothing and accidentally dropped his cell phone behind a nearby 7-11. The cell phone photos positively ID'd him.[2]

In yet another case, Adam Howe took a "selfie" photo of himself at the scene of a church burglary. This evidence led to a search of the suspect's property, which turned up the stolen goods from the church.

Our third case is in Raleigh, North Carolina, where Gennaro Salvatore Anastasio is charged with indecent liberties with a minor. Mr. Salvatore allegedly approached the boy and propositioned a sexual act. The boy refused, and Mr. Salvatore drove away, but the boy used his cell phone to photograph the suspect.[3]

Child pornography cases often have a cell phone component. It is not uncommon for perpetrators of child sex crimes to take photographs of the children and to keep such photographs with them. While extremely distasteful for a forensic examiner, such photos can absolutely lead to convictions.

GPS Records

The next case shows the use of GPS records. Mr. Derrick Lee, Jr. is charged with entering an apartment with a gun. He is accused of robbing and shooting the residents while in the apartment. It appears while allegedly committing the robbery, Mr. Lee was carrying a stolen cell phone. The GPS records for the phone confirm Mr. Lee was at the apartment at the time of the robbery and shooting.[4]

It is also becoming common practice in contentious divorce proceedings for one party (or both) to subpoena the other party's cell phone GPS records. If one suspects one's spouse of infidelity, cell phone records can help establish this. For example, if the spouse is supposed to be at work, but their cell phone is at a motel, this may not be absolute proof of infidelity, but it can certainly help to indicate infidelity.

EXAM TIP GPS on a phone is not actually GPS. GPS is an acronym for Global Positioning Satellite. That is not how phones determine location. Cell phones try to calculate distance from towers based on signal strength. Ideally, three or more towers are used. However, signal strength is affected by more than just distance. It is affected by weather conditions, terrain, large office buildings, etc. Therefore, the location is a best estimate and is not highly accurate. In some cases, a cell phone location will be accurate to 50 meters, but usually, it is closer to 100 meters. This means that it may not conclusively show a person was actually at the scene of a crime. I recommend that you not base a case solely on phone GPS location, but you might use phone location along with other clues.

Evidence from Apps

In our next case, a woman in Albuquerque was stealing cell phones. However, one of the cell phones she stole had a tracking app on it. Police were able to track the phone to the perpetrator and found a significant stash of stolen goods.[5] This occurred in 2014.

What You Should Look For

We have examined some specific cases that demonstrate the variety of evidence that can be gathered from cell phones. Let's look at some general principles as to what you should look for in a cell phone or other mobile device. Items you should attempt to recover from a mobile device include the following:

- Details of the phone itself
- Call history
- Photos and video
- GPS information
- Network information

Information about the phone should be one of the first things you document in your investigation. Just as you would document the specifics of a PC (model, operating system, etc.) you were examining, you should also document the phone's or tablet's specifics. This will include model number, serial number of the SIM card, operating system, etc. The more detailed descriptive information you can document, the better.

The call history will let you know who the user has spoken to and for how long. Obviously, call records by themselves are not sufficient to prove most crimes. With the exception of stalking or breaking a restraining order, just showing that one person called another is not enough to prove a crime. However, it can begin to build a circumstantial case.

As we have seen with some of the case studies, photos and video can provide direct evidence of a crime. In the case of child pornography, the relevance is obvious. However, it may surprise you to know that it is not uncommon for some criminals to actually photograph or videotape themselves committing serious crimes. This is particularly true of young criminals conducting unplanned crimes or conducting crimes under the influence of drugs or alcohol. There are numerous cases of perpetrators filming or photographing themselves performing crimes ranging from vandalism to burglary and rape.

GPS information has become increasingly important in a variety of cases. So many individuals have devices with GPS enabled, it would seem negligent for a forensic analyst to not retrieve this information. GPS cannot confirm that a suspect committed a crime, but it can show that the suspect, or at least their phone, was very near a location where a crime was committed. Of course, GPS can also help to exonerate someone. If a person is suspected of committing a crime, but his vehicle and cell phone GPS are both shown to be many miles away at the time of the crime, this can help establish an alibi.

 EXAM TIP Remember that any evidence that exonerates the accused is called exculpatory evidence. Law enforcement and prosecutors have a duty to turn over such evidence to the defense.

Network information is also important. What WiFi networks does the phone recognize? This might give you an indication of where the phone has been. If a phone has connected to a coffee shop that is near the scene of a crime, it at least shows the perpetrator was in the area. It is also possible that traditional computer crimes, such as denial of service, SQL injection, etc., might trace back to a public WiFi point and the perpetrator was clever enough to mask his computer's identity. If you can show his cellphone GPS was connected to that WiFi, it will help establish he had the opportunity to commit the crime.

Device Status

The NIST guidelines (http://csrc.nist.gov/publications/nistpubs/800-72/sp800-72.pdf) list four different states a mobile device can be in when you extract data. Those are

Nascent State/Factory Default State   Devices are in the nascent state when received from the manufacturer. The device contains no user data and observes factory configuration settings.

Active State   Devices that are in the active state are powered on, performing tasks, and able to be customized by the user and have their file systems populated with data.

Quiescent State   The quiescent state is a dormant mode that conserves battery life while maintaining user data and performing other background functions. Context information for the device is preserved in memory to allow a quick resumption of processing when returning to the active state.

Semi-Active State   The semi-active state is a state partway between active and quiescent. The state is reached by a timer, which is triggered after a period of inactivity, allowing battery life to be preserved by dimming the display and taking other appropriate actions.

You should document what state the device is in when you conduct your investigation and analysis. And if you change state (for example, by turning on the device), that should also be documented.

Seizing Evidence from a Phone

Now that we have discussed what kind of evidence you can find on a cell phone, we should discuss how to get that evidence. Once you are ready to seize evidence from the mobile device, the following steps should be taken:

1. If you are going to plug the phone into a computer, make sure the phone does not synchronize with the computer. This is particularly important with the iPhone that routinely auto-syncs.

2. Follow the same advice you do for PCs. Make sure you touch the evidence as little as possible, and document what you do to the device.

3. Create an image of the phone (actually of the SIM card).

4. Store the original phone in an evidence bag that prevents electromagnetic transmissions.

5. Document chain of custody.

Then the rest of your examination will take place in much the same way as examining a PC or laptop.

One of the most important things to do is make sure you don't accidentally write data to the mobile device. For example, if you plug an iPhone into your forensics workstation, you want to make sure you don't accidentally write information from your workstation to the iPhone.

If the forensics workstation is a Windows machine, you can use the Windows registry to prevent the workstation from writing to the mobile device. Before connecting to a Windows machine, you can find the registry key (HKEY_LOCAL_MACHINE\System\CurrentControlset\StorageDevicePolicies) and set the value to 0x00000001 and restart the computer. This will prevent that computer from writing to mobile devices that are connected to it.

Imaging a Phone

Regardless of the specific phone, the techniques for seizing it are essentially the same. There are two main types of data acquisition. In this section, we will examine those and then look at tools for doing an acquisition.

Logical Acquisition

Logical imaging refers to copying the active file system from the device into another file. Through this method, allocated data from the actual device is recovered and can later be analyzed. Logical techniques are often the first type of examination forensic analysts will run because they are easier to execute and often provide sufficient data for the case.

iPhone forensics physical techniques can provide far more data; however, they are more difficult to execute successfully and also take considerably more effort to analyze. Many of the mobile forensics tools that support iPhone logical acquisitions will also provide a reporting mechanism. Essentially, the tool will execute a logical acquisition of the device, and with this information, it will export commonly viewed files into a graphical user interface (GUI) or report. The problem with some of these tools is that the examiner can see the reported data, but cannot view the source of that data. For example, a report might show a website being visited, but not display the date and time. In such a case, the examiner would need to see the original source of the data in order to see other metadata associated with the file. For reasons such as this, it is helpful if an acquisition tool not only reports the data that was found, but also allows the investigator to view the raw files from which it was derived.

Physical Acquisition

Physical imaging has been widely used in forensics for many years, but is relatively new to the mobile device world. A physical acquisition creates a physical bit-by-bit copy of the file system, similar to the way a hard drive would be forensically imaged. For this reason, it has the greatest potential to recover large amounts of data, including deleted files. The release of iOS 4 brought up many issues from a mobile forensics standpoint. Hardware encryption is offered with iOS versions 4 and beyond. What this means is that even if a full physical disk image is possible, all the data may be encrypted.

Now that we have examined the types of acquisition you can do, let's take a look at a few of the most common tools used to do an acquisition.

 EXAM TIP   The test likes to use two terms: invasive and non-invasive techniques. Invasive techniques are any techniques that could change the data on the phone itself; for example, using the phone's own apps to learn about cellular activity.

Paraben

Paraben makes a number of forensics tools. They have SIM Card Seizure that has a free demo version that will work for 30 days. You can get this tool from www.paraben.com/. The process is pretty simple. There is a simple wizard you walk through, starting with the screen shown in Figure 10-7.

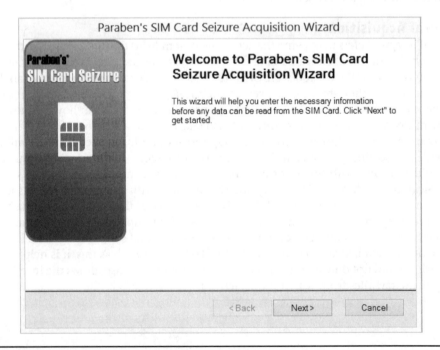

Figure 10-7   The welcome screen for the Paraben SIM Card Seizure wizard

Next, you simply select the files you wish to recover. This is shown in Figure 10-8.

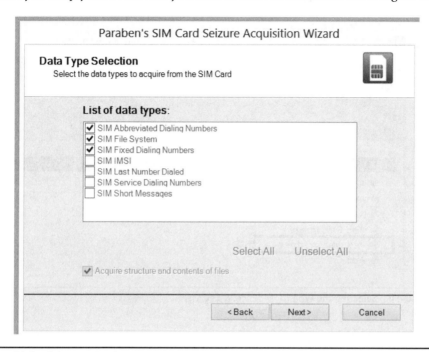

Figure 10-8   Selecting the data you want to recover

Then follow the wizard through to completion.

EnCase

EnCase from Guidance Software also has a utility to seize the data from a smartphone. The first step is to open a case and select Add Evidence, as shown in Figure 10-9.

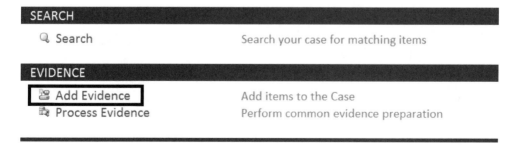

Figure 10-9   The Add Evidence button in EnCase

Then simply select the type of evidence you wish to add to the case file. This is shown in Figure 10-10.

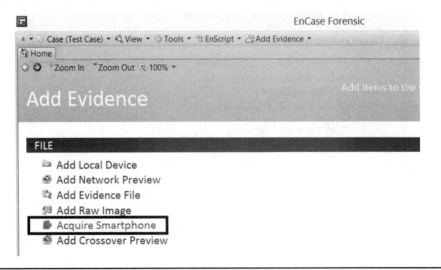

Figure 10-10   Selecting the type of evidence in EnCase

Then you select the type of mobile device you want to acquire. This is shown in Figure 10-11.

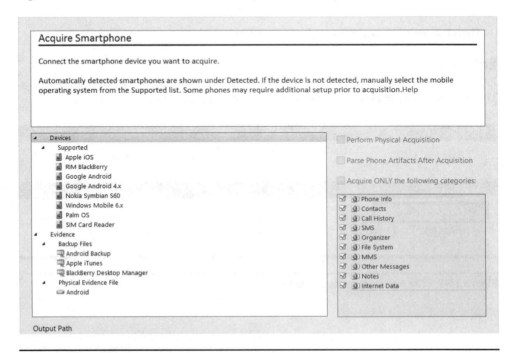

Figure 10-11   Selecting a smartphone in EnCase

EnCase will then acquire the smartphone and add the evidence to the case file.

Data Recovery

DDR Phone from Data Recovery Software (www.datarecoverysoftware.com) is also a simple-to-use program with an easy-to-use wizard. You simply select the type of search you want to perform. This is shown in Figure 10-12.

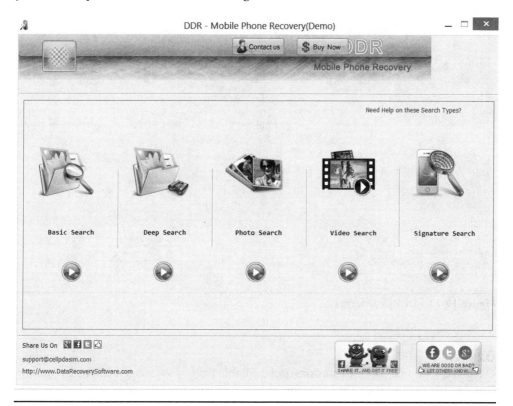

Figure 10-12 DDR Recovery

You can do a basic search or a deep search, as well as simply searching for photos or video. This is shown in Figure 10-13.

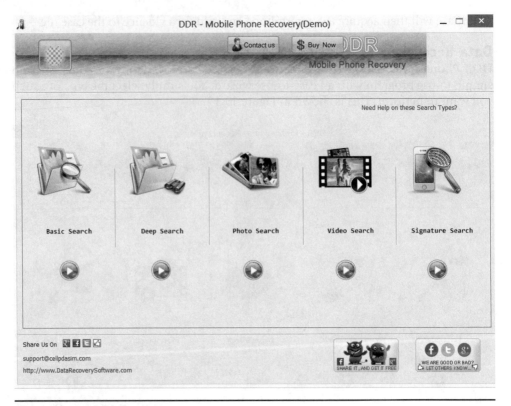

Figure 10-13 DDR Search types

Oxygen

Oxygen is a popular phone forensics tool available from www.oxygen-forensic.com/en/. It is fast becoming one of my favorite phone forensics tools because it is both easy to use and very thorough. There is also a limited free edition you can download from the vendor's website. We will walk through a complete acquisition and see what evidence we can find using Oxygen. In this demonstration, I use my own iPhone 5, and you will notice some information is redacted. The first step is to acquire a phone that you have connected to your PC. This is shown in Figure 10-14.

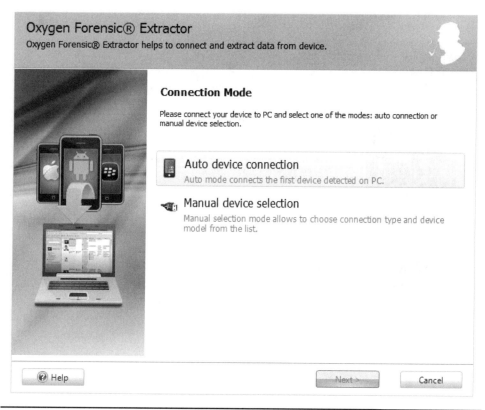

Figure 10-14 Acquire the phone.

Oxygen will immediately tell you a bit about the connected phone, as shown in Figure 10-15.

The next step is to enter the case details: who the investigator is, the case number, suspect name, etc. Notice this screen also shows the hashing algorithm being used and, by default, Oxygen uses SHA2 (recall our discussion of hashing algorithms in Chapter 7). You can see this in Figure 10-16.

Figure 10-15 The device

Next, Oxygen will prompt you to select what you wish to extract from the phone. I recommend extracting everything. This is shown in Figure 10-17.

After a few minutes, Oxygen will show you a results screen, shown in Figure 10-18. From this screen, you can view any piece of evidence that is of interest to you. For example, you can view messages, calls made, websites visited, etc.

It is interesting to note that Oxygen will recover deleted items as well. In this case, I had deleted all text messages and recent calls, but Oxygen recovered those as well. This can be very useful for a forensic investigation.

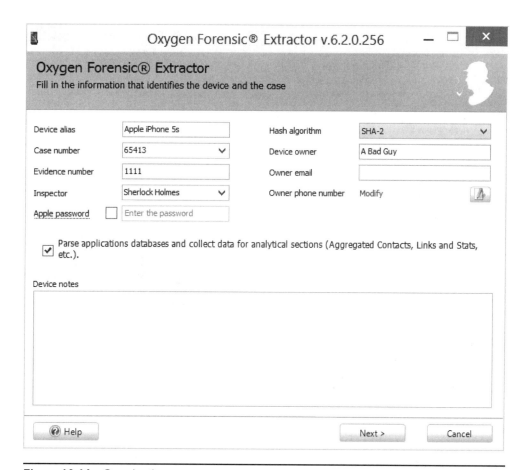

Figure 10-16 Case details

Also of interest is the network information Oxygen generates for you. For example, Oxygen will list all the WiFi networks that phone has connected to and the last date they were connected to. This can be seen in Figure 10-19.

NOTE As part of my own work in forensics, I frequently have discussions with various law enforcement officers. A U.S. Secret Service agent had a concern I wanted to pass along to all readers. The concern is that tools like the ones we just described may be too good. By that, I mean it is possible to extract evidence without knowing how the tool works internally or how evidence is to be handled. This can lead to mishandled cases. While I absolutely recommend using the tools, and the more automation, the better, it is critical that you know how the tool works and understand forensic procedure. That is one reason that certifications like the CCFP are so important.

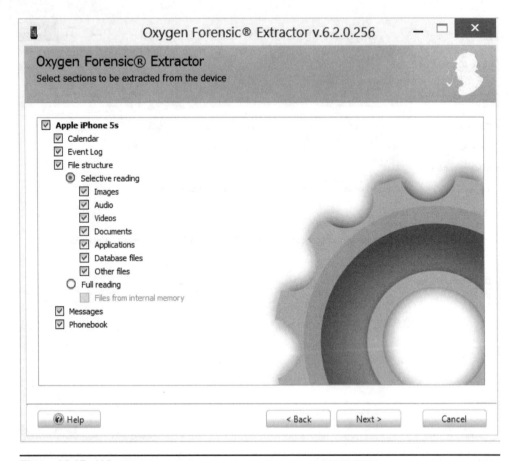

Figure 10-17 What to extract

Figure 10-18 Results

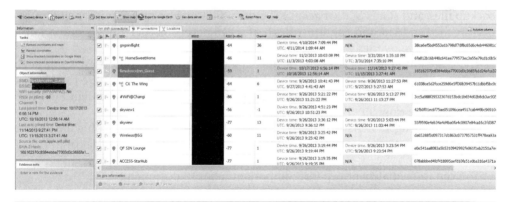

Figure 10-19 iPhone WiFi

Windows 8 Phone

Forensics for a Windows 8 phone is done in much the same way forensics for a Windows 8 PC or laptop is done. The most important issue is to make certain the phone does not synchronize with the forensic workstation. Usually, this is done by setting the phone itself, or the software on the forensic station, to not synchronize on connect. A similar issue arises with the Android. Since it is based on Linux, many of the same forensics techniques can be applied. Keep in mind that a handheld portable device probably will not have all the same logs that a PC or server has, but if the operating system is the same, then the forensics will be largely the same.

The iPhone

It is reasonable to assume that any information that can be viewed on an iPhone will be permanently stored on the device until it becomes overwritten. Most of this data is stored as part of an application installed on the device. There are various types of applications, including those that ship with the iPhone, those installed by the manufacturer, those installed by the wireless carrier, and those installed by the user through the iTunes App store (or those installed on a jailbroken phone through other sources).

Through a backup acquisition, data that has been backed up from the device onto a computer is retrieved. This method is used when the original device is not available. For example, if you cannot find the phone but you see the backup file on a computer you have seized, you can use backup recovery to ascertain what data was on the phone. It is not a perfect solution, since not every bit of data is backed up, and this should only be used in cases where the phone is not available. Because the source of the data is the backup files, only data that is explicitly backed up using Apple's synchronization protocol is recovered.

When an iPhone or iPad is backed up using iTunes, the files are stored in a default location that depends on the operating system being used. The status.plist, info.plist, and manifest.plist are all configuration files containing information about the device, backup files, and status of the backup. The main files that we care about for an acquisition are the *.mddata and *.mdinfo files (or for earlier versions of iTunes, *.mdbackup). These are the binary files that actually contain user data.

There are automated processes for breaking an iPhone passcode. XRY is one such tool (http://news.cnet.com/8301-1023_3-57405580-93/iphone-passcode-cracking-is-easier-than-you-think/). Keep in mind that the iPhone only has a four-digit PIN. This means there are only 9999 possibilities.

If you are using a forensics workstation with iTunes, you can simply plug the iPhone (or iPad/iPod) into the workstation and use iTunes to extract a great deal of information about the phone.

You can immediately notice three important items to document:

- The iOS version number
- The phone number
- The serial number

Notice you can also see where this phone is backed up to. That can indicate yet another place you should search during your forensic investigation. Some information in the figures shown has been redacted, since this image was taken from an actual phone.

If you have imaged the phone and then search for information, you may have to look more closely to find some data. For example, Library_CallHistory_call_history.db has the entire call history. If you cannot view that directly on the phone itself, the database file has all call information. Cookies can be found in the file Library_Cookies_Cookies .plist. This can give you a history of the phone user's Internet activities. These and other files are actually copied to a PC during synchronization. Here are a few of those files:

- Library_Preferences_com.apple.mobileipod.plist
- Library_Preferences_com.apple.mobileemail.plist
- Library_Preferences_com.apple.mobilevpn.plist

The mobileemail.plist has obvious forensic evidence. It will give you information about e-mail sent and received from the phone. The mobilevpn.plist can also be interesting. If the user has utilized the phone to communicate over a VPN, this file will have information about that.

Types of iPhone Analysis

There are three types of iPhone analysis. They are listed here in order of preference, from least preferred to most preferred:

- **Manual extraction** This means simply viewing on the phone the data it contains. This is the least preferred method. Just as with computers, you want to image a phone and work with the image. Also, manual extraction will not reveal deleted files.

- **Logical extraction** This was discussed previously in this chapter. It is normally done with software that connects to the computer and copies all files in the file structure.

- **Physical extraction** This was also discussed earlier in this chapter. It is a complete bit-by-bit copy of the entire phone's data storage. This is the most preferred method.

Deleted Files

When a file is deleted on the iPhone, iPad, or iPod, it is actually moved to the .Trashes\501 folder. Essentially, the data is still there until it is overwritten, so recently deleted files can be retrieved.

Android Forensics

Fortunately, the general concepts of phone forensics are essentially the same across models and brands. However, there are some specifics to each phone you should be aware of. The primary differences involve where to locate files, what happens with deleted files, and similar issues.

Key Directories

As with any operating system, there are certain directories that are more important than others. A listing of key Android directories is given here:

- **/data** This is the user data partition.
- **/data/data** This is data used by various apps.
- **/mnt/asec** These are encrypted apps.
- **/proc** This is process information, much like the standard Linux /proc directory.
- **/cache** This is the app cache and will often have useful information.

As you might suspect, the /data/data folder has useful information, and is itself divided into subdirectories, listed here:

- **/data/data /lib** Custom library files an application requires
- **/data/data /** Files the developer saves to internal storage
- **/data/data / cache** Files cached by the application, often cache files from the web browser or other apps that use the WebKit engine
- **/data/data /databases** SQLite databases and journal files

Each of these directories can have forensically interesting data.

File System

The Android file system is Yet Another Flash File System 2 (YAFFS2). This was the first file system developed for NAND (Not-AND) flash drive devices and was released in 2002. The file system of the Android device is stored in a few different places within /dev. You can image the drive using the dd Linux command we discussed in Chapter 1.

Embedded Devices

Embedded devices are computer systems with a dedicated function within an electrical system. Usually, it is designed to handle a specific function. These devices often use a Linux-like operating system; thus, Linux forensics may be applicable. Given the breadth of possible devices, it is impossible to cover them in detail.

There are a great many embedded devices. For example, medical devices such as insulin pumps are often embedded computer devices. It is not common to encounter these in a forensic situation, but that may change in the coming years. A number of potential attacks on medical devices have been documented by researchers. For example, insulin pumps and heart monitors have been successfully hacked by researchers.[6] It seems clear that eventually someone will use such attacks to commit a crime, and that will make these devices a subject of forensic analysis. If you are not well versed in the specific device, it is always advisable to get someone who specializes in that device to aid with your forensic examination.

SCADA devices are specialized computers used to manage industrial systems such as manufacturing systems. SCADA is an acronym for Supervisory Control and Data Acquisition. The Stuxnet virus was designed to attack a specific subset of SCADA devices used by Iran in the enrichment of uranium. Since there has already been an incident of a virus infecting these devices, it seems likely that there will be more. Just as with medical devices, you may want to secure the assistance of a specialist in the individual device to aid you in your forensic analysis.

With embedded devices the evidence can be found in locations that are remarkably similar to mobile devices. First you would need to search whatever permanent storage that device might have. This is the most obvious place to look for evidence. You should also check any log files the device might have.

Chapter Review

In this chapter, you have learned the basics of mobile forensics. Of critical importance is understanding the operating systems used in mobile devices. In this chapter, we looked at the basics of the operating systems for mobile devices. We also discussed at some length the types of evidence one can gather from a mobile device. In this chapter, you also received a basic introduction to how to retrieve data from a cell phone using three popular tools.

Questions

1. Why is it important to write-block a phone before doing forensic analysis?

   A. It is not.

   B. To make certain data is not copied to the phone.

   C. To make certain data is not copied to the forensic workstation.

   D. To ensure data on the SIM card is not changed.

2. Which of the following is a 4G standard?

   A. EDGE

   B. GSM

   C. LTE

   D. GSM4

3. SIM stores the _____.

   A. Phone serial number

   B. Mobile Subscriber Identity

   C. Cell network type (i.e., 3G/4G)

   D. Country and issuer

4. Where is the data for roaming phones stored?

   A. HLR

   B. GSM

   C. BTS

   D. VLR

5. The first seven digits of the ICCID identify the _____.

   A. Country and issuer

   B. Phone

   C. User

   D. Vendor

Answers

1. **B.** It is critical to ensure data is not copied to the phone, thus contaminating the phone (think Locard's principle).

2. **C.** LTE is the 4G standard. EDGE and GSM are earlier standards.

3. **B.** SIM is a chip that, among other things, stores the International Mobile Security Identity.

4. **D.** The visitor location register (VLR) stores roaming. HLR is for home users.

5. **A.** The first seven digits of the ICCID identify the country and issuer. After that is a variable-length number that identifies this chip/SIM and then a check digit.

References

1. http://www.forbes.com/sites/gordonkelly/2014/03/24/report-97-of-mobile-malware-is-on-android-this-is-the-easy-way-you-stay-safe/.

2. http://www.9news.com/news/article/351966/222/Cell-phone-pics-leads-to-arrest-in-Jewelry-heist.

3. http://www.utsandiego.com/news/2014/Feb/12/selfie-photo-burglary-arrest-chula-vista/.

4. http://www.wxii12.com/news/cell-phone-photo-leads-to-nc-child-sex-arrest/24978636.

5. http://www.wafb.com/story/24610756/gps-tracking-leads-to-arrest-in-br-shooting-armed-robbery.

6. http://www.timescall.com/longmont-local-news/ci_25303558/longmont-police-cell-phone-app-leads-arrest.

7. http://www.forbes.com/sites/ericbasu/2013/08/03/hacking-insulin-pumps-and-other-medical-devices-reality-not-fiction/.

PART IV

Application Forensics and Emerging Technologies

■ **Chapter 11** Application Forensics
■ **Chapter 12** Malware Forensics
■ **Chapter 13** New and Emerging Forensics Technology

263

Application Forensics

In this chapter you will learn:
- Details on file formats
- Details on the Windows registry
- Other files to find information in
- Web attacks and how to analyze them
- E-mail format and files
- How to analyze a database forensically

In this chapter, we will examine application forensics. This includes files that require specific forensic techniques, web-based application forensics, e-mail forensics, and database forensics. Fortunately, all of these various application issues still depend on the basic forensics methodologies you have been learning throughout this book.

File Formats

In previous chapters, we have discussed various file systems, and even briefly discussed file structure. In this section, we will be discussing files that are part of the operating systems. These include things like the Windows registry, index.dat, and related files.

The Registry

The registry is a repository of everything in Windows. It has all the settings, files you have opened, desktop settings, network information, and more. It is built in a hierarchical structure, consisting of five hives. Given that the Windows registry contains so much information, it is clearly of interest in a forensic investigation. Microsoft describes the registry as follows:

> A central hierarchical database used in the Microsoft Windows family of operating systems to store information necessary to configure the system for one or more users, applications, and hardware devices.

The registry contains information that Windows continually references during operation, such as profiles for each user, the applications installed on the computer, and the types of documents that each can create, property sheet settings for folders and application icons, what hardware exists on the system, and the ports that are being used.[1]

As you will see in this section, there is a great deal of forensic information one can gather from the registry. That is why it is important to have a good, thorough understanding of registry forensics. But first, how do you get to the registry? The usual path is through the tool regedit. In Windows 7 and Server 2008, you select Start and then Run and then type **regedit**. In Windows 8, you will have to go to the applications list and select All Apps and then find regedit. Most forensics tools provide a means for examining the registry as well.

The registry is organized into five sections referred to as *hives*. Each of these sections contains specific information that can be useful to you. The five hives are described here:

- **HKEY_CLASSES_ROOT (HKCR)**   This hive stores information about drag-and-drop rules, program shortcuts, the user interface, and related items.

- **HKEY_CURRENT_USER (HKCU)**   This will be very important to any forensic investigation. It stores information about the currently logged-on user, including desktop settings, user folders, etc.

- **HKEY_LOCAL_MACHINE (HKLM)**   This can also be important to a forensic investigation. It contains those settings common to the entire machine, regardless of the individual user.

- **HKEY_USERS (HKU)**   This hive is critical to forensics investigations. It has profiles for all the users, including their settings.

- **HKEY_CURRENT_CONFIG (HCU)**   This hive contains the current system configuration. This might also prove useful in your forensic examinations.

You can see the registry and these five hives in Figure 11-1.

Figure 11-1
The registry hives

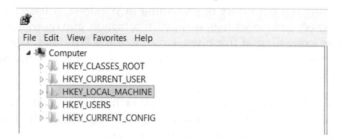

All registry keys contain a value associated with them called LastWriteTime. This value indicates when this registry value was last changed. Rather than a standard date/time, this value is stored as a FILETIME structure. A FILETIME structure represents the number of 100 nanosecond intervals since January 1, 1601. Clearly, this is important forensically.

Let's turn our attention to some specific registry entries that can be very useful forensically.

USB Information

One of the first things most forensic analysts learn about the Windows registry is that they can find out what USB devices have been connected to the suspect machine. The registry key HKEY_LOCAL_MACHINE\System\ControlSet\Enum\UBSTOR lists USB devices that have been connected to the machine. A criminal often will move evidence to an external device and take it with them. This could indicate to you that there are devices you need to find and examine. This registry setting will tell you about the external drives that have been connected to this system. You can see this in Figure 11-2.

Figure 11-2
USB devices in
the registry

>
>
> **NOTE** Just before the UBSTOR key is a key named USB. You might suspect that would be the place to look, but you would be wrong. That key contains information about the actual USB bus within the machine.

Autostart Locations

This key is frequently used by malware to remain persistent on the target system. It shows those programs that are configured to start automatically when Windows starts—for example: HKEY_CURRENT_USER\Software\Microsoft\Windows\CurrentVersion\Run. You can see this in Figure 11-3.

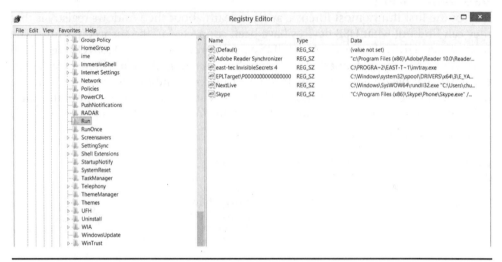

Figure 11-3 Autostart

Obviously, you should expect to see legitimate programs in this registry key. However, if there is anything you cannot account for, this could indicate malware.

Last Visited

The key HKCU\Software\Microsoft\Windows\CurrentVersion\Explorer\ComDlg32\Last-VisitedMRU will show recent sites that have been visited. The data is in hex format, but you can see the text translation when using regedit, and you will probably be able to make out the site visited just looking at regedit. You can see this registry key in Figure 11-4.

Recent Documents

Recent documents can be found at the following key: HKCU\Software\Microsoft\Windows\CurrentVersion\Explorer\RecentDocs. This can be quite forensically important, particularly in cases involving financial data or intellectual property. This key allows you to determine what documents have been accessed on that computer. You can see this key in Figure 11-5.

As you can see, it is first divided into document types. Then, once you select the type, you can see the recent documents of that type that have been accessed. In Figure 11-5, I selected docx as the type and then one specific document. You can see the document name in the image.

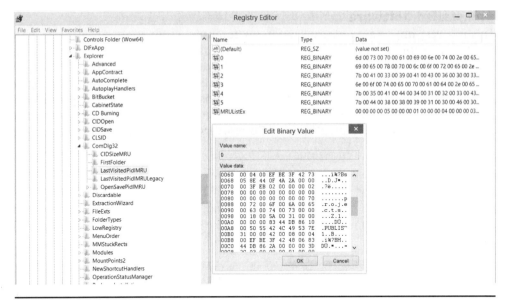

Figure 11-4 Last visited sites

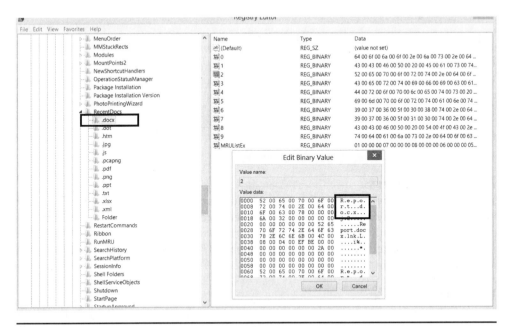

Figure 11-5 Recent documents

Uninstalled Software

This is a very important registry key for any forensic examination. An intruder who breaks into a computer might install software on that computer for various purposes, such as recovering deleted files or creating a back door. He will then most likely delete the software he used. Or, an employee who is stealing data might install steganography software so he can hide the data. He will subsequently uninstall that software. This key lets you see all the software that has been uninstalled from this machine: HKLM\SOFTWARE\Microsoft\Windows\CurrentVersion\Uninstall. You can see the key in Figure 11-6.

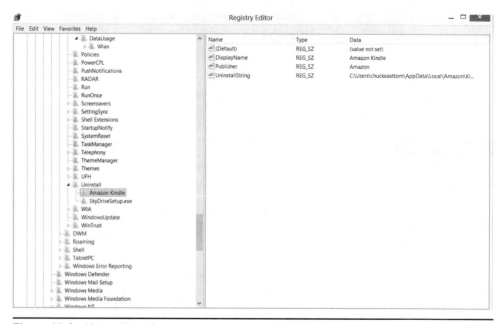

Figure 11-6   Uninstalled software

Network Adapters

This key contains recent settings for the network adapter, such as system IP address and default gateway for the respective network adapters. Each GUID subkey refers to a network adapter. This will tell you all about every network adapter on the suspect machine: HKLM\SYSTEM\CurrentControlSet\Services\Tcpip\Parameters\Interfaces\GUID. You can see this registry key in Figure 11-7.

Wireless Networks

Think, for just a moment, about connecting to a WiFi network. You probably had to enter some passphrase. But you did not have to enter that next time you connected to that WiFi network, did you? Obviously, that information is stored somewhere on the computer.

Figure 11-7 Network adapters

But where? You guessed it—it is stored in the registry. When an individual connects to a wireless network, SSID (Service Set Identification) is logged as a preferred network connection. This information can be found in the registry in the HKLM\SOFTWARE\Microsoft\ Windows NT\CurrentVersion\NetworkList\Profiles\ key. You can see this in Figure 11-8.

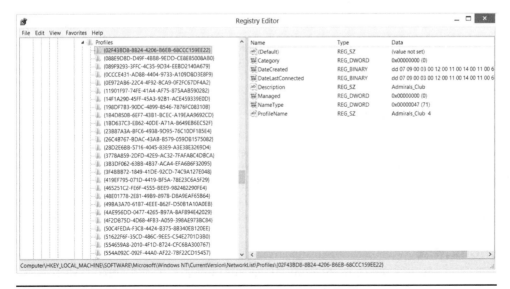

Figure 11-8 Individual network adapter

This can be quite important forensically. It can verify that a suspect was connecting to a specific WiFi network and even when they connected.

Passwords

If the user tells Internet Explorer (IE) to remember passwords, they are stored in the registry and you can retrieve them. The following key holds these values: HKCU\Software\Microsoft\Internet Explorer\IntelliForms\SPW. Note that in some versions of Windows, it will be \IntelliForms\Storage 1. You can see this key in Figure 11-9.

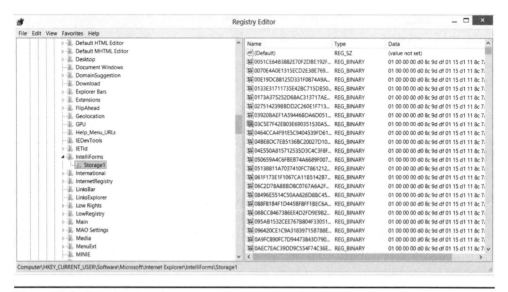

Figure 11-9   Stored passwords

Passwords are encrypted by the operating system. However, tools are available that can decrypt these values, such as Protected Storage PassView by NirSoft or Helix's incident response tools.

Windows Swap File

We have discussed the Windows swap file in previous chapters. It is essentially a special file in the hard drive used to store data temporarily so it can be retrieved by RAM quickly. The Windows swap file used to end in a .swp extension, but since Windows XP, it is now pagefile.sys. It is typically found in the Windows root directory. The swap file is a binary file. Given that the swap file is used to augment RAM, it is often referred to as virtual memory. Since it is a physical file, you can analyze it as you would any other file.

Index.dat

This is an amazing file from the point of view of forensics. It stores pretty much everything the user does using Windows Explorer or Internet Explorer. That includes cookies, websites visited, and even any files opened. Even if the person erases his history, it is still possible to retrieve it if they were using Internet Explorer. Even if a file is on a USB device but was opened on the suspect machine, index.dat would contain a record of that file.

You can download a number of tools from the Internet that will allow you to retrieve and review the index.dat file. Here are a few:

- http://www.eusing.com/Window_Washer/Index_dat.htm
- http://www.acesoft.net/index.dat%20viewer/index.dat_viewer.htm
- http://download.cnet.com/Index-dat-Analyzer/3000-2144_4-10564321.html

You can see Window Washer in Figure 11-10.

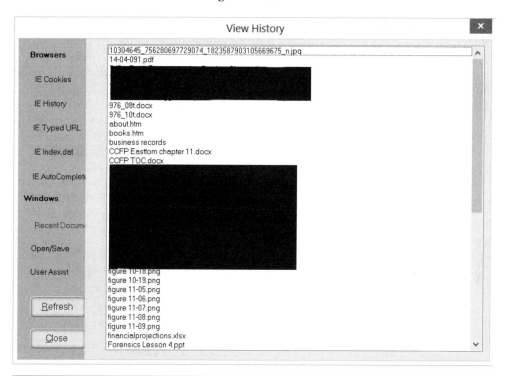

Figure 11-10   Window Washer and index.dat

Of course, many of the more advanced forensic software suites will also analyze the index.dat file for you.

Other Files That Provide Evidence

Many files in any operating system might contain data you can examine. For example, spool files, such as the print spool, can contain data. Print spools usually operate like a queue. That means the first data put in is the first data processed. Old data is not automatically flushed. It remains in the spool until that space is needed. In Windows, the print spool is found at %SystemRoot%\SYSTEM32\SPOOL\PRINTERS. This is a file like any other and can be analyzed using the file-carving techniques we discussed earlier in this book.

Temporary files can also contain valuable information. Windows will have a temporary directory where these are stored. This is usually found at %SystemRoot%\TEMP. Again, these are just files, like any other, and can be examined with any file-carving utility.

 EXAM TIP The CCFP refers to these types of files as either traces or application debris. They are essentially the byproducts of other applications.

Memory Analysis

Obviously, memory is not a file per se; however, there is data in memory. Since memory is volatile, this is referred to as volatile memory analysis. Volatile memory analysis requires you to get a physical dump of the memory. This can be done with many forensic tools. Let's take a look at one easy-to-use tool: RamCapture64 from Belkasoft (http://forensic.belkasoft.com/en/ram/download.asp). When you first launch the tool, it will prompt you for a location to put the output data. This is shown in Figure 11-11.

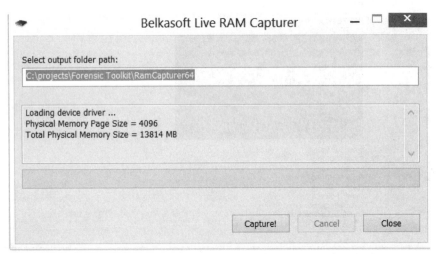

Figure 11-11 RamCapture output location

Then, just click the Capture button and the tool will do the rest. When the process is done, a .mem file will be generated, as seen in Figure 11-12.

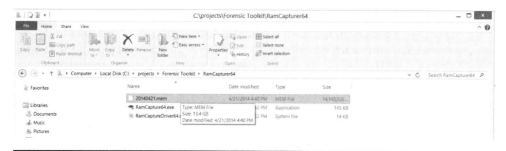

Figure 11-12   RamCapture file

This can be examined using one of the file-carving utilities discussed earlier in this book.

EXAM TIP   In the case of virtual machines, VMware allows you to simply suspend the virtual machine and use the .vmem file as a memory image.

Unlike with traditional hard drive forensics, you don't need to calculate a hash before data acquisition. Due to the volatile nature of running memory, the imaging process involves taking a snapshot of a "moving target." Memory is constantly changing, so computing the hash would be difficult anyway.

To produce digital data from a live system as evidence in court, it is essential to justify the validity of the acquired memory data. One common approach is to acquire volatile memory data in a dump file for offline examination. A dump is a complete copy of every bit of memory or cache recorded in permanent storage or printed on paper. You can then analyze the dump electronically or manually in its static state.

Maintaining data consistency is a problem with live system forensics in which data is not acquired at a unified moment and is thus inconsistent. If a system is running, it is impossible to freeze the machine states in the course of data acquisition. Even the most efficient method introduces a time difference between the moment you acquire the first bit and the moment you acquire the last bit. For example, the program may execute function A at the beginning of the memory dump and execute function B at the end.

The data in the dump may correspond to different execution steps somewhere between function A and function B. Because you didn't acquire the data at a unified moment, data inconsistency is inevitable in the memory dump.

PART IV

What Is Memory?

We have been discussing live memory as if it were a single amorphous entity. In fact, there are actually two types of memory:

- **Stack** (*S*)   Memory in the stack segment is allocated to local variables and parameters within each function. This memory is allocated based on the last-in, first-out (LIFO) principle. When the program is running, program variables use the memory allocated to the stack area again and again. This segment is the most dynamic area of the memory process. The data within this segment is discrepant and influenced by the program's various function calls.

- **Heap** (*H*)   Dynamic memory for a program comes from the heap segment. A process may use a memory allocator such as malloc (this is a C/C++ command to allocate memory) to request dynamic memory. When this happens, the address space of the process expands. The data in the heap area can exist between function calls. The memory allocator may reuse memory that has been released by the process. Therefore, heap data is less stable than the data in the data segment.

When a program is running, the code, data, and heap segments are usually placed in a single contiguous area. The stack segment is separated from the other segments. It expands within the memory-allocated space. Indeed, the memory comprises a number of processes of the operating system or the applications it is supporting. Memory can be viewed as a large array that contains many segments for different processes. In a live system, process memory grows and shrinks, depending on system usage and user activities.

 EXAM TIP   The CCFP won't ask you details regarding types of memory, but for your forensic career, it is useful to know the difference between stack and heap.

Windows File Copying

By default, an object inherits permissions from its parent object, either at the time of creation or when it is copied or moved to its parent folder. The only exception to this rule occurs when you move an object to a different folder on the same volume. In this case, the original permissions are retained.[2]

- Same partition/drive:
  - Copy/paste – Files/folders will inherit the rights of the folder they are being copied to.
  - Cut/paste (move) – Files/folders will retain the original permissions (even if the files/folders have the "Include inheritable permissions…"/" Allow inheritable permissions from parent to propagate to this object…" checked).

> This is because when the files/folders are on the same partition, they don't actually move; rather, the "pointers to their locations" are updated.

- Different partition:
  - Copy/paste OR cut/paste files/folders will inherit the rights of the folder they are being copied to.

 EXAM TIP The CCFP will definitely ask you about file permissions, particularly when files are copied or moved.

Web Forensics

A great many cybercrimes involve the World Wide Web. In this section, we will examine web forensics. We have already discussed IP addresses and protocols in previous chapters. In this chapter, we will discuss common web attacks and how to analyze them. In Chapter 8, we discussed some of these attacks. In this section, we will review what was discussed in Chapter 8, but add more detail and discuss some attacks not covered in Chapter 8. We will also be discussing how to forensically detect these attacks.

Basics of Web Applications

Before we delve deeper into web attacks, we should discuss how web applications are designed. It is often useful to take an historical approach to explaining this. When the Web was first invented, it consisted simply of HTML (Hypertext Markup Language) documents. This provided static, unchanging, and relatively simple web pages. Eventually, CGI (Common Gateway Interface) was created to allow the HTML page to initiate an application running on a server so the application could accomplish more robust tasks for the web page.

In the mid-1990s, a number of technologies emerged. JavaScript provided a scripting language for websites to enhance functionality. CSS (Cascading Style Sheets) provided a means to improve the layout and design of web pages. Eventually, robust programming languages that would run in a web browser emerged. These included Perl Scripts, Java, ASP (Active Server Pages), ASP.Net, and others. This allowed fully functioning and complex programs to be implemented on the Web. This advance led to the explosion of e-commerce, online banking, and other conveniences we take for granted today. However, it also led to the Web becoming the most popular target for hackers.

SQL Injection

SQL injection is a very common web attack. It is based on inserting SQL (Structured Query Language) commands into text boxes, often the user name and password text fields on the login screen. To understand how SQL injection works, you have to first understand the basics of how a login screen is programmed and to understand SQL.

Obviously, a login screen requires the user enter a user name and password and that user name and password have to be validated. Mostly likely, they are validated by checking a database that has a table of users to see if the password matches that user. Relational databases are the most common sort of databases, and they all use SQL. Most of the common databases you are familiar with such as Oracle, Microsoft SQL, MySQL, PostGres, etc., are all relational databases. Modern websites use databases to store data, including login information.

SQL is relatively easy to understand—in fact, it looks a lot like English. There are commands like SELECT to get data, INSERT to put data in, and UPDATE to change data. In order to log in to a website, the web page has to query a database table to see if that user name and password are correct. The general structure of SQL is this:

```
select column1, column2 from tablename
```

or

```
select * from tablename;
```

Conditions:

```
select columns from tablename  where condition;
```

For example:

```
SELECT * FROM tblUsers WHERE USERNAME = 'admin'
```

This statement retrieves all the columns or fields from a table named tblUsers where the user name is admin.

The problem arises because the website is not written in SQL. It is written in some programming language such as PHP, ASP.Net, etc. If you just place SQL statements directly in the web page code, an error will be generated. The SQL statements in the programming code for the website have to use quotation marks to separate the SQL code from the programming code. A typical SQL statement might look something like this:

```
"SELECT * FROM tblUsers WHERE USERNAME = '" + txtUsername.Text +' AND
PASSWORD = '" + txtPassword.Text +"'".
```

If you enter user name "jdoe" and the password "password," this code produces the SQL command:

```
SELECT * FROM tblUsers WHERE USERNAME = 'jdoe' AND PASSWORD = 'password'
```

This is fairly easy to understand, even for nonprogrammers. And it is effective. If there is a match in the database, that means the user name and password match. If no records are returned from the database, that means there was no match, and this is not a valid login.

SQL injection is basically about subverting this process. The idea is to create a statement that will always be true. For example, you enter in ' or '1' = '1 into the user name and password boxes. This will cause the program to create this query:

```
SELECT * FROM tblUsers WHERE USERNAME = '' or '1' = '1' AND PASSWORD = '' or
'1' = '1'.
```

So you are telling the database and application to return all records where user name and password are blank or if 1 = 1. The fact is that 1 always equals 1, so this will work. Now if the programmer wrote the login code properly, this will not work. But in all too many cases, it does work. And then the intruder has logged into your web application and can do whatever any authorized user can do.

The example of SQL injection we just described is the most basic version of SQL injection. SQL injection can be much more advanced than this, and can do quite a bit more than this. In fact, SQL injection is only limited by your own knowledge of SQL. If you wish to delve further into this topic, I suggest the following resources:

- http://www.w3schools.com/sql/sql_injection.asp
- http://www.techkranti.com/2010/03/sql-injection-step-by-step-tutorial.html
- My own YouTube video on this topic: http://www.youtube.com/watch?v=HbjMqs_cN-A

So how do you detect SQL injection? The most important step is to check out the logs for the firewall, web server, and database to look for telltale SQL injection commands, such as ' or '1' = '1. This is only one possible SQL injection technique—there are many others. But there is also some good news about this crime for forensic investigations. The goal of this attack is to gain access to the target site and to get data. Therefore, this is very difficult to do if spoofing your IP address. In other words, if you see evidence of this attack in the logs, the source IP address is likely to be a real IP address. It could be a free WiFi hotspot at some public location, but it will likely be a real IP address, allowing you to at least partially track down the perpetrator.

NOTE This sort of attack is easily prevented by good programming practices. One technique is to simply filter whatever the user types in before processing it. Unfortunately, as late as the writing of this book, I routinely find websites still vulnerable to this attack when I conduct penetration tests/security audits.

Cross-Site Scripting

This attack is closely related to SQL injection. It involves entering data other than what was intended, and it depends on the web programmer not filtering input. The perpetrator finds some area of a website that allows users to type in text that other users will see and then injects client-side script into those fields instead.

NOTE Before I describe this particular crime, I would point out that the major online retailers such as eBay and Amazon.com are not susceptible to this attack. They do filter user input.

To better understand this process, let's look at a hypothetical scenario. Let's assume ABC online book sales has a website. In addition to shopping, users can have accounts with credit cards stored, post reviews, etc. The attacker first sets up an alternative web page that looks as close to the real one as possible. Then the attacker goes to the real ABC online book sales website and finds a rather popular book. He goes to the review section, but instead of typing in a review, he types in this:

```
<script> window.location = "http://www.fakesite.com"; </script>
```

Now when users go to that book, this script will redirect them to the fake site, which looks a great deal like the real one. The attacker then can have the website tell the user that their session has timed out and to please log in again. That would allow the attacker to gather a lot of accounts and passwords. That is only one scenario, but it illustrates the attack.

The way to detect this forensically is two-fold. The most obvious is finding any script embedded in the web page. Another indication would be in the web server logs. Remember that earlier in this book when we discussed network forensics, we mentioned web server messages. The 300 series messages are redirect messages.

Cookie Manipulation

Many websites use what is called a cookie to store data. A cookie is basically a text file that has some information. One common thing they store is simply the user name and the fact that the user is currently logged in. For example, when you log in to a social media site, it might write a cookie that has your user name, the time of login, how long before your session expires, and the fact that you are logged in. It probably won't store the actual password. Unfortunately, this still leads to possible attacks.

A few years ago, one intrepid attacker created a tool called Firesheep. It was an add-on for the Mozilla Firefox browser. What this tool did was sniff the WiFi network the attacker was connected to, listening for a cookie from Facebook. This cookie did not contain a password, but it did contain the user name and that they were logged in. Firesheep would then show that user's profile in a window next to the Firefox browser. The attacker could, at will, simply click the profile in question and be logged on to Facebook as that user. This also worked for other social media sites like Twitter. You can see Firesheep in Figure 11-13. Accounts have been redacted and I used my own Facebook Fan Page image rather than an actual user's.

As far as computer crimes are concerned, hijacking someone's social media page is certainly less serious than some other crimes. However, it is a crime, and as you can see, it is relatively easy to perpetrate. The immediate evidence of this crime is tampering with the social media page, often to post items that would be considered embarrassing to the actual owner of that social media page.

Figure 11-13 Firesheep

Forceful Browsing

This technique is rather primitive. It is based on websites that don't protect files. The attacker types in the complete URL to a specific file in order to download it directly, without even logging into the site. Fortunately, improvements in web programming are making this attack less common. However, if a site is vulnerable to this attack, it is easy to perform. It also may not leave any trace in any logs unless the web server is logging every single request.

XML Injection

When a web user takes advantage of a weakness with SQL by entering values they should not, it is known as a SQL injection attack. Similarly, when the user enters values that query XML (known as XPath) with values that take advantage of exploits, it is known as an *XML injection attack*. XPath works similarly to SQL, except that it does not have the same levels of access control, and taking advantage of weaknesses within can return entire documents.

E-mail Forensics

E-mail forensics is a critical area to explore. A variety of crimes involve e-mail. Spam, cyber stalking, fraud, phishing—these are all e-mail–based cybercrimes. In this section, we will first examine how e-mail works and then look at how to forensically analyze it.

PART IV

How E-mail Works

Before we can begin delving into e-mail forensics, we have to understand how e-mail works. The sender will first type an e-mail message using their preferred e-mail software (i.e., Outlook, Eudora, etc.). The e-mail is sent first to that sender's e-mail server. Usually, that will be the company server or ISP server. That e-mail server will then send the e-mail to the recipient's e-mail server. When the recipient logs on to their e-mail program, they can retrieve the e-mail from their server. You can see this in Figure 11-14.

Figure 11-14
How e-mail
works

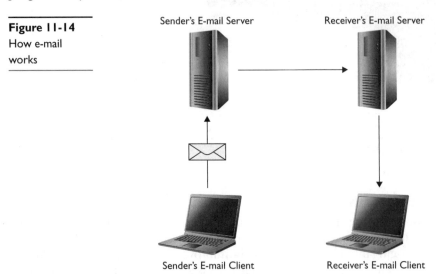

Sender's E-mail Server   Receiver's E-mail Server

Sender's E-mail Client   Receiver's E-mail Client

This process is important forensically. E-mail evidence can be found at any of these locations. It could be on the sender's computer, the sender's e-mail server, the recipient's e-mail server, or the recipient's computer. When investigating crimes that have an e-mail component, it is important to check all four sources. Obviously, a subpoena may be needed to get e-mail records from an Internet service provider. It also is possible that they have purged their records; however, they may still have backups of the server that would have records.

It is also important to keep in mind that the content of e-mail can be very important even in noncomputer crime cases. Given how common e-mail communications are, it should no surprise to you to find that criminals often communicate via e-mail. Some crimes, like cyber stalking, usually include an e-mail element. Other crimes, such as drug trafficking and terrorism, can utilize e-mail communication. In financial crimes, such as insider trading, as well as in civil litigation, e-mail is often a critical piece of evidence. Keep in mind that the sender and perhaps even the recipient may have deleted the e-mail, but it could still reside on an e-mail server or in the backup media for that server.

E-mail Protocols

Earlier in this book, we introduced you to basic e-mail protocols. Before we go deeper into e-mail forensics, it is necessary to refresh your memory on this topic. The first e-mail protocol we will look at is Simple Mail Transfer Protocol (SMTP) that is used to send e-mail. This typically operates on port 25. There is also secure SMTP that is encrypted with either SSL or TLS, and that protocol operates on port 465. For many years, Post Office Protocol version 3 (POP3) was the only means for retrieving e-mail. However, in recent years, there has been an improvement on POP3. That improvement is IMAP. Internet Message Access Protocol operates on port 143. One advantage of IMAP over POP3 is that it allows the client to download only the headers to the machine and then the user can choose which messages to fully download. This is particularly useful for smartphones.

Spoofed E-mail

The process of spoofing e-mail involves making an e-mail message appear to come from someone or somewhere other than the real sender or location. The e-mail sender uses a software tool that is readily available on the Internet to cut out his or her IP address and replace it with someone else's address. However, the first machine to receive the spoofed message records the sending machine's real IP address. Thus, the header contains both the faked ID and the real IP address (unless, of course, the perpetrator is clever enough to have also spoofed their IP address).

Many websites will let someone send an e-mail and choose any "from" address they want. Here are just a few:

- http://sendanonymousemail.net/
- http://theanonymousemail.com/
- http://send-email.org/

Even though e-mail can be spoofed, it is still important to forensically examine it. In many cases, including cyber stalking, civil litigation, etc., it is less common to find spoofed e-mails.

E-mail Headers

One of the first things to learn about is the headers. The header for an e-mail message tells you a great deal about the e-mail. The standard for e-mail format, including headers, is RFC 2822. It is important that all e-mail use the same format. That is why you can send an e-mail from Outlook on a Windows 8 PC and the recipient can read it from their Hotmail account on an Android phone (that runs Linux for an operating system!). All e-mail programs use the same format, regardless of what operating system they run on.

Make sure that any e-mail you offer as evidence includes the message, any attachments, and the full e-mail header. The header keeps a record of the message's journey as it travels through the communications network. As the message is routed through one or more mail servers, each server adds its own information to the message header. Each device in a network has an IP address that identifies the device and provides a location address. A forensic investigator may be able to identify the IP addresses from a message header and use this information to determine who sent the message.

Obviously, the content of the e-mail itself could be evidence of a crime. In the case of child pornography sent via e-mail, cyber stalking, or in civil cases where the e-mail has incriminating messages, the message itself (along with attachments) can be compelling evidence. But it is important to also examine the message header.

Consider the specifications for the e-mail format given in RFC 2822:

NOTE   RFCs are "request for comments," and they are the standards for various network protocols established by the Internet Engineering Task Force (IETF).

- The message header must include at least the following fields:
  - *From*: The e-mail address, and optionally, the name of the sender.
  - *Date*: The local time and date the message was written.
- The message header should include at least the following fields:
  - *Message-ID*: Also an automatically generated field.
  - *In-Reply-To*: Message-ID of the message that this is a reply to. Used to link related messages together.

RFC 3864 describes message header field names. Common header fields for e-mail include:

- *To*: The e-mail address.
- *Subject*: A brief summary of the topic of the message.
- *Cc*: Carbon copy; send a copy to secondary recipients.
- *Bcc*: Blind carbon copy; addresses added to the SMTP delivery list that are not shown to other recipients.
- *Content-Type*: Information about how the message is to be displayed, usually a MIME type.
- *Precedence*: Commonly with values "bulk," "junk," or "list"; used to indicate that automated "vacation" or "out of office" responses should not be returned for this mail, e.g., to prevent vacation notices from being sent to all other subscribers of a mailing list.
- *Received*: Tracking information generated by mail servers that have previously handled a message, but in reverse order (last handler first).
- *References*: Message-ID of the message that this is a reply to.
- *Reply-To*: Address that should be used to reply to the message.

- *Sender*: Address of the actual sender acting on behalf of the author listed in the From header.

The headers are to be read chronologically from bottom to top—the oldest are at the bottom. Every new server on the way adds its own message. One of the first issues is to see who sent the e-mail. Following is the header information from an e-mail I sent to myself from one e-mail address I have to another for testing purposes. I have bolded important items.

X-Apparently-To: chuck@chuckeasttom.com via 98.138.83.191; Tue, 22 Apr 2014 16:59:18 +0000
Received-SPF: none (domain of cec-security.com does not designate permitted sender hosts)
X-YMailISG: HnqC9kgWLDurJ7R3t2xKTOhqmJuptmbl1HkGtHSTNu8dS4M2
xMKy4SogkFof.zujJKGroSdCwC0.LFH.rc17CxJb63OYRkuNQ6ta6bq.bEyd
v.RryfHe_1hU04UU72BFufYJErl3.QimX4CNkGll14ty4kr2y1LRIUtEm8mf
BdtspKAQc.hk75UDi0wsbQtwBZa_T.fpQ5cyh4.GaK07lxFjpWOoTTnBGui_
yD6GTlz6eiDfAzAgx0tlhq0k48_bwZFZ6JsixZe6UUtRJyXE2u5.Z5QFfZ18
r2hxQqIonP1owUr0rK8WMcBHxHLRaXbpm.Bf1.o3Szsrd2epjLLmpv_ULeKz
yIjibV7zj9TFOlHr.67lQ5sJLavMqec.pki2oaZQBn1ULP27O7EgOsFN6ziM
jwgXNFY3Vvufj6mYWfzexU7b_8.BZo4fEj2cO1753a4HBMpKrDFMiZxfUphn

e68YjMgmPmXQlDKPKCvMMa3XRKYnaYsBqc0GDyQKKJ7GHQAxssCeI-
u4OZdS
9tRQOgY8JLHdtsX92wUD6kF4dG6ZfTvZc1eej50xNVWYZZxc17G6ZiA5O62l
uf4dd7VlAUstwF.AXsFyA7kNTOtTKVAdSPZxMJAEuF.qZfUWUrkPoENBe4gG
50NQ1v4yXkkqVn7w4Jx2ZRkIa6pgJ3jVyvvBgssS6jIEZeOw9.ef1juige6C
ikofU6EM3d7FF141Sx6CpRaCbX5IrD7rlYzdXkPmiFUgje914L_kchQSa9QX
JcBeM4cj6JqUf6QIgA6MBuSpX_eqkOFWNYHVJmsaszRbqeZftVvhjPoO_uE8
5s7XU41AZJ8J7xxUZv4DZUhqlVCPm2w4SOSpV5U49AbXSGQlDIjrIw.bxbso
GAXGqDuvAsa_F_rnsZOsxPBQKB2zQ8Pc1fSqhNnC6XbiWWuYD4AsSwe08_
UJ
IrpYCjW7oZ2J6NT3nFsKyMW3IOjKXJ.4I6._jpVoJa54TOs6.MrPAWLBWVzl
KA0rE9hxg7f2J8uXBJgDA5HKslV0JfmUF9oujCmMHdDQ9gM_NydiVsDKoxmg
MkHrN4j5CnMOFZllM4mcr2ivKlw521Hn.sbYoNprDng508eTNVFl.75Q774b
YD46b.llTJfsEslkRGzasm09sCWA12Z8WlSxVx1SJzGi7WbZ5PefsU1PsFcM
6Wdj.hL.gHvYBNXFP6oh39ABEkTP39hf86cy8VWp_Q2yWmz.z5WSfSd6jFyR
gQLH4W0KlygKRet.njaffo0qoYYayDa.pX43OGucAeOIfPFGn.Iv5cioLSM2
73sWC06iSYEZnz0UgfdYkwHRb_d_ctEti3f2Akkxs81TG.HIj3OlACvd68I8
nhdCpdBWxs7msndHtk5ViyTBu5SfpgI2SBRBxcshMIo0jINl6c2KAYM-
X-Originating-IP: [173.201.192.105]
Authentication-Results: mta1010.biz.mail.gq1.yahoo.com from=cec-security.com;
domainkeys=neutral (no sig); from=cec-security.com; dkim=neutral (no sig)
Received: from 127.0.0.1 (EHLO p3plsmtpa06-04.prod.phx3.secureserver.net)
(173.201.192.105)

by mta1010.biz.mail.gq1.yahoo.com with SMTP; Tue, 22 Apr 2014 16:59:17 +0000
Received: from cecmain ([173.64.206.194])
   by p3plsmtpa06-04.prod.phx3.secureserver.net with
   id t4zF1n00X4CB0Ed014zG7A; Tue, 22 Apr 2014 09:59:17 -0700
From: "Chuck Easttom" <ceasttom@cec-security.com>
To: "Chuck Easttom" <chuck@chuckeasttom.com>
Subject: Test Message
Date: Tue, 22 Apr 2014 11:59:15 -0500
Message-ID: <00a001cf5e4c$31fc56a0$95f503e0$@cec-security.com>
MIME-Version: 1.0
Content-Type: multipart/mixed;
   boundary="----=_NextPart_000_00A1_01CF5E22.492C6920"
X-Mailer: Microsoft Outlook 15.0
Content-Language: en-us
Thread-Index: Ac9eTC6Yocf6q6bIQPe+s7XJm2yRVg==
X-MS-TNEF-Correlator:
0000000042B94DC204F2AC4A836F291A4ABFD7EDC4E32200

The *Received from* line shows the e-mail server used to send the e-mail. The second line shows the IP address of the user who sent the e-mail using this server. The actual *From* field can be forged, so you want to look at the *Received from* field. *Date* shows the date and time the message was composed. *X-Mailer* tells you the e-mail client the sender used.

Return path and *Reply to* are the same, and this is where replies will be sent. Seeing any mismatches between Received from, From, Return path, and Reply is an indication this e-mail might be spoofed. It is also usually a good idea to trace any IP addresses. For example, an e-mail that purports to be from your local bank in Tampa, Florida, but that actually comes from an IP address in China is likely to be spoofed.

Get Headers in Outlook 2010

The simplest method that works in Outlook 2010 and Outlook 2013 is to first select a message and open it, as shown in Figure 11-15.

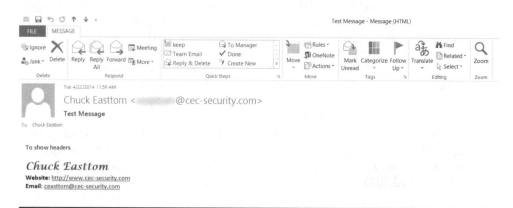

Figure 11-15 Outlook message

Then, with the message open, select File and then Properties, as shown in Figure 11-16.

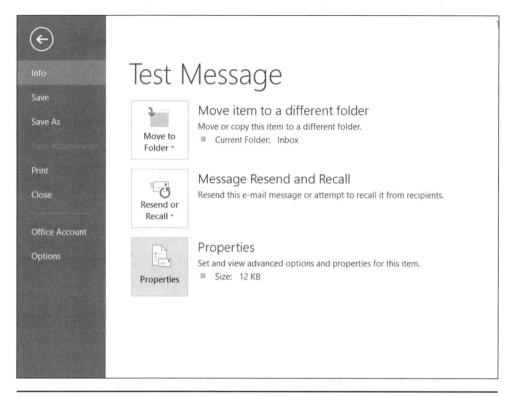

Figure 11-16 Outlook message properties

Then you will see the headers, shown in Figure 11-17.

Get Headers from Yahoo! E-mail
If you are working with Yahoo! e-mail, first open the message. Then select Actions and then Full Headers, as shown in Figure 11-18.

Then you can examine the header information.

Get Headers from Gmail
Viewing e-mail headers in Gmail is fairly simple and not that different from Yahoo! mail. You first open the message. Then, on the right, click the drop-down list, and select Show Original. This will give you the full headers, as shown in Figure 11-19.

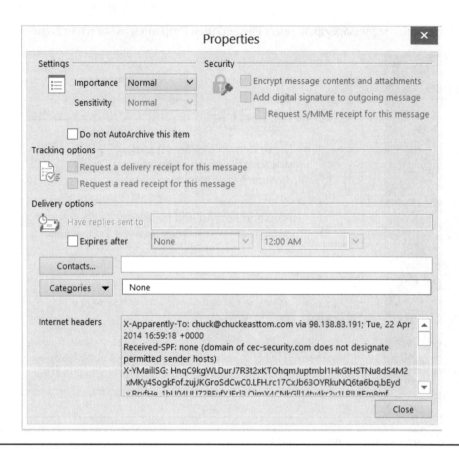

Figure 11-17 Outlook headers

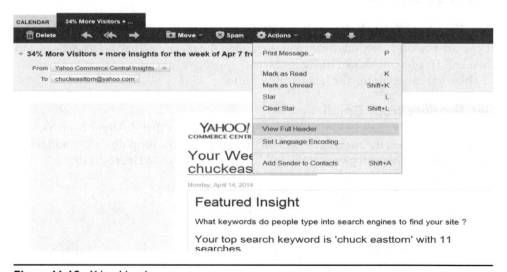

Figure 11-18 Yahoo! headers

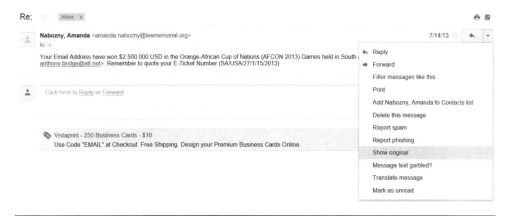

Figure 11-19 Gmail headers

E-mail Files

E-mail clients store the e-mail on the local machine. That means there is a file somewhere on your computer that has your entire mailbox. That includes all subfolders, calendars, etc. The file extension will depend on the e-mail client you are using. Here is a list of the most common e-mail client file extensions:

- .pst (Outlook)
- .ost (Offline Outlook Storage)
- .mbx or .dbx (Outlook Express)
- .mbx (Eudora)
- .emi (common to several e-mail clients)

If a person has multiple e-mails set up with an e-mail client, each e-mail will have its own file. For example, if you use Outlook and have jdoe@xyz.com and jdoe@abc.com, each will have a separate file. It is also possible for someone who wishes to hide e-mail communication to have a separate e-mail file that they leave detached from their client. So it is a good idea to scan the suspect drive(s) for any e-mail files. Most major forensics suites such as EnCase and FTK will examine e-mail and search for key terms.

Tracing E-mail

E-mail tracing involves examining e-mail header information to look for clues about where a message has been. This will be one of your more frequent responsibilities as a forensic investigator. You will often use audits or paper trails of e-mail traffic as evidence in court. One of the first steps is to trace where the e-mail came from. You will get the necessary IP addresses from the headers, but then you have to trace it to its origin. You can do this with a simple tracert command (traceroute in Linux and Unix). You can tracert either IP addresses or domain names, as shown in Figure 11-20.

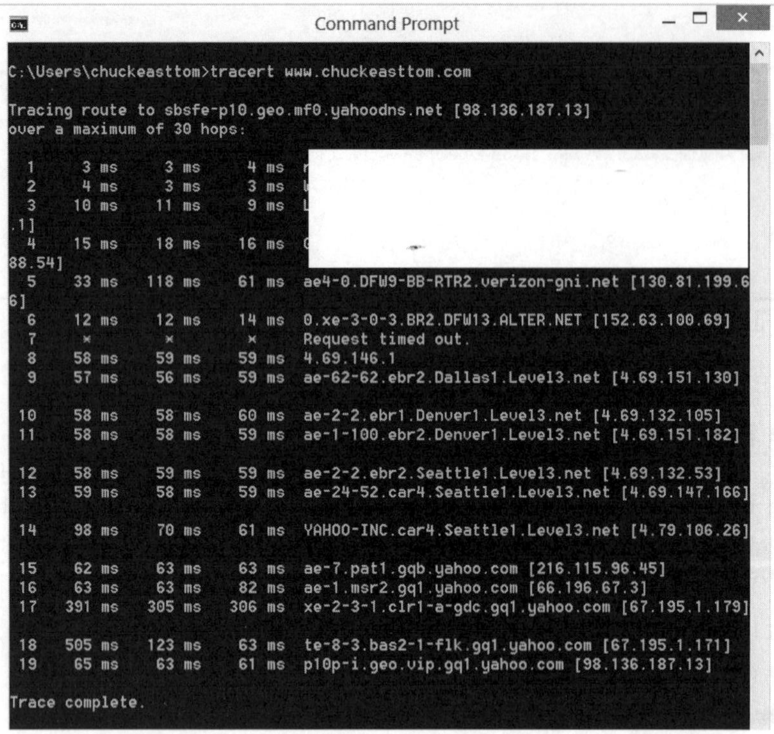

Figure 11-20 Using tracert to examine e-mail

You can also use the Whois tools described in Chapter 8 to track down who an IP address or domain name is registered to.

E-mail Server Forensics

At some point, you need to check the e-mail server. Both the sender and the recipient could have deleted relevant e-mails, but there is a good chance a copy is still on the e-mail server. When you examine an e-mail server, be aware that a variety of e-mail server programs could be in use. Microsoft Exchange is a common server. Lotus Notes and Novell Groupwise are also popular e-mail server products.

The file formats associated with the most widely used e-mail server software are listed here:

- Exchange Server (.edb)
- Exchange Public Folders (pub.edb)

- Exchange Private Folders (priv.edb)

- Streaming Data (priv.stm)

- Lotus Notes (.nsf)

- GroupWise (.db)

- GroupWise Post Office Database (wphost.db)

- GroupWise User databases (userxxx.db)

- Linux E-Mail Server Logs/var/log/mail.*

Obviously, tools like Forensic Toolkit and EnCase will allow you to add these files to a case and to work with them. You can also manually examine these files provided you have access to the relevant software (i.e., Exchange, Lotus Notes, etc.).

Database Forensics

Databases are often the focus of computer crime. This is because many crimes, like fraud and identity theft, center on information. Therefore, it is logical for the database to be a target. This means that database forensics is also important.

Database Types

We have already discussed relational databases earlier in this chapter and their reliance on SQL. Here we will provide just a little bit more information. Relational databases are constructed of columns or fields that are ordered by tables that, in turn, are organized into databases. For example, you might have a table that has student data. It would have columns such as last name, first name, city, state, etc. Then you might have another table with class information. It would have columns such as class name, description, prerequisites, etc. These tables would be linked via key columns. You can see this in Figure 11-21.

There are several widely used, well-known relational databases that you are likely to encounter in your forensic career. Each are briefly described here:

- **Microsoft SQL Server**   This is Microsoft's database server for medium to large-scale databases. It is a full-featured relational database that is widely used.

Figure 11-21

How relational databases work

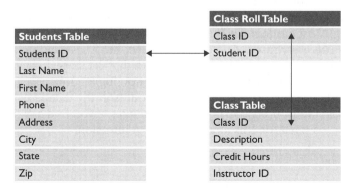

- **Oracle**   Oracle and Microsoft SQL Server are the two most widely used commercial relational database systems. They both have a robust and complex structure.

- **Microsoft Access**   This system is meant for small databases, no more than 2 gigabytes in size. It lacks some of the more advanced features found in Microsoft SQL Server.

- **MySQL**   This is a popular open-source database management system. It is very popular in the web development community. In fact, one will often see jobs for a LAMP developer, LAMP being an acronym for Linux, Apache, MySQL, and PHP. So when investigating web crimes, you are likely to see MySQL.

- **PostGres**   This is another popular open-source database management system, especially Linux/Unix users.

Another type of database is the NoSQL database. The book *Getting Started with NoSQL* (Packt Publishing, 2013) describes NoSQL as follows: "In computing, NoSQL (mostly interpreted as 'not only SQL') is a broad class of database management systems identified by its non-adherence to the widely used relational database management system model; that is, NoSQL databases are not primarily built on tables, and as a result, generally do not use SQL for data manipulation."[3] MongoDB is a common implementation of the NoSQL database.[4]

A hierarchical database is one in which the data is linked from parent to child data.[5] Forensically, this does not significantly change the analysis. Hierarchical structures were widely used in the first mainframe database management systems, but have been mostly supplanted by relational databases.

There are also object-oriented databases. These databases are built using the same principles applied in object-oriented programming. This entails child objects inheriting properties or data from parent objects and then modifying or adding to those properties or data. This method has been around for many years, but has not gained wide use. The relational database model is the most widely used.

What to Look For

Databases often are stored on their own servers, so you should start with the same examinations you would do for any server. That means looking at logs, checking for malware, restoring deleted files, etc. However, some items are unique to databases.

One of the best places to seek forensic evidence regarding a database is the transaction log. Most modern database systems are set up to log every transaction that occurs. That means every insert, delete, update, select, etc. These transaction logs will provide a very good picture of what has occurred with that database. In any forensic examination involving databases, reviewing the transaction log is a must.

It is also important to look at user accounts in the database. It is possible to add a new user via advanced SQL injection techniques. If you find any user accounts that cannot be accounted for, this might indicate an intrusion.

Database backups are also an important source of forensic evidence. Databases are usually backed up quite frequently. This is to allow the system to be restored to operation should there be a database crash. Fortunately for forensic analysts, this also provides a means to potentially find data that may have been deleted from the current running database system.

 NOTE Databases are often the ultimate target for financially motivated cybercrimes. Being at least basically proficient in a few of the most widely used database management systems is definitely recommended for any forensic analyst.

Record Carving and Database Reconstruction

It is not uncommon to uncover a database that has damaged data. This can occur because data has been deleted or because the database has become corrupted.

Record carving is a process to recover deleted records from a database. This occurs not just in traditional relational database systems, but also in smaller systems like the SQLite used in some smartphones. In some cases, the records are carved from a disk image in an attempt to restore data. The process is similar to file carving. Record carving requires specialized tools—wdsCarve is one such tool.

One can also reference transaction logs to attempt to recover missing data. For example, Microsoft SQL Server has the main database file (.mdf file) and a log file (.ldf). By reviewing the transactions that brought the database to its current state, it might be possible to reconstruct damaged or missing data. Continuing with Microsoft SQL Server as an example database management system, you can see multiple fields in the log. The transaction ID and the operation are the two most important. The first identifies the transaction, and the second tells you what was done (update, delete, insert, etc.). The SANS institute publishes a paper that provides a walk-through of recovering an SQL database.[6]

Chapter Review

A number of crimes can be perpetrated via databases, e-mail, files, etc. Each of these has its own specific forensic challenges and techniques. It is important that you have a working knowledge of these various forensic issues. Web attacks such as SQL injection are quite common, and you will likely encounter these during your career.

Questions

1. Firesheep is an example of:

   A. SQL injection

   B. Cookie manipulation

   C. Forceful browsing

   D. XML injection

2. What is the most common type of database management system?

   A. SQL Server

   B. Object oriented

   C. NoSQL

   D. Relational

3. Which of the following protocols encrypts outgoing e-mail?

   A. SMTPS

   B. POP3

   C. IMAP

   D. POP4

4. If you copy a file between two folders on different partitions, what permissions will the file have after being copied?

   A. The source folder

   B. Neither folder

   C. The destination folder

   D. The source partition

5. Which of the following is the extension of a local Microsoft Outlook e-mail file?

   A. MDB

   B. MFT

   C. PST

   D. XML

Answers

1. **B.** Firesheep works by manipulating cookies, specifically copying them.

2. **D.** Relational databases are the most common.

3. **A.** The last S in SMTPS is for "secure," and it is SMTP encrypted with either SSL or TLS.

4. **C.** When copying or moving between partitions, the file always inherits the properties of the destination folder.

5. **C.** Microsoft Outlook stores mailboxes locally in .pst files.

References

1. Microsoft Computer Dictionary.

2. http://support.microsoft.com/kb/310316.

3. *Getting Started with NoSQL* by Gaurav Vaish.

4. http://www.mongodb.org/.

5. http://codex.cs.yale.edu/avi/db-book/db6/appendices-dir/e.pdf.

6. https://www.sans.org/reading-room/whitepapers/application/forensic-analysis-sql-server-2005-database-server-1906.

CHAPTER 12

Malware Forensics

In this chapter you will learn about
- Viruses, how they work, and the various types
- Various malware, including spyware, logic bombs, and Trojan horses
- How to understand advanced persistent threats
- How to perform malware analysis

Malware is a term for software that does some malicious action. It takes many forms: viruses, Trojan horses, spyware, root kits, logic bombs, ransomware, etc. These are so common that it is guaranteed your forensic career will be replete with cases involving malware. In this chapter, we will examine the various forms of malware, how one finds evidence of them, and how to conduct malware analysis.

Viruses

The first issue to address is to define what a virus is. A virus is any software that self-replicates. This might seem incomplete to you. You might think that in order for software to be classified as a virus, it must do some terrible misdeed to the host computer—perhaps alter the Windows registry, delete files, or perform some other sort of attack. While many viruses do cause harm to the infected computer, the definition of a virus is simply self-replication.

How a Virus Spreads

With self-replication being the defining factor for a virus, the next question is how do they spread? This is an interesting topic because at one time, a virus was considered separate from a worm, based on how each spreads. Today, the line between virus and worm is quite blurry, and we will assume the two terms mean essentially the same thing. A virus will usually spread in one of two ways. The first method is to read your e-mail address book and e-mail itself to everyone in it. The second method is to simply scan your computer for connections to a network and then copy itself to other machines on the network to which your computer has access. This is actually the most efficient way for a virus to spread. However, this method requires more programming skill than other methods.

Microsoft Outlook is a common target for virus writers. The reason is not so much a security flaw in Outlook as it is the ease of working with Outlook. All Microsoft Office products are made so that a legitimate programmer who is writing software for a business can access many of the application's internal objects and thereby easily create applications that integrate with the Microsoft Office suite. For example, a programmer could write an application that accesses a Word document, imports an Excel spreadsheet, and then uses Outlook to automatically e-mail the resulting document to interested parties. Microsoft has worked to make this process easy. There are numerous code examples on the Internet, including in the Microsoft Developer Network (MSDN), that illustrate how to automate Outlook as well as other Office products. Essentially, the ease of programming Outlook is why there are so many virus attacks that target Outlook.

Real-World Cases

The following are a few recent examples of viruses. It is important to consider real-world cases and understand how they work in order to be prepared for the viruses you might encounter during your investigations.

Fake Antivirus

FakeAV is a virus that spreads by purporting to be an antivirus software program for several versions of Windows. The various versions of FakeAV appear to be Windows antivirus programs and have an interface that is consistent with the version of Windows they were written for. This lures many end users into thinking these are legitimate antivirus products, perhaps even official Microsoft products. This leads to the user downloading and installing the software. FakeAV usually takes over the browser, thus preventing the user from going to the Web and downloading a legitimate tool, such as Malware Bytes.

 NOTE   Malware Bytes (www.malwarebytes.org) is a popular tool for removing malware on an infected machine. There is a free version and a commercial version.

There is now a version for Windows 8 called Windows 8 Security System. One of the tasks it accomplishes is to make FakeAV even more entrenched in the system and harder to remove. You can see a screen shot in Figure 12-1.

The virus installs as a driver. It also takes over the Action Center, supplanting its fake Action Center for the real one. The fake Action Center tells the victim the computer is not properly protected against viruses and spyware, as you can see in Figure 12-2.

Mac Defender and Mac Security are two viruses that both purport to be antivirus programs for Macintosh. Starting in 2011, these viruses began to appear more often. There have also been newer versions. The file is labeled as "safe" for the Safari browser, so it can be executed immediately upon download without needing the administrator password. This makes it a dangerous piece of malware. Macintosh has

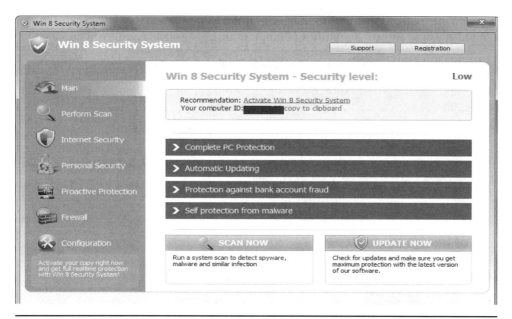

Figure 12-1   Windows 8 Security System virus

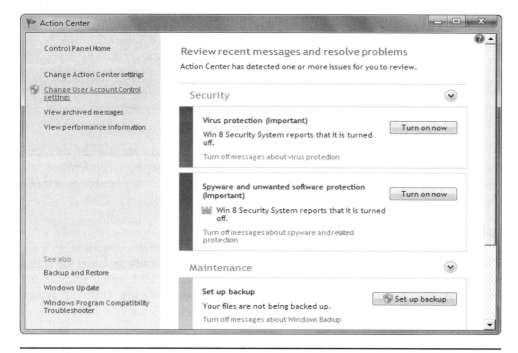

Figure 12-2   Fake Action Center

released instructions on cleaning this virus from an infected system.[1] You can see one version of this malware in Figure 12-3.

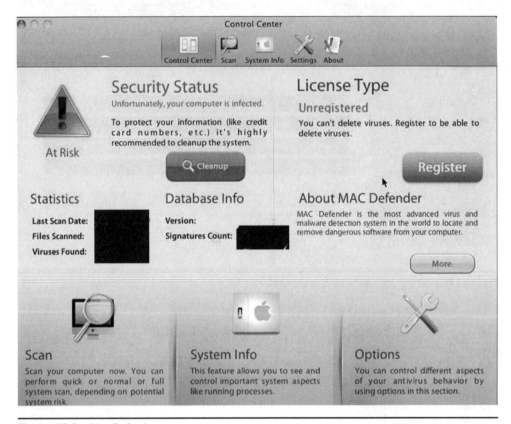

Figure 12-3   Mac Defender

The purpose of this, and most fake antivirus software, is to convince the user that their system is infected with a virus that only this "antivirus" program can remove. The user then pays for the full version because the trial/free version is not able to remove the virus infecting the system. You can see this in Figure 12-4.

Famous Recent Viruses

The Flame virus first appeared in 2012 and was targeting Windows operating systems. The first item that makes this virus notable is that it was specifically designed for espionage. Flame is spyware that can monitor network traffic and take screen shots of the infected system. It was first discovered at an Iranian government site. This virus is also notable because it used a forged digital certificate to trick systems into accepting it as legitimate software.

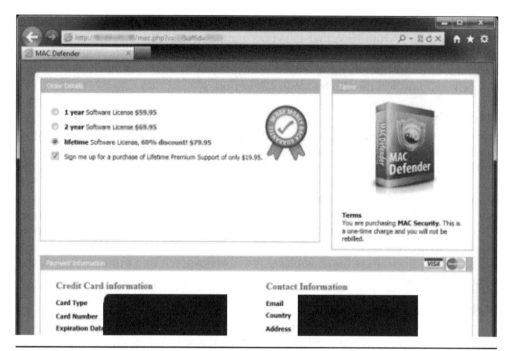

Figure 12-4   User credit card

Types of Viruses

You will need to understand several different types of viruses. A brief description of the most common types is given here.

Armored Virus

An *armored virus* uses techniques that make it hard to analyze. Code confusion is one such method. The code is written such that if the virus is disassembled, the code won't be easily followed. Compressed code is another method for armoring the virus.

Sparse Infection Virus

A *sparse infection virus* will only be active intermittently and for short periods. This makes it much harder to detect. The virus is dormant much of the time and only causes whatever malicious actions it has sporadically. If it is well written, it will only infect at random intervals, not at regular intervals. The intermittent nature of the attack is what makes them so difficult for antivirus to detect. For example, the virus may not be active when a virus scan is run.

In some cases the sparse infector targets a specific program but the virus only executes every 10th time or 20th time that target program executes. Or a sparse infector may have a burst of activity and then lay dormant for a period of time. There are a number of variations on the theme, but the basic principle is the same: to reduce the frequency of attack and thus reduce the chances for detection.

Macro Virus

A *macro virus* is written into a macro in some business application. For example, Microsoft Office allows users to write macros to automate some tasks. Microsoft Outlook is designed so that a programmer can write scripts using a subset of the Visual Basic programming language, called Visual Basic for Applications (VBA). This scripting language is, in fact, built into all Microsoft Office products. Programmers can also use the closely related VBScript language. Both languages are quite easy to learn. If such a script is attached to an e-mail and the recipient is using Outlook, then the script can execute. That execution can do any number of things, including scanning the address book, looking for addresses, sending out e-mail, deleting e-mail, and more.

Multipartite Virus

A *multipartite virus* attacks your system in multiple ways, but usually infects the boot sector as well as some other portion of the system. File infection viruses are made to infect some file on the computer, and they spread when the user runs the infected file. Boot sector viruses run when the computer boots up. A multipartite virus does both. For example, a multipartite virus might affect the boot sector and make changes to a specific file or the Windows registry.

Polymorphic

Polymorphic viruses derive their name from the fact that they change form in order to avoid detection. The virus will attempt to hide from your antivirus software, often by encrypting parts of itself. When the virus does this, it's referred to as *mutation*. The mutation process makes it hard for antivirus software to detect common characteristics of the virus.

It is not uncommon for modern viruses to have more than one modality. For example, a polymorphic virus might be armored and multipartite.

History of Viruses

Viruses are not a new problem. They have been around for many years. However, the behavior of viruses and the frequency of infections have definitely changed. The following table reviews some significant milestones in virus history.

1981	Apple Viruses 1, 2, and 3 are some of the first viruses "in the wild" or public domain. Found on the Apple II operating system, the viruses spread through Texas A&M via pirated computer games.
1980s	In the early 1980s, Fred Cohen did extensive theoretical research on viral-type programs in addition to setting up and performing numerous practical experiments. His dissertation was presented in 1986 as part of the requirements for a doctorate in electrical engineering from the University of Southern California. This work is foundational, and any serious student of viral programs disregards it at his own risk. Dr. Cohen's definition of a computer virus is "a program that can 'infect' other programs by modifying them to include a ... version of itself."
1987	In November, the Lehigh virus was discovered at Lehigh University in the United States. It was the first "memory resident file infector." A file-infecting virus attacks executable files and gets control when the file is opened. The Lehigh virus attacked a file called Command.com. When the file was run (usually by booting from an infected disk), the virus stayed in the resident memory.
1988	In March, the first antivirus software was written. It was designed to detect and remove the Brain virus and immunized disks against Brain infection.
1990	Viruses combining characteristics spring up. They included polymorphism (involves encrypted viruses where the decryption routine code is variable), armoring (used to prevent antivirus researchers from disassembling a virus), and multipartite (can infect both programs and boot sectors).
1991	Symantec releases Norton Anti-Virus software.
1992	Media mayhem greeted the virus Michelangelo in March. Predictions of massive disruptions were made, and antivirus software sales soared. As it turned out, the cases of the virus were far and few between.
1994	A virus called Kaos4 was posted on a pornography news group file. It was encoded as text and downloaded by a number of users.
1996	Concept, a macro-virus, becomes the most common virus in the world.
1999	The Melissa virus, which is a macro, appears. It uses Microsoft Word to infect computers and is passed on to others through Microsoft Outlook and Outlook Express e-mail programs.
2000	The "I Love You Virus" wreaks havoc around the world. It is transmitted by e-mail and, when opened, is automatically sent to everyone in the user's address book.
2001	The "Anna Kournikova" virus, promising digital pictures of the young tennis star, was relatively harmless. It simply clogged networks by spreading, much like the I Love You Virus, e-mailing itself to every person in the victim's Microsoft Outlook address book.
July 2001	The Code Red worm infects tens of thousands of systems running Microsoft Windows NT and Windows 2000 server software, causing an estimated $2 billion in damages. The worm is programmed to use the power of all infected machines against the White House website at a predetermined date. In an ad hoc partnership with virus hunters and technology companies, the White House deciphers the virus's code and blocks traffic as the worm begins its attack.
2002	Melissa virus author David L. Smith, 33, is sentenced to 20 months in federal prison.

PART IV

January 2003	The "Slammer" worm infects hundreds of thousands of computers in less than three hours. The fastest-spreading worm ever wreaks havoc on businesses worldwide, knocking cash machines offline and delaying airline flights.
2004	The "MyDoom" worm becomes the fastest-spreading e-mail worm as it causes headaches—but very little damage—almost a year to the day after Slammer ran rampant in late January 2003. MyDoom uses social engineering, or low-tech psychological tricks, to persuade people to open the e-mail attachment that contains the virus. It claims to be a notification that an e-mail message sent earlier has failed and prompts the user to open the attachment to see what the message text originally said. Many people fall for it.
	A new type of virus attack was seen—the virus hoax. A virus hoax is a fake report there is a virus when none exists. The jdbgmgr.exe virus hoax was an example of this. It encouraged the reader to delete a file that the system actually needed. Surprisingly, a number of people followed this advice and not only deleted the file, but promptly e-mailed all their friends and colleagues to warn them to delete the file from their machines. Virus hoaxes are becoming more common.
2007	A PDF virus named Peachy was first reported in August 2007. It only spreads when creating PDFs, not simply reading them. It was one of the first PDF-based viruses.
2010	Java.Backdoor is a virus written with Java. It is usually found as a JAR file with a number of class files and is wrapped into an executable using jshrink. That executable is downloaded by the user as an applet, when then infects the host machine. It sets up an Internet relay chat (IRC) connection that allows the infected system to be controlled, thus becoming part of a botnet.
2013	PDF:Exploit.CVE-2013-5065.A is another PDF virus that first showed up in late 2013. It allows attackers to run code with elevated privileges on systems that are using Windows XP or Windows Server 2013.

Modern Virus Creation

For many years, one needed significant programming skills in order to create a virus. However, in recent years, a number of tools have been developed that create viruses. These tools allow the end user to click a few buttons and create a virus. This is one reason viruses are becoming so prevalent. One such tool is the Terabit Virus Maker, shown in Figure 12-5.

Tools like this make it easy for even a novice to create a virus. When tools like this become prevalent, tools that automate some specific computer attack, then one can expect a great many more such attacks.

Figure 12-5 Terabit Virus Maker

Trojan Horses

A Trojan horse is a program that appears innocuous but actually has a malicious purpose. It derives its name from the famous story of the wooden horse the Greeks gave to Troy. When the Trojans went to sleep, soldiers hidden in the wooden horse came out and opened the gates of Troy from the inside, allowing the Greek army to enter the city.

There are two ways to create a Trojan horse. The first is to write a program entirely from scratch. The program would appear to have some benign purpose and then perform its malfeasance when installed on the target system. The second method is to use a program that wraps a piece of malware to an innocuous program, making the two appear to be a single program (the benign one).

A number of tools on the Web allow one to create a Trojan horse. For example, the free tool EliteWrap works from the command line and allows a person to tie any two programs together. It is easy to use, as you can see in Figure 12-6.

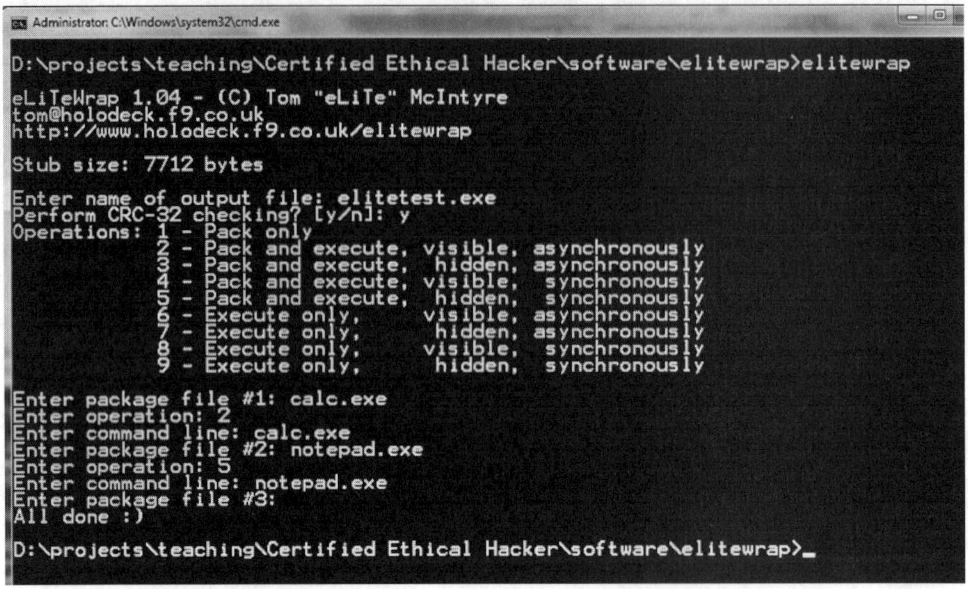

```
Administrator: C:\Windows\system32\cmd.exe

D:\projects\teaching\Certified Ethical Hacker\software\elitewrap>elitewrap

eLiTeWrap 1.04 - (C) Tom "eLiTe" McIntyre
tom@holodeck.f9.co.uk
http://www.holodeck.f9.co.uk/elitewrap

Stub size: 7712 bytes

Enter name of output file: elitetest.exe
Perform CRC-32 checking? [y/n]: y
Operations: 1 - Pack only
            2 - Pack and execute, visible, asynchronously
            3 - Pack and execute, hidden, asynchronously
            4 - Pack and execute, visible, synchronously
            5 - Pack and execute, hidden, synchronously
            6 - Execute only,     visible, asynchronously
            7 - Execute only,     hidden, asynchronously
            8 - Execute only,     visible, synchronously
            9 - Execute only,     hidden, synchronously

Enter package file #1: calc.exe
Enter operation: 2
Enter command line: calc.exe
Enter package file #2: notepad.exe
Enter operation: 5
Enter command line: notepad.exe
Enter package file #3:
All done :)

D:\projects\teaching\Certified Ethical Hacker\software\elitewrap>_
```

Figure 12-6   Using EliteWrap to create a Trojan horse

Spyware

This is any software that monitors your computer activities. For example, it may be a key logger (software that logs keystrokes) or software that records all the websites you visit. There are some perfectly legal uses for spyware. Some employers have embraced it as a means of monitoring employee use of company technology. Many companies have elected to monitor phone, e-mail, or web traffic within the organization. Keep in mind that the computer, network, and phone systems are the property of the company or organization, not of the employee. These technologies are supposedly only used for work purposes; therefore, company monitoring might not constitute any invasion of privacy. While courts have upheld this monitoring as a company's right, it is critical to consult an attorney before initiating this level of employee monitoring and to consider the potential negative impact on employee morale.

Some sources believe searchprotocolhost.exe is related to Windows indexing—this is not true; it is spyware.[2] Yes, there is a Windows process with this name, but there is also spyware with this name.[3] Based on the over 2GB of memory this file is consuming, it is far more likely to be spyware than a normal process.

Most modern antivirus systems will also detect spyware. However, they can only detect software-based spyware, not hardware-based spyware. Such systems are installed in the back of a PC and plug into the keyboard port. The keyboard is then plugged into the device. The device copies all keystrokes. Since this is not software installed on the target system, antispyware cannot detect it. Software-based spyware, including key loggers, are far more common than hardware-based spyware. This is because of the difficulty in getting hardware-based spyware on the target machine.

The Buffer Overflow

A buffer overflow attack happens when one tries to put more data in a buffer than it was designed to hold. Any program that communicates with the Internet or a private network must take in some data. This data is stored, at least temporarily, in a space in memory called a *buffer*. If the programmer who wrote the application was careful, when you try to place too much information into a buffer, that information is either simply truncated or outright rejected. Given the number of applications that might be running on a target system and the number of buffers in each application, the chances of having at least one buffer that was not written properly are significant enough to cause any prudent person some concern.

Someone who is moderately skilled can write a program that purposefully writes more into the buffer than it can hold. For example, if the buffer can hold 1024 bytes of data and you try to fill it with 2048 bytes, the extra 1024 bytes is simply loaded into memory. If that extra data is actually a malicious program, then it has just been loaded into memory and is now running on the target system. Or, perhaps the perpetrator simply wants to flood the target machine's memory, thus overwriting other items that are currently in memory and causing them to crash. Either way, the buffer overflow is a serious attack.

Fortunately, buffer overflow attacks are a bit harder to execute than a denial of service (DoS) or a simple Microsoft Outlook script virus. To create a buffer overflow attack, you must have a good working knowledge of some programming language (C or C++ is often chosen) and understand the target operating system/application well enough to know whether it has a buffer overflow weakness and how that weakness might be exploited.

Rootkit

A rootkit is a collection of tools that a hacker uses to mask her intrusion and obtain administrator-level access to a computer or computer network. The intruder installs a rootkit on a computer after first obtaining user-level access, either by exploiting a known vulnerability or cracking a password. The rootkit then collects user IDs and passwords to other machines on the network, thus giving the hacker root, or privileged, access.

The presence of a rootkit on a network was first documented in the early 1990s. At that time, Sun and Linux operating systems were the primary targets for a hacker looking to install a rootkit. Today, rootkits are available for a number of operating systems and are increasingly difficult to detect on any network.

Logic Bombs

Logic bombs are programs or snippets of code that execute when a certain predefined event occurs. There are some real-world examples of logic bombs.

In June 1992, defense contractor General Dynamics employee Michael Lauffenburger was arrested for inserting a logic bomb that would delete vital rocket project data. Another employee of General Dynamics found the bomb before it was triggered. Lauffenburger was charged with computer tampering and attempted fraud and faced potential fines of $500,000 and jail time, but was actually only fined $5,000.

In June 2006 Roger Duronio, a system administrator for UBS, was charged with using a logic bomb to damage the company's computer network. His plan was to drive the company stock down due to damage from the logic bomb; thus, he was charged with securities fraud. Duronio was later convicted and sentenced to eight years and one month in prison, as well as a $3.1 million restitution to UBS.

Logic bombs are usually crafted for a specific purpose and are extremely difficult for antivirus software to detect. Of course, some viruses did not perform their misdeeds until a specific date, but those are not what we generally think of when we speak of logic bombs. Usually, a logic bomb is created by a skilled programmer, and often it is someone within the organization who has some grudge against it. Detecting that kind of logic bomb can only be done with thorough software testing, including code reviews.

Ransomware

With ransomware, software—often delivered through a Trojan—takes control of a system and demands that a third party be paid before the control is released. The "control" can be accomplished by encrypting the hard drive, by changing user password information, or by any of a number of other creative ways. Users are assured that by paying the extortion amount (the ransom), they will be given the code needed to revert their systems back to normal operations.

The first known ransomware was the 1989 PC Cyborg Trojan, which only encrypted filenames with a weak symmetric cipher. The notion of using public key cryptography for these attacks was introduced by Young and Yung in 1996. This involved using public key cryptography to encrypt sensitive files on the infected computer. Then the user had to send money to the attacker to get the files decrypted.

More recently, the Reveton virus spread in 2013, and it asked victims to pay $100 to the U.S. Department of Justice. It presented an official-looking interface in an attempt to fool users. This ransomware did not actually encrypt files on the users' computers; instead, it simply tried to trick them into sending money. You can see Reveton in Figure 12-7.

Figure 12-7 Reveton

Advanced Persistent Threats

This term, often abbreviated APT, is a relatively new term for a continuous process of attacking. It can involve hacking, social engineering, malware, or combination of attacks. The key is that the attack must be relatively sophisticated—thus the term advanced—and it must be ongoing—thus the term persistent.

It just so happens that while writing this chapter, there was a news release about a significant APT being launched against American companies by members of the Chinese military.[4]

The security firm Mandiant tracked several APTs over a period of seven years, all originating in China—specifically, Shanghai and the Pudong region. These APTs were simply named APT1, APT2, etc.

The attacks were linked to Unit 61398 of the Chinese military. The Chinese government regards this unit's activities as classified, but it appears that offensive cyber warfare is one of its tasks. Just one of the APTs from this group compromised 141 companies in 20 different industries. APT1 was able to maintain access to victim networks for an average of 365 days, and in one case for 1,764 days. APT1 is responsible for stealing 6.5TB of information from a single organization over a ten-month time frame.

Malware Analysis

Malware analysis consists of far more than simply identifying that malware is present on a given machine. It also involves studying the malware to understand how it functions. This can provide insight into the purpose of the malware, and perhaps even the perpetrator who created it, or at least how a given system was infected.

The major antivirus vendors have to use malware analysis so that they can fully understand a virus. When antivirus vendors release a new virus signature and update the virus definitions, it is the results of the malware analysis that allow this information to be utilized to prevent the spread of the virus.

 EXAM TIP The test will ask you questions about the difference between static and dynamic analysis.

Static Analysis

Static analysis is the process of studying a program—in this case malware—without actually executing it. One common technique is to attempt to decompile the malware. Static analysis can be used on the source code of malware, if it is available.

Dynamic Analysis

Dynamic analysis involves studying the program as it is executing. While the malware is running on an isolated test machine, you can use a variety of tools to analyze exactly what the code is doing. One common technique is to use function call analysis.[5] This involves using a process viewer or similar tool to see what functions the malware is calling, particularly API (application programming interface) function calls.

Particular attention is usually paid to system calls. For example, when malware is calling Windows system calls, this can be interesting for the malware analyst. When functions are called, it is important to also note the parameters that are passed to those functions. Parameter information can reveal a great deal about the malware in question.

Monitoring the use of system resources is also important. How is the malware utilizing RAM, processor time, and any other system resources? I must also recommend making a backup of the registry prior to running the malware and then using a file compare utility to see what changes the malware made to the registry. Many sources on dynamic malware analysis overlook registry issues, but most malware that infects Windows systems also makes alterations to the Windows registry. Knowing exactly what changes the malware makes may be critical to removing the virus from live, infected machines.

NOTE It is imperative that malware be analyzed in a safe environment. Virtual machine environments are ideal for this sort of analysis. If not using a virtual machine, then at least use a machine that is completely isolated from the network.

There are a variety of live system analysis tools, many specifically for Windows operating systems. Windows Sysinternals is a suite of tools that gives you a very good picture of what is happening in a live Windows system.[6] We will look at a few of the Sysinternals tools that are most useful for dynamic malware analysis.

Procmon

This tool has a graphical user interface (GUI) and gives you a live view of all running processes on a system. You can see this in Figure 12-8. You can see process name, ID, time it was executed, whether or not it was successful in its operation, and related information. This can tell you what a virus is actually doing on a system. For example, is it launching additional processes?

PART IV

Time o...	Process Name	PID	Operation	Path	Result	Detail
11:36:28...	SearchIndexer....	4648	ReadFile	C:\Windows\System32\mssrch.dll	SUCCESS	Offset: 1,940,480, Le...
11:36:28...	SearchIndexer....	4648	FileSystemCont...C:		SUCCESS	Control: FSCTL_RE...
11:36:28...	SearchIndexer....	4648	FileSystemCont...C:			Control: FSCTL_RE...
11:36:28...	LMS.exe	4684	RegOpenKey	HKLM\System\CurrentControlSet\Control...	SUCCESS	Desired Access: Al...
11:36:28...	LMS.exe	4684	RegOpenKey	HKLM\System\CurrentControlSet\Control...	NAME NOT FOUND	Desired Access: Q...
11:36:28...	LMS.exe	4684	RegCloseKey	HKLM\System\CurrentControlSet\Control...	SUCCESS	
11:36:28...	LMS.exe	4684	RegOpenKey	HKLM\System\CurrentControlSet\Control...	SUCCESS	Desired Access: Q...
11:36:28...	LMS.exe	4684	RegOpenKey	HKLM\System\CurrentControlSet\Control...	NAME NOT FOUND	Desired Access: Q...
11:36:28...	LMS.exe	4684	RegCloseKey	HKLM\System\CurrentControlSet\Control...	SUCCESS	
11:36:28...	dwm.exe	6604	Thread Exit		SUCCESS	Thread ID: 10788, ...
11:36:28...	Explorer.EXE	5356	Thread Exit		SUCCESS	Thread ID: 8572, U...
11:36:28...	svchost.exe	860	RegOpenKey	HKLM\System\CurrentControlSet\Control...	REPARSE	Desired Access: R...
11:36:28...	svchost.exe	860	RegOpenKey	HKLM\System\CurrentControlSet\Control...	SUCCESS	Desired Access: R...
11:36:28...	svchost.exe	860	RegCloseKey	HKLM\System\CurrentControlSet\Control...	SUCCESS	
11:36:28...	svchost.exe	860	RegOpenKey	HKLM\System\CurrentControlSet\Control...	REPARSE	Desired Access: R...
11:36:28...	svchost.exe	860	RegOpenKey	HKLM\System\CurrentControlSet\Control...	SUCCESS	Desired Access: R...
11:36:28...	svchost.exe	860	RegCloseKey	HKLM\System\CurrentControlSet\Control...	SUCCESS	
11:36:28...	svchost.exe	860	RegOpenKey	HKLM\System\CurrentControlSet\Control...	REPARSE	Desired Access: R...
11:36:28...	svchost.exe	860	RegOpenKey	HKLM\System\CurrentControlSet\Control...	SUCCESS	Desired Access: R...
11:36:28...	svchost.exe	860	RegCloseKey	HKLM\System\CurrentControlSet\Control...	SUCCESS	
11:36:28...	svchost.exe	860	RegOpenKey	HKLM\System\CurrentControlSet\Control...	REPARSE	Desired Access: R...
11:36:28...	svchost.exe	860	RegOpenKey	HKLM\System\CurrentControlSet\Control...	SUCCESS	Desired Access: R...
11:36:28...	svchost.exe	860	RegCloseKey	HKLM\System\CurrentControlSet\Control...	SUCCESS	
11:36:28	svchost.exe	860	RegOpenKey	HKLM...	SUCCESS	Desired Access: M...

Showing 7,112 of 17,823 events (39%)   Backed by virtual memory

Figure 12-8 Procmon

Rammap

This tool gives you a detailed map of what is happening in memory. You can easily view every process and every file and how much RAM they are consuming. Malware often consumes more RAM than a normal file. You can see Rammap in Figure 12-9.

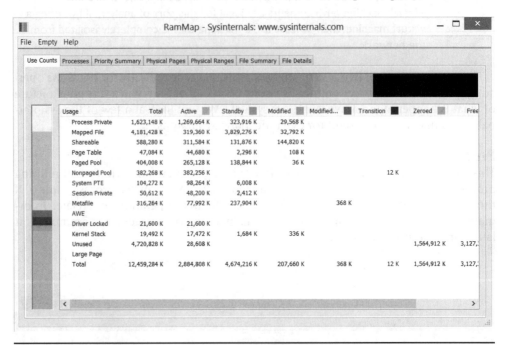

Usage	Total	Active	Standby	Modified	Modified...	Transition	Zeroed	Free
Process Private	1,623,148 K	1,269,664 K	323,916 K	29,568 K				
Mapped File	4,181,428 K	319,360 K	3,829,276 K	32,792 K				
Shareable	588,280 K	311,584 K	131,876 K	144,820 K				
Page Table	47,084 K	44,680 K	2,296 K	108 K				
Paged Pool	404,008 K	265,128 K	138,844 K	36 K				
Nonpaged Pool	382,268 K	382,256 K				12 K		
System PTE	104,272 K	98,264 K	6,008 K					
Session Private	50,612 K	48,200 K	2,412 K					
Metafile	316,264 K	77,992 K	237,904 K		368 K			
AWE								
Driver Locked	21,600 K	21,600 K						
Kernel Stack	19,492 K	17,472 K	1,684 K	336 K				
Unused	4,720,828 K	28,608 K					1,564,912 K	3,127,
Large Page								
Total	12,459,284 K	2,884,808 K	4,674,216 K	207,660 K	368 K	12 K	1,564,912 K	3,127,

Figure 12-9 Rammap

These are just a few of the tools you will find in Sysinternals. These can be invaluable when conducting dynamic malware analysis.

Chapter Review

In this chapter, you have seen an overview of the major types of malware. You have seen viruses, Trojan horses, spyware, rootkits, ransomware, logic bombs, and other types of malware. Specific types of viruses were also described. Finally, we discussed malware analysis, including both static and dynamic analysis.

Questions

1. Which of the following is the best definition of virus?

    A. A program that causes harm on your computer

    B. A program that self-replicates

    C. A program used in a DoS attack

    D. A program that deletes files

2. What is a Trojan horse?

    A. Software that self-replicates

    B. Software that appears to be benign but really has some malicious purpose

    C. Software that deletes system files and then infects other machines

    D. Software that causes harm to your system

3. A virus that changes as it spreads is called what?

    A. Multipartite

    B. Armored

    C. Changeling

    D. Polymorphic

4. A key logger is what type of malware?

    A. Virus

    B. Buffer overflow

    C. Trojan horse

    D. Spyware

5. What is dynamic analysis?

    A. Studying malware while it is running

    B. Studying malware with a variety of tools

    C. Studying malware while it is off

    D. Studying the source code of malware

Answers

1. B. The hallmark of a virus is self-replication.

2. B. A Trojan horse is software that appears to have a benign function but delivers malware.

3. D. A polymorphic virus is a virus that changes as it spreads.

4. **D.** A key logger logs all your keystrokes and is a common type of spyware.

5. **A.** Dynamic analysis is studying malware while it is executing.

References

1. http://www.macworld.com/article/1160098/macdefender.html.

2. http://www.neuber.com/taskmanager/process/searchprotocolhost.exe.html.

3. http://answers.microsoft.com/en-us/windows/forum/windows_xp-performance/searchprotocolhostexe-consumes-95-of-cpu/1651e73e-fa99-4761-9c82-e4778e068207.

4. http://intelreport.mandiant.com/Mandiant_APT1_Report.pdf.

5. https://iseclab.org/papers/malware_survey.pdf.

6. http://technet.microsoft.com/en-US/SysInternals.

New and Emerging Forensics Technology

In this chapter you will learn:

- How to conduct forensics involving social media
- What threats exist to control systems
- How our infrastructure can be the scene of a computer crime
- Online gaming and its relevance to forensics
- The new issues in electronic discovery

There are a number of new and interesting technologies that affect the field of cyber forensics. New devices, new methods, new legal processes—all of these affect the forensic process. In this chapter, we will explore these areas in detail.

Social Networks

We have briefly mentioned social media earlier in this book. It is certainly a fact that social media has become ubiquitous. Thus, it is natural to consider what effect this will have on cyber forensics. In this section, we will examine this issue.

Types and Applications of Social Networks

There are a few main types of social networks. The first are general social connection sites. These portals allow people to create profiles and interact with others who also have created profiles. Facebook and LinkedIn are the two most well-known social networks. There are also social networks that allow one to broadcast messages, with Twitter being the most well known of this type. Finally, there are media sharing networks, such as YouTube that allow a user to share video and for other users to leave comments. Evidence can reside in any of these networks in the form of text postings, pictures, video, or even GPS location information.

There are a number of issues to be aware of when forensically examining social networks. The first is jurisdiction. By their very nature, social networks allow users in diverse locations to interact. This means the users are likely to be in different jurisdictions, and perhaps even different countries. It is important to be aware of the laws in the various jurisdictions before proceeding with an investigation. The specific networks' terms of service are also important. Do those terms of service allow the sharing of information with law enforcement without the users' specific consent? A few terms of service issues are listed and discussed next.

Facebook

Facebook has the following statement in its terms of service:

> Facebook complies with the U.S.-EU and U.S.-Swiss Safe Harbor frameworks as set forth by the Department of Commerce regarding the collection, use, and retention of data from the European Union. To view our certification, visit the U.S. Department of Commerce's Safe Harbor website.
>
> As part of our participation in the Safe Harbor program, we agree to resolve disputes you have with us in connection with our policies and practices through TRUSTe.[1]

Safe Harbor means the site complies with the European Union Directive 95/46/EC on the protection of personal data. This entails seven areas, but four are most important to privacy issues:

- Subjects must be notified if data is collected.
- Data can only be used for the purpose stated.
- Data cannot be disclosed without the user's consent.
- Users are informed of who is collecting their data.

 EXAM TIP The test does not ask about specific European Union laws, but might ask general questions. For example, you should know that the EU has specific privacy laws that exceed the laws of most other jurisdictions.

LinkedIn

LinkedIn does not claim to adhere to EU Directive 95/46/EC; instead, they have crafted their own privacy policy:

> At LinkedIn, our fundamental philosophy is "members first." That value powers all of the decisions we make, including how we gather and respect your personal information.
>
> We protect your personal information and will only provide it to third parties: (1) with your consent; (2) where it is necessary to carry out your instructions; (3) as reasonably necessary in order to provide our features and functionality to you; (4) when we reasonably believe it is required by law, subpoena or other legal process; or (5) as necessary to enforce our User Agreement or protect the rights, property, or safety of LinkedIn, its Members and Visitors, and the public.

You may note there is no mentioning of notifying the user of who is collecting data, how it is being used, or why it is being collected.

Direct Evidence of Crimes

It may seem shocking to you that some people actually place evidence of crimes they have committed in their own social media accounts. A classic example is shown in Figure 13-1. This individual posted a Facebook photo of themselves drinking and driving.[2]

Figure 13-1
Facebook drinking and driving

In some cases, Facebook or other social media is not the source of the crime, but rather, the source of the evidence. For example, Andrew Curry was convicted of battery after posting a picture of his 22-month-old daughter bound with duct tape.[3]

One particular female robber, 19-year-old Hannah Sabata, chose to make a seven-minute video detailing her crimes. In the video, she is sitting on the floor in a bedroom and holds up a series of handwritten signs. The first states that she stole a car; the next that she robbed a bank with a gun. Then she shows a large sum of cash supposedly stolen from the bank. She was arrested a few hours after uploading the video.[4]

Nineteen-year-old Jonathan Parker broke into a home, and while there decided to take time out to use their computer to log onto Facebook. He neglected to log off prior to leaving, and thus the police had no trouble tracking him down.[5]

Maxi Sopo was in hiding in Mexico. A fugitive facing charges of bank fraud in Seattle, Sopo chose to update his Facebook status advising that he was "living in paradise" in

Mexico. He provided even more details that made it relatively easy for authorities to track his location and have him arrested and then extradited to the United States.[6]

And these crimes are just the tip of the iceberg. Some sources claim there is a crime linked to Facebook every 40 minutes. These crimes include pedophiles, assaults, witness intimidation, and even murder.[7]

Commission of Crimes

In some cases, the use of social media is an element of the crime itself. It is actually quite common for pedophiles to attempt to lure their victims via social media. Cyber stalking often involves social media. And, of course, a number of financial-based scams utilize social media.

Child Predators

Adults who prey on children often initiate contact via social media. The initial conversation the predator has with a minor will probably be about an innocuous topic that is of interest to that minor. During this initial phase, the predator is often looking for key signs that this child might be a likely target—for example, children who feel like they don't belong, are not getting enough attention from parents, or are going through some major life issue such as parental divorce.

Once the predator has identified a potential target, he will then begin trying to extend the conversations outside the chat room or social page into private chats or e-mails. He will also likely be very sympathetic to whatever the child's problem is. Predators often use flattery with their intended victims. Children who feel like they don't belong or who have low self-esteem are susceptible to these sorts of tactics.

The next step is to begin easing sexual content into the conversation. Their intent is to gradually get the child comfortable discussing sexual topics. Usually, they are careful to take this phase carefully so as not to cause the targeted child to panic. If this process proceeds to a point the predator feels comfortable, they will then suggest a face-to-face meeting. In some cases, the face-to-face meeting is expressly for the purpose of sex; in others, they lure the child to a location with the promise of some seemingly benign activity such as video games or a movie.

Of course, there are deviations from this pattern. Some predators move much quicker to meet with the child face to face. They may also avoid sexual conversations altogether and simply try to lure the child out of their house with the intent of forcibly molesting the child. Whether the predator chooses to lure the child and then force a sex act or attempts to seduce the child depends on how the predator views the act. It may surprise some readers to discover that some pedophiles actually view themselves, not as child molesters, but rather, as being in a relationship with the child. They actually think their behavior is acceptable, and it is simply society that fails to understand them. This sort of pedophile is much more likely to use a method of gradually increasing the sexual content and explicitness of the online conversation. Their intent is to seduce the child.

Cyber Stalking

Cyber stalking cases often involve social media too. Social media provides a means for interacting with other people and thus makes a useful vehicle for inappropriate contact. Before we discuss specific real-world cases, we should make a few points about cyber stalking. The courts have not given a clear definition of what "stalking" is, much less cyber stalking, so there are some gray areas. However, a few general guidelines can help you determine if something is cyber stalking or not.

The first is the content of the communication. For example, someone routinely messaging you on Facebook that they could get you a good deal on a car may be annoying, but is probably not stalking. However, if the e-mail is something that a reasonable person would consider to be threatening, then it might be stalking.

The next issue will be frequency of communication. Sometimes, people lose their temper, even in online chats, forums, bulletin boards, etc. If someone makes a single vague but hostile comment, that may not be stalking. If they repeat it, however, particularly after having had time to cool off, it might be stalking.

NOTE You may notice that I keep stating this "might or might not be" cyber stalking. Unfortunately, this issue is not clear and definite. It can be difficult to tell if some cases are actually cyber stalking or not.

Real Stalking Cases

Seventy-year-old Joseph Medico met a 16-year-old girl at church.[7] The girl was at the church volunteering, helping to prepare donations for homeless shelters. Mr. Medico followed the girl to her car and tried to talk her into going to dinner with him and then back to his home. When she spurned his advances, he began calling and texting her several times a day.

When she realized he was not going to stop, she called the police. Mr. Medico was arrested and charged with stalking. This case illustrates how easy it is for an unstable person to become obsessed with their victim. It also demonstrates the proper way to handle this sort of situation. This is definitely a case to report to the police. An adult who is making romantic overtures to a minor is a matter of grave concern.

An honors graduate from the University of San Diego terrorized five female university students over the Internet for more than a year. The victims received hundreds of violent and threatening e-mails, sometimes receiving four or five messages a day. The graduate student, who pled guilty, told police he committed the crimes because he thought the women were laughing at him and causing others to ridicule him. In fact, the victims had never met.

In the first successful prosecution under California's new cyber stalking law, prosecutors in the Los Angeles District Attorney's Office obtained a guilty plea from a 50-year-old former security guard who used the Internet to solicit the rape of a woman who rejected his romantic advances. The defendant terrorized his 28-year-old victim by impersonating her in various Internet chat rooms and online bulletin boards, where he posted, along with her telephone number and address, messages that she fantasized being raped. On at least six occasions, sometimes in the middle of the night, men knocked on the woman's door saying they wanted to rape her. The former security guard pleaded guilty in April 1999 to one count of stalking and three counts of solicitation of sexual assault. He faces up to six years in prison.

 NOTE Another phenomenon is thieves using social media to identify when someone might be gone and if they have valuables in their home. If you tweet about your purchase of a new Rolex and then post on Facebook that you are off having a good time in Cancun, thieves can put these two pieces of information together and burglarize your home while you are gone. There is a website that documents the oversharing people do on social media in an attempt to educate people. The site is http://pleaserobme.com/.

New Devices

In addition to new technologies such as social media, there are new devices available today that did not exist a short time ago. These devices will clearly affect the field of cyber security, although the exact level remains to be seen. In this section, we will look briefly at some of the new devices.

Google Glass

Google Glass is a new device, just released to the public in 2013. It is not clear yet if it will be popular and gain widespread use or simply fade. However, it is clear that new technologies are coming, so understanding Google Glass is important. The most obvious forensic issue is that Google Glass has the potential to record video.

Google Glass includes permanent storage in the form of a small hard drive. It also has the ability to record images and video. Those two facts make it a possible target for a forensic investigation. At a minimum, Google Glass could contain photographic or video evidence of a crime.

The operating system is Android, which is Linux based. This means that the same Linux knowledge you would apply to an Android phone or Linux desktop, can be used with Google Glass.

Cars

For several years, cars have become increasingly sophisticated. For example, GPS devices within cars are now commonplace. Many vehicles have hard drives for storing music to be played. These technological advances can also be repositories for forensic evidence. For example, GPS data might establish that a suspect's car was at the scene of a crime when it took place. That alone would not lead to a conviction, but it does help to build a case.

Medical Devices

An increasing number of medical devices are built to communicate data. For example, there are insulin pumps that send data regarding usage to a computer via a wireless connection. There are pacemakers that operate similarly. This leads to the question as to whether or not that wireless communication can be compromised. The unfortunate fact is they can. Multiple news sources have carried the story of a researcher who discovered he could hack into wireless insulin pumps and alter the dosage, even to fatal levels. To date, there is no known case of someone being murdered through hacking a medical device. However, it is difficult to believe that it will not happen eventually.

With the increasing complexity of medical devices, it could eventually become commonplace to forensically examine them in cases where foul play is suspected, just as it is now commonplace to forensically examine any phone seized in relation to a crime.

Control Systems and Infrastructure

Control systems are systems used to control devices—one good example is computers that control manufacturing equipment. For example, a computer might be used to control factory equipment or refining equipment. Programmable logic controllers (PLCs) are one example.

SCADA (Supervisory Control and Data Acquisition) systems are another example. These systems remotely monitor and control equipment via some communication channel. These are used in manufacturing, refining, and power generation systems.

The Stuxnet virus was designed to affect PLCs that handled refining of nuclear material. It has been claimed that Stuxnet shut down one-fifth of Iran's nuclear refining capability. This is one case of an attack on a control system. It is likely that other attacks on control systems will be seen in the future.

It is important to use the same forensic processes we have studied throughout this book. However, control systems likely will require specialized knowledge that the forensic analyst may not have. If you have no experience with a specific control system, you should enlist the aid of a specialist who does.

Much of our infrastructure is dependent upon computer systems. These systems run dam operations, traffic signals, power generation, and related systems. Obviously, infrastructure is a serious concern, as someone shutting down power in a region, for example, is deeply disconcerting.

In 2010, *60 Minutes* broadcast a report on hacking and cyber terrorism. They clearly showed that our power plants, and perhaps our hardware, are vulnerable. In this broadcast, penetration testers from the Department of Energy were able to take control of power generation equipment and potentially shut down power to large areas.

Online Gaming

Online gaming is becoming quite popular. This includes online gambling as well as what are termed massively multiplayer online (MMO) games, such as *World of Warcraft, Everquest*, and *Sims*. In these games, players create identities that interact with both other players and computer-generated characters in a fantasy environment.

One issue that has become important for the vendors of these games is online cheating. Certainly, cheating in an online fantasy game is not a crime, but this could require an administrative investigation (we will discuss those in detail in the next section). The game vendor wishes to ferret out cheaters and terminate their accounts. More frequently, the gaming companies are turning to cyber forensics to track down cheaters.[8]

Aside from administrative investigations into possible cheating, there can be criminal activities involved in these fantasy worlds. It is important to first understand how these games work. Players spend significant time developing characters and forging relationships with other players' characters in the online fantasy world. It must be remembered that this is a social environment, just like any other. There will be disputes, arguments, terminated friendships, etc.—all the things you would expect to see in any social environment.

The web of social interaction facilitated by online gaming can also lead to issues such as threats, cyber stalking, and related crimes. These games provide a social network, but with the added element that members can remain anonymous. This anonymity can embolden some people to be more likely to make threatening comments, or even stalk people who they feel animosity toward.

Electronic Discovery

Electronic discovery is the process of producing evidence that is stored electronically. Often, this occurs in administrative and civil investigations. Essentially, it is an extension of traditional civil discovery rules into ESI (electronically stored information). ESI includes e-mails, word processing documents, spreadsheets, web pages, etc.—any data that can be stored electronically.

Normally, the electronic discovery process begins with notification of some civil or administrative procedure and then the custodian of the data or some related person gathers the ESI to produce to the opposing party. This does not involve a forensic analyst seizing possible evidence and analyzing it to find clues. It also will not usually involve hidden evidence (i.e., steganography or cryptography). This traditional e-discovery process is nonforensic; it does not utilize normal forensic techniques such as recovering deleted files.

Regardless of the investigation type, spoliation is a major concern. Spoliation simply means the evidence is no longer available or no longer useable. The more time that elapses before evidence is secured, the more likely it is that some of the evidence could become damaged, altered, or unavailable. In the case of e-mails, deletion is a significant issue. Even e-mail server backups are only retained for a finite period.

 EXAM TIP   The CCFP will ask questions about spoliation in a general/ conceptual manner.

Types of Investigation

As we mentioned, electronic discovery can involve either civil litigation or administrative investigations. Both of these have been briefly mentioned earlier in this chapter, but will be described in more detail here.

Civil Litigation

Any time one party files a lawsuit against another, this is a civil process. The penalties are only financial, and do not also involve imprisonment. Any type of lawsuit could involve electronic discovery; however, the following are some areas of litigation that commonly involve electronic discovery:

- **Copyright infringement**   One party accuses another of using copyright-protected material without permission. The U.S. federal courts have established that for software copyright cases, the best test to use is the abstraction-filtration-comparison test. In this test, the expert must first abstract the accused product to identify the expression of the idea. U.S. copyright law allows a person to copyright the expression of an idea, but not the idea itself. The next step is to filter out aspects of the software that are not subject to copyright protection. Then finally, the accused product is compared with the product it is accused of copying.

- **Patent infringement**   One party accuses the other of using a process or device that has been patented by the accusing party. When accusing a party of patent infringement, one of the first steps is to create a claim chart. That is a table that lists the asserted claims of the patent in question (often even breaking those claims down into smaller parts) and showing how the accused product is infringing. There are two defenses against patent infringement claims. The first is noninfringement. This is the argument that the accused product functions differently from the patent in some significant way. The second is invalidity. It is the claim that there was prior art, published before the patent, that renders the patent invalid. In other words, it is the argument that the patent should never have been granted in the first place.

 EXAM TIP   Both copyright infringement and patent infringement are intellectual property cases. Intellectual property involves the protection of novel ideas (patent) or the expression of those ideas (copyright) and includes software, devices, processes, books, etc.

- **Discrimination**   Workplace discrimination encompasses a number of different scenarios. Employers can discriminate based on race, religion, gender, disability, or sexual orientation. These cases often involve electronic discovery, particularly targeting e-mail and other electronic communications.

PART IV

• **Divorce**   When there are significant assets at stake, divorce proceedings will often involve electronic discovery. Parties will want e-mails to confirm or refute infidelity allegations and bank records to confirm assets. In recent years, GPS records have even become quite common targets of electronic discovery in divorce cases.

Administrative Investigation

An administrative investigation is an internal investigation. Often, an organization wishes to examine some issue within it. This could be to ensure there are no issues that could lead to litigation (such as discrimination or copyright infringement) or to investigate the termination of a key employee. The process is usually a bit easier in these cases because the organization is investigating itself and therefore has unfettered access to all data.

Administrative investigations can also include forensic investigations of the organization's response to disaster. For example, if there was a network server crash, there might be an investigation into the causes of that crash and how well the company responded. This type of e-discovery may involve traditional forensic techniques such as recovering deleted files and file carving.

Recovery after a virus will also often involve forensic e-discovery. The analyst has complete access to the system in question, and the system's owner is certainly not attempting to hide any evidence. However, the malware itself may be elusive. It may be necessary to check slack space, search the registry for specific keys, look for hidden files, etc. If it is discovered that the malware infection began with an e-mail attachment, there may be a need to trace the e-mail to its source. So while issues like warrants and seizing evidence may not be present, the same forensic techniques we have discussed throughout this book could be used.

The role of an expert in an administrative investigation is a bit different. In administrative investigations, the expert is not called upon to draw legal conclusions, formulate theories of the crime, or generate reports for court proceedings. Rather, the expert serves as an advisor. This means his or her role is to assist management, investigators, and technical personnel in clearly understanding the relevant issues. For example, if an administrative investigation requires the review of archived Microsoft Exchange records, it may be prudent to enlist the aid of an expert in Microsoft Exchange to aid in understanding relevant technological nuances.

Criminal Investigations

While electronic discovery is a part of civil proceedings or administrative investigations, it is always possible that a civil proceeding could lead to criminal charges. A search for assets in a divorce case could yield evidence of tax fraud. Scanning e-mails in an administrative investigation could find evidence of embezzlement. Because this is always a possibility, it is important that electronic discovery be conducted as if it were a criminal investigation. Most importantly, this means always maintaining the chain of custody.

In the preceding sections, we discussed e-discovery in relation to evaluating the response to disaster recovery and recovering from a virus. Both of these start off as administrative investigations, but could easily result in a criminal investigation. For example, it could be determined that a malware investigation began with a disgruntled employee, or that a server crash was due to an attempt (successful or not) to breach the server.

Limitations of Investigations

All investigations will have limits as to what data can be acquired. The most obvious limit is privilege. One cannot demand information that is covered by attorney-client privilege, doctor-patient privilege, or spousal privilege. These are all areas where opposing counsel will move to block the production of any evidence. Another area is attorney-client work product. If one is asking for records of the work between an attorney and an expert they hired, or another attorney, this is likely to be considered attorney-client work product.

Liability and Proof

In all civil litigation, one needs to first establish who is liable. That is just a legal term meaning *who is responsible*. It is entirely possible to have joint liability. For example, if I drive a car and the brakes fail, but I was also driving too fast and had not kept up with maintenance on the car, it could be found that both myself and the auto/brake manufacturer were liable. In such circumstances, the jury must determine percentage of liability for each party.

In civil cases, the burden of proof is a bit different. I am sure you have watched televised crime/courtroom dramas where the burden of proof was "beyond a reasonable doubt." That is the burden of proof in criminal cases. The burden of proof in civil cases is a bit less onerous. In civil cases, it is by a *preponderance of the evidence*. This just means that the allegation is more likely to be true than not true.

This all begs the question of what is being proved. Civil cases usually begin with what is called a tort. A tort is short for a tortious act, and it is an act that causes someone harm. That harm can be physical or financial. The harm may even be accidental through negligence. The person accused of committing the tort is referred to as the tortfeasor.

The term delict is similar to tort, at least in some jurisdictions. It essentially means to commit some wrong. That is not a term commonly used in the U.S. legal system. In most jurisdictions where this term is used, a delict refers to an intentional wrong and a quasi-delict is an unintentional wrong.

Relevant Laws

According to Fed. R. Civ. P. 34(a): [the term] "document" includes "data compilations from which information can be obtained [and] translated, if necessary, by the respondent through detection devices into reasonably usable form."

In 2006, the Federal Rules of Civil Procedure were amended in part to deal with the rapidly rising costs and burden of electronic discovery, as the following sections explain.

Rule 26(f)

Rule 26(f) *In General.* Except as exempted by Rule 26(a)(1)(B) or as otherwise stipulated or ordered by the court, a party must, without awaiting a discovery request, provide to the other parties

> (i) the name and, if known, the address and telephone number of each individual likely to have discoverable information—along with the subjects of that information—that the disclosing party may use to support its claims or defenses, unless the use would be solely for impeachment;

> (ii) a copy—or a description by category and location—of all documents, electronically stored information, and tangible things that the disclosing party has in its possession, custody, or control and may use to support its claims or defenses, unless the use would be solely for impeachment;

> (iii) a computation of each category of damages claimed by the disclosing party—who must also make available for inspection and copying as under Rule 34 the documents or other evidentiary material, unless privileged or protected from disclosure, on which each computation is based, including materials bearing on the nature and extent of injuries suffered; and

> (iv) for inspection and copying as under Rule 34, any insurance agreement under which an insurance business may be liable to satisfy all or part of a possible judgment in the action or to indemnify or reimburse for payments made to satisfy the judgment.[9]

Rule 30(b)(6)

This rule involves depositions. In a civil case, the parties must provide each side with someone from their organization with knowledge of the issues in dispute. The other party can then take the deposition of that person in order to gather information/evidence. For example, if a company is being sued regarding hiring practices, they will need to provide someone who is familiar with their hiring practices for a deposition by opposing counsel. These are often simply called 30(b)(6) depositions by attorneys.

Rule 37(f)

This rule governs electronically stored information and how courts might deal with the production or lack of production of such information. Absent exceptional circumstances, a court may not impose sanctions under these rules on a party for failing to provide electronically stored information lost as a result of the routine, good-faith operation of an electronic information system.

In *Zubulake v. UBS Warburg,* a female employee filed a lawsuit against her former employer (UBS) alleging gender discrimination, failure to promote, and retaliatory discharge. When Zubulake brought an EEOC (Equal Employment Opportunity Commission) charge in August 2001, UBS counsel gave instructions to UBS employees to preserve relevant materials (including e-mails).

It was not until August 2002, however, that Zubulake requested e-mails stored on backup tapes. UBS counsel then issued instructions to preserve backup tapes. Over time, without proper structure, e-mails, backup tapes, and relevant evidence were destroyed. While some evidence was recovered through expensive technologies, other evidence was lost for good.

The *Zubulake* Court held that UBS violated its discovery duties to preserve, protect, and disclose relevant evidence.

The Court ordered UBS to

- Pay for the redeposition of relevant UBS personnel and key players, limited to the subject of newly discovered e-mails over time
- Restore and produce relevant documents from relevant backup tapes
- Pay the plaintiff's reasonable expenses, including attorney's fees related to these issues

Consequences in the wake of *Zubulake v. UBS Warburg* include:

- To avoid court sanctions for failing to produce relevant electronic information, be aware of the implications of the amended Federal Rules of Civil Procedure regarding discovery of ESI.
- Take steps to identify and preserve ESI if litigation may be reasonably anticipated.

Big Data

Electronic discovery often entails large amounts of data. As the industry has progressed and terabytes of data storage have become common, a phrase has been developed for this: *Big Data*. Formally, the definition of Big Data is any data set that is too large to be handled via standard tools and techniques. This data normally cannot fit on a single server and is instead stored on a storage area network (SAN).

The most obvious location to find Big Data is in the SAN. SANs are so called because they are separate networks set up to appear as a server to the main organizational network. Usually, a SAN will consist of servers and network storage devices connected via high-speed cabling and switches. Users can access the data in the SAN without being concerned about the associated complexities involved. SANs usually have redundant storage.

When analyzing SANs for forensic data, you would take the same steps as with any server, but with one exception. The data in question is likely spread over multiple storage devices and they will all have to be examined in order to collect all the evidence. Other than this nuance, SAN forensics is not very different from standard server forensics.

PART IV

Steps in Electronic Data Discovery

Regardless of the purpose of the electronic discovery or the specific nuances of the investigation, there are essentially five steps to this process:

- **Identify**   Identify what evidence is relevant. Does the investigation necessitate gathering e-mails? Spreadsheets? Server logs?
- **Collect**   Once the relevant data has been identified, it needs to be collected. It is in this phase that you should pay particular attention to the chain of custody.
- **Reduce**   There is a significant chance that you will have collected more data than you need. Then you need to reduce the evidence down to just those items that provide meaningful insight for the investigation.
- **Review**   Review the evidence and determine what conclusions can be garnered from the data collected.
- **Produce**   The evidence will ultimately need to be produced, usually along with some report summarizing what was found and the conclusions drawn.

Follow these five steps in all electronic discovery cases.

Disaster Recovery

Disaster recovery can also require forensic techniques. It is common to have an administrative investigation after a disaster in order to ascertain the causes. In the course of recovery operations, it may be necessary to use forensic techniques to recover lost or damaged data. But that is only one way forensics affects disaster recovery.

Another aspect of forensically investigating a disaster involves basic electronic discovery. The company's business continuity and disaster recovery plans will need to be produced, along with relevant meeting notes, tape backups, plans, and other related documents. Usually, an internal audit team will use these items to conduct an investigation into the disaster and issue a report.

Chapter Review

In this chapter, we have investigated the latest trends in cyber forensics. Social networks play an increasing role in forensic investigations. They can be a source of evidence or the actual scene of the crime. New devices also pose challenges for forensic analysts. Cars now routinely have computers and GPS, medical devices can be WiFi enabled, and new devices are being created every day. Any device that can electronically store information could be part of a cyber forensic investigation.

We briefly reviewed control systems along with their infrastructure. These systems are vulnerable to malware and other attacks and thus could be the subject of a cyber forensic investigation. We also looked at the world of online gaming and how that social environment can be pertinent to an investigation, and even be part of a cybercrime.

We also discussed electronic discovery, which is quickly becoming a significant part of cyber forensics. Large organizations routinely have internal needs for examining data in a forensic manner, and civil litigation almost always involves electronic discovery. These areas will continue to grow in importance for cyber forensics.

Questions

1. What federal rule discusses depositions in civil litigation?

    A. 26(f)

    B. 27(f)

    C. 30(b)(6)

    D. Daubert

2. What is Big Data?

    A. Data that is more than 100GB in size

    B. Data that is too large for traditional tools

    C. Data that is distributed

    D. Data that is more than 1TB in size

3. What is a PLC?

    A. Programmable Logic Controller

    B. Partial Logic Controller

    C. Pre-CPU Linear Controller

    D. Programmable Linear Controller

4. What is SCADA?

    A. Supervisory Control and Data Acquisition

    B. System Corrupt Analysis Data Acquisition

    C. It is not an acronym but rather a term

    D. European privacy law

5. Is all unwanted contact via social media considered stalking?

    A. Yes, any unwanted contact is stalking.

    B. Yes, if you have warned the person to quit contacting you.

    C. No, it must meet additional criteria.

    D. No, social media contact is never stalking.

PART IV

Answers

1. **C.** Rule 30(b)(6) governs depositions of corporate representatives in civil litigation.
2. **B.** Big Data is any data that is too large to be dealt with using traditional tools.
3. **A.** A PLC is a Programmable Logic Controller.
4. **A.** SCADA is an acronym for Supervisory Control and Data Acquisition.
5. **C.** While the definition of stalking is not clear, it takes more than simply unwanted communication. Usually, law enforcement will look for repeated threats.

References

1. https://www.facebook.com/about/privacy/other.
2. http://happyplace.someecards.com/2013/07/26/facebook/people-accidentally-confessing-to-criminal-activity-on-facebook/.
3. http://www.cbsnews.com/pictures/facebook-related-crimes/.
4. http://theweek.com/article/index/227257/7-suspected-criminals-who-got-themselves-caught-via-facebook.
5. http://fusion.net/modern_life/entertainment/story/criminals-caught-social-media-7700.
6. http://www.theguardian.com/technology/2009/oct/14/mexico-fugitive-facebook-arrest.
7. http://www.dailymail.co.uk/news/article-2154624/A-Facebook-crime-40-minutes-12-300-cases-linked-site.html.
8. http://caveon.com/df_blog/forensics-analysis-moves-to-online-games.
9. http://www.law.cornell.edu/rules/frcp/rule_26.

About the CD-ROM

The CD-ROM included with this book comes complete with Total Tester customizable practice exam software and a PDF copy of the book.

System Requirements

The software requires Windows XP or higher and 30MB of hard disk space for full installation, in addition to a current or prior major release of Chrome, Firefox, Internet Explorer, or Safari. To run, the screen resolution must be set to 1024 × 768 or higher. The PDF copy of the book requires Adobe Acrobat, Adobe Reader, or Adobe Digital Editions.

Total Tester Premium Practice Exam Software

Total Tester provides you with a simulation of the live exam. You can also create custom exams from selected certification objectives or chapters. You can further customize the number of questions and time allowed.

The exams can be taken in either Practice Mode or Exam Mode. Practice Mode provides an assistance window with references to the book, explanations of the correct and incorrect answers, and the option to check your answer as you take the exam. Exam Mode provides a simulation of the actual exam. The number of questions, the types of questions, and the time allowed are intended to be an accurate representation of the exam environment. Both Practice Mode and Exam Mode provide an overall grade and a grade broken down by certification objectives.

To take an exam, launch the program and select the exam suite from the Installed Question Packs list. You can then select Practice Mode, Exam Mode, or Custom Mode. After making your selection, click Start Exam to begin.

Installing and Running Total Tester Premium Practice Exam Software

From the main screen you may install Total Tester by clicking the Total Tester Practice Exams button. This will begin the installation process and place an icon on your desktop and in your Start menu. To run Total Tester, navigate to Start | (All) Programs | Total Seminars, or double-click the icon on your desktop.

To uninstall the Total Tester software, go to Start | Settings | Control Panel | Add/ Remove Programs (XP) or Programs And Features (Vista/7/8), and then select the Total Tester program. Select Remove, and Windows will completely uninstall the software.

PDF Copy of the Book

The entire contents of the book are provided in PDF on the CD-ROM. This file is viewable on your computer and many portable devices. Adobe Acrobat, Adobe Reader, or Adobe Digital Editions is required to view the file on your computer. A link to Adobe's web site, where you can download and install Adobe Reader, has been included on the CD-ROM.

 NOTE For more information on Adobe Reader and to check for the most recent version of the software, visit Adobe's web site at www.adobe.com and search for the free Adobe Reader or look for Adobe Reader on the product page. Adobe Digital Editions can also be downloaded from the Adobe web site.

To view the PDF copy of the book on a portable device, copy the PDF file to your computer from the CD-ROM, and then copy the file to your portable device using a USB or other connection. Adobe offers a mobile version of Adobe Reader, the Adobe Reader mobile app, which currently supports iOS and Android. For customers using Adobe Digital Editions and an iPad, you may have to download and install a separate reader program on your device. The Adobe web site has a list of recommended applications, and McGraw-Hill Education recommends the Bluefire Reader.

Technical Support

Technical Support information is provided in the following sections by feature.

Total Seminars Technical Support

For questions regarding Total Tester software or operation of the CD-ROM, visit www.totalsem.com or e-mail support@totalsem.com.

McGraw-Hill Education Content Support

For questions regarding the PDF copy of the book, e-mail techsolutions@mhedu.com or visit http://mhp.softwareassist.com.

For questions regarding book content, e-mail customer.service@mheducation.com. For customers outside the United States, e-mail international_cs@mheducation.com.

burden of proof   A term that defines how much evidence is needed to prove a case. In criminal cases, the burden is "beyond a reasonable doubt"; in civil cases, it is "by a preponderance of the evidence."

capture point   The point in time at which evidence is seized.

chain of custody   The complete documentation of the path evidence takes from the moment of seizure to presentation at trial.

cluster   A cluster is a logical grouping of sectors. Clusters can be 1 sector in size to 128 sectors. That means 512B up to 64KB. The minimum size a file can use is one cluster. If the file is less than the size of a cluster, the remaining space is simply unused.

Daubert standard   In laymen's terms, the Daubert standard is that you should only use tests, software, and equipment that has gained wide acceptance in the industry.

discovery   Discovery is the process of each litigant finding out what evidence the other party has. In a criminal case, the prosecutor has a legal obligation to turn over all evidence to the defense attorney. The defense attorney does not have a reciprocal obligation.

drive geometry   This term refers to the functional dimensions of a drive in terms of the number of heads, cylinders, and sectors per track.

ELF   Executable and Linkable Format (ELF, formerly called Extensible Linking Format) is a common standard file format for executables (i.e., programs, applications, etc.), object code, and shared libraries for Unix-based systems.

EMI   Electromagnetic interference.

evidence return   According to the SWGDE Model Standard Operation Procedures for Computer Forensics, this is the fourth of four steps in a forensic examination. Exhibits are returned to the appropriate location, usually some locked or secured facility.

exculpatory evidence   Exculpatory evidence is evidence that proves the accused innocent.

EXT   Extended File System was the first file system created specifically for Linux. There have been many versions of EXT—the current version is 4.

Faraday bag   A bag that prevents electronic signals from entering or exiting. It is used to secure evidence such as cell phones.

FAT   FAT (File Allocation Table) is an older system that was popular with Microsoft operating systems for many years. It was first implemented in Microsoft Stand-alone Disk BASIC. FAT stores file locations by sector in a file called, eponymously, the File Allocation Table.

forensic duplication According to the SWGDE Model Standard Operation Procedures for Computer Forensics, this is the second of four steps in a forensics examination. This is the process of duplicating the media before examination. It is always preferred to work with a forensic copy and not the original.

forensic report This is a report of every step in the investigation. Even before you begin your actual analysis, you will document the crime scene and the process of acquiring the evidence. You should also document how the evidence is transported to your forensic lab. From there, you continue documenting every step you take, starting with documenting the process you use to make a forensic copy. Then document every tool you use, every test you perform. You must be able to show in your documentation everything that was done.

forensics The use of science and technology to investigate and establish facts in criminal or civil courts of law.

GUID Windows Office files have a GUID (Globally Unique Identifier) to identify them.

high-level format This is the process of setting up an empty file system on the disk and installing a boot sector. This takes little time, and is sometimes referred to as a "quick format."

hub The simplest connection device is the hub. A hub is a device into which you can plug network cables. It will have four or more ports, most likely RJ 45 jacks. You can also connect one hub to another; this strategy is referred to as "stacking" hubs. If you send a packet from one computer to another, a copy of that packet is actually sent out from every port on the hub.

IDE Integrated Drive Electronics is an older standard, but one that was commonly used on PCs for many years. It is obvious you are dealing with an IDE drive if you see a 40-pin drive connector. This was supplanted years ago by Extended IDE (EIDE). Chances are if you find any IDE drives, they will be EIDE. However, neither standard has been used in a long time.

iOS The Apple operating system for mobile devices, including the iPhone and iPad.

ipconfig This is the Windows command-line command to view and configure the settings for the network card. In Linux, the command is ifconfig.

Locard's principle of transference This principle states that one cannot interact in any environment without leaving something behind.

low-level format This creates a structure of sectors, tracks, and clusters.

media examination According to the SWGDE Model Standard Operation Procedures for Computer Forensics, this is the third of four steps in a forensic examination. This is the actual forensic testing of the application. By media, we mean hard drive, RAM, SIM card—any item that can contain digital data.

netstat   Netstat is short for network status. It shows the current connections that a machine is engaged in.

NTFS   New Technology File System. This is the file system used by Windows NT 4, 2000, XP, Vista, 7, Server 2003, Server 2008, Windows 8, and Server 2012. One major improvement of NTFS over FAT was the increased volume sizes NTFS could support.

OC   Optic cable. The cabling used with fiber optics. OC 3 and OC 12 are examples.

PE   Portable Executable (PE) is used in Windows for executables and DLLs (dynamic linked libraries).

ping   A command-line or shell command that sends one or more ICMP packets to a target to see if a response is sent back.

RAM   RAM, or random access memory, is the main memory of a computer.

Reiser   The Reiser File System is a popular journaling file system used primarily with Linux. Reiser was the first file system to be included with the standard Linux kernel, and first appeared in kernel version 2.4.1.

router   A router is much like a switch, except that it routes traffic based on the IP address. Routers can also incorporate all types of network functionality such as a firewall.

SATA   Serial Advanced Technology Attachment. SATA and solid state are the two most common drives in use today. These devices are commonly found in workstations and many servers. The internals of the hard drive are similar to IDE and EIDE—it is the connectivity to the computer's motherboard that is different. Also, unlike IDE or EIDE drives, this type of drive has no jumpers to set the drive.

SCSI   Small Computer Systems Interface—the acronym is pronounced "scuzzy." This has been around for many years, and is particularly popular in high-end servers. This standard is actually pretty old—it was established in 1986. SCSI devices must have a terminator at the end of the chain of devices to work and are limited to 16 chained devices. There is also an enhancement to the SCSI standard called Serial SCSI.

sector   A sector is the basic unit of data storage on a hard disk, usually 512 bytes. Newer hard drives using the Advanced Format have sector sizes of 4096 bytes.

solid state   These drives are becoming more common—in fact, many tablets use solid-state drives (SSDs) because they have a longer battery lifespan (they use less electricity). Unlike other drive types, SSDs don't have moving parts, such as platters, spindles, etc. Since 2010, most SSDs use NAND (Negated AND gate)–based flash memory, which retains memory even without power. Unfortunately, this type of memory has a shorter lifespan than traditional hard drives.

switch A switch is basically an intelligent hub. It works and looks exactly like a hub, but with one significant difference. When the switch receives a packet, it will send that packet out only on the port it needs to go out on. A switch accomplishes this routing by using the MAC address to determine where the packet should be routed to.

tort Torts are civil wrongs recognized by law as grounds for litigation.

tracert The Windows command-line command to send an ICMP packet to a target and trace the route it takes to the target. The Linux command is traceroute.

visual inspection According to the SWGDE Model Standard Operation Procedures for Computer Forensics, this is the first of four steps in a forensic examination. The purpose of this inspection is to verify the type of evidence, its condition, and relevant information to conduct the examination. This is often done in the initial evidence seizure. For example, if a computer is being seized, you want to document if the machine is running, its condition, and the general environment.

warrant
A legal document signed by a judge that authorizes law enforcement to search and/or seize certain evidence. A warrant must specify the particular place to be searched and what is being searched for.

3-DES (triple-DES), 160
7-Zip files, 92
802.11 Wi-Fi standards, 14, 198
802.11a standard, 14, 198
802.11b standard, 14, 198
802.11g standard, 14, 198
802.11n standard, 14, 198
802.11n-2009 standard, 14, 198

A

AAFS (American Academy of
   Forensic Science), 37–38
academic training, 48
access control, 69, 71
access time, 130
AccessData certifications, 28, 118
AccessData Certified Examiner
   (ACE) exam, 118
AccessData Forensic Toolkit. See
   FTK entries
ACE (AccessData Certified
   Examiner) exam, 118
ACK bit, 184, 185, 200
ACPI (Advanced Configuration and
   Power Interface), 134
Active Directory, 187
active partitions, 128
Address Resolution Protocol
   (ARP), 17
Adleman, Len, 164
administrative investigations,
   44–45, 324
ADRAM (asynchronous DRAM), 8
Advanced Configuration and Power
   Interface (ACPI), 134
Advanced Encryption Standard
   (AES), 14–15, 161
Advanced Forensics Format (AFF), 91
Advanced Format technology, 86
advanced persistent threats (APTs),
   309–310
AES (Advanced Encryption
   Standard), 14–15, 161
AFF (Advanced Forensics Format), 91
air conditioning, 68
Al-Qaeda, 176
American Academy of Forensic
   Science
   (AAFS), 37–38
American Society of Crime
   Laboratory Directors.
   See ASCLD
analysis. *See* forensic analysis

AND operation, 158
Android OS, 11, 239–240, 320
Android phones. *See also* smart
   phones
      considerations, 11, 259
      file system, 260
      forensics, 259–260
      key directories, 259
      malware, 239
      OS versions, 239
      overview, 239–240
      "rooting," 238
APIs (application programming
   interfaces), 138
Apple iOS. *See* iOS
Apple Mac systems. *See* Mac
   OS–based systems
application debris, 274
application logs, 190, 206
application programming interfaces
   (APIs), 138
applications, 265–295
      database software, 291–293
      e-mail programs. *See* e-mail
      file formats, 265–276
      log files, 190, 206
      mobile device apps, 243, 244
      uninstalled, 270
      web browsers, 277, 280–281
      web-based, 277–281
      Windows file copying, 276–277
APTs (advanced persistent threats),
   309–310
archival storage, 71
area density, 11, 90
armored viruses, 301
ARP (Address Resolution
   Protocol), 17
ASAP systems, 66
ASCII strings, 130
ASCLD (American Society of Crime
   Laboratory Directors), 115–116
ASCLD accreditation, 115–116
ASCLD/LAB program, 115–116
asymmetric cryptography, 158,
   163–167
asynchronous DRAM (ADRAM), 8
Atbash cipher, 155
attacks. *See also* malware; viruses
      buffer overflow, 307
      Chinese miltary, 309–310
      chosen plain text, 178
      cipher text only, 178
      denial-of-service, 199
      DoS attacks, 199

known plain text, 177
ping floods, 199, 205
ping of death attacks, 199
rainbow table, 169
related-key, 178
rootkit, 307–308
router, 202–204
smurf attacks, 200
SYN flood attacks, 200, 205
teardrop attacks, 199
war driving, 198
war flying, 198
web-based, 193
wireless network, 198–200, 202
attorney-client privilege, 325
attorney-client work product, 325
audit monitor, 222
auditing, 179, 222, 289
Auditpol tool, 179
authentication logs, 190
automobiles, 320
Autopsy tool, 97–99, 111, 130
Autostart locations, 268

B

B02K (Back Orifice 2K) port, 187
Back Orifice 2K (B02K) port, 187
background checks, 47–48, 119–120
backups
      databases, 293
      e-mail, 282
      iPhone, 257–258
      RAID, 130, 131
      tape, 86, 327
barcode scanners, 67
barcode tracking, 67
Base Transceiver Station (BTS), 235
Beast port, 187
BEDO (Burst EDO), 8
Bellaso, Giovan Battista, 156
Berkley Fast File System, 12, 89
BGP (Border Gateway Protocol),
   16, 187
Big Data, 327
Biham, Eli, 178
bin Laden, Osama, 176
binary files, 147
binary numbers, 158–159
binary operations, 158–159
BIOS/CMOS, 133–134
Birthday paradox, 160
bitmaps, 145
black hole bags, 64

BlackBerry devices, 241, 242
block ciphers, 158, 160–162, 178
blocks, 145
Blowfish cipher, 161
Blu-Ray drives, 86, 87
boot process, 133–134
boot sectors, 7, 302
Border Gateway Protocol (BGP), 16, 187
Bosselaers, Antoon, 168
browsers. *See* web browsers
BTS (Base Transceiver Station), 235
buffer, 307–308
buffer overflow attacks, 307
burden of proof, 5, 325, 331
"burner phone," 243
Burst EDO (BEDO), 8
bus topology, 210
bytes, 7, 12, 16

C

cables
coax, 13
Ethernet, 13
fiber-optic, 13–14
overview, 13–14
purpose of, 15
RG, 13
RJ, 13
Thicknet, 13
Thinnet, 13
USB, 87
UTP, 13
Caesar cipher, 154–155
capture point, 331
carriers, 170
cars, 320
Carver-Recovery utility, 96–97
carving, 96–97, 293
Cascading Style Sheets (CSS), 277
case notes, 108–109. *See also* reports
case-re-examination, 120, 121
CASP (CompTIA Advanced Security Practitioner) certification test, 117
Cat-4 cables, 13
Cat-5 cables, 13
Cat-6 cables, 13
Cat-7 cables, 13
CCFP (Certified Cyber Forensics Professional) test, 4, 28
CCMP protocol, 14–15
CD drives, 86
cell phones. *See also* mobile devices; smart phones
"burner phone," 243
call records, 243
DDR Phone tool, 251–252
identification information, 234–235
imaging, 247–260
Oxygen tool, 252–257
SIM cards, 234
SMS, 235
type of evidence on, 243–246

centralized networks, 210
certification tests, 27–28
certifications, 117–118
AccessData, 28
forensic lab, 115–116
Guidance Software, 28
industry, 48–49
(ISC)², 49, 117
need for, 27–28
personnel, 27–28, 48–49
purpose of, 28
vendor, 118
Certified Cyber Forensics Professional (CCFP) test, 4, 28
Certified Ethical Hacker certification, 117–118
Certified Hacking Forensic Investigator certification, 118
Certified Information Systems Security Professional (CISSP), 117
CGI (Common Gateway Interface), 277
chain of custody, 31–33
basics, 31–32
considerations, 4, 33, 65
damaged media and, 133
defined, 4, 32, 331
while transporting evidence, 64–65
channels, 170
cheating, online, 322
child pornography, 50, 107, 176, 244, 284
child predators, 27, 318
Chinese military attacks, 309–310
The Chinese Wall, 41–42
chi-square analysis, 176
chkdsk utility, 95
chosen plain text attacks, 178
ChuckEasttom.com, 220
cipher text only attacks, 178
ciphers, 154–157. *See also* cryptography
asymmetric algorithm, 158, 163–167
block, 158, 160–162, 178
Caesar, 154–155
described, 153
Feistel, 160–161
historical, 154–157
modern, 157–159
overview, 157–158
stream, 158, 163
symmetric algorithm, 158, 159–163
transposition ciphers, 157
Cisco routers, 201
CISSP (Certified Information Systems Security Professional), 117
civil investigations, 44
civil law, 24
civil lawsuits, 40, 44
civil litigation, 44, 323–324
civil matters, 40
client/server networks, 210

clipper chip, 162
cloud systems, 217, 222–229, 227
clusters
considerations, 83, 86, 128
described, 7, 331
FAT file system and, 138–139
slack space and, 130
CMOS (Complementary Metal-Oxide Semiconductor), 134
CMOS/BIOS, 133–134
coax cables, 13
code, compressed, 301
code confusion, 301
code of ethics, 36–39
COFF (Common Object File Format), 90
college degrees, 117
color pairs, 175–176
Common Gateway Interface (CGI), 277
Common Object File Format (COFF), 90
community clouds, 223
CommView tool, 190
Complementary Metal-Oxide Semiconductor. *See* CMOS
compressed code, 301
compressed files, 92
CompTIA Security+/CASP certification, 117
computer forensics. *See* cyber forensics
Computer Hacking Forensic Investigator test, 28
computer shares, 205
computers. *See also* devices
assessing suspect computer, 55–57
condition/status of target computer, 55
consent to search, 25–26
devices connected to, 55–57
evidence found on, 82
IP address of. *See* IP addresses
knowledge of, 6
searching/seizing, 25–26
widespread use of, 3
conflicts of interest, 41–42, 50
connection devices, 15
connectionless protocols, 184
connection-oriented protocols, 184
consultants. *See* expert consultants
contacts, 238
contamination, 80
contractors, 39
control systems/infrastructure, 321
cookies, 280–281
copyright infringement, 323
CRC (cyclic redundancy check), 186
CRC-32 checksum, 14
credentials, 38, 50
credibility, 49
credit card laws, 229
credit checks, 119
crime scene
associating person with, 81

documenting, 55–57
environmental conditions, 57
personnel present at, 57
photographing, 55–57
removing evidence from, 64–65
securing, 21–22, 33
sketching, 57
video recording, 57
crimes
building theories about, 77–78
burden of proof, 5, 325, 331
comissioned via social media, 318–320
cybercrimes, 3, 199–200
elements of, 5–6
emergence of computer crime, 3
exculpatory evidence, 6, 245, 331
intent, 5
laws broken, 5
posted on social media, 317–318
reconstructing, 81
criminal conduct, 40
criminal investigations, 43–44, 324–325
criminal law, 24
criminal matters, 40
cross-site scripting, 193, 279–280
cryptanalysis, 176–178
CryptoCorner.com, 157
cryptographic hashes, 167–168
cryptography, 153–169. *See also* encryption
AES, 14–15, 161
asymmetric, 158, 163–167
binary operations, 158–159
Birthday paradox, 160
ciphers. *See* ciphers
DES, 159–160
Enigma Machine, 157
GOST algorithm, 162
history of, 154–157
IDEA, 162
modern, 157–159
multialphabet substitution, 155–156
overview, 153
public key, 308
Scytale, 155
Serpent algorithm, 162
Skipjack algorithm, 162–163
vs. steganography, 170
symmetric, 158, 159–163
CSS (Cascading Style Sheets), 277
curriculum vitae (CV), 113
Curry, Andrew, 317
CV (curriculum vitae), 113
cyber forensics. *See also* crimes; forensics
considerations, 4
defined, 3
federal guidelines, 26–27
fundamental principles of, 21–23
Inman-Rudin Paradigm, 81
introduction to, 3–30
knowledge base needed for, 6–21

legal issues, 23–26
Locard's principle of transference, 79–80, 81, 332
mobile. *See* mobile devices
network. *See* network forensics
new/emerging technology, 315–330
overview, 3–4
cyber forensics certification. *See* certification
cyber stalking, 284, 318, 319–320
cybercrimes, 3, 199–200
cybercrimes5 web page, 27
cyclic redundancy check. *See* CRC

D

DAT (digital audio tape) drives, 86
.dat extension, 92
data. *See also* evidence; files
backing up. *See* backups
Big Data, 327
encrypted. *See* encryption
finding on hard drives, 130
formats, 82
hidden, 85
magnetic, 7, 8
metadata, 97–99
payload, 170
recovering. *See* data recovery
salt, 169
storing. *See* storage devices/media
data carving, 96–97
Data Encryption Standard (DES), 159–160
data files, 92
data recovery, 95–99
from damaged media, 132–135
data carving, 96–97
iBoot recovery mode, 238–239
iPhone, 238–239
known file filtering, 99
logical damage, 95, 133
metadata, 97–99
physical damage, 95, 133
Windows files, 138–144, 145
databases, 291–293
backups, 293
evidence from, 82, 292–293
hierarchical, 292
log files, 293
Microsoft Access, 292
MySQL, 292
NoSQL, 292
object-oriented, 292
Oracle Server, 292
PostGres, 292
reconstruction, 293
record carving, 293
SQL Server, 291
SQLite, 92
transaction ID, 293
transaction logs, 292, 293
types of, 291–292
user accounts, 292

datagrams, 184
Daubert standard, 23–24, 46, 331
.db extension, 92
.dbx extension, 289
DCFLdd utility, 133
DDR (Double Data Rate), 8
DDR Phone tool, 251–252
debris, application, 274
defendants, 24
degaussing hard drives, 181
deleted files
considerations, 78
e-mail, 290
iPhone, 259
logs, 179
recovering (Linux), 145–147
recovering (Mac), 147
recovering (Windows), 138–144, 145
delict, 325
denial-of-service (DoS) attacks, 199
Department of Defense (DoD), 144
depositions, 24, 326
DES (Data Encryption Standard), 159–160
device drivers, 137–138
devices. *See also* drives
assessing condition/status of, 55–57
embedded, 260
Google Glass, 320
GPS, 320
hard drives. *See* hard drives
log files, 190, 191
medical, 321
mobile. *See* mobile devices
new technology, 320–321
SCADA, 260
storage. *See* storage devices
USB, 267
write-blocking, 63
differential cryptanalysis, 178
Diffie, Whitfield, 166
Diffie-Hellman protocol, 166
digital audio tape (DAT) drives, 86
digital forensics, 4, 39. *See also* cyber forensics
Digital Visual Interface. *See* DVI
disaster recovery, 328
discovery
defined, 331
e-discovery, 25, 322–328
overview, 24–25
relevancy, 25
scope of, 25
discrimination, 323
disk controllers, 63
Disk Digger, 140–142
disk images. *See* images
disk striping, 131–132
Disk Utility, 95, 133
disks. *See* drives
district attorney, 24
divorce cases, 324
DLL format, 92

DLLs (Dynamic Linked Libraries), 11
DNS (Domain Name Service), 16, 187
Dobbertin, Hans, 168
doctor-patient privilege, 325
documentation. *See also* reports
    evidence, 43, 55–57
    overview, 33–35
    photographic, 35, 55–57
    possible crime scene, 55–57
    video, 35, 57
documents, recently visited, 268–269
DoD (Department of Defense), 144
DOD 5220.22-M standard, 144
Domain Name Service (DNS), 16, 187
DoS (denial-of-service) attacks, 199
DOS commands, 9
DOS operating system, 9
Double Data Rate (DDR), 8
DRAM (Dynamic Random Access
    Memory), 8
drive geometry, 7, 8, 331
drivers, 137–138
drives. *See also* devices
    Blu-Ray, 86, 87
    CD, 86
    DAT, 86
    DVD, 86
    encrypted, 150
    hard. *See* hard drives
    optical, 86–87
    SATA, 333
    tape, 86, 327
Duronio, Roger, 308
DVD drives, 86
DVI (Digital Visual Interface), 88
DVI connectors, 88
dynamic analysis, 310–311
Dynamic Linked Libraries. *See* DLLs
dynamic memory, 276
Dynamic Random Access Memory
    (DRAM), 8

E

EC Council, 28, 117–118
EC Council Certifications, 117–118
ECC (elliptic curve cryptography), 167
e-commerce servers, 106
EDGE (Enhanced Data Rates for
    GSM Evolution), 236
e-discovery, 25, 322–328
EDO (Extended Data Out) DRAM, 8
education, 48, 117, 118
EFS (Encrypting File System),
    148–149
EIDE (Extended IDE), 6–7, 83
EIDE drives, 6–7, 83
electromagnetic interference (EMI),
    64, 69–70, 331
electronic discovery, 25, 322–328
Electronic Serial Number (ESN), 234
electrostatic discharge (ESD), 64
ELF (Executable and Linkable
    Format), 11, 90, 331
EliteWrap tool, 306

elliptic curve cryptography (ECC), 167
e-mail, 281–291
    basics, 282–283
    content of, 282
    deleted, 290
    evidence from, 282
    file formats, 290–291
    on iPhone, 258
    Outlook, 298
    protocols, 283
    spoofed, 283
    storage of, 289
    tracing, 289–290
    virus spread via, 297–298
e-mail files, 289
e-mail headers, 283–289
e-mail records, 282
e-mail server, 282, 290–291
e-mail server forensics, 290–291
embezzlement, 324
EMI (electromagnetic interference),
    64, 69–70, 331
.emi extension, 289
employees. *See* forensics staff
EnCase Certified Examiner (EnCE)
    certification, 118
EnCase forensic tool
    acquiring RAID arrays, 132
    disk imaging with, 60–62
    evidence preservation, 60–62
    forensic reports, 110
    mobile devices, 249–251
Encase format, 91
EnCE (EnCase Certified Examiner)
    certification, 118
encrypted drives, 150
encrypted files, 148–150
encrypted partitions, 129
Encrypting File System (EFS),
    148–149
encryption. *See also* cryptography
    AES, 14–15, 161
    cryptanalysis, 176–178
    DES, 159–160
    IDEA, 162
    traffic, 181
end of chain (EOC) character, 138
Enhanced Data Rates for GSM
    Evolution (EDGE), 236
Enigma Machine, 157
environmental conditions/hazards,
    57, 67–69, 70
EOC (end of chain) character, 138
errors, 106
ESD (electrostatic discharge), 64
ESN (Electronic Serial Number), 234
Ethernet cables, 13
Ethernet connections, 13
Ethernet headers, 186
ethical conduct
    AAFS guidelines, 37–38
    The Chinese Wall, 41–42
    civil matters, 40
    code of ethics, 36–39
    conflicts of interest, 41–42, 50

    considerations, 36–37
    criminal matters, 40
    during investigation, 41–43
    ISC guidelines, 37
    ISO Code of Ethics, 38–39
    lab accreditation, 39
    outside investigation, 40–41
    regulations for, 42–43
ETSI (European Telecommunications
    Standards Institute), 236
EU (European Union) has strict
    privacy laws, 228
Euler's totient, 164–165
European Telecommunications
    Standards Institute (ETSI), 236
European Union (EU) has strict
    privacy laws, 228
evidence, 55–74
    access to, 69, 71
    administrative investigations,
        44–45
    admissibility of, 42
    analyzing. *See* forensic analysis
    associating person with, 81
    authentication, 43
    authority to acquire, 25, 42
    barcodes, 67
    chain of custody. *See* chain
        of custody
    civil investigations, 44
    classifying, 81, 82
    collection of, 55–64, 105–106
    completeness of, 107
    on computer. *See* computers
    contamination, 80
    copies of. *See* forensic imaging
    criminal investigations, 43–44
    data format, 82
    database, 82, 292–293
    Daubert standard, 23–24, 46
    disposing of, 71
    documenting. *See*
        documentation
    electromagnetic interference,
        64, 69–70
    e-mail. *See* e-mail
    environmental conditions/
        hazards, 57, 67–69, 70
    ethical considerations. *See*
        ethical conduct
    examination of, 36
    exculpatory, 6, 245, 331
    extrinsic, 45, 113
    fragility, 43
    hiding. *See* cryptography;
        encryption
    identifying, 81, 82
    intrinsic, 45, 113
    latent, 3
    limiting interaction with, 22–23
    Locard's principle of
        transference, 79–80, 81, 332
    management of, 55–71
    on mobile devices. *See* mobile
        devices

network traffic, 82
in plain sight, 44
posted on social media, 317–318
preponderance of, 5, 325
preservation of, 57–64
probative value, 82
proper handling of, 107
provenance, 42
radio frequency interference,
  64, 69–70
reliability of, 42
removing from crime scene,
  64–65
return of, 36, 331
RFID chips, 67
searching/seizing, 42, 43–44
securing, 21–23, 32, 33
source of, 82
spoliation, 322
storing, 67–70, 71
trace, 80
tracking, 65–67
transporting, 64–67
type of, 82
validation of findings,
  106–107, 113
visual inspection, 36, 334
volatile, 43
where to find, 82–94
evidence bags, 64
evidence logs, 65–66
evidence return, 36, 331
evidence room, 68–70
evidence tags, 32
Evidence Tracker, 66
evidence transfer, 32
exaggeration, 38
examination quality control, 120–121
examination steps, 36
Exchangeable Image File Format
  (EXIF) format, 91
exculpatory evidence, 6, 245, 331
EXE format, 92
Executable and Linkable Format
  (ELF), 11, 90, 331
executables, 11, 92
EXIF (Exchangeable Image File
  Format) format, 91
"expert as a learner," 48
expert consultants. See also expert
  witness
    background check, 47–48,
      119–120
    conduct. See ethical conduct
    conflicts of interest, 41–42, 50
    credentials, 38, 50
    credibility, 49, 120
    curriculum vitae, 113
    experience, 49
    misrepresentation, 37–38
    multiple, 106
    personality traits, 50–51
    personal/professional conduct,
      36, 37
    qualities of, 47–51

testimony, 46, 51, 191
  training, 48–49
expert report, 113–114
expert testimony, 46, 51, 191
expert witness. See also expert
  consultants
    forensic investigator as, 46–51
    vs. forensics investigator, 47
    honesty/integrity of, 51, 120
    testimony, 46, 51, 191
EXT (Extended File System),
  12, 89, 331
EXT3 partitions, 147
EXT4 partitions, 147
Extended Data Out (EDO) DRAM, 8
Extended File System. See EXT
Extended IDE. See EIDE
extended partitions, 128
Extensible Linking Format. See ELF
extensions. See file extensions
extrinsic evidence, 45, 113
ExtUndelete tool, 147

F

Facebook, 41, 214, 215, 316
facts, 77–78
FakeAV virus, 298–300, 301
falsifiability, 78
Faraday bags, 64, 331
Faraday cage, 64, 69–70
Faraday, Michael, 64
FAT (File Allocation Table), 12, 89,
  138–139, 331
FAT12 systems, 12, 89
FAT16 systems, 12, 89, 138
FAT32 systems, 12, 89, 138, 238
FBI (Federal Bureau of
  Investigation), 26–27
FBI forensic guidelines, 26–27
FBI Regional Computer Forensics
  Laboratory (RCFL), 115
Federal Bureau of Investigation.
  See FBI
federal guidelines, 26–27
Federal Information Processing
  Standard (FIPS), 166
federal laws, 23
Federal Rules of Civil Procedure,
  325–327
Feistel ciphers, 160–161
fiber-optic cables, 13–14
Fibre Channel, 84
Fibre Channel Arbitrated loops, 84
File Allocation Table. See FAT
file carving, 96
file extensions, 11, 92
file formats, 90–91, 265–276
file headers, 11, 90
file permissions, 276–277
file signatures, 92
File System Check (FSCK) utility,
  12, 89
file systems
    Android phones, 260

Berkley Fast File System, 12, 89
EFS, 148–149
EXT, 12, 89, 331
FAT, 12, 89, 138–139, 331
HFS, 238
journaling, 11, 90
Linux, 89
Mac OS, 238
nonjournaling, 11
NTFS, 12, 89, 139, 333
overview, 11–12, 89–90
Reiser File System, 12, 89, 333
slack space, 7
Windows, 89, 138–139
YAFFS2, 260
File Transfer Protocol (FTP), 16, 186
files. See also images
AFF, 91
basics, 11–12
binary, 147
compressed, 92
considerations, 90
copied/moved, 276–277
data, 92
deleted. See deleted files
described, 90
e-mail, 289
encrypted, 148–150
executable, 92
filtering, 99
graphics, 90
hidden messages in. See
  steganography
log. See log files
.mdf, 293
media, 99–102
.mem, 275
MP3, 175
Office, 11, 91
overview, 11–12
PNG, 94
RAR, 92
raster, 91
recently visited, 268–269
SAM, 169
scrubbing, 144
spool, 273–274
swap, 134–135, 272
tar, 92
temporary, 274
.vmem, 275
.zip, 92
FIN bit, 185, 186
findings, validation of, 106–107, 113
fingerprints, 80
FIPS (Federal Information
  Processing Standard), 166
fire protection, 68–69
Firefox browser, 280–281
Firesheep tool, 215, 280, 281
firewall logs, 205
firewalls, 193, 200, 204–205
FireWire connectors, 89
Flame virus, 300
floods/flooding, 68

floppy disks, 12
forensic analysis, 105–123
  analyzing evidence, 106–108
  case notes, 108–109
  case-re-examination, 121
  collecting evidence, 105–106
  legal compliance, 108
  planning, 105–108
  proper evidence handling, 107
  quality control, 114–121
  reports. *See* reports
forensic analysts, 119
forensic copies, 22
forensic disk controllers, 63
forensic duplication, 36, 332
forensic imaging
  considerations, 57
  with EnCase, 60–62
  with Forensic Toolkit, 58–60
  invasive vs. non-invasive, 248
  logical, 247
  mobile devices, 247–260
  physical, 248
  virtual machines, 225
forensic investigations. *See*
  investigations
forensic investigators. *See also*
  forensics staff
  authority to investigate, 35
  background checks, 47–48,
    119–120
  conflicts of interest, 41–42, 50
  credibility, 49
  credit checks on, 119
  criminal record and, 40, 119
  ethical conduct. *See* ethical
    conduct
  experience, 49
  as expert witness, 46–51
  vs. expert witness, 47
  federal guidelines, 26–27
  ideal elements of, 118–119
  lawsuits and, 40
  misrepresentation, 36–37
  multiple, 106–107
  personal/professional conduct,
    36, 37
  public statements, 41, 51
  quality control, 116–120
  training/education, 48–49,
    117–119
forensic lab machines, 8
forensic labs
  access controls, 69, 71
  accreditation/certification, 39,
    115–116
  American Society of Crime
    Laboratory Directors,
    115–116
  evidence storage, 67–70, 71
  new technology and, 39
  physical access, 69
  quality of, 114–116
  Regional Computer Forensics
    Laboratory, 115

  training/education options,
    115–116
  U.S. Army guidelines, 70
  validation of findings,
    106–107, 113
  video surveillance, 69
forensic reports, 109–113, 332. *See
  also* reports
Forensic Toolkit. *See* FTK
forensics. *See also* cyber forensics
  analysis. *See* forensic analysis
  Daubert standard, 23–24, 46, 331
  defined, 3, 332
  elements of a crime, 5–6
  peer reviews, 78–79, 120
  science of, 4–5, 77–81
forensics staff
  background checks, 47–48,
    119–120
  certifications, 117–118
  conflicts of interest, 41–42, 50
  credibility, 49
  credit checks on, 119
  ethical conduct. *See* ethical
    conduct
  experience, 49
  experts. *See* expert consultants;
    expert witness
  investigators. *See* forensic
    investigators
  misrepresentation, 36–37
  outside contractors, 39
  peer reviews, 78–79, 120
  personality traits, 50–51
  personal/professional conduct,
    36, 37
  present at crime scene, 57
  quality control, 116–120
  training/education, 39, 48,
    117–119
formatting hard drives, 86
Fourth Amendment, 25, 43
Fourth Amendment "search," 25
frames, 184
FreeBSD, 10, 147
frequency analysis, 177
fsck utility, 95, 133
FSCK (File System Check) utility, 12, 89
FTK (Forensic Toolkit)
  disk imaging with, 58–60
  evidence preservation, 58–60
  reports, 111
FTK certifications, 28, 118
FTP (File Transfer Protocol), 16, 186
function call analysis, 310
Fusion RMS software, 66

G

gaming, online, 321–322
Generic Forensic Zip (GfZIP)
  format, 92
GET requests, 195
GfZIP (Generic Forensic Zip) format, 92
GIF format, 91

Gigabit Ethernet, 13
Global Positioning Satellite. *See* GPS
Global System for Mobile
  Communications (GSM), 236
Globally Unique Identifier (GUID),
  11, 91, 332
glossary, 331–334
Gmail headers, 287, 289
GNU (GNU is Not Unix), 10
GNU is Not Unix (GNU), 10
"GNU Manifesto," 10
Google Glass, 320
Google Scholar, 49, 79
GOST algorithm, 162, 168
GPS (Global Positioning Satellite), 244
GPS devices, 320
GPS records, 244, 245
graphical user interface (GUI), 137
graphics files, 90
grep command, 146–147
grep flags, 147
GSM (Global System for Mobile
  Communications), 236
GUI (graphical user interface), 137
GUID (Globally Unique Identifier),
  11, 91, 332
Guidance Software certifications, 28
Guidance Software EnCase. *See
  EnCase entries*

H

hacking, 117–118
hard drives, 83–86
  boot process, 133–134
  clusters. *See* clusters
  components, 127–128
  connectors, 83–85
  considerations, 8
  data organization, 86
  data structure, 128
  degaussing, 181
  drive geometry, 7, 8, 331
  EIDE, 6–7, 83
  external, 85
  failed, 95
  finding data on, 130
  forensics procedures, 85–86
  formatting, 86
  free space, 130
  high-level format, 7, 332
  IDE, 6–7, 83, 332
  logical damage, 95, 133
  logical drives, 128
  low-level format, 7, 332
  magnetic, 83–85
  overview, 6–8, 83
  partitions, 85, 86–87, 128–130
  physical damage, 95, 133
  physical drives, 128
  platters, 127–128
  "quick format," 7
  RAID, 130–132
  SATA, 7
  SCSI, 6

sectors. *See* sectors
slack space, 86, 130
specifications, 127–132
SSDs, 7, 85, 333
swap files, 134–135
unallocated space in, 85, 130
USB, 85, 267
wiping, 181
hard links, 146
hardware basics, 6–9
hardware interfaces, 87–89
hashes, 167–168, 169
HCU (HKEY_CURRENT_CONFIG),
266
HDDs. *See* hard drives
header analysis, 92–94
Health Insurance Portability and
Accountability Act (HIPAA),
228–229
heap memory, 276
Hellman, Martin, 166, 169
hex editors, 92, 93–94
HexEdit, 92
hexidecimal format, 93–94
HFS (Hierarchical File System), 238
HFS+ File System, 238
hidden data, 85
hidden partitions, 129
Hierarchical File System. *See* HFS
high-level format, 7, 332
HIPAA (Health Insurance Portability
and Accountability Act), 228–229
hives, 266
HKCR (HKEY_CLASSES_ROOT), 266
HKCU (HKEY_CURRENT_USER),
266, 268–269, 272
HKEY_CLASSES_ROOT (HKCR), 266
HKEY_CURRENT_CONFIG
(HCU), 266
HKEY_CURRENT_USER (HKCU),
266, 268–269, 272
HKEY_LOCAL_MACHINE (HKLM),
266, 267, 270–272
HKEY_USERS (HKU), 266
HKLM (HKEY_LOCAL_MACHINE),
266, 267, 270–272
HKU (HKEY_USERS), 266
HLR (Home Location Register), 235
Home Location Register (HLR), 235
honesty, 51
host machine, 218
host-protected area (HPA), 85
HPA (host-protected area), 85
HTTP (Hypertext Transfer Protocol),
16, 187, 194, 277
HTTP messages, 194–196
HTTP Sniffer, 190, 194
HTTPS (Hypertext Transfer Protocol
Secure), 16, 187
hubs, 15, 201, 332
HyperTerminal tool, 202
Hypertext Transfer Protocol. *See* HTTP
Hypertext Transfer Protocol Secure
(HTTPS), 16, 187
hypervisor, 218, 222

hypotheses
considerations, 4–5
scientific approach to, 77–81
testing, 5, 78

I

IaaS (infrastructure as a service),
221–222
iBoot recovery mode, 238–239
ICCID (Integrated Circuit Card
Identification), 234
ICMP packets, 199
ICMP (Internet Control Message
Protocol) packets, 199
ICMP requests, 200
IDE (Integrated Drive Electronics),
6–7, 83, 332
IDE drives, 6–7, 83, 332
IDEA (International Data Encryption
Algorithm), 162
iDEN (Integrated Digitally Enhanced
Network), 236–237
IE (Internet Explorer), 272–273
IEEE 802.11n-2009 standard, 14, 198
ifconfig command, 18
images. *See also* files
copying, 22–23
hidden messages in, 175–176
photos on mobile devices,
243–244, 245
pornographic, 50, 176, 244, 284
IMAP (Internet Message Access
Protocol), 187, 283
IMEI (International Mobile
Equipment Identity), 234, 235
IMSI (International Mobile
Subscriber Identity), 234
index.dat file, 272–273
infrastructure as a service (IaaS),
221–222
Inman-Rudin Paradigm, 81
inodes, 145
inspections, visual, 36, 334
Integrated Circuit Card Identification
(ICCID), 234
Integrated Digitally Enhanced
Network (iDEN), 236–237
Integrated Drive Electronics. *See* IDE
integrity, 51
intellectual property, 45–46, 323
intellectual property investigations,
45–46
intent, 5
interference, electromagnetic,
64, 69–70
interference, radio frequency,
64, 69–70
International Data Encryption
Algorithm (IDEA), 162
International Mobile Equipment
Identity (IMEI), 234, 235
International Mobile Subscriber
Identity (IMSI), 234
Internet Control Message Protocol.
See ICMP

Internet Explorer (IE), 272–273
Internet Message Access Protocol
(IMAP), 187, 283
Internet Protocol. *See* IP
Internet Relay Chat (IRC), 187
Internet Service Providers (ISPs), 16
interrogatories, 24
interrupts, 137–138
intrinsic evidence, 45, 113
investigations, 31–53
administrative, 44–45, 324
authority to perform, 35
case re-examination, 121
chain of custody. *See* chain
of custody
civil litigation, 44, 323–324
completeness of, 107
criminal, 43–44, 324–325
documentation, 33–35, 43
ethical requirements. *See* ethical
conduct
examination steps, 36
FBI forensic guidelines, 26–27
hypotheses, 4–5
intellectual property, 45–46
jurisdiction, 35, 215, 227, 228
laws. *See* laws
limitations of, 325
nature of, 228
objectives, 35
Secret Service "golden rules," 27
securing crime scene, 21–22, 33
standard operating
procedures, 107
types of, 323–325
investigators. *See* forensic
investigators
investigators, private, 33
Invisible Secrets tool, 171–175
iOS, 11, 237–239, 332. *See also* iPhone
IP addresses
considerations, 17
overview, 16–17
private, 17
public, 17
spoofing, 279, 283
tracing, 17
IP headers, 185
ipconfig command, 18–19, 332
iPhone. *See also* iOS; smart phones
backup files, 257–258
considerations, 257
deleted files, 259
device data, 258
e-mail on, 258
iBoot recovery mode, 238–239
imaging, 257–258
iOS, 237–239
"jailbreaking," 238
types of analysis, 258–259
IPv4 addresses, 16–17
IPv6 addresses, 16, 17
IRC (Internet Relay Chat), 187
(ISC)² certification, 49, 117
(ISC)² Ethics, 37

ISO Code of Ethics, 38–39
ISO format, 92
ISPs (Internet Service Providers), 16
iStumbler, 199
iTunes, 257–258

J

"jailbreaking," 238
JavaScript, 277
journaling file systems, 11, 90
JPEG format, 91
jurisdiction, 35, 215, 227, 228

K

Kasiski examination, 177
Kasiski, Friedrich, 177
Kerberos, 187
kernel, 136–137
key loggers, 306, 307
key-scheduling algorithm (KSA), 163
KFF (known file filtering), 99
Kindle devices, 241, 242
Kindle Fire, 241, 242
known file filtering (KFF), 99
known plain text attacks, 177
Koblitz, Neal, 167
Kravitz, David W., 166
KSA (key-scheduling algorithm), 163

L

labs. See forensic labs
LANs (local area networks), 201
last-in, first-out (LIFO) principle, 276
latency period, 130
latent evidence, 3
Lauffenburger, Michael, 308
law enforcement, 33, 255
laws. See also legal issues/proceedings
    civil, 24
    criminal, 24
    cyber forensics and, 23
    federal, 23
    forensic investigations, 23
    relevant, 325–327
    state, 23
lawsuits. See also litigation
    civil, 40, 44
    considerations, 40
    grounds for, 24
    liability, 24
    monetary damages, 24
    sexual harassment, 44
LDAP (Lightweight Directory Access
    Protocol), 187
.ldf files, 293
least significant bits (LSB), 170
legal compliance, 108
legal issues/proceedings. See also laws
    cloud systems and, 227–229
    cyber forensics, 23–26
    Daubert standard, 23–24, 46
    defendants, 24
    depositions, 24

discovery, 24–25
    Fourth Amendment, 25, 43
    general, 24
    interrogatories, 24
    laws broken, 5
    liability, 24
    litigants, 24
    plaintiffs, 24
    "under oath" concept, 24, 25
    warrants, 25–26, 43–44, 334
liability, 24, 325
LIFO (last-in, first-out) principle, 276
Lightweight Directory Access
    Protocol (LDAP), 187
linear cryptanalysis, 178
LinkedIn, 214, 316–317
links, types of, 145–146
Linux-based systems
    copying drive images, 22–23
    file systems, 89
    history, 10
    log files, 206
    overview, 10
    run levels, 146
    undeleting files, 145–147
litigants, 24
litigation. See also lawsuits
    civil, 44, 323–324
    patent, 45–46
live memory captures, 8, 9
local area networks (LANs), 201
Locard, Edmond, 79–80
Locard's principle of transference,
    79–80, 81, 332
log files
    application logs, 190, 206
    authentication logs, 190
    considerations, 191
    databases, 293
    deletion of, 179
    device logs, 190, 191
    evidence tracking, 65–66
    firewall logs, 205
    Linux logs, 206
    network, 190–191, 205–207
    operating system logs, 190
    tampering with, 179
    Windows logs, 205–206
log tampering, 179
logic bombs, 308
logical drives, 128
logical imaging, 247
logical journaling, 11, 90
logical network perimeter, 222
logical partitions, 129
Long-Term Evolution (LTE), 236
low-level format, 7, 332
LSB (least significant bits), 170
LTE (Long-Term Evolution), 236

M

MAC (Media Access Control), 17
MAC addresses, 17, 180, 186
Mac Defender virus, 298, 300, 301

Mac OS–based systems
    considerations, 10
    file systems, 238
    overview, 10
    undeleting files, 147
Mac Security virus, 298
MacKeeper tool, 147
macro viruses, 302
MacStumbler, 199
magic numbers, 94
magnetic data, 7, 8
magnetic hard drives, 83–85
magnetic storage devices, 83–85
mail. See e-mail
malware, 297–314. See also attacks;
    viruses
    advanced persistent threats,
        309–310
    analysis of, 310–311
    buffer overflow attacks, 307
    logic bombs, 308
    mobile devices, 239
    ransomware, 308–309
    rootkit attacks, 307–308
    spyware, 306–307
    Trojan horses, 305–306
    viruses. See viruses
Malware Bytes, 298
MAP (Mobile Application Part), 235
Markman hearing, 45–46
massively multiplayer online (MMO)
    games, 321
Master Boot Record (MBR), 85
Master File Table (MFT), 139
Matsui, Mitsura, 178
MBR (Master Boot Record), 85
.mbx extension, 289
MCC (mobile country code), 234
MD5 hashes, 168
.mdb extension, 92
.mdf extension, 92
.mdf files, 293
media. See also storage devices/media
    damaged, 132–135
    examination, 36, 332
    forensic duplication, 36
    recovering, 132–135
Media Access Control. See MAC
media files, 99–102
medical devices, 321
Medico, Joseph, 319
.mem files, 275
memory
    ADRAM, 8
    analysis, 274–276
    BEDO, 8
    considerations, 276
    DDR, 8
    DRAM, 8
    dynamic, 276
    EDO DRAM, 8
    heap, 276
    live memory captures, 8, 9
    NAND, 7, 85
    protected, 136

PSRA, 9
RAM, 8–9, 200, 312, 333
RAM-9, 8
RLDRAM, 9
SDRAM, 8
SGRAM, 9
stack, 276
types of, 276
virtual, 134–135
volatile, 274–275
memory dumps, 275
memory management, 136
mesh topology, 211
message history, 238
Meta File Table. *See* Master File Table
metadata, 97–99
MFT (Master File Table), 139
microdots, 171
micro-kernel architecture, 136
Microsoft Access, 92, 292
Microsoft Developer Network
　(MSDN), 298
Microsoft Office files, 11, 91
Microsoft Office products, 298, 302
Microsoft Outlook, 298
Microsoft SQL Server, 92, 291
Microsoft Virtual PC, 218, 219, 227
Microsoft Windows. *See*
　Windows systems
Miller, Victor, 167
MIMO (multiple-input multiple-
　output), 14
Minix operating system, 10
misrepresentation, 36–37
MiTeC Hexadecimal Editor, 93–94
mixed mode networks, 210
MMO (massively multiplayer online)
　games, 321
MMS (Multimedia Messaging
　Service), 235
Mobile Application Part (MAP), 235
mobile country code (MCC), 234
mobile devices, 233–262
　apps, 243, 244
　basics, 234–235
　"burner phone," 243
　call history, 245
　call records, 243, 245
　concepts, 243
　considerations, 233
　contacts, 238
　DDR Phone tool, 251–252
　device information, 245
　device status, 246
　embedded devices, 260
　Encase tools, 249–251
　evidence, from apps, 244
　evidence, seizing, 246–260
　evidence, types of, 243–246
　GPS records, 244, 245
　identification information,
　　234–235
　imaging, 247–260
　local acquisition, 247
　malware, 239

message history, 238
networks, 236–237, 246
operating systems, 237–242
Oxygen tool, 252–257
Paraben tools, 248–249
photos/video on, 243–244, 245
physical acquisition, 248
remote wipe feature, 64, 243
signal isolation precautions, 64
SIM cards, 234
smartphones. *See* smart phones
SMS, 235
what to look for, 245–246
mobile subscription identifier
　number (MSIN), 234
Mobile Switching Center (MSC), 235
modulo, 165
monitor connectors, 88
monolithic-kernel architecture, 136
MP3 files, 175
MP3Stego tool, 175
MSC (Mobile Switching Center), 235
MSDN (Microsoft Developer
　Network), 298
MSIN (mobile subscription identifier
　number), 234
multialphabet substitution, 155–156
Multimedia Messaging Service
　(MMS), 235
multipartite viruses, 302
multiple-input multiple-output
　(MIMO), 14
multiprocessing OS, 135
multitasking OS, 135
multithreading OS, 135
multiuser OS, 135
MySQL, 292

N

NAND (Negated AND gate) memory,
　7, 85
National Institute of Standards and
　Technology (NIST), 222
National Security Agency (NSA),
　162–163
Negated AND gate (NAND) memory,
　7, 85
negligence, 325
net sessions, 102, 208–209
NetBIOS, 16, 187
NetIntercept tool, 190
netstat command, 20–21, 101, 208, 333
NetStumbler, 199
network adapters, 270, 271
network attacks
　DoS attacks, 199
　ping floods, 199, 205
　ping of death attacks, 199
　smurf attacks, 200
　SYN flood attacks, 200, 205
　teardrop attacks, 199
　war driving, 198
　war flying, 198
network cards, 188–190

network device logs, 191
network forensics, 183–216
network interface cards (NICs), 13, 201
network packets, 184–186
network proxies, 214
network services, 214
network shares, 213–214
network topology, 210–213
network traffic evidence, 82
network trailers, 186
network utilities, 17–21
　ipconfig command, 18–19
　netstat command, 20–21
　ping command, 19
　tracert command, 19–20
networks, 13–21
　basic communications, 185–186
　centralized, 210
　client/server, 210
　connection devices, 15
　considerations, 13
　firewalls, 193, 200, 204–205
　hubs, 15
　LANs, 201
　mixed mode, 210
　mobile devices, 236–237, 246
　P2P, 210, 214
　packets, 15, 183–198
　payload, 186
　physical connections, 13–14
　ports. *See* ports
　protocols, 16
　routers, 15, 200–204
　SANs, 214, 223–224, 327
　social, 214–215, 315–320
　structure, 210–214
　switches, 15
　traffic analysis, 188–190
　tunneling, 181
　types of, 210
　VPNs, 181
　WANs, 201
　wireless. *See* wireless networks
New Technology File System. *See* NTFS
ngrep tool, 190
NICs (network interface cards), 13, 201
NIST (National Institute of Standards
　and Technology), 222
nmap tool, 196–197
nonjournaling file systems, 11
NoSQL database, 292
notes, case, 108–109
NSA (National Security Agency),
　162–163
.nsf extension, 92
NTFS (New Technology File System),
　12, 89, 138, 333
NTFS Undelete tool, 144, 145

O

object code, 11
obscurity, 170
OC3 cables, 14
OC12 cables, 14

OC48 cables, 14
OCs (optic cables), 14, 333
Office files, 11, 91
Office products, 298, 302
onion routing, 179–180
online cheating, 322
online gaming, 321–322
openfiles command, 102, 209
operating system logs, 190
Operating System–Directed
    Configuration and Power
    Management (OSPM), 134
operating systems, 9–12
    considerations, 9
    defined, 135
    DOS, 9
    fundamentals, 135–138
    interrupts, 137–138
    kernel, 136–137
    Linux. See Linux-based systems
    Mac OS. See Mac OS–based
        systems
    Minix, 10
    mobile devices, 237–242
    multiprocessing, 135
    multitasking, 135
    multithreading, 135
    multiuser, 135
    types of, 135–136
    Unix-based, 10, 12, 89, 90
    virtual. See virtual systems
    Windows. See Windows systems
optic cables. See OC
optical drives, 86–87
OR operation, 158
Oracle Server, 292
Oracle VirtualBox, 218, 219, 226
"The Origin of Evidence," 81
OS utilities, 207–209
OS X. See Mac OS–based systems
OSPM (Operating System–Directed
    Configuration and Power
    Management), 134
.ost extension, 289
Outlook, 298
Outlook e-mail headers, 286–287, 288
Oxygen tool, 252–257

P

P2P (peer-to-peer) networks, 210, 214
PaaS (platform as a service), 221
pacemakers, 321
packet filters, 204
packet sniffers, 188–190
packets, 184–186
    communications, 185–186
    described, 15
    headers, 185–186
    overview, 183–186
    payload, 185–186
    trailers, 185–186
pagefile.sys, 134
Paraben tools, 248–249
Parallel Advanced Technology
    Attachment (PATA), 84

parallel ports, 88
parameter tampering, 193
Parker, Jonathan, 317
partitions, 85, 86–87, 128–130
passwords
    considerations, 150
    Internet Explorer, 272
    Windows systems, 169, 272
PATA (Parallel Advanced Technology
    Attachment), 84
PATA connectors, 84
patent infringement, 323
patent litigation, 45–46
payload, 170, 186
Payment Card Industry (PCI), 229
p-box (permutation box), 161
PC Cyborg Trojan, 308
PCI (Payment Card Industry), 229
PCI standards, 229
PE (Portable Executable), 11, 90
PE Explorer, 92–93
pedophiles, 27, 318
peer reviews, 78–79, 120
peer-to-peer (P2P) networks, 210, 214
permissions, 276–277
permutation box (p-box), 161
personal identification number
    (PIN), 234
Personal Unlock Number (PUK),
    234, 235
personality traits, 50–51
personal/professional conduct, 36, 37
personnel. See forensics staff
PHI (protected health
    information), 228
philosophy of science, 78
phone lines, 13
phones, cell. See mobile devices
photographic documentation, 35,
    55–57
photos, on mobile devices, 243–244, 245
physical access controls, 69
physical drives, 128
physical imaging, 248
physical journaling, 11, 90
PIN (personal identification
    number), 234
ping command, 19, 333
ping floods, 199, 205
ping of death attacks, 199
plain old telephone service
    (POTS), 234
plaintiffs, 24
planning, 105–108
platform as a service (PaaS), 221
PLCs (programmable logic
    controllers), 321
PNG files, 94
PNG format, 91
Pocket PC 2000, 239
point-to-multipoint topology, 212
point-to-point topology, 211–212
polymorphic viruses, 302
POP3 (Post Office Protocol Version 3),
    16, 187, 283

Popper, Karl, 78
pornography, 50, 107, 176, 244, 284
Portable Executable (PE), 11, 90
ports, 186–188
    common, 16, 186–187
    considerations, 187–188
    described, 16
    overview, 186
    parallel, 88
    serial, 87
    "well-known," 16
POST (power-on self test), 134
Post Office Protocol Version 3
    (POP3), 16, 187, 283
POST requests, 195
PostGres, 292
POTS (plain old telephone
    service), 234
power plants, 321
power-on self test (POST), 134
predators, child, 27, 318
Preneel, Bart, 168
preponderance of evidence,
    5, 325
PRGA (pseudo-random generation
    algorithm), 163
primary partitions, 128
privacy issues, 25
privacy laws, 228
private clouds, 223
private investigators, 33
private key, 163, 166
probative value, 82
processes, 100–101, 136
Procmon tool, 311
professional conduct, 36, 37
programmable logic controllers
    (PLCs), 321
promiscuous mode, 188
proof, 5, 325, 331
protected health information
    (PHI), 228
provenance, 42
proxies, network, 214
PS2 connectors, 89
pseudo-random generation algorithm
    (PRGA), 163
pseudo-static RAM (PSRAM), 9
PSRAM (pseudo-static RAM), 9
.pst extension, 289
PSTN (Public Switched Telephone
    Network), 235
public clouds, 223
public key, 163, 166
public key cryptography, 308. See
    also asymmetric cryptography
Public Switched Telephone Network
    (PSTN), 235
PUK (Personal Unlock Number),
    234, 235

Q

quality control, 114–121
quasi-delict, 325

R

RACE Integrity Primitives Evaluation Message Digest (RipeMD), 168
radio frequency ID (RFID) chips, 67
radio frequency interference (RFI), 64, 69–70
Radio Guide. *See* RG
RAID (Redundant Array of Inexpensive Disks), 130
RAID drives, 130–132
rainbow table attacks, 169
rainbow tables, 169
RAM (random access memory), 8–9, 200, 312, 333
RamCapture64 tool, 274–275
random access memory (RAM), 8–9, 200, 312, 333
ransomware, 308–309
RAR files, 92
raster files, 91
Raw Quick Pair (RQP) method, 175–176
RC (Ron's Cipher), 163
RC4 cipher, 14, 163
RCFL (Regional Computer Forensics Laboratory), 115
Reachout port, 187
reasonable doubt, 5
reconstruction, 81
record carving, 293
recovering data. *See* data recovery
recovery, disaster, 328
Recycle Bin, 139
Reduced Latency DRAM (RLDRAM), 9
Redundant Array of Independent Disks. *See* RAID
Regional Computer Forensics Laboratory (RCFL), 115
registered jack. *See* RJ
registry. *See* Windows registry
Reiser File System, 12, 89, 333
Reiser, Hans, 89
related-key attacks, 178
reliable protocols, 184
reports, 109–114. *See also* case notes; documentation
    Autopsy tool, 111
    clarity of, 114
    completeness, 114
    enCase, 110
    example of, 34
    expert, 113–114
    forensic, 109–113, 332
    FTK, 111
    guidelines for, 34–35
    length of, 114
    sample, 34–35
request for comments (RFCs), 284
Reveton virus, 308–309
RFCs (request for comments), 284
RFI (radio frequency interference), 64, 69–70
RFID (radio frequency ID) chips, 67
RG (Radio Guide), 13
RG 8 cables, 13

RG 58 cables, 13
Rijndael algorithm, 161
RipeMD (RACE Integrity Primitives Evaluation Message Digest), 168
Rivest, Ron, 163, 164, 168
RJ (registered jack) connections, 13
RJ11 jacks, 13
RJ45 jacks, 13
RLDRAM (Reduced Latency DRAM), 9
Rmmap tool, 312
Ron's Cipher. *See* RC
"rooting" Android phones, 238
rootkit attacks, 307–308
ROT 13 cipher, 155
router commands, 203–204
routers, 200–204
    attacks on, 202–204
    basics, 200–201
    Cisco, 201
    considerations, 15
    described, 201, 333
    getting evidence from, 202–204
RQP (Raw Quick Pair) method, 175–176
RSA algorithm, 164–166
RST bit, 184
run levels, 146

S

SaaS (software as a service), 220–221
Sabata, Hannah, 317
Safe Harbor program, 316
salt data, 169
SAM (Security Accounts Manager) file, 169
SANs (storage area networks), 214, 223–224, 327
SATA (Serial Advanced Technology Attachment), 7, 84, 333
SATA connectors, 84
SATA drives, 7, 333
s-box (substitution box), 161
SCADA devices, 260
SCADA (Supervisory Control and Data Acquisition) systems, 321
Scalpel tool, 96–97
scholarly sources, 79
Scientific Working Group on Digital Evidence. *See* SWDGE
scope of discovery, 25
scrubbing files, 144
SCSI (Small Computer System Interface), 6, 84, 333
SCSI connectors, 84, 89
SCSI drives, 6
Scytale, 155
SDRAM (synchronous dynamic random access memory), 8
search warrants, 25–26, 43–45, 334
searches, 42, 43–44
searchprotocolhost.exe, 306
Secret Service, 27, 255
sectors
    boot, 7, 302

considerations, 83, 86, 128, 331
described, 7, 333
slack space and, 130
Secure FTP, 186
Secure Hash Algorithm. *See* SHA
Secure Shell (SSH), 16, 186
Secure SMTP, 16
Security Accounts Manager (SAM) file, 169
Security+ certification, 117
security through obscurity, 170
seek time, 130
segments, 184
seizure of property, 25
Serial Advanced Technology Attachment. *See* SATA
serial connectors, 87
serial ports, 87
Serpent algorithm, 162
servers
    e-commerce, 106
    e-mail, 282, 290–291
    virtual, 222
service-based systems, 220–222
sexual harassment lawsuits, 44
SGRAM (Synchronous Graphics RAM), 9
SHA (Secure Hash Algorithm), 168
SHA-1 hashes, 168
SHA-2 hashes, 168
SHA-3 hashes, 168
Shamir, Adi, 164, 178
shared libraries, 11
shares
    computer, 205
    network, 213–214
Short Message Service (SMS), 235
signatures, file, 92
SIM (Subscriber Identity Module), 234
SIM cards, 234
Simple Mail Transfer Protocol. *See* SMTP
Simple Network Management Protocol (SNMP), 16, 187
single-key encryption. *See* symmetric cryptography
single-mode fiber (SMF), 13
sketches, crime scene, 57
Skipjack algorithm, 162–163
slack space, 7, 86, 130
Sleuth Kit, 95
Small Computer System Interface. *See* SCSI
smart phones. *See also* mobile devices
    Android. *See* Android phones
    "burner phone," 243
    call records, 243
    DDR Phone tool, 251–252
    identification information, 234–235
    imaging, 247–260
    iPhone. *See* iPhone
    Oxygen tool, 252–257
    photos/video on, 243–244, 245
    prepaid, 243

smart phones (*Cont.*)
    remote wipe feature, 64, 243
    SIM cards, 234
    SMS, 235
    type of evidence on, 243–246
SMF (single-mode fiber), 13
SMS (Short Message Service), 235
SMTP (Simple Mail Transfer
    Protocol), 16, 186, 283
SMTP over SSL, 187
smurf attacks, 200
SNMP (Simple Network Management
    Protocol), 16, 187
snort tool, 197–198
social networks, 214–215, 315–320
soft links, 146
Softperfect Network Protocol
    Analyzer, 190
software as a service (SaaS), 220–221
software, uninstalled, 270
solid-state drives (SSDs), 7, 85, 333
Sopo, Maxi, 317–318
SOPs (standard operating
    procedures), 107
sparse infection viruses, 301–302
SPI (stateful packet inspection)
    firewalls, 204–205
spoliation, 322
spoofing
    described, 180
    e-mail, 283
    IP addresses, 279, 283
    MAC addresses, 180
spool files, 273–274
spot checks, 121
spousal privilege, 325
spyware, 300, 306–307
SQL (Structured Query Language),
    191–193, 277–278
SQL injection, 191–193, 277–279
SQL Server, 291
SQLite database, 92
SS7 protocol, 235
SSDs (solid-state drives), 7, 85, 333
SSH (Secure Shell), 16, 186
stack memory, 276
staff. *See* forensics staff
stalking, 284, 318, 319–320
Stallman, Richard, 10
standard operating procedures
    (SOPs), 107
star topology, 210–211
state laws, 23
stateful packet inspection (SPI)
    firewalls, 204–205
static analysis, 310
static electricity, 64
steganalysis, 175–176
steganography, 170–176
    vs. cryptography, 170
    historical, 170–171
    Invisible Secrets, 171–175
    methods/tools, 171–175
    MP3Stego, 175
    overview, 170

steganophony, 171
storage area networks (SANs), 214,
    223–224, 327
storage devices/media, 83–87. *See
also* media
    evidence storage, 67–70, 71
    hard drives. *See* hard drives
    hardware interfaces, 87–89
    labeling, 63
    magnetic, 83–85
    WORM storage, 64
    write-protecting, 63
storage, virtual, 222
stream ciphers, 158, 163
striped disks, 131–132
Structured Query Language. *See* SQL
Stuxnet virus, 321
Subscriber Identity Module. *See* SIM
substitution box (s-box), 161
superblock, 145
supervisor review, 120
Supervisory Control and Data
    Acquisition. *See* SCADA
Supervisory Control and Data
    Acquisition (SCADA) systems, 321
s-video connectors, 88
swap files, 134–135, 272
SWDGE (Scientific Working Group
    on Digital Evidence), 4, 34–35, 36
SWGDE standards, 36
switches, 15, 201, 334
.swp extension, 134, 272
symbolic links, 146
symmetric cryptography, 158, 159–163
SYN bit, 184–185, 200
SYN floods, 200, 205
SYN packets, 200
synchronous dynamic random access
    memory (SDRAM), 8
Synchronous Graphics RAM
    (SGRAM), 9
system calls, 310
system resources, 310

T

tables, rainbow, 169
Tanenbaum, Andrew S., 10
tape backups, 86, 327
tar files, 92
tax fraud, 324
TCP headers, 184–185
TCP/IP (Transmission Control
    Protocol/Internet Protocol), 16
teardrop attacks, 199
Telnet, 16, 186
temperature control, 68
Temporal Key Integrity Protocol
    (TKIP), 14
temporary files, 274
Terabit Virus Maker, 304–305
terms, glossary of, 331–334
TestDisk tool, 95
testifying, preparation for, 22
testimony
    Daubert standard, 46

    expert, 46, 51, 191
    impugning, 40
    trial, 22
texting, 235
TFTP (Trivial FTP), 187
theories, 77–78
Thicknet cables, 13
Thinnet cables, 13
TIFF format, 91
Timbuktu port, 187
time to live (TTL), 19, 185
TKIP (Temporal Key Integrity
    Protocol), 14
tool quality control, 116
tortious acts. *See* torts
torts, 24, 325, 334
Torvalds, Linus, 10
trace evidence, 80
tracert command, 19–20, 290, 334
traces, 274
tracing e-mail, 289–290
tracking evidence, 65–67
tracks, described, 7
training, 39, 48–49
transaction logs, 292, 293
transfer rates, 130
transference, 332
Transmission Control Protocol/
    Internet Protocol (TCP/IP), 16
transposition ciphers, 157
tree topology, 212–213
trial testimony. *See* testimony
triple-DES (3-DES), 160
Trithemius, Johannes, 170
Trivial FTP (TFTP), 187
Trojan horses, 305–306
TrueCrypt tool, 149–150
TTL (time to live), 19, 185
tunneling, 181
Twitter, 214

U

UMTS (Universal Mobile
    Telecommunications
    Systems), 236
UNICODE strings, 130
Universal Mobile
    Telecommunications Systems
    (UMTS), 236
Unix-based systems, 10, 12,
    89, 90
unreliable protocols, 184
unshielded twisted-pair (UTP)
    cables, 13
URG bit, 184
U.S. Army Digital Evidence
    Storage, 70
U.S. Attorney, 24
U.S. Secret Service, 27, 255
USB cables/connectors, 87
USB devices, 267
USB drives, 85, 267
UTP (unshielded twisted-pair)
    cables, 13

V

validation of findings, 106–107, 113
VBA (Visual Basic for
    Applications), 302
VBScript language, 302
vendor certifications, 118
verification, 78
VGA (Video Graphics Array), 88
video connectors, 88
video documentation, 35, 57
Video Graphics Array (VGA), 88
video, on mobile devices,
    243–244, 245
video recording, 57
video surveillance, 69
Vigenere cipher, 156–157
virtual addressing, 136
virtual machines (VMs), 217–220,
    226, 275
virtual memory, 134–135
Virtual PC, 218, 219, 227
Virtual Private Networks (VPNs), 181
virtual servers, 222
virtual storage, 222
virtual systems, 217–231
    cloud-based, 217, 222–229, 227
    considerations, 217
    described, 217
    forensic issues, 225–229
    host machine, 218
    host operating system, 218
    hypervisor, 218
    legal/procedural issues, 227–229
    service-based, 220–222
    technical issues, 225
    types of, 217–225
    virtual machines, 217–220,
        226, 275
    Virtual PC, 219, 227
    VirtualBox, 218, 219, 226
    VMWare, 218, 220, 226
VirtualBox, 218, 219, 226
virtualization, 217
viruses, 297–305. *See also* attacks;
  malware
    armored, 301
    child pornography and, 107
    chronical list of, 303–304
    definition of, 297
    FakeAV, 298–300, 301
    Flame, 300
    history of, 302–304
    Mac Defender, 298, 300, 301
    Mac Security, 298
    macro, 302
    modern virus creation, 304–305
    multipartite, 302
    mutation, 302
    polymorphic, 302
    recent examples of, 298–301
    Reveton, 308–309
    sparse infection, 301–302
    spread of, 297–298
    Stuxnet, 321
    types of, 301–302

Visitor Location Register (VLR), 235
Visual Basic for Applications
    (VBA), 302
visual inspection, 36, 334
VLR (Visitor Location Register), 235
.vmem files, 275
VMs (virtual machines), 217–220,
    226, 275
VMWare, 218, 220
VMWare virtual machines, 218, 220, 226
volatile evidence, 43
volatile memory, 274–275
VPNs (Virtual Private Networks), 181

W

WAP (wireless access point), 14
war driving, 198
war flying, 198
warrants, 25–26, 43–44, 334
wdsCarve tool, 293
web applications, 277–281
web browsers, 277, 280–281
web forensics, 277–281
web traffic
    analyzing, 194–196
    websites, 191–193
web-based attacks, 193
websites
    cookies, 280–281
    cross-site scripting, 193,
        279–280
    embedded scripts and, 280
    fake, 280
    forceful browsing, 281
    parameter tampering, 193
    recently visited, 268, 269
    web traffic, 191–193
    XML injection, 281
"well-known ports," 16
WEP (Wired Equivalent Privacy), 14
WhoIS command, 186
Whois tools, 290
wide area networks (WANs), 201
Wi-Fi networks. *See* wireless
  networks
WiFi Protected Access (WPA), 14
Window Washer, 273
Windows 7 Phone, 239
Windows 8 partitions, 129
Windows 8 phone, 239–240, 257
Windows 8 Security System, 298, 299
Windows CE, 239
Windows Explorer, 272–273
Windows registry, 265–272
    Autostart locations, 268
    hives, 266
    information in, 9
    issues, 310–311
    network adapters, 270, 271
    overview, 265–266
    recent documents, 268–269
    recent sites, 268, 269
    stored passwords, 272
    uninstalled software, 270

    USB information in, 267
    wireless network information,
        270–272
Windows Remote Desktop, 187
Windows swap file, 272
Windows Sysinternals, 311–312
Windows systems
    copying files, 276–277
    file systems, 89, 138–139
    log files, 205–206
    mobile devices, 240–241
    Office files, 11, 91
    overview, 9
    passwords, 169, 272
    recovering deleted files,
        138–144, 145
    Recycle Bin, 139
    registry. *See* Windows registry
    running processes in, 100–101
WinUndelete tool, 142–143
WinZapper tool, 179, 205
wiping hard drives, 181
wiping mobile devices, 64, 243
Wired Equivalent Privacy (WEP), 14
wireless access point (WAP), 14
wireless networks, 198–200. *See also*
  networks
    attacks on, 198–200, 202
    firewalls, 193, 200, 204–205
    log files, 205–207
    mobile devices, 236–237, 246
    overview, 198
    protocols, 14–15
    routers, 200–204
    stored information on, 270–272
wireless standards, 14–15
Wireshark sniffer, 188–190
witness of fact, 46
witnesses, expert. *See* expert witness
workplace discrimination, 323
WORM storage, 64
WPA (WiFi Protected Access), 14
WPA2 standard, 14–15
write blockers, 63
Write Once Read Many. *See* WORM
write-blocking devices, 63

X

XML injection, 281
XOR operation, 159

Y

YAFFS2 (Yet Another Flash File
    System 2), 260
Yahoo! e-mail headers, 287, 288
Yet Another Flash File System 2
    (YAFFS2), 260
YouTube, 214

Z

.zip files, 92
Zubulake v. UBS Warburg, 326–327